T0358621

EQUALITY OF OPPORTUNITY

The Economics of Responsibility

World Scientific Series in Economic Theory
(ISSN: 2251-2071)

Series Editor   Eric Maskin, *Harvard University, USA*

Published*

Vol. 1   Equality of Opportunity: The Economics of Responsibility
         by Marc Fleurbaey and François Maniquet

World Scientific Series in Economic Theory – Vol. 1

EQUALITY OF OPPORTUNITY

The Economics of Responsibility

Marc Fleurbaey

Princeton University, USA

François Maniquet

Université catholique de Louvain, Belgium
University of Warwick, UK

World Scientifi

NEW JERSEY · LONDON · SINGAPORE · BEIJING · SHANGHAI · HONG KONG · TAIPEI · CHENNAI

Published by

World Scientific Publishing Co. Pte. Ltd.

5 Toh Tuck Link, Singapore 596224

USA office: 27 Warren Street, Suite 401-402, Hackensack, NJ 07601

UK office: 57 Shelton Street, Covent Garden, London WC2H 9HE

Library of Congress Cataloging-in-Publication Data
Fleurbaey, Marc.
    Equality of opportunity : the economics of responsibility / by Marc Fleurbaey &
François Maniquet.
       p. cm. -- (World scientific series in economic theory, 2251-2071 ; vol. 1)
    ISBN-13 978-981-4368-87-2
    ISBN-10 981-4368-87-3
    1. Distributive justice.   2. Welfare economics.   3. Equality.   4. Poor.   5. Opportunity.
I. Maniquet, François, 1965–   II. Title.
    HB523.F588 2012
    330.12'6--dc23

                                                                          2012005124

British Library Cataloguing-in-Publication Data
A catalogue record for this book is available from the British Library.

In-house Editor: Alisha Nguyen

Typeset by Stallion Press
Email: enquiries@stallionpress.com

Printed in Singapore.

Acknowledgments

The idea of publishing a selection of our papers on equality of opportunity came from Professor Eric Maskin, Editor-in-Chief of this series in Economic Theory. We are most grateful to him for his invitation, his advice, and the foreword he accepted to write. We also would like to take this opportunity to thank him for the many influential discussions we held with him about the topic of this book.

Among the ten publications that are gathered in this book, the oldest one was published in 1994 and the most recent one in 2011. During this long period of time, our ideas and opinions have evolved. This evolution is mainly due to the influence of many researchers, whose comments, remarks and criticisms have been immensely valuable.

Serge Kolm and John E. Roemer have been the most influential, and Amartya Sen has had a considerable impact, too. They are among the first economists having introduced the theme of equality of opportunity, compensation and responsibility in welfare economics (even if they use different terms). Without their seminal contributions, and without the many discussions we shared with them, we would have failed to develop a consistent set of works on this theme. Their whole works have always been a source of inspiration.

The same can be said about the philosophers who have brought the idea of equal resources or equal opportunity to the fore and with whom exchanges of ideas have been very helpful, in particular Richard Arneson, the late Gerald Cohen, Ronald Dworkin, Martha Nussbaum, Peter Vallentyne, Philippe Van Parijs, and Andrew Williams.

Our immense gratitude also goes to those who encouraged and helped us a lot at the time of our early efforts. Philippe Mongin and the late Louis Gevers, our dissertation supervisors, have shaped our understanding of welfare economics. Hervé Moulin and William Thomson, who pioneered the development of the economic theory of fair resource allocation, have deeply influenced our research agenda.

We are also grateful to the researchers who developed similar ideas as ours during that period of time, Walter Bossert, Iñigo Iturbe-Ormaetxe,

Yves Sprumont, Bertil Tungodden, Dirk Van de Gaer, and Alex Voorhoeve. Some of them have become co-authors. All of them have helped us clarify our ideas and improve our works.

We would like to thank all those who have commented on and forced us to revise our manuscript. They are too numerous to be all mentioned here. This large set contains many anonymous referees. It also contains colleagues and friends who devoted a considerable amount of time discussing with us on the topic of equality of opportunity, Claude d'Aspremont, John Weymark, Peter Hammond, Kotaro Suzumura, Koichi Tadenuma, Daniel Hausman, Matthew Clayton, Paula Casal, Naoki Yoshihara, Reiko Gotoh, and Thomas Christiano.

Finally, we are thankful to younger researchers, Juan de Dios Moreno-Ternero, Giacomo Valletta, and Timos Athanasiou, who claim to have been influenced by our works. By the questions they have raised, by their doubt on some parts of the work and their enthusiasm about other parts, as well as by their own contributions to the field, they have had a decisive impact on the evolution of the ideas that are contained in this book.

Last but not least, we thank Fabienne Henry for her meticulous editing of the proofs, and Zvi Ruder, Alisha Nguyen, and Sherry Tang, from World Scientific Publishing, for their help and assistance during the preparation of the manuscript.

Foreword

In a just society, accidents of birth, having impoverished parents, for example, should not disadvantage a person for life. Appropriate compensation, e.g., state-financed pre-school education for underprivileged children, is often warranted.

But these days almost no one except a die-hard socialist, and perhaps not even he, would claim that justice requires equalizing well-being (utility) across people: those with lazy or extravagant habits need not fare as well as the diligent and moderate. According to an important line of contemporary thought, the just society takes *personal responsibility* as well as equality seriously. Or, put another way, society should aspire to equality of *opportunity* not utility.

For nearly two decades, Marc Fleurbaey and Francois Maniquet have been among our foremost thinkers about equality of opportunity. Their work, together and separately, elucidates the uneasy tension between the demands of egalitarianism and responsibility. But it also shows that one can obtain a sharp conception of equal opportunity — not to mention crisp policy prescriptions — if one is willing to relax these demands a bit.

I am delighted that Fleurbaey and Maniquet have collected ten of their major articles in this volume. Equally significant, they have provided an incisive introduction that details the connections between the various strands of their own papers and those of other researchers.

Eric Maskin

Editor-in-Chief, *World Scientific Series in Economic Theory*

Contents

Acknowledgments   v

Foreword   vii

Introduction   xiii

Part 1 The Pure Compensation Problem   1

Chapter 1   On Fair Compensation   3
1 Introduction   3
2 The Framework   6
3 Compensation Properties   8
4 General Impossibilities   10
5 No-Envy   13
6 Weaker Criteria and Existence Results   17
7 Concluding Remarks   21
Appendix   22
References   29

**Chapter 2   Three Solutions for the Compensation
          Problem**   33
1 Introduction   33
2 The Model   35
3 Properties of Solutions   36
4 Consequences of Consistency   39
5 A Dual Characterization of Two Solutions   41
6 A Third Solution   44
Appendix: Proofs   48
References   50

**Chapter 3   On the Equivalence between Welfarism
          and Equality of Opportunity**   53
1 Introduction   53
2 Model and Notations   56
3 Properties   58

4   The Result   65
5   Ordinal Non-Comparability   67
6   Proofs   69
   6.1   Theorem 1   70
   6.2   Theorem 2   72
   6.3   Theorem 5   73
7   Conclusion   75
References   76

Part 2   Unequal Earning Abilities and Income Redistribution

Part 2   Unequal Earning Abilities and Income
      Redistribution   **79**

**Chapter 4   Fair Allocation with Unequal Production
           Skills: The No Envy Approach
           to Compensation   81**
1   Introduction   81
2   Two Basic Requirements   85
3   Introducing Reference Preferences   88
4   Weakening the Basic Requirements   95
5   Concluding Remarks   98
Appendix 100
   A.1 Non-emptiness of RWEB 100
   A.2 Non-emptiness of S^Y 104
References 105

**Chapter 5   Cooperative Production with Unequal
           Skills: The Solidarity Approach
           to Compensation   109**
1   Introduction 109
2   Skill Solidarity 112
3   Non-Discrimination Among Preferences 115
4   Limited Self-Ownership of Skill 122
5   Conclusion 124
References 125

**Chapter 6   An Equal Right Solution to the
           Compensation–Responsibility Dilemma   127**
1   Introduction 127
2   Model and Basic Definitions 130
3   The x^*-Equal Right 131

4 Full Compensation or Full Responsibility Requirements 136
5 Two Polar Classes of Simple Rules 143
References 147

**Chapter 7   Fair Social Orderings When Agents Have
             Unequal Production Skills   149**
1 Introduction 149
2 Model and Basic Definitions 155
3 Ethical Principles 157
4 Fair Social Ordering Functions 162
    4.1 The Compensation-Equal Access dilemma 162
    4.2 Social ordering functions of the leximin type 162
    4.3 Social ordering functions of the utilitarian type 166
5 Relationship with the Literature 167
6 Conclusion 172
Appendix: Proofs and Independence of the Axions 173
References 187

Chapter 8   Fair Income Tax   191
1 Introduction 191
2 The Model 194
3 Fair Social Preferences 196
    3.1 Fairness requirements 196
    3.2 Social preferences 200
4 Tax Redistribution 206
    4.1 Setting 206
    4.2 Two agents 210
    4.3 General population 211
5 Conclusion 219
Appendix: Proofs 220
References 234

**Chapter 9   Help the Low Skilled or Let
             the Hardworking Thrive? A Study
             of Fairness in Optimal Income Taxation   237**
1 Introduction 238
2 The Model 241
3 Social Preferences 244
4 Optimal Tax: The Two-by-Two Case 252
5 Optimal Tax: The General Case 258

5.1 The Case $w_m = 0$ 258
5.2 EE Tax When $w_m > 0$ 260
5.3 EB Tax When $w_m \geq 0$ 263
6 Conclusion 266
Appendix: Proofs 267
References 273

Chapter 10 Kolm's Tax, Tax Credit, and the Flat Tax   275
1 Introduction 275
2 The Model 277
3 Axiomatic Foundations 283
4 Second Best: Observable Labor Time 285
5 Second Best: Unobservable Labor Time 291
6 Concluding Comments 296
Appendix 298
References 300

Author Index   **303**

Subject Index   **307**

Introduction

There seems to be a consensus among economists that our discipline should not be confined to describing or explaining societies. Economics should also provide help to those whose mission is to make recommendations for better institutions.

The consensus is weaker, though, when it comes to specifying how such help should be conceived. Many would claim that only efficiency should matter: economists should allow themselves to make recommendations only if all the interested parties would gain from the proposed decision.

Welfare economists, on the contrary, think that economics can be used to elucidate the underpinnings of prescriptive conclusions even when some interested agents gain whereas others lose. This clearly calls for introducing other values in addition to efficiency in the discipline. When efficiency and fairness considerations are combined, then justifications can be provided for policies that bring about some reallocation of resources from those who will eventually suffer welfare losses to those who will eventually gain from the policy.

The first, immediate, and major difficulty one faces when trying to combine efficiency with fairness is that fairness cannot receive a unique, undebatable, definition. While there is a consensus on the definition of efficiency as Pareto efficiency, many different definitions of fairness have been proposed and discussed.

Of course, economists themselves are not the ones having to choose, ultimately, which notion of fairness is the one that should prevail to inspire this or that policy. The role of economists should be restricted to conditional statements: if the policymaker is interested in promoting this or that value of fairness, then this or that policy should be implemented. Welfare economics is then the discipline that studies the possible combinations of efficiency and fairness requirements, and the relationship between a choice of such requirements and the policy recommendation that should follow.

Several notions of fairness have an egalitarian flavor. They embody the intuition that societies should equalize something. The question is then: what should be equalized? The works that are gathered in this book are grounded on the view that fairness is a matter of equalizing resources which agents can use to follow their own goals.

Notions of fairness based on equality of resources differ from those that are based on equality of utilities. By utilities, we mean any notion of individual welfare (including notions of happiness) that is entirely subjective and inherently comparable among individuals.

A policymaker could prefer the objective of resource equality over that of utility equality for at least two reasons. First, she could argue that no such utilities exist. That is, one could claim that there exists no objective way (by objective we mean a way that would be accepted by all impartial ethical observers) of building a measure of welfare that is only grounded on subjective feelings and that allows the observer to make interpersonal comparisons.

Second, she could argue that even if such a measure existed, fairness is not a question of how utilities are distributed in societies. Rather, fairness is a question of how resources are distributed in societies. That is, the motivation to design institutions to help our societies become fair should not be, for instance, that redistribution or social benefits should be targeted towards low utility agents. Experiencing a low utility level, being depressed, reaching a low level of happiness, if it does not come from a lack in resources, does not justify, according to that view, any special treatment from social institutions. John Rawls and Ronald Dworkin have developed theories of justice around this idea, and related theories of equality of opportunities have been proposed by Amartya Sen, John Roemer, and others.[1]

Again, is only brings a new question: how to define the resources that are to be equalized? In this book, we study notions of fairness that require that resources societies should be interested in include internal resources. By this we mean the set of non-transferable personal resources that are crucial in determining what opportunities people have in life. Depending on the kind of applications (and, therefore, on the kind of policy choice faced by the policymaker), and depending on the policymaker's ethical positions, internal resources may include health conditions, gender, ethnicity, genetic endowment, family background, or education.

This implies that resources are both external, like financial resources, infrastructures, publicly provided public goods, and internal. The theories that are presented in this book are consistent with the ethical position that societies should try equalize the total bundle of resources that agents have at their disposal in order to follow their goals. Internal resources,

---

[1]See Rawls (1971, 1982), Dworkin (2000), Sen (1999), Roemer (1998), Arneson (1989, 2000), Cohen (1989).

by definition, cannot be redistributed. Consequently, the social objective should be to allocate external resources in an unequal way so as to compensate inequalities in the individuals' endowments in internal resources.

It is time, here, to bring efficiency back into the picture. Even if a policy is claimed to be consistent with some fairness notion, it cannot conflict with efficiency. Such a policy, indeed, would be objected to by everyone in society. This means that individual preferences are a key ingredient in the analysis. Note that incentive issues also force us to take preferences into account. We come back on this issue later on.

Preferences, however, given that they differ among agents, are an additional source of inequality. For instance, think of differences in preferences for leisure, which lead agents with equal skill levels to end up at different income levels. Some policymakers would object against suppressing such income inequalities.

More generally, looking again at philosophical theories of equality of resources and opportunities, there seem to be ethical arguments for the view that not all inequalities are unfair, that is, not all inequalities call for compensation. Using the terms introduced above, in the large set of internal resources, or internal characteristics that influence the set of outcomes an individual can reach, some will be considered as calling for compensation, whereas others will be considered as failing to justify any special redress by society.

Consequently, fairness can be defined as the requirement that external resources be allocated in order to compensate inequalities in the particular internal resources that are viewed as yielding unfair inequalities. This has come to be called the principle of compensation. On the other hand, external resources should be allocated independently of internal resources that are viewed as yielding inequalities that are not unfair. That is a principle of responsibility or neutrality that has also been called the principle of natural (or liberal) reward in view of the fact that under application of this principle the individuals reap the direct consequences of their own endowments in such internal resources.[2]

---

[2]The economic literature has also considered the related "utilitarian" reward principle, according to which the situation of subgroups of individuals differing only in characteristics that do not generate unfair inequalities can be evaluated by an inequality-neutral social objective. This is a very different sort of responsibility principle. To see the difference, observe that this principle warrants transfers from individuals with low marginal utility to individuals with high marginal utility when differences in marginal utility are due to characteristics that generate fair inequalities, whereas the neutrality principle advocates the absence of redistribution between them. For general surveys on these approaches, see Fleurbaey (2008) and Fleurbaey and Maniquet (2011).

All the works gathered in this book study the possibility of combining efficiency with the principles of compensation and responsibility. All these works have in common that agents are characterized by two elements. One element calls for compensation, the other does not. All the works also have in common that the characteristic that does not call for compensation is the agents' preferences. That is, these works study the consequences of adopting the ethical position that differences in preferences, for instance preferences towards leisure, lead to inequalities, for instance income inequalities, that are not unfair.

It could also be argued, on the contrary, that differences in preferences at least partly reveal differences in education or family background, and, therefore, could lead to unfair inequalities. However, this is just a way of saying that certain individual preferences do not fully deserve to be respected, and that the state of society could be improved by constraining the choice of individuals over the use of their resources. This is an important problem that can be dealt with by identifying the ideal (as opposed to actual) individual preferences that should be used in the evaluation of individual situations.

The works presented here could be extended to address this problem of imperfect preferences, but they retain the assumption of perfectly respectable preferences and draw the attention of the reader to another important difficulty: the principles of compensation and responsibility are generally incompatible with each other. That is, as long as one is interested in efficiency, no policy recommendation can be designed that guarantees that inequalities due to differences in the compensation characteristic be eliminated whereas inequalities due to differences in preferences are kept unchanged. This fundamental dilemma is at the heart of the works that are gathered here. Each chapter contains a study of one possible compromise between compensating for some characteristics and letting the individuals bear the consequences of the other characteristics.

The main distinction to be made among the works gathered in this book has to do with the models. Two different models are studied. In part I, the three chapters deal with the so-called pure compensation model. That is the most fundamental, general, and therefore, abstract model in which the compensation-responsibility dilemma can be studied. The individuals are assumed to have non-transferable characteristics, collectively called talent or handicap, and individual preferences are defined over all possible combinations of talent and a transferable good (money). The question is then the following: assuming that there is a fixed budget to allocate among these individuals, how should it be allocated to compensate for differences in talent if the policymaker considers that no individual can claim to deserve any special amount of money in virtue of her preferences. An important literature (Bossert 1995, Bossert and Fleurbaey 1996, Iturbe-Ormaetxe and Nieto 1996, Iturbe-Ormaetxe 1997, Sprumont 1998, Cappelen and Tungodden 2002, 2003, 2007) has studied the special case in which preferences are quasi-linear in money. This particular model can be used to study how monetary transfers can be used to suppress income inequalities due to specific characteristics of talent while remaining neutral about inequalities generated by characteristics of effort, assuming that such characteristics are fixed and unaffected by the redistributive policy, or to make transfers between jurisdictions of a federation so as to compensate the inequalities in budget due to certain local characteristics.

In part II, seven chapters deal with a more applied model. This is the canonical model in which issues of labor income taxation can be addressed. Recall that labor income has by far the largest share of average income in all western societies. The question that is addressed in these works is that of what Serge Kolm (2004) calls "macrojustice": how should individual contributions to the welfare state be computed and who should deserve welfare benefits and in which quantity? In Mirrlees' classical approach to this problem (Mirrlees 1971), a utilitarian objective defined over individual utilities is maximized over the set of incentive-compatible policies. As Mirrlees assumes that all individuals have the same preferences (and utility function), his model does not leave any room for a differential treatment of internal characteristics that influence the individuals' earning abilities and internal characteristics of preferences over consumption and leisure. The classical analysis of fair allocations by Pazner and Schmeidler (1974), in which fairness is defined as no-envy over consumption-leisure bundles, contains the main ingredients of such a distinction and the chapters of part II can be viewed as developments of their approach.

In this second set of works, agents differ in their productive skill, that is, their ability to earn income, or the wage rate at which they are able to find a job. Agents also differ in their preferences, which bear on consumption-leisure bundles. We study fairness in the following sense: how is it possible to compensate for differences in productive skills and, at the same time, not compensate for differences in preferences?

A second important distinction has to be made. In half of the works that are presented here, the objective is to define an efficient and fair allocation rule, that is, a fair selection of the best allocations for society. In the other half of the works, the objective is to define a social ordering function, that is, a complete ranking of the allocations, based on efficiency and fairness considerations.

Looking for an allocation rule is a limited objective. Indeed, as efficiency is part of the policymaker's objective, the allocations that will be considered best for society are first-best efficient allocations. The theory of fair allocation has traditionally focused on the selection of first-best allocations and developed an axiomatic methodology that nicely analyzes the ethical underpinnings of various allocation rules.[3] As it is well known, however, first-best allocations may not be implementable, when individual preferences are the agents' private information. The Gibbard-Satterthwaite theorem reveals the difficulty of combining Pareto-efficiency and incentive-compability. It has been proven, though, that certain forms of implementation are possible if agents know each other sufficiently well.[4] However, this assumption is valid only in small groups of agents. Consequently, the methodology of fair allocation rules does not really enable us to discuss policy recommendations for large societies. On the other hand, given that the objective of finding fully optimal allocations is limited, the models that are studied are more general (in particular, regarding returns to scale), and that has allowed us to highlight more fundamental tensions among principles of fairness. That, in turn, has paved the way to the second set of works.

Looking for social ordering functions is more challenging. Some scholars would even claim that it is impossible, as it requires to aggregate individual preferences into social preferences, an exercise that is often thought to be impossible. This widespread view is grounded on Arrovian social choice theory. What is correct is that aggregating individual preferences is problematic as long as one retains Arrow celebrated independence property, according to which social preferences between two allocations should only depend on individual preferences about these two allocations. In the works we present here, the independence property is weakened in such a way that it becomes possible to combine it with efficiency and fairness principles. Moreover, contrary to the social choice literature, the emphasis in the works here is shifted from independence conditions to fairness conditions, and independence conditions are taken into account only when they are compatible with basic fairness conditions.[5]

---

[3]See Thomson (2011) for a survey.
[4]See Jackson (2001) and Maskin and Sjöström (2002) for recent surveys.
[5]The independence condition we retain was proposed by Hansson (1973) and Pazner (1979). There has been a heated debate on the possibility of Bergson-Samuelson social welfare functions in relation to independence conditions (see Fleurbaey and Mongin 2005).

In principle, social ordering functions, by themselves, solve the implementation problem. Indeed, the policy recommendation that can be deduced from an objective that takes the shape of a social ordering function merely follows from the maximization of the orderings under appropriate incentive-compatibility constraints. Practically speaking, though, such a maximization problem needs to be explicitly solved, which may turn out to be possible only numerically. In the last three chapters of this book, we show that even if the maximization problem cannot be fully solved, some interesting properties of optimal taxation schemes can be deduced. Moreover, we show how it is sometimes possible to derive simple criteria for the evaluation of tax reforms, an exercise that is arguably more relevant to policymakers than the determination of the optimal tax.

We believe there are three main lessons that can be drawn from the list of works that follow in this book. The first lesson, which we already mentioned above, is that the principles of compensation and responsibility are incompatible with each other when combined with efficiency. Consequently, compromises have to be found, that is, weakenings of the principles have to be accepted, and admissible solutions (allocation rules or social ordering functions) are those that are justified by a combination of weakened conditions of compensation and responsibility. Many such solutions are presented in this book. In particular, Chapters 4 and 10 focus on solutions leaning on the responsibility side, Chapters 5 and 8 focus on solutions leaning on the compensation side, whereas the remaining chapters analyze solutions pertaining to both sides of the dilemma.

The second lesson is that the precise notion of egalitarian social objective that we study can only take the shape of an infinite aversion to inequality. This is the most striking lesson of the book. Let us explain. Egalitarianism in the first place, as it is embodied for instance in the Pigou-Dalton transfer principle, simply states that transferring resources from a richer agent to a poorer agent is a social improvement. In a nutshell, different degrees of inequality aversion emerge as different answers to the following question: how large a resource loss to the richer agent do we agree on, in exchange of a given resource gain to the poorer agent? The degree of inequality aversion is infinite when we claim that an arbitrarily small gain for the poorer agent justifies an arbitrarily large loss for the richer. The requisite of infinite inequality aversion is typically embedded in the so-called maximin social objective.

The classical literature on income inequality measurement has taught us in the last decades that the egalitarian principle could lead to any degree of inequality aversion. The results gathered here teach us that if well-being indices depend on more dimensions than just income, then the egalitarian principle necessarily leads to an infinite degree of inequality aversion. To put it differently, only maximin social preferences are compatible with the efficiency, fairness and independence conditions stated here. This does not tell us which well-being index should be "maximinned", but it tells us that, whatever the well-being index one derives from basic fairness conditions, social aggregation needs to take the form of a maximin if these conditions are combined with the efficiency and independence conditions we study. This is developed in Chapters 8 and 9 — in Chapter 7, in contrast, the infinite inequality aversion is directly assumed. We find it an important future research question whether other independence conditions could lead us to social objectives that are not of the maximin type.

The third lesson comes from the last three chapters of the book. They are the most practical conclusions of this inquiry into the ethics of compensation and responsibility. They have to do with the schemes of labor-income taxation that can be derived from social orderings based on compensation and responsibility conditions. The results are that the policymaker needs to focus on maximizing the situation of low incomes in some specific way, and the marginal rate of taxation that turns out to receive the strongest support is a zero marginal tax rate. That is, low incomes should be treated in such a way that the benefit that agents get when they do not work should still be transferred to all agents earning income below some threshold (the threshold corresponds more or less to the level of earning of an agent working full time at the minimal wage rate). This result identifies a possible ethical justification to policies of earned income tax credit, like the ones that have been implemented in the US or the UK.

One surprising feature of this result is that it can be derived from the maximization problem of social preferences either when those preferences give priority to the compensation principle or when they give priority to the responsibility principle. That is, in spite of the impossibility of combining these two principles at the stage of the definition of a well-behaved objective for the policymaker, in spite of the need to choose between the two principles the one that will be given priority, once we reach the stage of implementing the social objective and once we face incentive-compatibility constraints, we reach similar conclusions from either approach. This can be seen in particular in Chapters 9 and 10. Moreover, these conclusions take the simple shape of a zero marginal rate of taxation on low incomes.

This zero marginal rate of taxation is not the only policy that may receive justification from our inquiry. Although from less general ethical justifications, we present the result that a negative marginal rate of taxation on low incomes is also consistent with some combination of ethical principles (Chapter 8). Finally, we find combinations of fairness conditions that would lead the policymaker to maximize the minimal income, a policy recommendation that looks similar to the basic income proposal (Chapter 9).

The works that are gathered here offer a consistent summary of our works on fairness, when fairness is defined as a combination of the principle of compensation and the principle of responsibility. Maybe the main achievement of these works is to prove that it is possible to define policy objectives that follow from this definition of fairness and to derive policy recommendations from those objectives. On the other hand, the main limitation of these works is that the application that is studied, mainly that of labor-income taxation, however important it is, is only one policy issue among many others. In other words, this set of works calls for generalizations and applications to further issues of interest. May this book inspire future research along these lines.

References

1. R. J. Arneson. 'Equality and equal opportunity for welfare', *Philosophical Studies* **56** (1989), 77–93.
2. R. J. Arneson. 'Luck egalitarianism and prioritarianism', *Ethics* **110** (2000a), 339–349.
3. W. Bossert. 'Redistribution mechanisms based on individual characteristics', *Mathematical Social Sciences* **29** (1995), 1–17.
4. W. Bossert and M. Fleurbaey. 'Redistribution and compensation', *Social Choice and Welfare* **13** (1996), 343–355.
5. A. W. Cappelen and B. Tungodden. 'Responsibility and reward', *FinanzArchiv* **59** (2002), 120–140.
6. A. W. Cappelen and B. Tungodden. 'Reward and responsibility: How should we be affected when others change their effort?', *Politics, Philosophy & Economics* **2** (2003), 191–211.
7. A. W. Cappelen and B. Tungodden. 'Local autonomy and interregional equality', *Social Choice and Welfare* **28** (2007), 443–460.
8. G. A. Cohen. 'On the currency of egalitarian justice', *Ethics* **99** (1989), 906–944.

9. R. Dworkin. *Sovereign Virtue. The Theory and Practice of Equality*, Cambridge, MA: Harvard University Press. 2000.

10. M. Fleurbaey. *Fairness, Responsibility, and Welfare*, Oxford: Oxford University Press. 2008.

11. M. Fleurbaey and F. Maniquet. 'Compensation and responsibility', in K. J. Arrow, A. K. Sen and K. Suzumura (eds.), *Handbook of Social Choice and Welfare*, Vol. 2, Amsterdam: North-Holland. 2011.

12. M. Fleurbaey and P. Mongin. 'The news of the death of welfare economics is greatly exaggerated', *Social Choice and Welfare* **25** (2005), 381–418.

13. B. Hansson. 'The independence condition in the theory of social choice', *Theory and Decision* **4** (1973), 25–49.

14. I. Iturbe-Ormaetxe. 'Redistribution and individual characteristics', *Review of Economic Design* **3** (1997), 45–55.

15. I. Iturbe-Ormaetxe and J. Nieto. 'On fair allocations and monetary compensations', *Economic Theory* **7** (1996), 125–138.

16. M. Jackson. 'A crash course in implementation theory', *Social Choice and Welfare* **18**(4) (2001), 655–708.

17. S. C. Kolm. *Macrojustice. The Political Economy of Fairness*, New York: Cambridge University Press. 2004.

18. E. Maskin and T. Sjöström, 'Implementation theory', in K. J. Arrow, A. K. Sen and K. Suzumura (eds.), *Handbook of Social Choice and Welfare*, Vol. 1, Amsterdam: North-Holland. 2002.

19. J. Mirrlees. 'An exploration in the theory of optimum income taxation', *Review of Economic Studies* **38** (1971), 175–208.

20. E. Pazner. 'Equity, Nonfeasible Alternatives and Social Choice: A Reconsideration of the Concept of Social Welfare', in J. J. Laffont (ed.), *Aggregation and Revelation of Preferences*, Amsterdam: North-Holland. 1979.

21. E. Pazner and D. Schmeidler. 'A difficulty in the concept of fairness', *Review of Economic Studies* **41** (1974), 441–443.

22. J. Rawls. *A Theory of Justice*, Cambridge, MA: Harvard University Press. 1971.

23. J. Rawls. 'Social unity and primary goods', in A. K. Sen, B. Williams (eds.), *Utilitarianism and Beyond*, Cambridge: Cambridge University Press. 1982.

24. J. E. Roemer. *Equality of Opportunity*, Cambridge, MA: Harvard University Press. 1998.

25. A. K. Sen. *Development as Freedom*, New York: Alfred A. Knopf. 1999.

26. W. Thomson. 'Fair allocation', in K. J. Arrow, A. K. Sen and K. Suzu-mura (eds.), *Handbook of Social Choice and Welfare*, Vol. 2, Amsterdam: North-Holland. 2011.

Sources of the chapters:

The chapters are reproduced from the following articles and chapter, with the permission of the publishers (Elsevier, John Wiley and Sons, Oxford University Press, Springer), to whom we are very grateful.

1. M. Fleurbaey. 'On fair compensation', *Theory and Decision* **36** (1994), 277–307 (Springer).
2. M. Fleurbaey. 'Three solutions for the compensation problem', *Journal of Economic Theory* **65** (1995), 505–521 (Springer).
3. F. Maniquet. 'On the equivalence between welfarism and equality of opportunity', *Social Choice and Welfare* **23** (2004), 127–147 (Springer).
4. M. Fleurbaey and F. Maniquet. 'Fair allocation avec unequal production skills: The no-envy approach to compensation', *Mathematical Social Sciences* **32** (1996), 71–93 (Elsevier).
5. M. Fleurbaey and F. Maniquet. 'Fair allocation with unequal production skills: The solidarity approach to compensation', *Social Choice and Welfare* **16** (1999), 569–583 (Springer).
6. F. Maniquet. 'An equal-right solution to the compensation-responsibility dilemma', *Mathematical Social Sciences* **35** (1998), 185–202 (Elsevier).
7. M. Fleurbaey and F. Maniquet. 'Fair social orderings when agents have unequal production skills', *Social Choice and Welfare* **24** (2005), 93–128 (Springer).
8. M. Fleurbaey and F. Maniquet, 'Fair income tax', *Review of Economic Studies* **73** (2006), 55–83 (Oxford University Press).
9. M. Fleurbaey and F. Maniquet. 'Help the low-skilled or let the hard-working thrive? A study of fairness in optimal income taxation', *Journal of Public Economic Theory* **9** (2007), 467–500 (Wiley and Sons).
10. M. Fleurbaey and F. Maniquet, 'Kolm's tax, tax credit, and the flat tax', in M. Fleurbaey, M. Salles and J. Weymark (eds.), *Social Ethics and Normative Economics. Essays in honor of Serge-Christophe Kolm*, Springer. 2011.

PART 1

The Pure Compensation Problem

CHAPTER 1

On Fair Compensation

Marc Fleurbaey

ABSTRACT. This paper analyses the problems arising in the pure exchange fair division model, when some dimensions of the resources are personal, fixed, and cannot be redistributed. The remaining resources must then be allocated in a compensatory way. A set of desirable normative properties is defined. No-envy satisfies these properties, but is not generally non-empty in this setting and other criteria are examined, for which existence results are given. General impossibility results obtain. In particular, it is generally impossible to compensate fully and only for differential personal resources, when preferences differ.

Keywords: Compensation, justice, equality of resources, extended preferences, no-envy.

1. Introduction

The traditional problem of fair division involves agents who have equal claims on the resources to be shared. Although many difficulties may arise when one attempts to devise an equal sharing scheme compatible with efficiency or with other ethical requisites [see 23], in most cases the equal income Walrasian equilibrium appears as an outstanding solution [35], and can even suggest general rules for the organization of a 'just' society [38].

The situation in which the agents have unequal claims over the resources is more complicated. It has been mostly examined through the rights arbitration problem, in which the individual claims are directly expressed as amounts of the resource to be shared (see e.g. [3, 6, 24, 39]). But unequal claims may arise in a more indirect way, when the agents have differential access to other resources than those under consideration. The agents'

Theory and Decision **36**: 277–307, 1994.

preferences should then be taken into account, and the allocation of the
resources to be shared can then be selected so as to compensate the
agents. The case of differential productive talents is a well trodden although
extremely specific example of such a situation. A more abstract and general
framework has been proposed by Roemer [31], but little further research
has been made on this model.

The purpose of this paper is to revisit Roemer's general framework, in
order to pursue the exploration of the general issue of compensation. A revision of Roemer's model is proposed, in order to clarify the informational
assumptions made in this approach. This allows a formulation of general
ethical properties related to the goal of compensation, and two impossibility results obtain, which reveal the feasibility constraints bearing on such
a goal. It is shown, in particular, that it is in general impossible to compensate the agents fully, so that no handicap justify a loss in welfare, if
one wants to compensate them only for such handicaps, and not for other
personal parameters that do not call for compensation.

The paper then focuses on a particular family of ethical solutions that
may be applied to this model, namely, the solutions related to the concept of no-envy. The properties of the no-envy solution are studied first,
and the results, although mainly negative, give interesting perspectives on
other parts of the literature dealing with no-envy. In particular, as was
already argued by Roemer [30], the incompatibility between no-envy and
efficiency pointed out by Pazner and Schmeidler [26] in the production
model is essentially due to the presence of non-transferable talents rather
than production, since almost identical results obtain in a pure exchange
framework. More positive results are obtained with solutions weakening the
requirements of no-envy. A critical assessment of several solutions of this
kind is made in the paper, as well as a presentation of existence results. In
particular, a refinement of solutions and existence results by Daniel, Iturbe
and Nieto [8, 18] is proposed.

The applications that can be made of this research concern two fields.
First, the philosophical question of equalizing the social condition of people with different gifts and handicaps may receive some clarification from
an inquiry into its formal logic. Although this issue was alluded to in [28],
interest in it has been triggered by Dworkin [10], who advocated 'equality of resources' while acknowledging that in the real world the individuals
have unequal abilities to make use of the resources. Dworkin discussed two
mechanisms designed to achieve an equality of resources encompassing the
individuals' internal resources (gifts and handicaps). But Roemer [29, 31]
discovered flaws and inconsistencies in these mechanisms, and reached the

somewhat disappointing conclusion that only equality of welfare could make sense as an equality of resources. More recently, this question has been revived with a new proposal by Arneson and Cohen [2, 7]. According to them, the adequate formulation of equality of resources has to do with opportunities: the allocation of resources should give equal opportunity for welfare (or 'advantage', for Cohen) to all individuals. The analysis presented in this paper applies directly to these debates. First, this analysis shows that most of Roemer's negative results do not hold in the revised framework, and second, it turns out that the impossibility result briefly described above applies to Dworkin's first mechanism, and also to Arneson's and Cohen's solution.

Besides, this research can help us cope with more concrete fair division problems, when they display characteristics close to a set-up of non-transferable resources combined with a desire to compensate agents for that. One can think of problems linked to education or health, or of situations in which some investment has been made in a particular assignment. For instance, some specialized skills may have been acquired in jobs, and differential wages may be a simpler way to satisfy the workers than a costly shift in their positions. Or, households who have settled in different apartments may not be willing to move, while considering normal some compensation for a new nuisance in the neighborhood. As a matter of fact, many problems of fair division probably involve a dimension of compensation. In many real-life cost-sharing problems, for instance, the agents have an unequal need for or access to the facility whose cost must be shared. Imagine the construction of a large swimming pool for a group of villages. Their population size, their distance from the pool will vary, and some villages may already have their own small pool: such parameters should probably be taken into account in the allocation of cost burdens. By contrast, other parameters (such as the usual per capita taxes of each village) might very well be deliberately disregarded, although they matter in the utility each village will derive from building the facility. Similarly, airline companies sharing the cost of a runway may be willing to take account of the length of the runway each of them actually uses, and (for commercial reasons) to disregard the value of the freight they make or expect to make with it (cf. [21]). All of these philosophical and practical problems could be more easily handled if a general theory of fair compensation were developed. This paper tries to defend the project of such a theory.

Section 2 below presents the framework, and desirable compensation properties are proposed in Section 3. The impossibility results are described in Section 4. The discussion of the no-envy solution is made in Section 5,

and the next section presents the other related solutions and their existence
theorems. The last section gives a few indications about other kinds of solutions, and suggestions for further research. Most of the proofs are gathered
in the Appendix.

2. The Framework

We consider pure exchange economies, with finite numbers of agents. There
are two types of resources. Some (the 'personal resources') are already
distributed to the agents and cannot be transferred, whereas some other
resources (the 'external resources') are still freely transferable, and raise
the allocation problem under consideration. The personal resource of individual i, for $i = 1, \ldots, n$, is denoted y_i, and $y = (y_1, \ldots, y_n)$ is the population profile of personal resources. The external resources consist of only one
good x, and the extended consumption of agent i is (x_i, y_i). The consumption set of all individuals is assumed to be a product set $X \times Y$, with $X \subset \mathbb{R}$
and $Y = \{y_1, \ldots, y_n\}$. Unless otherwise stated, it will be assumed $X = \mathbb{R}_+$.
Individual i's extended preferences are assumed to generate a preordering
R_i over $X \times Y$ (with associated strict preference and indifference relations
P_i and I_i). In other words, the distribution of personal resources among the
agents is irreversible and arbitrary, but nothing prevents the agents from
imagining how they would feel with personal resources different from what
they are actually endowed with. A profile of extended preferences for the
economy is denoted $R = (R_1, \ldots, R_n)$. The preferences are assumed to be
strictly monotonic w.r.t. the external resource x. Most of the analysis of
this paper is ordinal, and the preferences provide sufficient information, but
it is useful to note that a cardinal version of the model could also be used,
with agents characterized by utility functions u_i defined over $X \times Y$. Let
$\bar{x} \in \mathbb{R}_{++}$ be the total amount of external resources which is available in the
economy. An economy is then denoted $\mathscr{E} = \langle n, y, R, \bar{x} \rangle$. Let $\mathscr{D}$ be the set of
economies satisfying these assumptions.

Formally, this model is similar to the model of large indivisibles studied
by Svensson, Maskin and Alkan [1, 22, 33], and others, with the additional
assumption that the indivisible goods y_i are already allocated.

A solution φ is a function defined over a set D_φ of economies, such
that for any $\mathscr{E}$ in $D_\varphi, \varphi(\mathscr{E}) \subset X^n$. The feasibility solution Z is defined
by $Z(\mathscr{E}) = \{x \in X^n : \Sigma_{i=1}^n x_i = \bar{x}\}$. A solution φ is feasible if for any $\mathscr{E}$
in $D_\varphi, \varphi(\mathscr{E}) \subset Z(\mathscr{E})$. From now on, all solutions examined are implicitly
defined as feasible.

Notice that what is called 'preferences' here could be any kind of performance function as well, and the results obtained in the current model can be directly applied to various settings. The most general setting would simply involve a performance function $f(x, y, z)$, the same for every agent, where z would denote the parameter which, contrary to y, does not elicit compensation. The more precise framework we adopt here for mere convenience assumes that f is welfare, and z a preference parameter. But all the results of this paper can be applied to the more general setting. As a consequence this paper does not deal with the debates concerning what outcome f is ethically relevant (welfare, capability, advantage, etc.) or where to locate the cut between y and z (circumstances vs. ambitions, responsibility, etc.).

The essence of the compensation problem, as it is modelled here, is that differential personal resources y may warrant different quantities of external resource x between the individuals.

By drawing a clear line between personal resources and preferences, this model provides the information that resourcist egalitarians need. In this respect, this model differs from that adopted by Roemer [29–31]. Indeed, Roemer rewrites this model as one in which all resources are transferable, but the personal endowments take the form of personalized goods, which only their holder likes. That is, if u_i is agent i's utility function, then $u_i(x_i, y_i)$ is rewritten as $w_i(x_i, y_1, \ldots, y_n)$, with w_i constant in y_j for all $j \neq i$, and $w_i(x_i, y_1, \ldots, y_n) \equiv u_i(x_i, y_i)$. This amounts to representing the handicapped agents as agents who particularly like scarce resources, i.e. who display expensive tastes. Obviously, in this second framework, any Pareto-optimal allocation will give the personal resources to their original holders. But the comparison of the two frameworks highlights two problems in Roemer's analysis.

First, most ethical criteria are sensitive to what is an endowment and what is a preference, and they will thus select different allocations x in the two frameworks. For instance, if the agents have identical utility functions u_i, an equal income Walrasian equilibrium will give them equal welfare in the first framework, whereas it will disadvantage the handicapped agents in Roemer's formulation, because their handicap is modelled as an expensive taste. The counter-compensation paradox presented in [29] for this equal division mechanism is therefore due only to this peculiar formulation of the problem.

Second, the consistency axiom (CONRAD), on which Roemer's reduction of resource equality to welfare equality relies, can be defended in his model because it means that cases of expensive tastes and cases of lack of cheerfulness should be treated the same way. But its translation to the problem of personal resources would simply mean that the solution must be insensitive to the presence of handicaps, and that is clearly inconsistent with the idea of compensation.

3. Compensation Properties

Before considering various compensation schemes inspired by some equity criteria, one can a priori define some desirable properties which capture the idea of compensating for an arbitrary distribution of personal resources by an adequate distribution of external resources.

The general idea of 'equal treatment of equals' leads to two desirable properties. The first one may be named 'Equal Welfare for Equal Preferences' (EWEP), and relies on the principle that individuals who happen to differ only in their endowments of personal resources should suffer no welfare gap from that fact. The strongest form of this property states that this applies to any pair of individuals:

EWEP: $\forall \mathscr{E} \in D_\varphi, \forall i, j, [R_i = R_j \Rightarrow \forall x \in \varphi(\mathscr{E}), (x_i, y_i) I_i (x_i, y_j)]$

Note that this single property forbids, in this pure exchange framework, the phenomena of over-compensation and counter-compensation identified in [29]. A weaker form stipulates that this applies only when all the individuals have identical preferences:

EWEP*: $\forall \mathscr{E} \in D_\varphi, [\forall i, j, R_i = R_j]$
$$\Rightarrow [\forall x \in \varphi(\mathscr{E}), \forall i, j, (x_i, y_i) I_i (x_i, y_j)]$$

In models with equal claims, it is simply a matter of symmetry or anonymity that two agents with the same preferences should be placed on the same indifference surface. EWEP requires this property to hold even in the presence of differential personal resources, which seems indeed warranted if one wants the agents to be fully compensated. This property may seem strong when some agents are badly handicapped and need so huge an amount of external resources that all agents end up quite badly off. But if EWEP is dropped in such cases that means that the goal of full compensation is indeed abandoned then, and that some agents are deemed entitled to a higher welfare because of their good personal resources. This in turn may be difficult to justify.

The second property related to 'equal treatment of equals' requires that, if the compensation scheme is motivated only by the arbitrary distribution of ys, the individuals who benefit from the same endowment of personal resources should receive the same amount of variable resources. Indeed, an unequal distribution in that case would mean that something else matters (for instance, the tastes of the individuals, which however are not eligible for compensation). Again, this property, whose name might be 'Equal Resource for Equal Handicap' (EREH), can be stated in various versions:

$$\text{EREH:} \quad \forall \mathscr{E} \in D_\varphi, \quad \forall i, j, [y_i = y_j \Rightarrow \forall x \in \varphi(\mathscr{E}), x_i = x_j]$$

$$\text{EREH}^*: \quad \forall \mathscr{E} \in D_\varphi, \quad [\forall i, j, y_i = y_j] \Rightarrow [\forall x \in \varphi(\mathscr{E}), \forall i, j, x_i = x_j]$$

In models with equal claims, all ordinal anonymous solutions select the egalitarian allocation $x = (\bar{x}/n, \ldots, \bar{x}/n)$, so that EREH* appears as a simple consistency requirement between the current model and the equal-claim model: since the current model contains the equal-claim model as a particular case, EREH* states that the solution should behave as all usual solutions do in this particular case. EREH is a pairwise version of this idea, and also captures the ethical goal of compensating the agents only for their personal resources, and not for preference characteristics. Notice that, in the rights arbitration model, anonymity requires agents with equal claims to receive equal shares.

The EREH axiom can nonetheless be considered as insufficient since the idea of compensation should imply differential external resources for differential personal endowments, with the adequate direction of inequality. More specifically, if in some sense i's fixed endowment is better than j's, x_j should then be greater than x_i. Since different meanings can be assigned to the phrase 'better than', this property, which may be called 'Compensation for Acknowledged Handicap' (CAH), may have several formulations. Here we will consider a particular family of such properties. For $m \geqslant 2$, let $I_{ij}(m)$ denote the set of subsets I of $\{1, \ldots, n\}$ such that $|I| = m, \{i, j\} \subset I$.

$$\text{CAH}^*(m): \quad \forall \mathscr{E} D_\varphi, \quad \forall i, j,$$
$$[\exists I \in I_{ij}(m), \forall k \in I, \forall x \in X, (x, y_i) P_k, (x, y_j)]$$
$$\Rightarrow [\forall x \in \varphi(\mathscr{E}), x_i < x_j]$$

The axiom CAH$^*(m)$ means that agent j must receive more resources than agent i if there are at least m agents, including i and j, who always prefer y_i to y_j. If $m = 2$, such a differential is warranted whenever i and

j agree that j is relatively handicapped. If $m = n$, only unanimity among the population guarantees a bigger share for agent j.

Observe that EWEP $\Rightarrow$ EWEP*, EREH $\Rightarrow$ EREH*, and CAH*(m) $\Rightarrow$ CAH*$(m + 1)$ for $m < n$. An important fact to be noted is that none of the above properties can be fulfilled by a welfarist criterion such as utilitarianism or leximin. Indeed, such criteria do not take account of the information contained in the distinction between the endowment y_i and the preference R_i. However, such a distinction is crucial in the compensation problem under scrutiny, if one seeks to compensate the agents especially for their personal endowments y_i. This is why non-welfarist criteria are examined in the sequel.

4. General Impossibilities

It is obvious that EWEP is not always possible, because some handicaps may be so unbearable that the existing resources may be insufficient to put agents with the same preferences on the same indifference surface. However, if enough resources are available, and if the preferences are sensitive enough to the external resource, this difficulty can be removed. Specifically, consider the domain $\mathcal{D}_1$ of economies in $\mathcal{D}$ which satisfy the following property:

$$\forall i, j, \quad (\bar{x}/(n-1), y_i) R_i(0, y_j).$$

Lemma 1.   *There exists at least one solution φ such that $\mathcal{D}_\varphi \supset \mathcal{D}_1, \varphi$ is non-empty on $\mathcal{D}_1$ and satisfies EWEP.*

On the other hand, EREH can always be satisfied. And the two properties are strongly consistent in some circumstances. Indeed, if all of the agents have the same preferences, EWEP implies EREH; and if all the handicaps are the same, EREH implies EWEP.

But EWEP and EREH are generally incompatible, and this is our first impossibility result. Let $\mathcal{D}_2$ be the subset of $\mathcal{D}_1$ containing economies with at least four agents.

Proposition 1.   *There is no solution φ such that $\mathcal{D}_\varphi \supset \mathcal{D}_2, \varphi$ is non-empty on $\mathcal{D}_2$ and satisfies EWEP and EREH.*

Proof.   Two slightly different examples may be used to prove this result. Assume four agents A, B, C, D, are characterized by these personal resources and preferences: A and B have the same personal resource y_1, and C and D the same resource y_2, while A and C have an identical utility function u_1, and B and D similarly share a utility function u_2. EREH requires that $x_A = x_B$ and $x_C = x_D$, while EWEP requires $u_A = u_C$ and $u_B = u_D$.

Example 1. Assume that these four agents form the whole population. One must then take account of the feasibility constraint $x_A + x_B + x_C + x_D = \bar{x}$. After elimination of variables, one gets the following system of equations:

$$\begin{cases} u_1(x_A, y_1) = u_1(x_C, y_2) \\ u_2(x_A, y_1) = u_2(x_C, y_2) \\ x_A + x_C = \bar{x}/2 \end{cases}$$

There are three equations for two unknowns, and unless the agents all have the same preferences ($u_1 = u_2$), the existence of a feasible allocation satisfying EREH and EWEP is very unlikely. This example easily generalizes: in any population with $n \geqslant 4$, the constraints induced by EWEP and EREH may add up to bring about the nonexistence of a solution.

Example 2. The subsystem formed with the first two equations above may have no solution. This is straightforward if, e.g., $u_1 = x + \alpha y, u_2 = x + \beta y$, with $\alpha \neq \beta$. As Figure 1 illustrates, it may be the case that any pair of indifference curves which intersect a point (x, y_1) never intersect for $y = y_2$.

$\square$

The examples of the proof show that the result holds in fact on much smaller domains than $\mathcal{D}_2$. There is no unappealing feature in these examples which one could easily drop. There is therefore little hope of turning the impossibility into a possibility by narrowing the domain. The incompatibility would also remain even if one restricted the application of EWEP so as to equalize only the welfare of agents with identical cardinally comparable utility functions.[1]

Moreover, although such a four-agent configuration is quite unlikely in a small population, it is bound to occur in large populations. This is obvious if one thinks of a continuum of agents each characterized by a pair (y, z) on a support, with z denoting a preference index. The only way to avoid such a configuration would be to assume a perfect correlation between y and z, but then the idea of compensating for y while holding the agents responsible for their preferences (z) would hardly make any sense.

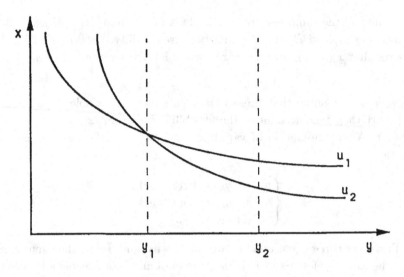

Fig. 1.

In conclusion, the general incompatibility displayed by EREH and EWEP suggests that serious limitations hinder the project of a partial compensation. EREH expresses the requirement that only handicaps y should be compensated (and not the preferences, parameters z). EWEP stipulates that the handicaps should be fully compensated (a difference in y should not by itself entail a difference in outcome or welfare). It turns out that it is in general impossible to compensate only but fully for given handicaps. In other words, the project of compensating only and fully for some handicaps y fails to provide a third way between (external) resource equality and welfare equality. If all agents have identical handicaps, an equal resource allocation will be chosen. If they all have the same preferences, the allocation should put them on the same indifference surface (ordinal welfare equality). But if both preferences and handicaps may differ between agents, the project breaks down.

The second impossibility result concerns $CAH^*(m)$.

Proposition 2.   *Unless $m = n$, there is no solution φ such that $\mathfrak{D}_\varphi \supset \mathfrak{D}_1$, φ is non-empty on $\mathfrak{D}_1$ and satisfies $CAH^*(m)$.*

Proof.   Consider $CAH^*(2)$ and assume there are three agents i, j, k, who rank their personal resources as shown in Table 1.

If one applies $CAH^*(2)$, one obtains:

— i and j consider y_i is better than y_j, and then $x_i < x_j$;

Table 1.1.

i	j	k
y_k	y_i	y_j
y_i	y_j	y_k
y_j	y_k	y_i

— j and k consider y_j is better than y_k, and then $x_j < x_k$;
— i and k consider y_k is better than y_i, and then $x_k < x_i$.

Hence a contradiction. Similarly, for CAH$^*(m)$, $m > 2$, the same cyclical problem may arise with $m + 1$ agents. Therefore only CAH$^*(n)$ avoids this impossibility, and it is immediate to check that indeed there always exists an allocation satisfying CAH$^*(n)$. □

This again may be considered a sobering result for the general problem of compensation. The usual domain restrictions of social choice theory (such as single-peaked preferences) could however be applied here in order to render CAH$^*(m)$ non-empty. The interpretation of such restrictions would have to be adapted to the context of extended preferences. Such refinements will not be considered here.

5. No-Envy

The criterion of no-envy [15, 19] stipulates that no agent should prefer any other agent's bundle to his own one. In the current framework, such bundles include the external and personal resources, and an envy-free allocation $x = (x_1, \ldots, x_n)$ satisfies:

$$\forall\, i, j, \quad (x_i, y_i) R_i (x_j, y_j)$$

Although this formulation suggests that this criterion does not represent the psychological phenomenon of 'envy' or 'jealousy', since no consumption externality appears in the individuals' preferences [16, 20], the now usual terminology [34] is referred to here, rather than the former 'equity' and 'fairness' terms, which are inappropriately general.

In a similar context of compensation for internal non-transferable endowments, no-envy has been introduced by Champsaur, Dworkin and Van Parijs [5, 10, 36]. The application of the no-envy criterion by Champsaur and Laroque is restricted to the transferable resources, which amounts to the following, in the current framework: $\forall i, j, (x_i, y_i) R_i(x_j, y_j)$. With one good and monotonic preferences, an envy-free allocation is then trivially defined by an equal distribution of the transferable good x, whatever the distribution of ys may be, and no compensation is enforced. But this results from the fact that, in this formulation, the internal endowments are unduly merged with the preference characteristics. The application of the no-envy criterion to the complete bundle (x, y) seems more appropriate.

This is what Dworkin and Van Parijs consider, and Dworkin proposes to implement an envy-free allocation through an 'extended auction', namely an equal-income Walrasian equilibrium in which the internal resources would also be virtually traded among the agents. Although Dworkin has in mind a production economy in which the internal resources are mainly skills (for this case, see also [29, 37]), this idea can be introduced into the current pure exchange framework. Let the good x be the numeraire, and let $q_i \in \mathbb{R}$ denote the value of the (total) personal endowment y_i. Let an extended equilibrium be a vector $(x, y, q) \in Z \times Y^n \times \mathbb{R}^n$, such that:

$$\forall i, j, \forall x' \in X, x' + q_j \leqslant x_i + q_i \Rightarrow (x_i, y_i) R_i(x', y_j)$$

$x_i + q_i$ may be called agent i's extended income. An interesting result, due to [33] in a related context, is that in this pure exchange framework there is an equivalence between envy-free allocations and equal-income extended equilibria. The extended auction imagined by Dworkin is not a particular way to realize an envy-free allocation: it realizes all and only the envy-free allocations.

Proposition 3. *For $y \in Y^n$ being given, $x \in Z$ is an envy-free allocation if and only if there exists $q \in \mathbb{R}^n$ such that (x, y, q) is an extended equilibrium with equal extended incomes.*

Proof.   Svensson (33, Theorem 4).   □

Now, consider how the no-envy criterion performs as far as the compensation properties introduced in Section 3 are concerned.

Lemma 2.   *The no-envy solution satisfies the properties EWEP, EREH, and $CAH^*(2)$.*

The no-envy criterion (and its subsolutions) thus ensures a seemingly adequate compensation of individuals with bad fixed endowments, and an 'equal treatment of equals'. In the corresponding equal-income extended equilibrium, the difference $x_j - x_i$ exactly compensates for the differential value $q_i - q_j$. However, the no-envy criterion does nothing to prevent agents with 'adaptive preferences' to accept abnormally low compensations: if an individual tends to adapt his preferences in order to be satisfied with his fixed endowment, he will easily be non-envious, although this may be ethically questionable. This criticism is very similar to Sen's ([32], p. 45), and in this sense, the no-envy criterion remains too welfarist.

All in all, as suggested by Lemma 2 and the above impossibility results, one runs into trouble as soon as the existence of envy-free allocations is dealt with. In fact, no-envy satisfies a much stronger (and thus unfeasible) property than CAH*(2), which is the following:

$$\forall i, j, \quad [(x_j, y_i)P_j(x_j, y_j) \Rightarrow x_i < x_j]$$

This guarantees a positive differential in variable resources to any agent who considers himself as having an unfavorable fixed endowment. It is then obvious that no-envy is empty if there exists a pair i, j of agents in which each one considers himself handicapped compared to the other one ('the grass is greener on the other side of the fence'):

$$\forall x, \quad (x, y_i)P_j(x, y_j) \quad \text{and} \quad (x, y_j)P_i(x, y_i)$$

But even if there is a configuration of preferences and personal resources so as to avoid the impossibility problems presented in the previous section, the set of envy-free allocations may still be empty, as the following example, adapted from [30], shows. Assume $u_i(x, y) = x^\alpha y^{1-\alpha}$ and $u_j(x, y) = x^\beta y^{1-\beta}$, with $0 < \alpha < 1$, $0 < \beta < 1$. It is straightforward that no allocation (x_i, x_j) can ensure no-envy between the two agents whenever $(\alpha - \beta)(y_i - y_j) > 0$, i.e. whenever the allocation of personal resources is inversely related to the intensity of preferences regarding these resources. In the language of extended equilibrium, non-existence occurs when it is impossible to find an equilibrium in which the agents have equal incomes and at the same time accept to buy the personal resource.

This example can be shown to be formally very close to those proving the incompatibility of no-envy and Pareto optimality in production economies combining different skills and different preferences [26, 37]. Indeed, it can equivalently represent the case in which the goods y are transferable but personalized (only i likes y_i, and only j likes y_j), so that Pareto optimality implies that i must receive the whole amount y_i, and j the whole y_j. But then no-envy cannot be achieved if the agents compare their bundles without taking account of the personalized character of the goods y, and if $(\alpha - \beta)(y_i - y_j) > 0$. Now, this is akin to what happens in production models when agents compare consumption-leisure bundles without taking into account that different persons' leisures are not the same goods if their skills differ (see Roemer, 1985b, for a more precise discussion). As the current model shows, the origin of the non-existence of efficient envy-free allocations first noticed by Pazner and Schmeidler is not so much the introduction of production as the presence of personal resources.

How unlikely the existence of envy-free allocations is appears clearly in the case of quasilinear utility functions, since it requires the current distribution of fixed resources y to be a maximizer, *ceteris paribus*, of the sum of the individual utilities.

Proposition 4. *Assume that for all $i, u_i(x, y) = x + v_i(y)$, where v_i is a real function on Y. Then the set of envy-free allocations is not empty only if*:

$$\forall \sigma \text{ permutation on } \{1, \ldots, n\}, \quad \sum_{i=1}^{n} v_i(y_{\sigma(i)}) \leqslant \sum_{i=1}^{n} v_i(y_i) \qquad (4\text{-a})$$

Proof. This is a corollary of Proposition 3. It can also be checked directly. If x is envy-free, for any permutation σ,

$$\forall i, x_i + v_i(y_i) \geqslant x_{\sigma(i)} + v_i(y_{\sigma(i)})$$

The conclusion obtains by summing over i.   □

Notice that the converse is true if $X = \mathbb{R}$ or if $\bar{x}$ is large enough (see [1]).

As with production economies, envy-free allocations can be proved to exist if the agents are identical in their personal resources (skills in production economies), or in their preferences. This latter condition obtains in particular when all the personal characteristics are ranked as endowments eligible to compensation. What remains as a preference ordering is then a 'fundamental preference' [17, 19], representative of the common nature of the agents under scrutiny. The EWEP* property (satisfied by no-envy) then implies that they are all located on the same indifference curve, which is the ordinal version of equality of welfare.

Proposition 5. *Envy-free allocations exist in the economy $\mathscr{E}$ if one of the following conditions is satisfied*:

$$\forall i, j, \quad y_i = y_j \qquad (5\text{-a})$$

$$\mathscr{E} \in \mathscr{D}_1 \quad \text{and} \quad \forall i, j, \quad R_i = R_j \qquad (5\text{-b})$$

Proof. (a) In this case, the egalitarian allocation $x = (\bar{x}/n, \ldots, \bar{x}/n)$ is envy-free.

(b) Since EWEP implies EWEP*, and EWEP* implies no-envy in this case, the existence result is a direct corollary of Lemma 1. □

6. Weaker Criteria and Existence Results

Other criteria have been proposed in the literature, either to solve the existence problem raised by no-envy in production economies, or to better tackle the question of compensating for internal endowments. They can be applied to the current model. Here are some existence results concerning these criteria, as well as an assessment of how well they compensate for bad fixed endowments. In this paper, only criteria inspired by the no-envy concept are examined. Other types of criteria are briefly mentioned in the concluding section.

Feldman and Kirman [11] have proposed to minimize the number of occurrences of envy, when the no-envy solution is empty. For a given economy $\mathcal{E}$ and an allocation x, let $C(\mathcal{E}, x) = |\{(i, j) : (x_j, y_j) P_i(x_i, y_i)\}|$. Formally, Feldman and Kirman's criterion is based on a mapping μ from the set of solutions into itself, defined by:

$$\mu(\varphi(\mathcal{E})) = \{x \in \varphi(\mathcal{E}) : \forall x' \in \varphi(\mathcal{E}), C(\mathcal{E}, x) \leqslant C(\mathcal{E}, x')\}$$

Existence results are easily obtained for solutions derived from μ, thanks to the following lemma.

Lemma 3. *If φ is non-empty on a domain D_φ, so is $\mu(\varphi)$.*

The particular solution that Feldman and Kirman examine is the application of this mapping to the feasibility solution, i.e. $\mu(Z)$. But this solution is ethically very weak. Consider the domain

$$\mathcal{D}_3 = \{\mathcal{E} \in \mathcal{D} : \forall i, j, (0, y_i) I_i(0, y_j) \quad \text{and} \quad \forall x \in Z(\mathcal{E}), C(\mathcal{E}, x) \geqslant n - 1\}$$

For instance, the economy of the two-agent example given in the previous section belongs to this domain.

Proposition 6. *On $\mathcal{D}$, the solution $\mu(Z)$ satisfies none of the compensation properties defined in Section 3. On $\mathcal{D}_3, \mu(Z)$ accepts all allocations in which one agent receives $\bar{x}$.*

The allocations described in the second part of this proposition are extremely inegalitarian. One agent receives the whole aggregate resource, and is therefore not envious, while all other agents have nothing and envy him. These $n - 1$ agents are envious without being envied by anybody.

A solution can be proposed, based on the idea that such situations should be avoided. It would require that each agent be either not envious, or envied by someone else:

$$\forall i, \quad [\forall j, (x_i, y_i) R_i(x_j, y_j)] \quad \text{and/or} \quad [\exists j, (x_i, y_j) P_j(x_j, y_j)]$$

In other words, this criterion would prevent any agent from being dominated, in the sense of being envious without being envied.

Proposition 7. *This solution satisfies $EWEP^*$, $EREH^*$, but none of the other properties. It is non-empty for economies such that:*

$$\forall i, j, \quad (\bar{x}/(n - 1), y_j) P_i(0, y_i) \tag{7-a}$$

Notice that in the two-agent case, this solution implies that either no agent is envious, or they envy each other. As a consequence, it satisfies $CAH^*(n)$ when $n = 2$. The fact that in the general case it does not satisfy $CAH^*(n)$ is due to the fact that it focuses on the worst-off agent only. Indeed, the reader will check that it only implies:

$$\forall j \neq i, \quad \forall k, \quad (x_i, y_j) P_k(x_i, y_i) \Rightarrow \exists j, \quad x_i > x_j$$

By taking care mostly of the worst-off agents, this solution allows very unequal positions at the top of the distribution. It even allows allocations in which one agent receives $\bar{x}$, is not envious and is envied by all other agents, while these agents have nothing and are indeed envious, but they are each envied by at least one other agent.

Such asymmetries are avoided by the 'balanced' solution proposed by Daniel [8]. This solution indeed selects the allocations such that for any agent, the number of agents she envies equals the number of agents who envy her. Pazner [25] has criticized this solution on the ground that it may accept allocations in which there are more envy occurrences than needed. For instance, it may admit allocations with envy when envy-free allocations exist. I think that this problem can be remedied while preserving the symmetry properties of the balanced solution. Define the 'μ-balanced' solution as the image of the balanced solution by the mapping μ. This solution selects the set of envy-free allocations when it is not empty, and minimizes the occurrences of envy otherwise, among the balanced allocations.

Proposition 8. *The μ-balanced solution is a subsolution of the previous solution, and satisfies the same compensation properties. But for $n \leqslant 3$, it satisfies EWEP, EREH, and $CAH^*(n)$. It is non-empty in economies $\mathscr{E}$ such that:*

$$\forall x \in Z(\mathscr{E}), \quad \forall i \text{ s.t. } x_i = 0$$

$$|\{j : (x_j, y_j) P_i(x_i, y_i)\}| > |\{j : (x_i, y_i) P_j(x_j, y_j)\}| \qquad (8\text{-a})$$

$$\forall x \in Z(\mathscr{E}), \quad |\{(i,j) : (x_i, y_i) I_i(x_j, y_j)\}| < n \qquad (8\text{-b})$$

Assumptions (8-a) and (8-b) are Daniel's assumptions, and are necessary with his method of proof. Although they do not imply a serious restriction in Daniel's analysis, in the current model they exclude important cases. In particular, (8-b) is falsified by an allocation satisfying EWEP* when all agents have the same preferences, and also by the egalitarian allocation (satisfying EREH*) when all agents have the same handicap. Fortunately, they can be weakened so as to be consistent with such cases, as shown by the following result, which relies on a different method of proof.

Lemma 4. *In Proposition* 8, (8-a) *and* (8-b) *can be replaced by the weaker assumption:*

$$\exists \delta > 0, \quad \forall x \in Z(\mathscr{E}), \quad \exists i, x_i > 0$$

$$|\{j : (x_j, y_j) P_i(x_i, y_i)\}| \leqslant |\{j : (x_i, y_i) R_j(x_j + \delta, y_j)\}| \qquad (8\text{-c})$$

This latter assumption is true in particular when there always is a non-envious agent (with positive x_i), as in the equal-preference or equal-handicap cases.

Instead of balancing and minimizing the occurrences of envy, one may focus on the quantities envied by the agents. An allocation with some imbalance or some unnecessary envy relations may be judged preferable if the intensity of envy is made lower in this way. Diamantaras and Thomson [9] have recently followed this alternative approach and proposed a solution which might be called minimax envy, since it amounts to minimizing the maximal degree of envy which the agents feel. In the present framework their formulation has to be slightly modified. For a given allocation x, let t_{ij} denote the minimal amount of external resource such that: $x_i + t_{ij} \in X$ and $(x_i + t_{ij}, y_i) R_i(x_j, y_j)$. Let $t_i = \max_j t_{ij}$, and $t = (t_1, \ldots, t_n)$. Then choose the allocation x in Z which corresponds to the leximin of $-t$. That is, minimize the greatest t_i, and then the second greatest one, and so forth until the last one.

This solution selects an envy-free allocation whenever the set of envy-free allocations is not empty, and tries to minimize the level of envy when envy is unavoidable. It is a subsolution of the μ-balanced solution when $n = 2$.

Proposition 9. *The minimax-envy solution satisfies $EWEP^*$ (on $\mathscr{D}_1$), $EREH^*$, but none of the other properties. It is non-empty in economies such that:*

$$\forall i, j, \exists M \in \mathbb{R}_+, (M, y_i)R_i(\bar{x}, y_j) \tag{9-a}$$

Still another weakening of no-envy has been proposed by van Parijs [36], under the label 'undominated diversity'. The idea is to exclude allocations in which all agents consider that some agent j is better off than some other agent i. In other words, any agent i should not envy j for some preferences R_k available in the population profile:

$$\forall i, j, \exists k, \quad (x_i, y_i)R_k(x_j, y_j)$$

Proposition 10. *The undominated diversity solution satisfies $EWEP^*$, $EREH$ and $CAH^*(n)$. It is non-empty in economies such that:*

$$\forall i, j, \exists k, \quad (\bar{x}/(n-1), y_i)R_k(0, y_j) \tag{10-a}$$

This criterion performs better than the previous ones in terms of compensation properties. But it remains quite minimal since only situations of unanimous dominance are excluded. It can be strengthened in two ways. A first idea is to require that i be fully non-envious for some preferences R_k:

$$\forall i, \exists k, \forall j, \quad (x_i, y_i)R_k(x_j, y_j)$$

Proposition 11. *This solution is a subsolution of the previous one, and satisfies the same compensation properties. It is non-empty in economies such that:*

$$\forall i, \exists k, \forall j, (\bar{x}_i/(n-1), y_i)R_k(0, y_j). \tag{11-a}$$

Another subsolution of undominated diversity has been proposed by Iturbe and Nieto [18]. For some given integer $K \leqslant n$, it excludes allocations in which for some pair i, j, there is a group of K agents (including i) who all consider j to be better off than i. When $K = 1$, this is simply no-envy. And when $K = n$, this is undominated diversity. The problem is that the choice of K has to be specified, and the smaller K, the more stringent the existence assumptions. One can define a new solution simply by choosing the smallest K, in each economy, which allows Iturbe and Nieto's solution to be non-empty. The following proposition is then a direct corollary of Proposition 10:

Proposition 12. *This solution is a subsolution of undominated diversity, satisfies the same compensation properties, and is not empty under assumption* (10-a).

7. Concluding Remarks

Further research may be undertaken in at least four directions. First, the incompatibility between EWEP and EREH can be applied to various cases in which it may not have been noticed in the literature. For instance, it has a more precise formulation when applied to equal opportunity problems, and impossibility results can then be obtained even when all agents differ in their personal resources and preferences [see 12].

Second, the pure exchange case is the basic one, but the results obtained here can in no way pretend to directly apply to problems involving production, and a specific examination of the production model seems necessary [see 14].

Third, the list of compensation properties which is referred to here is surely not exhaustive. In particular, although the EREH and CAH-like properties, to some extent, deal with the problems of expensive tastes and adaptive preferences, they certainly do not close the problem, as the flaws of no-envy regarding adaptive preferences show. More generally, a general theory of the various abstract properties which may be considered as ethically desirable in a compensation problem is still to be elaborated. Besides, other ethical properties commonly studied in the fair division literature can be introduced into this framework, such as consistency, resource monotonicity and population monotonicity.

Fourth, other criteria and compensation schemes than those studied here deserve attention. In a companion paper [13], three other solutions are studied which satisfy either EWEP, or EREH and CAH*(n). A characterization of such solutions is even possible by retaining one of these axioms while weakening the other one. One of these solutions is the egalitarian-equivalent solution, which has been introduced in the literature precisely because of the negative results obtained about envy-free efficient allocations in production economies [27]. Among other possible approaches, let us mention the insurance schemes such as the ones proposed by Zeckhauser and Dworkin [10, 40], and examined by Roemer [29].

Appendix

Proof of Lemma 1. Partition the set of agents into subsets $G_1, \ldots, G_m$ containing agents with identical preferences (and such that no two different subsets contain agents with identical preferences). Take any subgroup G_k. If $|G_k| = 1$, give this agent $\bar{x}/n$. Now assume $|G_k| > 1$. Let the function $u: X \times Y \to \mathbb{R}$ represent the common preference preordering of those agents, such that for all y in Y, $u(\cdot, y)$ is continuous and increasing w.r.t. x. There is an i_0 in G_k such that $\forall i \in G, u(0, y_{i_0}) \geqslant u(0, y_i)$. Let $\tilde{x}$ be the (unique) allocation over G_k such that $\forall i \in G, u(\tilde{x}_i, y_i) = u(0, y_{i0})$. Necessarily

$$\sum \tilde{x}_i \leqslant \frac{|G_k|}{n} \bar{x},$$

since otherwise

$$\exists j, \tilde{x}_j > \frac{|G_k|}{n} \frac{\bar{x}}{(g-1)} \geqslant \bar{x}/(n-1) \quad \text{and}$$

$$u(\tilde{x}_j, y_j) = u(0, y_{i_0}),$$

which contradicts the domain assumption $u(\bar{x}/(n-1), y_j) \geqslant u(0, y_{i_0})$. For each i in G_k define the function $f_i: [\tilde{x}_i, +\infty) \to \mathbb{R}$ by $f_i(x) = u(x, y_i) - u(0, y_{i_0})$. It is easily checked that the allocation

$$(\hat{x}_i)_{i \in G_k} = \left(f_i^{-1} \left[\left(\sum f_i^{-1} \right)^{-1} \left(\frac{|G_k|}{n} \bar{x} \right) \right] \right)_{i \in G_k}$$

is well defined, satisfies

$$\sum_{i \in G} \hat{x}_i = \frac{|G_k|}{n} \bar{x},$$

and equalizes the $|G_k|$ agents' welfare. This procedure can be applied to all subsets G_k, and one then obtains a feasible allocation satisfying EWEP. This can be done for any economy in $\mathscr{D}_1$, which provides the desired solution.

Proof of Proposition 6: The first part is a corollary of the second one, but deserves a separate proof since counterexamples abound outside $\mathscr{D}_3$.

Consider the economy $\mathscr{E}_x$, with $n = 3$, such that $R_2 = R_3$, and for $x = (\bar{x}/n, \bar{x}/n, \bar{x}/n)$, 2 envies 3, there is no other envy instance. Thus $C(\mathscr{E}_1, x) = 1$. Let there be $x' = (\bar{x}/n, x_2', x_3')$ such that 2 and 3 are indifferent to each other. Necessarily $x_2' > \bar{x}/n > x_3'$. One can assume that in x', 1 envies 2 and 3 envies 1. Thus, for any allocation in which 2 and 3 are indifferent to each other, either 1 envies 2 or 3 envies 1. There is no envy-free allocation, and then $x \in \mu(Z(\mathscr{E}_1))$, violating EWEP. (Notice that $\mathscr{E}_1$ can belong to $\mathscr{D}_1$.)

Consider the economy $\mathscr{E}_2$, with $n = 3$, such that $R_2 = R_3, y_2 = y_3$, and for any $x = (x_1, x_2, x_2)$, either 1 envies 2 and 3, or 2 and 3 envy 1. For such x, one has $C(\mathscr{E}_2, x) \geqslant 2$. But if $\mathscr{E}_2$ belongs to $\mathscr{D}_1$, one can also have $C(\mathscr{E}_2, x') = 2$ for $x' = (\epsilon, \epsilon, \bar{x} - 2\epsilon)$, ϵ small enough. Therefore $\mu(Z(\mathscr{E}_2))$ contains allocations with $x_2 \neq x_3$, violating EREH.

The economy $\mathscr{E}_1$ can serve as a counterexample for CAH$^*(n)$, just by assuming that all agents agree that y_3 is better than y_2.

The second part of the proposition is easily checked.

Proof of Proposition 7. The proof of the compensation properties is left to the reader.

For the existence, take a family of utility functions (u_i) representing the agents' preferences, and continuous in x. Let

$$E_i^\epsilon = \{x \in Z(\mathscr{E}) : [\forall j, (x_i, y_j) R_i(x_j, y_i)] \quad \text{and/or}$$
$$[\exists j, u_j(x_i, y_i) \geqslant u_j(x_j, y_j) + \epsilon]\}$$

We will show that there exists an envy-free allocation, and/or there is an $\epsilon > 0$ such that $\cap E_i^\epsilon \neq \emptyset$ (in both cases, this means the existence of an allocation without dominance). First, for any $\epsilon > 0$, E_i^ϵ is closed. For any subset I of $\{1, \ldots, n\}$, let $Z_I = \{x \in Z(\mathscr{E}) : \forall i \notin I, x_i = 0\}$. Then, if there is no envy-free allocation, one has: $\exists \epsilon > 0, \forall I, Z_1 \subset \cup_{i \in I} E_i^\epsilon$. The contrary would imply: $\forall \epsilon > 0, \exists x \in Z(\mathscr{E}), \forall i$ s.t. $x_i > 0, \forall j, u_j(x_i, y_i) < u_j(x_j, y_j) + \epsilon$. By continuity of the utility functions and compactness of $Z(\mathscr{E})$, one easily derives: $\exists x \in Z(\mathscr{E}), \forall i$ s.t. $x_i > 0, \forall j, u_j(x_i, y_i) \leqslant u_j(x_j, y_j)$. But in view of (7-a), this requires $x_i > 0$ for all i. As a consequence, $\exists x \in Z(\mathscr{E}) \cap \mathbb{R}_{++}^n, \forall i, j, u_j(x_i, y_i) \leqslant u_j(x_j, y_j)$. But this is an envy-free allocation. Therefore, either there is an envy-free allocation, or, by the Knaster–Kuratowski–Mazurkiewicz Lemma (see [4], 5.2), there is an $\epsilon > 0$ such that $\cap E_i^\epsilon \neq \emptyset$.

Proof of Proposition 8 and Lemma 4. Consider the economy $\mathscr{E}_1$, with $n = 4, \bar{x} = 20$, and assume the agents have quasi-linear utility functions

$u_i(x_i, y_i) = x_i + v_i(y_i)$, where the $v_i(y_i)$s are given by this matrix:

$$\begin{pmatrix} 2 & 3 & 0 & 2 \\ 0 & 0 & 2 & 4 \\ 0 & 0 & 2 & 4 \\ 2 & 4 & 0 & 1 \end{pmatrix}$$

One can check that $x = (5, 5, 5, 5)$ is μ-balanced, which violates EWEP because $u_2 = u_3$ and $u_2(x_2, y_2) \neq u_3(x_3, y_3)$. This also violates CAH$^*(n)$, because all agents prefer y_4 to y_3, but $x_3 = x_4$.

Consider the economy $\mathscr{C}_2$, with $n = 4, \bar{x} = 20, y_2 = y_3$, and quasi-linear utility functions $u_i(x_i, y_i) = x_i + v_i(y_i)$, defined by the following matrix:

$$\begin{pmatrix} 0 & 1 & 1 & 0 \\ 1 & 2 & 2 & 0 \\ 3 & 0 & 0 & 1 \\ 3 & 1 & 1 & 2 \end{pmatrix}$$

One can check that $x = (5, 4.5, 5.5, 5)$ is μ-balanced, which violates EREH because $y_2 = y_3$ and $x_2 \neq x_3$.

The case $n \leqslant 3$ is easy, because the balanced solution already satisfies EWEP, EREH, and CAH$^*(n)$, and therefore the μ-balanced solution as well.

Now to the existence result. We will directly prove existence under assumption (8-c), and then show that (8-c) is implied by (8-a) and (8-b). This will prove Proposition 8 and Lemma 4 simultaneously. Take an economy $\mathscr{C}$ and choose a δ as in Assumption (8-c). For any i, define:

$$E_i = \{x \in Z(\mathscr{C}) : |\{j : (x_j, y_j)P_i(x_i, y_i)\}| \leqslant |\{j : (x_i, y_i)R_j(x_j + \delta, y_j)\}|\}$$

Step one. We first show that E_i is closed. Let $\tilde{x} \notin E_i$. There is a neighborhood V of $\tilde{x}$ such that:

$$\forall x \in V, \quad \forall j \neq i, \quad (\tilde{x}_j, y_j)P_i(\tilde{x}_i, y_i) \Rightarrow (x_j, y_j)P_i(x_i, y_i)$$

This implies:

$$\forall x \in V, \quad |\{j : (\tilde{x}_j, y_j)P_i(\tilde{x}_i, y_i)\}| \leqslant |\{j : (x_j, y_j)P_i(x_i, y_i)\}|$$

Similarly, there is a neighborhood W of $\tilde{x}$ such that:

$$\forall x \in W, \quad \forall j \neq i, \quad (\tilde{x}_j + \delta, y_j)P_j(\tilde{x}_i, y_i) \Rightarrow (x_j + \delta, y_j)P_j(x_i, y_i)$$

This implies:

$$\forall x \in W, \quad |\{j : (\tilde{x}_j + \delta, y_j) P_j(\tilde{x}_i, y_i)\}| \leqslant |\{j : (x_j + \delta, y_j) P_j(x_i, y_i)\}|$$

or equivalently:

$$\forall x \in W, \quad |\{j : (\tilde{x}_i, y_i) R_j(\tilde{x}_j + \delta, y_j)\}| \geqslant |\{j : (x_i, y_i) R_j(x_j + \delta, y_i)\}|$$

Recalling that $\tilde{x} \notin E_i$, one gets:

$$\forall x \in V \cap W, \quad |\{j : (x_j, y_j) P_i(x_i, y_i)\}| \geqslant |\{j : (\tilde{x}_j, y_j) P_i(\tilde{x}_i, y_i)\}|$$
$$> |\{j : (\tilde{x}_i, y_i) R_j(\tilde{x}_j + \delta, y_j)\}| \geqslant |\{j : (x_i, y_i) R_j(x_j + \delta, y_j)\}|$$

Hence $\forall x \in V \cap W, x \notin E_i$.

Step two. For $I \subset \{1, \ldots, n\}$, let $Z_I = \{x \in Z(\mathscr{E}) : \forall i \notin I, x_i = 0\}$. Assumption (8-c) directly implies: $\forall x \in Z_I, \exists i \in I, x \in E_i$. This also reads: $\forall I, Z_I \subset \cup_{i \in I} E_i$.

Step three. By the Knaster–Kuratowski–Mazurkiewicz Lemma, one concludes from Steps One and Two that there exists an x^* in $\cap E_i$. Notice that for all x, by monotonicity of preferences:

$$|\{j : (x_i, y_i) R_j(x_j + \delta, y_j)\}| \leqslant |\{j : (x_i, y_i) P_j(x_j, y_j)\}|$$

Therefore x^* is such that:

$$\forall i, \quad |\{j : i \text{ envies } j \text{ at } x^*\}| \leqslant |\{j : j \text{ envies } i \text{ at } x^*\}|$$

Now, for any x:

$$\sum_i |\{j : i \text{ envies } j \text{ at } x\}| = \sum_i |\{j : j \text{ envies } i \text{ at } x\}|$$

As a consequence:

$$\forall i, \quad |\{j : i \text{ envies } j \text{ at } x^*\}| = |\{j : j \text{ envies } i \text{ at } x^*\}|$$

i.e. x^* is a balanced allocation. That there is a μ-balanced allocation then follows from Lemma 3.

We now show that, under (8-a), not (8-c) implies not (8-b). Thus, assume (8-a) holds and (8-c) is false. This means:

$$\forall \delta, \exists x, \forall i, x_i > 0, \quad |\{j : (x_j, y_j) P_i(x_i, y_i)\}| > |\{j : (x_i, y_i) R_j(x_j + \delta, y_j)\}|$$

Take any sequence (δ^k) converging to 0, and a related sequence (x^k) derived from this assertion. By compactness of $Z(\mathscr{E})$, one can assume that (x^k) converges to some x^*.

Consider any i. Let j be such that $(x_i^*, y_i) P_j(x_j^*, y_j)$, and J be the set of such agents j. There is a neighborhood V_j of x^*, and a $\delta_j > 0$ such that:

$$\forall x \in V_j, \quad \forall \delta < \delta_j, \quad (x_j, y_i) R_j(x_i + \delta, y_j)$$

Let $\bar{V} = \cap_{j \in J} V_j$, and $\bar{\delta} = \min_{j \in J} \delta_j$. $\bar{V}$ is a neighborhood of x^*, and $\bar{\delta} > 0$.

$$\forall x \in \bar{V}, \quad \forall \delta < \bar{\delta}, \quad \forall j \neq i, \quad (x_i^*, y_i) P_j(x_j^*, y_j) \Rightarrow (x_i, y_i) R_j(x_j + \delta, y_j)$$

As a consequence,

$$\forall x \in \bar{V}, \quad \forall \delta < \bar{\delta}, \quad |\{j : (x_i^*, y_i) P_j(x_j^*, y_j)\}| \leq |\{j : (x_i, y_i) R_j(x_j + \delta, y_j)\}|$$

Define:

$$k_i = |\{j : j \text{ envies } i \text{ at } x^*\}| - |\{j : i \text{ envies } j \text{ at } x^*\}|$$
$$L = \{i : k_i < 0\}$$
$$B = \{i : k_i = 0\}$$
$$H = \{i : k_i > 0\}$$

Notice that $\Sigma_i k_i = 0$.

If $x_i^* = 0$, i belongs to L by assumption (8-a). If $x_i^* > 0$, i may belong to L, B or H. Consider this second case. Let $\bar{V}$ and $\bar{\delta}$ be as defined above.

By construction of (x^k), and $x^* > 0$:

$$\forall V \subset \bar{V}, \quad \exists \delta < \bar{\delta}, \quad \exists x \in V,$$
$$|\{j : (x_j, y_j)P_i(x_i, y_i)\}| > |\{j : (x_i, y_i)R_j(x_j + \delta, y_j)\}|$$
$$\geqslant |\{(j : x_i^*, y_i)P_j(x_j^*, y_j)\}|$$
$$= |\{(j : x_j^*, y_j)P_i(x_i^*, y_i)\}| + k_i$$

Summing up:

$$\forall V \subset \bar{V}, \quad \exists x \in V, \quad |\{j : (x_j, y_j)P_i(x_i, y_i)\}| > |\{j : (x_j^*, y_j)P_i(x_i^*, y_i)\}| + k_i$$

Therefore:

$$\forall i, x_i^* > 0, \quad |\{j : (x_j^*, y_j)I_i(x_i^*, y_i)\}| \geqslant 1 + k_i$$

As a consequence, and since $\Sigma_{i \in L \cup H} k_i = 0$:

$$\sum_i |\{j : (x_j^*, y_j)I_i(x_i^*, y_i)\}| \geqslant \sum_{i \in B \cup H} |\{j : (x_j^*, y_j)I_i(x_i^*, y_i)\}|$$
$$\geqslant \sum_{i \in B \cup H} (1 + k_i)$$
$$= |B| + |H| + \sum_{i \in H} k_i$$
$$= n - |L| - \sum_{i \in L} k_i$$

But $|L| + \Sigma_{i \in L} k_i < 0$, hence $\Sigma_{i \in B \cup H}(1 + k_i) \geqslant n$.

As a conclusion: $|\{(i, j) : (x_i^*, y_i)I(x_j^*, y_j)\}| \geqslant n$. This contradicts (8-b).

Proof of Proposition 9. EWEP* and EREH* are satisfied because (under the additional assumption for EWEP*) minimax envy selects an envy-free allocation when the premises of these properties hold.

The following example shows that EWEP is not satisfied. Assume $n = 3$, $u_i(x, y) = x + v_i(y)$, with $v_i(y_j)$ given in this matrix:

$$\begin{pmatrix} 2 & 1 & 0 \\ 20 & 2 & 0 \\ 2 & 1 & 0 \end{pmatrix},$$

and $\bar{x} = 20$. Then minimax envy selects $x = (0, 9.5, 10.5)$, implying $t = (8.5, 8.5, 0)$. One sees that although $u_1 = u_3, u_1(x_1, y_1) = 2 \neq u_3(x_3, y_3) = 10.5$.

That EREH is not implied by minimax envy requires another example. Assume $n = 3, u_1(x, y) = y\sqrt{x}, u_2(x, y) = x + 10y, u_3(x, y) = x + y/10,$ $y_1 = 2, y_2 = y_3 = 1,$ and $\bar{x} = 20$. In this economy minimax envy selects $x = (1.25, 10, 8.75),$ with $t = (1.25, 1.25, 1.25)$. Thus, inspite of $y_2 = y_3,$ $x_2 \neq x_3$. By slightly perturbing this example, the reader will observe that one can have $y_2 > y_3$ and $x_2 > x_3$, which means that $CAH^*(n)$ is no more implied by this criterion than EREH.

The existence proof derives from the continuity of the t_{ij} as functions of x, over $Z(\mathscr{E})$, which is compact.

Proof of Proposition 10. The properties are straightforward. For existence, let $E_i = \{x \in Z(\mathscr{E}): \forall\, j, \exists\, k, (x_i, y_i) R_k(x_j, y_j)\}$.

First, E_i is closed for all i.

Second, for any $I \subset \{1, \ldots, n\}, Z_I \subset \cup_{i \in I} E_i$, with $Z_I = \{x \in Z(\mathscr{E}): \forall\, i \notin I, x_i = 0\}$. Assume the contrary. There would be an x such that for all i with $x_i > 0, x \notin E_i$. That is, $\exists\, j, j\bar{P}i$, where $\bar{P}$ is the transitive and unreflexive relation defined by: $j\bar{P}i$ iff $\forall\, k, (x_j, y_j) P_k(x_i, y_i)$. The allocation x cannot be strictly positive, since otherwise $\forall\, i, \exists\, j, j\bar{P}i$. This would imply the existence of a cycle for $\bar{P}$, which is impossible since $\bar{P}$ is unreflexive. Thus there is some j with $x_j = 0$, and some i with $x_i \geqslant \bar{x}/(n-1)$. Since $x_i > 0$, there is $i_1\bar{P}i$, and so on until one reaches some j with $x_j = 0$. By transitivity, $j\bar{P}i$, which implies $\forall\, k, (0, y_j) P_k(\bar{x}/(n-1), y_i)$. But this contradicts assumption (10-a).

By the KKM Lemma, there is $x^* \in \cap_i E_i$, which completes the proof.

Proof of Proposition 11. The method of proof is very similar to that of the previous proposition.

Acknowledgments

This paper was written when the author was visiting U.C. Davis under the program 'Economy, Justice and Society'. I would like to thank the department, and especially J. Roemer, for their hospitality. Comments and criticisms on earlier drafts by C. Arnsperger, W. Bossert, S. Kolm, I. Iturbe, Ph. Mongin, H. Moulin, J. Nieto, J. Roemer, W. Thomson, Ph. van Parijs, and an anonymous referee are gratefully acknowledged. I also thank the participants in seminars in Delta (Paris), U.C. Davis, Rochester, and in the Econometric Society European Meeting in Cambridge, September 1991.

The remaining errors and shortcomings are mine. Financial support has been provided by NATO.

Note

1. One might think that with several transferable goods the impossibility would vanish, but this is not the case. The problem, however, is that EREH has various possible extensions to the multidimensional case. One such extension is to require equality of bundles $x_i = x_j$ when $y_i = y_j$. A more sensible idea is to require only equality of shadow budgets. But in both cases, the counterexample in the proof can be applied directly, if for instance one specifies $u_1 = u(x) + y$, $u_2 = u(x) + 2y$, for some strictly quasi-concave function u.

References

1. A. Alkan, G. Demange and D. Gale. 'Fair allocations of indivisible goods and criteria of justice', *Econometrica* **59**(4) (1991), 1023–1040.
2. R. J. Arneson. 'Equality and equal opportunity for welfare', *Philosophical Studies* **56** (1989), 77–93.
3. R. Aumann and M. Maschlter. 'Game theoretic analysis of a bankruptcy problem from the Talmud', *Journal of Economic Theory* **36** (1985), 195–213.
4. K. C. Border. *Fixed Point Theorems with Applications to Economics and Game Theory*, Cambridge: Cambridge University Press. 1985.
5. P. Champsaur and G. Laroque. 'Fair allocations in large economies', *Journal of Economic Theory* **25** (1981), 269–282.
6. Y. Chun. 'The proportional solution for rights problems', *Mathematical Social Sciences* **15** (1988), 231–246.
7. G. A. Cohen. 'On the currency of egalitarian justice', *Ethics* **99** (1989), 906–944.
8. T. E. Daniel. 'A revised concept of distributional equity', *Journal of Economic Theory* **11** (1975), 94–109.
9. D. Diamantaras and W. Thomson. 'A refinement and extension of the no-envy concept', *Economic Letters* **33** (1990), 217–222.
10. R. Dworkin. 'What is equality? Part 2: Equality of resources', *Philosophy and Public Affairs* **10**(4) (1981), 283–345.

11. A. Feldman and A. Kirman. 'Fairness and envy', *American Economic Review* **64**(6) (1974), 995–1005.

12. M. Fleurbaey. 'The requisites of equal opportunity', forthcoming in W. Barnett, H. Moulin, M. Salles and N. Schofield (eds.), *Advances in Social Choice Theory and Cooperative Games*, Cambridge: Cambridge University Press, 1992.

13. M. Fleurbaey. 'Three solutions for the compensation problem', forthcoming in *Journal of Economic Theory.* 1993.

14. M. Fleurbaey and E. Maniquet. 'Fair allocations with unequal skills', mimeo. 1993.

15. D. K. Foley. 'Resource allocation and the public sector', *Yale Economic Essays* **7** (1967), 45–98.

16. S. Goldman and C. Sussangkarn. 'Dealing with envy', *Journal of Public Economics* **22** (1983), 103–112.

17. J. C. Harsayni. *Essays on Ethics, Social Behavior, and Scientific Explanation,* Reidel, Dordrecht. 1976.

18. I. Iturbe and J. Nieto. 'On fair allocations and monetary compensations', mimeo. 1992.

19. S. C. Kolm. *Justice et Equité,* Editions du CNRS, Paris. 1972.

20. S. C. Kolm. 'The ethical economics of envy', mimeo. 1991.

21. S. C. Littflechild and G. Owen. 'A simple expression for the Shaley value in a special case', *Management Science* **20** (1973), 370–372.

22. E, Maskin. 'On the fair allocation of indivisible goods', in G. R. Feiwel (ed.), *Arrow and the Foundations of the Theory of Economic Policy,* London: Macmillan Press. 1987.

23. H. Moulin. 'Stand alone and unanimity tests: A reexamination of fair division', Workshop on Ethics and Economics, University of Siena, July 1991.

24. B. O'Neill. 'A problem of rights arbitration in the Talmud', *Mathematical Social Sciences* **2** (1982), 345–371.

25. E. Pazner. 'Pitfalls in the theory of fairness', *Journal of Economic Theory* **14** (1977), 458–466.

26. E. Pazner and D. Schmeidler. 'A difficulty in the concept of fairness', *Review of Economic Studies* **41** (1974), 441–443.

27. E. Pazner and D. Schmeidler. 'Egalitarian-equivalent allocations: A new concept of economic equity', *Quarterly Journal of Economics* **92** (1978), 671–687.

28. J. Rawls. *A Theory of Justice*, Cambridge, MA: Harvard University Press. 1971.

29. J. E. Roemer. 'Equality of talent', *Economics and Philosophy* **1** (1985a), 151–187.

30. J. E. Roemer. 'A note on interpersonal comparability and the theory of fairness', Working Paper No. 261, Department of Economics, University of California, Davis. 1985b.

31. J. E. Roemer. 'Equality of resources implies equality of welfare', *Quarterly Journal of Economics* **101** (1986), 751–784.

32. A. Sen. *On Ethics and Economics*, Oxford: Basil Blackwell. 1987.

33. L. G. Svensson. 'Large indivisibles: An analysis with respect to price equilibrium and fairness', *Econometrica* **51** (1983), 939–954.

34. W. Thomson. 'Equity concepts in economics', mimeo, University of Rochester. 1990.

35. W. Thomson and H. Varian. 'Theories of justice based on symmetry, in L. Hurwicz, D. Schmeidler and H. Sonnenschein (eds.), *Social Goals and Social Organizations*, Cambridge: Cambridge University Press. 1985.

36. P. Van Parijs. 'Equal endowments as undominated diversity', *Recherches Economiques de Louvain* **56** (1990), 327–355.

37. H. Varian. 'Equity, envy and efficiency', *Journal of Economic Theory* **9** (1974), 63–91.

38. H. Varian. 'Distributive justice, welfare economics, and the theory of fairness', *Philosophy of Public Affairs* **4**(3) (1975), 223–247.

39. H. P. Young. 'On dividing an amount according to individual claims or liabilities', *Mathematics of Operations Research* **12** (1987), 398–414.

40. R. Zeckhauser. 'Risk spreading and distribution', in H. M. Hochman and G. E. Peterson (eds.), *Redistribution through Public Choice*, New York: Columbia University Press. 1974.

CHAPTER 2

Three Solutions for the Compensation Problem*

Marc Fleurbaey

ABSTRACT. A model of fair division in which differential claims are grounded in talents and handicaps is studied, and a characterization of three solutions is provided. The first two solutions, conditional equality and egalitarian-equivalence, display dual properties. The consistency axiom is shown to have strong consequences in one-good models. *Journal of Economic Literature.*
Classification Number(s): D63. D71. 131.

1. Introduction

The problem of differential claims has been dealt with in the fair division literature in a very specific way. The claims have been supposed to be expressed in the same unit as the resource to be distributed among agents (see, e.g., O'Neill [7], Aumann and Maschler [2], and Chun [3]). This is appropriate for describing problems of bankruptcy, when creditors' claims add up to more than is left. To some extent, this can also be applied to taxation issues, where income differentials are similar to claims. But in many problems of fair division, the claims consist in non-transferable differences that affect the benefit the agents can derive from the resource to be shared. In such cases, the claims cannot be directly translated into amounts requested.

---

*I thank an anonymous referee, F. Maniquet, P. Mongin, and especially W. Thomson for valuable comments; H. Moulin for helpful suggestions; and participants in a seminar in Leuven. The usual disclaimer applies.
Journal of Economic Theory **65**: 505–521 (1995).

For instance, when a group of agents share the cost of a facility, it is commonly the case that differences of distance, access, type, and amount of use justify unequal shares in a way that cannot be dealt with simply by registering monetary claims or by applying a model of cost sharing with equal claims. Consider the following example. An elevator undergoes a costly repair, whose cost has to be shared among the building inhabitants. It is likely that their willingness to pay for the use of the elevator depends on many factors, such as the floor at which they live, their frequency of going in and out, their bodily mobility, their income, and their genuine preference regarding stairs vs lift. Would the residents accept the use of a standard cost sharing model? That would imply that, for instance, the disabled tenant of the third floor should pay a big share, while the person living on the sixth floor would pay little just because he greatly values not being bothered by charity demands and environmental activists (who come more often when the elevator is operational). A more reasonable method should instead sort out among these factors those that should not affect the value derived by an agent from the repair (including cost paid): floor, possibly income, and rate of use. The cost shares should then compensate for the influence of these factors on the willingness to pay, so that the persons living on a high floor, or with a high income or frequent use of the lift, should pay more. In contrast, there would be no compensation for the other factors, and it might be deemed normal that the disabled person on the third floor derive a high utility from the repair and that the tenant on the sixth floor derive little utility from it. But this selective approach cannot be easily translated into differential monetary claims. A more comprehensive model seems necessary in order to take account of the relevant information.

In this paper, I will not address the difficult question of how the factors should be sorted out[1] and will examine only the methods by which the partial compensation can be performed. Moreover, I will restrict my attention to the basic case of a pure exchange economy, in which a one-dimensional resource has to be divided among a finite population. Each agent is characterized by a personal parameter which denotes a non-transferable talent or handicap that must be compensated for by an adequate allocation of external resource. The agents have preferences over bundles of external resources *cum* handicaps, so that they can assess how well off they would be with other possible personal parameters and other amounts of external resource.

---

[1] The classification made in the above example has only an illustrative purpose and may not satisfy the reader.

In a companion paper [4], I introduce this model in more detail and discuss its relevance not only for microeconomic fair division problems, but also for the issue of equality of resources vs equality of welfare (see, e.g., Roemer [9]) and the concept of equal opportunities.[2] All solutions studied there are inspired by the no-envy approach to equity. Here, three other solutions are examined, which are not directly related to no-envy. One of them, Pazner and Schmeidler's egalitarian-equivalent solution, is well known in the fairness literature. A characterization result is given for each of them.

Here substantial use is made of the axiom of (subgroup) consistency. The no-envy solution is consistent, but turns out be generally empty in this model (see Fleurbaey [4]). The main solutions which are based on weakened definitions of no-envy and display reasonable existence conditions, however, are not consistent. In this paper, it is shown that the consistency axiom has strong implications in any one-good model and that, nonetheless, reasonable solutions can be characterized in this model if consistency is combined with other mild ethical requisites.

The paper is organized as follows. The next section presents the model and the notation. The main properties that are desirable for a solution in this context are presented in Section 3. Section 4 proceeds with the analysis of the implications of consistency. Section 5 then presents a dual characterization of two consistent solutions. Section 6 introduces and characterizes a third solution, which is not consistent but satisfies other appealing requisites.

2. The Model

Consider a pure exchange economy, in which a given amount ω ($\omega \in \mathbb{R}_{++}$) has to be shared among n agents. Each agent i is characterized by a parameter y_i, which represents her non-transferable talent or handicap, and by preferences R_i (strict preferences P_i and indifference I_i) over pairs (x_i, y_i) in $\mathbb{R}_+ \times Y$. The set Y contains all possible parameters y that the agents may have. No particular mathematical structure is assumed for this set; we only assume that it contains at least three elements. The preference relation R_i is assumed to be strictly monotonic w.r.t. x_i, and representable by a utility

---

[2]A precise application of this approach to the equal opportunity concept is made in Fleurbaey [5].

function defined over $\mathbb{R}_+ \times Y$, and continuous in x_i. Let $\mathscr{R}$ denote the set of such preferences.[3]

Let $y = (y_1, \ldots, y_n), R = (R_1, \ldots, R_n)$ denote the population profiles of handicaps and preferences. An economy is denoted $\mathscr{E} = (y; R; \omega)$ (the number of agents is given by the dimension of y and R). Let $\mathscr{D}$ denote the domain of economies satisfying the above assumptions.

A solution φ is a function defined over a set D_φ of economies, such that for any economy $\mathscr{E}$ of this set, $\varphi(\mathscr{E}) \in \mathbb{R}_+^n$ and $\sum_{i=1}^n \varphi_i(\mathscr{E}) = \omega$. In other words, in this paper only single-valued[4] solutions yielding feasible allocations are considered.

Let z be an n vector, G a subset of $\{1, \ldots, n\}$. and k an n vector of natural numbers. Then $\#G$ denotes the cardinal of G, z_G denotes the $\#G$ vector of components of z which belong to G, and $z^{(k)}$ denotes the $\sum_{i=1}^n k_i$ vector obtained from z by replicating k_i times the ith component of z. It is assumed throughout this paper that the domain D_φ is such that if $\mathscr{E} = (y; R; \omega) \in D_\varphi$, then $(y_G; R_G; \sum_{i \in G} \varphi_i(\mathscr{E})) \in D_\varphi, (y^{(k)}; R^{(k)}; \sum_i k_i \varphi_i(\mathscr{E})) \in D_\varphi$, and $(y; R; \omega') \in D_\varphi$, for any $\omega' > \omega$. All solutions considered in this paper have domains satisfying these assumptions.

3.   Properties of Solutions

This section introduces the properties of solutions that will appear in subsequent analysis. The first one is a standard anonymity requisite.

Anonymity. If σ is a permutation over $\{1, \ldots, n\}$, for any economy $\mathscr{E} = (y; R; \omega)$ in D_φ,

$$\sigma(\varphi(\mathscr{E})) = \varphi(\sigma(y); \sigma(R); \omega).$$

Another requisite is continuity w.r.t. total resources.

Continuity. The function φ is continuous in ω over D_φ.

The consistency axiom means that the allocation selected in a given economy is still selected if only a subeconomy is considered.

---

[3]The ordinal framework adopted here is not essential to the results. See below.
[4]Single-valuedness is not a strong requirement in a one-good model with monotone preferences.

Consistency. For any $G \subset \{1, \ldots, n\}$, and any $\mathscr{E} = (y; R; \omega)$ in D_φ,

$$\varphi_G(\mathscr{E}) = \varphi\left(y_G; R_G; \sum_{i \in G} \varphi_i(\mathscr{E})\right).$$

The axiom of expansion invariance roughly has a converse meaning: any allocation selected by the solution can be retained in a larger economy obtained by addition of agents identical to some agents of the original economy.

Expansion invariance. For any k in $\mathbb{N}^n$, and any $\mathscr{E} = (y; R; \omega)$ in D_φ,

$$\varphi^{(k)}(\mathscr{E}) = \varphi\left(y^{(k)}; R^{(k)}; \sum_i k_i \varphi_i(\mathscr{E})\right).$$

When $k = (m, \ldots, m)$, we get the property of replication invariance (Thomson [15]), stipulating that the replicated allocation of a solution is the solution allocation for the replicated economy.

The next two axioms express an idea of solidarity among the agents of an economy. If the total resources expand, or if the number of agents decreases. all (remaining) agents should be weakly better off. The former idea has been introduced by Roemer [10], and the latter by Thomson [14].[5]

Resource monotonicity. For any $\mathscr{E} = (y; R; \omega)$ and $\mathscr{E}' = (y; R; \omega')$ in D_φ,

$$\omega \geqslant \omega' \Rightarrow \varphi(\mathscr{E}) \geqslant \varphi(\mathscr{E}')$$

Population monotonicity. For any $\mathscr{E} = (y; R; \omega)$ in D_φ and $G \subset \{1, \ldots, n\}$,

$$\varphi_G(\mathscr{E}) \leqslant \varphi(y_G; R_G; \omega).$$

The properties to be introduced now are more specific to this model. They express the aim of compensating *only* but *fully* for the handicap differentials of the agents.[6] If the compensation is made only for handicaps, then two agents with identical handicaps should receive the same amount of resource:

Equal resource for equal handicap (EREH). $\forall \mathscr{E} \in D_\varphi, \forall i, j, y_i = y_j \Rightarrow \varphi_i(\mathscr{E}) = \varphi_j(\mathscr{E})$.

---

[5] For vectors, the signs $\geqslant$ and $\leqslant$ mean that the same holds for all components.
[6] They are discussed at length in Fleurbaey [4]. See also Iturbe and Nieto [6].

On the other hand, if full compensation is performed, then two agents who differ only in their handicaps should obtain the same welfare, or at least, the allocation should maximin their welfare[7]:

Equal welfare for equal preference (EWEP). $\forall \mathscr{E} \in D_\varphi, \forall i, j, R_i = R_j \Rightarrow$ $(\varphi_i(\mathscr{E}), y_i) I_i(\varphi_j(\mathscr{E}), y_j)$, or $\varphi_i(\mathscr{E}) = 0$ and $(0, y_i) R_i(\varphi_j(\mathscr{E}), y_j)$, or $\varphi_j(\mathscr{E}) = 0$ and $(0, y_j) R_i(\varphi_i(\mathscr{E}), y_i)$.

A fundamental limitation to the ethical goal of compensation, in the current framework, is that these two axioms are in general incompatible: no solution defined on a reasonably large domain can compensate strictly and fully for handicap differentials.

Proposition 1.   *There is no solution on $\mathscr{D}$ satisfying EREH and EWEP.*

Proof.[8]   The counterexamples given in the proof of Fleurbaey [4, Proposition 1] can be adapted easily to the present context. Here is a simple numerical example. Consider $\mathscr{E} = ((1, 1, 3, 3); (R, R', R, R'); 5)$, with R and R' respectively represented by $u(x, y) = x + y$ and $u'(x, y) = x + 2y$. By EREH, $x_1 = x_2$ and $x_3 = x_4$. If EWEP is to be satisfied, there are several possibilities. If all x's are positive, one must have $u(x_1, y_1) = u(x_3, y_3)$, i.e., $x_1 = x_3 + 2$, and $u'(x_1, y_1) = u'(x_3, y_3)$, i.e., $x_1 = x_3 + 4$. That is impossible. If $x_1 = 0, u(x_1, y_1) \geqslant u(x_3, y_3)$ implies $0 \geqslant x_3 + 2$, which is impossible. If $x_3 = 0$, one must have $u(x_1, y_1) \leqslant u(x_3, y_3)$, i.e., $x_1 \leqslant 2$. But then $2x_1 + 2x_3 \leqslant 4 < \omega = 5$. EWEP cannot be satisfied. $\square$

As a consequence, it is useful to consider weakened versions of these axioms, which require compensation "only" or "fully", only when all agents have the same handicap or the same preferences:

EREH.* $\forall \mathscr{E} \in D_\varphi, [\forall i, j, y_i = y_j] \Rightarrow [\forall i, j, \varphi_i(\mathscr{E}) = \varphi_j(\mathscr{E})]$.

EWEP.* $\forall \mathscr{E} \in D_\varphi, [\forall i, j, R_i = R_j] \Rightarrow [\forall i, j, (\varphi_i(\mathscr{E}), y_i) I_i(\varphi_j(\mathscr{E}), y_j)$, or $\varphi_i(\mathscr{E}) = 0$ and $(0, y_i) R_i(\varphi_j(\mathscr{E}), y_j)$, or $\varphi_j(\mathscr{E}) = 0$ and $(0, y_j) R_i(\varphi_i(\mathscr{E}), y_j)]$.

Many reasonable solutions satisfy these two requisites simultaneously.

---

[7]This weakens the definition of EWEP given in Fleurbaey [4] and Iturbe and Nieto [6]. A further weakening would he possible if comparable utility functions were used: the maximin of welfare might be asked only for two agents displaying the same utility functions. For further reference, let us call this weaker axiom EWEU.

[8]The proof actually shows that EREH and EWEU are incompatible, which means that adding utility information does not affect this result.

4. Consequences of Consistency

The consistency axiom, in a one-good model, has strong consequences in terms of invariance, continuity, monotonicity, and compensation. Propositions 2 through 5 below apply to any one-good model, not only to the current one.

Proposition 2. *Any anonymous consistent solution is expansion invariant.*

Proof. Take any k in $\mathbb{N}^n$ and any economy $\mathcal{E} = (y; R; \omega)$ in D_φ. Let $k^* = \max\{k_1, \ldots, k_n\}$ and $\bar{k} = (k^*, \ldots, k^*)$. Consider the economy $\mathcal{E}^{(\bar{k})} = (y^{(\bar{k})}; R^{(\bar{k})}; k^*\omega)$. In view of anonymity, necessarily there is an allocation $x \in \mathbb{R}^n_+$ such that $\varphi(\mathcal{E}^{(\bar{k})}) = x^{(\bar{k})}$. Due to consistency, one must have $x = \varphi(\mathcal{E})$. The economy $(y^{(k)}; R^{(k)}; \sum_i k_i \varphi_i(\mathcal{E}))$ is then a subeconomy of $\mathcal{E}^{(\bar{k})}$ as defined in the consistency property, so that applying consistency again, one gets a solution allocation for this subeconomy which equals $\varphi^{(k)}(\mathcal{E})$. □

Take some given values of y and R. Then the solution φ is said here to be Lipschitzian if each component of the function $\varphi(y; R; \cdot)$ is Lipschitzian on the set $\{\omega \mid (y; R; \omega) \in D_\varphi\}$. Similarly, "the set of discontinuity points of the solution" is a short expression standing for the set of discontinuity points of the function $\varphi(y; R; \cdot)$. An element of $X \subset \mathbb{R}$ is said to be *isolated* if there is a neighborhood of this point containing no other element of X.

Proposition 3. *If a solution is anonymous and consistent, then, for any (y, R), either it is Lipschitzian or its set of discontinuity points has no isolated point.*

The proof is given in the Appendix. This proposition shows that consistency (with anonymity) precludes all cases of weak continuity or weak discontinuity. Therefore, to combine consistency and continuity in a one-good model is somewhat redundant. It is enough to resort to a mild regularity condition stipulating that the set of discontinuity points of φ, for any (y, R), is empty or has an isolated point. Let us say that a solution is *regular* if it satisfies this condition.

The next lemma is then a corollary of Proposition 3 and of a result obtained by Young on the bankruptcy model [17, Lemma 2]. A direct proof is given in the Appendix.

Proposition 4. *Any anonymous, consistent, regular solution is resource monotonic.*

It may be asked whether the regularity condition is actually necessary in this proposition, and whether the discontinuous case in Proposition 3 is possible. This is indeed the case, and here is an example of a solution which, for some economies, is neither continuous nor resource monotonic, although it is always anonymous and consistent. Partition the set Y into two subsets Y_1 and Y_2. For a given profile y, let $\alpha_1(y) = \#\{i \mid y_i \in Y_1\}$ and $\alpha_2(y) = \#\{i \mid y_i \in Y_2\}$. The solution is defined as follows. For any economy $\mathscr{E}$, if $(\omega \in \mathbb{Q}$, then $\varphi(\mathscr{E}) = (\omega/n, \ldots, \omega/n)$. If $\omega \in \mathbb{R} \backslash \mathbb{Q}, \varphi_i(\mathscr{E}) = (\omega + \alpha_1(y) - \alpha_2(y))/n - 1$ if $y_i \in Y_1$, and $\varphi_i(\mathscr{E}) = (w + \alpha_1(y) - \alpha_2(y))/n + 1$ if $y_i \in Y_2$.

The representation theorems of Young [17] can be translated into the current framework, but more structure must be assumed for the set Y. This is not examined here, because the representations obtained are still quite general and do not have a direct ethical meaning.

Proposition 5. *Any consistent solution satisfying resource monotonicity is also population monotonic.*

Proof. Consider an economy $\mathscr{E} = (y; R; \omega)$. Suppose p agents are added to the population, with profiles y' and R'. Let $\mathscr{E}' = (y, y'; R, R'; \omega)$. Necessarily $\omega' = \sum_{i=1}^{n} \varphi_i(\mathscr{E}') \leqslant \omega$. By consistency, for any $i \leqslant n, \varphi_i(\mathscr{E}') = \varphi_i(y; R; \omega')$. By resource monotonicity, $\varphi_i(\mathscr{E}') \leqslant \varphi_i(\mathscr{E})$. This entails population monotonicity. □

This result is in fact true for a large class of economic models (with several goods, production, etc.). It is also easy to check that, in the present model, resource monotonicity alone implies that the solution is Lipschitzian. It is worth noting that, contrary to what happens in most models of fair division, in this model the monotonicity properties are more easily satisfied than no-envy: they are practically implied by consistency, whereas no-envy (which implies EREH and EWEP) is generally empty. The incompatibility between EREH and EWEP is even strengthened by consistency.

Proposition 6. *Any consistent solution satisfying* EREH* *(resp.* EWEP*) satisfies* EREH *(resp.* EWEP).

Proof. Consider two agents i and j. If $y_i = y_j$, then by EREH* $x_i = x_j$ in the reduced economy formed by these two agents, and by consistency this allocation (x_i, x_j) is the same as that in the full economy.

If $R_i = R_j$, then by EWEP* (x_i, x_j) maximins the welfare of i and j in the subeconomy formed by these two agents, and by consistency again this is also true in the full economy. □

An important consequence of this proposition is the following corollary of Proposition 1:

Corollary 1. *There is no consistent solution on $\mathscr{D}$ satisfying EREH* and EWEP*.*

Therefore if one seeks to compensate as strictly and as fully as possible with a consistent solution, further weakening of the EREH and EWEP requisites is needed. This is the topic of the next section.

5. A Dual Characterization of Two Solutions

Assume that a benchmark handicap $\tilde{y} \in Y$ and a benchmark preference ordering $\tilde{R} \in \mathscr{R}$ are chosen. One can further weaken EREH* and EWEP* so as to require equal resource or equal welfare only when all agents have the benchmark parameter.

$\tilde{y} - EREH^*$. $\forall \mathscr{E} \in D_\varphi, [\forall i, y_i = \tilde{y}] \Rightarrow [\forall i, j, \varphi_i(\mathscr{E}) = \varphi_j(\mathscr{E})]$.

$\tilde{R} - EWEP^*$. $\forall \mathscr{E} \in D_\varphi, [\forall i, R_i = \tilde{R}] \Rightarrow [\forall i, j, (\varphi_i(\mathscr{E}), y_i)\tilde{I}_i(\varphi_j(\mathscr{E}), y_j)$, or $\varphi_i(\mathscr{E}) = 0$ and $(0, y_i)\tilde{R}_i(\varphi_j(\mathscr{E}), y_j)$, or $\varphi_j(\mathscr{E}) = 0$ and $(0, y_j)\tilde{R}_i(\varphi_i(\mathscr{E}), y_i)]$.

It may be noted that it would not be of much use to strengthen these axioms so as to require equal resource (or welfare) for two benchmark values of the parameters. For instance, equal resource would be required if all agents had the handicap $\tilde{y}_1$, or if they all had $\tilde{y}_2$. The same counterexample as in the proof of Proposition 1 can in fact be used to show that, with such strengthening, EREH* and $\tilde{y}_{1,2}$-EWEP*, or $\tilde{R}_{1,2}$-EREH* and EWEP*, are then incompatible (under consistency).

The benchmark parameters can also serve to define two solutions. The first one, *conditional equality*, has been introduced in a taxation model by Roemer [11]. Although Roemer's formulation is rather complex due to the model he studies, one can derive a much simpler definition in the current framework.

$\tilde{R}$-*Conditional equality.* Choose x such that $\forall i, j, (x_i, y_i)\tilde{I}(x_j, y_j)$, or $x_i = 0$ and $(0, y_i)\tilde{R}(x_j, y_j)$, or $x_j = 0$ and $(0, y_j)\tilde{R}(x_i, y_i)$.

This solution simply applies the leximin[9] criterion referring to $\tilde{R}$, and leximin here coincides with maximin. Indeed, all agents who have a higher welfare (measured by any representation of $\tilde{R}$) than the minimum level have a zero resource and then no redistribution can be made to increase the minimum level of welfare or any intermediate level (without decreasing the minimum level).

This solution may also be interpreted as representing Sen's criterion of equal capabilities.[10] Assume there is a function C which measures the capability index of a person, depending on her resources (x, y). This function directly defines a preordering like $\tilde{R}$, and equalizing the capability index across agents amounts to enforcing the conditional equality solution. It may look strange that this solution is independent of the preference profile of the population, but this is mainly because there is only one transferable good. In a more general setting, this solution would only define the distribution of *income* independently of the agents' personal preferences about handicaps,[11] but of course the allocation of transferable *goods* would depend on the agents' preferences over these goods.

Proposition 7. *The $\tilde{R}$-conditional equality solution is non-empty over $\mathscr{D}$. It satisfies anonymity, continuity, consistency, expansion invariance, population monotonicity, resource monotonicity, EREH, and $\tilde{R}$-EWEP*.*

The proof is in the Appendix.

The other solution is the *egalitarian-equivalent* solution proposed by Pazner and Schmeidler [8]. Applied to this context, the common bundle with which every agent is (at least) indifferent is an extended bundle containing the benchmark handicap.

$\tilde{y}$-*Egalitarian-equivalent.* Choose x such that $\exists \tilde{x}, \forall i, (x_i, y_i) I_i(\tilde{x}, \tilde{y})$, or $x_i = 0$ and $(0, y_i) R_i(\tilde{x}, \tilde{y})$.

Define the function $\gamma(y_i, R_i) = \inf\{x_i \in \mathbb{R}_+ \mid (x_i, y_i) R_i(0, \tilde{y})\}$. By convention, if this set is empty, then $\gamma(y_i, R_i) = +\infty$. Let $\mathscr{R}'$ be the subset of

---

[9]On this criterion, see, e.g., Sen [13]. Note that in a framework with utility functions, nothing has to be changed in the definition.

[10]See Sen [12].

[11]But not necessarily independently of their opinions: there may be a political process which decides on the function C democratically.

$\mathscr{R}$ whose elements R_i satisfy

$$\forall\, x \in \mathbb{R}_+, \quad \forall\, y \in Y, \quad \exists\, x' \in \mathbb{R}_+, \quad (x', \tilde{y})R_i(x, y).$$

This assumption simply excludes preferences for which $\tilde{y}$ is an overwhelming handicap that no amount of external resource can compensate. We can then define the domains $\mathscr{D}' = \{\mathscr{E} \in \mathscr{D} \mid R \in \mathscr{R}'\}$ and $\mathscr{D}'' = \{\mathscr{E} \in \mathscr{D}' \mid \sum_{i=1}^{n} \gamma(y_i, R_i) \leqslant \omega\}$.

Proposition 8. *The $\tilde{y}$-egalitarian-equivalent solution is non-empty for $\mathscr{E} \in \mathscr{D}'$ if and only if $\mathscr{E} \in \mathscr{D}''$. It satisfies anonymity, continuity, consistency, expansion invariance, population monotonicity, resource monotonicity, $\tilde{y}$-EREH*, and EWEP.*

The proof is in the Appendix.

These two solutions have a symmetric behavior as regards the compensation properties (compensation "only" and "fully"). As a matter of fact, and this is the main result of this paper, they can be dually characterized by this particular feature.[12]

Proposition 9. *$\tilde{R}$-Conditional equality is the only consistent solution over $\mathscr{D}$ which satisfies EREH* and $\tilde{R}$-EWEP*. The $\tilde{y}$-egalitarian-equivalent solution is the only consistent solution over $\mathscr{D}''$ which satisfies $\tilde{y}$-EREH* and EWEP*.*

Proof. Let $\mathscr{E} = (y; R; \omega) \in \mathscr{D}$. Let $\tilde{R}^{(n)}$ denote the n vector $(\tilde{R}, \ldots, \tilde{R})$. Consider the economy $\mathscr{E}' = (y, y; R, \tilde{R}^{(n)}; 2\omega)$. Due to Proposition 6, the solution φ satisfies EREH, and therefore there is $x' \in \mathbb{R}_+^n$ such that $\varphi(\mathscr{E}) = (x', x')$. In the reduced economy $(y; \tilde{R}^{(n)}; \omega)$, by $\tilde{R}$-EWEP*, φ yields an allocation x such that $\forall\, i, j, (x_i, y_i)\tilde{I}(x_j, y_j)$ or $[x_i = 0$ and $(0, y_i)\tilde{R}(x_j, y_j)]$ or $[x_j = 0$ and $(0, y_j)\tilde{R}(x_i, y_i)]$. Now, by consistency, $x = x' = \varphi(\mathscr{E})$. In conclusion, φ coincides with the conditional equality solution.

Let $\mathscr{E} = (y; R; \omega) \in \mathscr{D}''$. Let $\tilde{y}^{(n)}$ denote the n vector $(\tilde{y}, \ldots, \tilde{y})$. By Proposition 8 there exists an egalitarian-equivalent allocation x for $\mathscr{E}$. Let $f(x)$ be defined as in the proof of Proposition 8 and consider the economy $\mathscr{E}' = (y, \tilde{y}^{(n)}; R, R; \omega + nf(x))$. Since $\sum_{i=1}^{2n} \gamma(y_i, R_i) = \sum_{i=1}^{n} \gamma(y_i, R_i) \leqslant \omega \leqslant \omega + nf(x), \mathscr{E}'$ belongs to $\mathscr{D}''$. Let $x' = \varphi(\mathscr{E}')$ and $x'' = (x_1', \ldots, x_n')$.

---

[12]The characterizations can be extended in a straightforward way to the model with comparable utility functions, using the related versions of EWEU instead of EWEP. Since the two solutions remain ordinal anyway, this means that ordinalism is implied by the axioms, even if it is not assumed in the model.

By consistency and $\tilde{y}$-EREH*, for all $i, j > n, x_i' = x_j' = \tilde{x}$ for some $\tilde{x}$.

By Proposition 6, φ satisfies EWEP and then, for all $i \leqslant n, (x_i', y_i)$ $I_i(\tilde{x}, \tilde{y})$ or $[x_i' = 0$ and $(0, y_i)R_i(\tilde{x}, \tilde{y})]$ or $[\tilde{x} = 0$ and $(0, \tilde{y})R_i(x_i', y_i')]$.

Consider the possibility of $\tilde{x} = 0$. Then for all $i \leqslant n$, either $(0, \tilde{y})R_i(x_i', y_i')$ or $x_i' = 0$ and $(0, y_i)R_i(0, \tilde{y})$. In both cases, $\gamma(y_i, R_i) \geqslant x_i'$. We then have $\omega \geqslant \sum_{i \leqslant n} \gamma(y_i, R_i) \geqslant \sum_{i \leqslant n} x_i' = \omega + nf(x) \geqslant \omega$. This implies $\gamma(y_i, R_i) = x_i'$. for all i, and $f(x) = 0$. But that means that either $(0, \tilde{y})I_i(x_i', y_i)$ or $x_i' = 0$ and $(0, y_i)R_i(0, \tilde{y})$. But this property is precisely satisfied by x, and therefore $x'' = x$. By consistency, φ coincides with the egalitarian-equivalent solution on $\mathscr{E}$.

Now examine the case $\tilde{x} > 0$. We have, for all $i \leqslant n, (x_i', y_i)I_i(\tilde{x}, \tilde{y})$ or $[x_i' = 0$ and $(0, y_i)R_i(\tilde{x}, \tilde{y})]$. But recall that, for all $i \leqslant n, (x_i, y_i)I_i(f(x), \tilde{y})$ or $[x_i = 0$ and $(0, y_i)R_i(f(x), \tilde{y})]$. Therefore, if $\tilde{x} \geqslant f(x)$, necessarily $x_i' \geqslant x_i$, for all i, and then $\sum_{i \leqslant n} x_i' + n\tilde{x} \geqslant \omega + nf(x)$. But since $\sum_{i \leqslant n} x_i' + n\tilde{x} = \omega + nf(x)$, one must have $x_i' = x_i$ for all i. The same reasoning applies in the case $\tilde{x} \leqslant f(x)$. As a consequence, $x'' = x$. By consistency, φ must coincide with the egalitarian-equivalent solution. $\qquad \square$

In fact, much more than Proposition 9 is proved here. Any solution satisfying the assumptions of the first assertion of the proposition, and non-empty for $\mathscr{E} = (y; R; \omega)$ and $(y, y; R, \tilde{R}^{(n)}; 2\omega)$, must coincide with conditional equality on $\mathscr{E}$. A similar statement holds for the egalitarian-equivalent solution. As a consequence, there is no risk that by restraining the domain assumptions other reasonable solutions satisfying the assumptions of the theorem can be found.

In contrast, it is easy to check that if consistency or one of the compensation properties is dropped, then the result no longer holds and other solutions can be imagined.

6. A Third Solution

It is possible to find solutions satisfying EREH and EWEP*, or EREH* and EWEP, simultaneously, but in view of Corollary 1 such solutions cannot be consistent. Solutions of this kind can be derived from conditional equality and the egalitarian-equivalent solution. Indeed, it is enough to make the benchmark parameter ($\tilde{R}$ or $\tilde{y}$) depend on the economy, and more precisely, to choose it among the preferences and handicaps of the agents in the population. The trouble is that if the solution is to be anonymous, the choice of the agent whose parameter will be taken as a benchmark must follow an anonymous procedure, and there may be no obvious candidate in this respect.

This section is devoted to another solution, which satisfies EREH and EWEP*, but is not inspired by conditional equality, A peculiar feature of conditional equality is that it does not take account of the agents' preferences, or, in its revised version just proposed, it uses only one agent's preferences as a "norm," This feature may be useful when the preferences of the agents are not supposed to differ too much from the benchmark and when strong problems of revelation may occur. But in some cases, it may be desirable to register all agents' evaluations of the handicap profile of the population and to aggregate these evaluations in the selection of the allocation of resources. On the other hand, it is also desirable not to rely only on i's preferences to evaluate y_i, because of the possibility of expensive tastes and adaptive tastes which might lead i to make unreasonable demands on society's resources, or oppositely to be content with too little. The *average compensation* solution tries to satisfy all these requisites.

Average compensation. Select the allocation

$$x = \frac{1}{n} \sum_{i=1}^{n} x^i,$$

with $x^i \in \mathbb{R}^n_+$ satisfying $\sum_{j=1}^{n} x^i_j = \omega$ and, for all $j, k, (x^i_j, y_j) I_i (x^i_k, y_k)$ or $[x^i_j = 0$ and $(0, y_j) R_i (x^i_k, y_k)]$ or $[x^k_i = 0$ and $(0, y_k) R_i (x^i_j, y_j)]$.

In words, each agent i proposes an allocation x^i which leximins the welfare of the population according to her own preferences, and the final allocation that is chosen is simply the mean of such proposals.

Proposition 10. *The average compensation solution is non-empty over $\mathscr{D}$. It satisfies anonymity, continuity, resource monotonicity, EREH, and EWEP*. It does not satisfy consistency, expansion invariance, and population monotonicity.*

The proof of existence is similar to that of Proposition 7. The rest is omitted here.

This solution is sensitive to every agent's valuation of the handicap profile. Here is a brief axiomatic analysis of this issue, and from now on fixed values of y and ω are retained, since we concentrate on responses of the solution to variations of preferences only. To simplify notations, the profile of preferences R will appear as the only argument of a solution $\varphi : \varphi(R)$.

One way to represent valuations of handicaps in view of particular preferences is to use a preordering $\succsim$ over $\mathscr{R} \times \{y_1, \dots, y_n\}$, with $(R_i, y_j) \succsim (R_k, y_l)$ meaning that y_j is deemed a deeper (or equivalent) handicap by R_i than y_l, by R_k. A solution φ will be said to be sensitive if it responds to changes of preferences in a way compatible with some preordering of this kind (the preordering may be specific to the solution). That is, if only i's preferences change, implying a (weak) worsening of her valuation of agent j's handicap, agent j's consumption must not decrease, and if there are unanimous preferences in the economy, then a strict worsening of the valuation made by all agents must entail an increase in consumption:

Sensitiveness. There exists a preordering $\succsim$ over $\mathscr{R} \times \{y_1, \dots, y_n\}$, such that for any agents i and j, any profile R, and preferences R_i', one has

$$(R_i', y_j) \succsim (R_i, y_j) \Rightarrow \varphi_j(R_{-i}, R_i') \geqslant \varphi_j(R)$$

$$(R_i', y_j) \succ (R_i, y_j) \Rightarrow \varphi_j(R_i', \dots, R_i') > \varphi_j(R_i, \dots, R_i).$$

Here is an example of a solution which is sensitive by mimicking a social security system. There is an ex ante allocation $\bar{x}$, which is accepted by the population except that it does not take into account the handicaps y. A group of experts is asked numerical valuations of the various y_j. The weight of agent i in the expert group is α_i, and $\sum_i \alpha_i = 1$. Each expert makes the valuation of handicaps on the basis of her own preferences, and there is a function $f : \mathscr{R} \to \mathbb{R}_+^n$, with $f_j(R_i)$ being the "points" of handicap given by i to the agent j. A proportional tax is levied on the population, with rate τ, yielding an amount $\tau\omega$ which is distributed to the agents depending on the points allotted by the experts. The final allocation is given by the formula

$$x_j = (1 - \tau)\bar{x}_j + \tau\omega \sum_i \alpha_i \frac{f_j(R_i)}{\sum_k f_k(R_i)}.$$

This solution is sensitive, and the related preordering may be defined by

$$(R_i, y_j) \succsim (R_k, y_l) \Leftrightarrow \frac{f_j(R_i)}{\sum_s f_s(R_i)} \geqslant \frac{f_l(R_k)}{\sum_s f_s(R_k)}.$$

The sensitiveness axiom is rather weak, since it does not guarantee that the preordering $\succsim$ is well behaved in the sense of giving more resource to an agent if his handicap is really deemed worse (rather than better) by the agents, in terms of welfare. A minimal way to introduce such a guarantee is to require that the solution φ also satisfy EWEP*. Another weakness of the axiom is that it allows great inequalities in the weight of individual preferences, as exemplified by the above solution (in which the expert group may have only one member). An anonymity requirement seems therefore also warranted. But then the following proposition shows that there is not much of a choice as regards the solution.

Proposition 11.   *For economies in $\mathscr{D}$ with at least three different handicaps, average compensation is the only anonymous[13] solution satisfying sensitiveness and EWEP*.*

Proof.   Let $\hat{\varphi}(R_i)$ denote the leximin function which computes x^i, on the basis of R_i, for the average compensation solution.

Let j, R_i, and R_i' be such that $\hat{\varphi}_j(R_i') = \hat{\varphi}_j(R_i)$. By EWEP*, $\varphi_j(R_i', \ldots, R_i') = \varphi_j(R_i, \ldots, R_i)$. By the second part of sensitiveness, this implies $(R_i', y_j) \sim (R_i, y_j)$. By the first part, one deduces $\varphi_j(R_{-i}, R_i') = \varphi_j(R_{-i}, R_i)$, for any profile R_{-i}, of the $n-1$ agents other than i.

This entails that $\varphi_j(R)$ depends only on $\hat{\varphi}_j(R_i), i = 1, \ldots, n$. That is, there is a function ψ such that

$$\varphi_j(\mathscr{E}) = \psi_j(\hat{\varphi}_j(R_1), \ldots, \hat{\varphi}_j(R_n)).$$

Consider any agent j and any preferences R_i, such that $\hat{\varphi}_j(R_i) = 0$. By EWEP*, if all agents had preferences R_i, then $\psi(\hat{\varphi}_j(R_i)), \ldots, \hat{\varphi}_j(R_i)) = \hat{\varphi}_j(R_i)$. But this also reads $\psi_j(0, \ldots, 0) = 0$.

By anonymity, ψ must be symmetric. Assume i and j have identical handicaps $y_i = y_j$. By the symmetry of ψ, x_i and x_j, must be unchanged if R_i, and R_j, are permuted. But by anonymity they must be permuted because this is also equivalent to permuting (y_i, R_i) and (y_j, R_j). Therefore they can only be equal: $x_i = x_j$. In other words, φ satisfies EREH.

Consider the m different handicaps of the population $(m > 2)$, and let them be indexed by k. Let h_k be the number of agents endowed with y_k. For any preference R_i, an m vector x^i can be derived from $\hat{\varphi}(R_i)$ by letting $x_k^i = h_k \hat{\varphi}(R_i)$ whenever $y_j = y_k$. One has $\sum_{k=1}^m x_k^i = \omega$. By varying the preferences R_i, x^i can reach any point in the set $\{x \in \mathbb{R}_+^m \mid \sum_{k=1}^m x_k = \omega\}$.

From the function ψ and the EREH property, one can define m functions g_k such that for all $k, g_k(x_k^1, \ldots, x_k^n)$ satisfies $\varphi_j(R) = g_k(x_k^1, \ldots, x_k^n)/h_k$ whenever $y_j = y_k$. The functions g_k satisfy two properties: $\sum_{k=1}^m g_k(x_k^1, \ldots, x_k^n) = \omega$, and $\forall k, g_k(0, \ldots, 0) = 0$.

---

[13]More precisely, the form of anonymity that this result relies upon is that the solution must be invariant to permutations of preferences.

As $m \geqslant 3$, one can then apply Theorem 2 of Aczél [1, p. 8], and therefore there exist non-negative $\alpha_1, \ldots, \alpha_n$, with $\sum_{i=1}^{n} \alpha_i = 1$, such that for any profile R, $g_k(x_k^1, \ldots, x_k^n) = \sum_{i=1}^{n} \alpha_i x_k^i$. That implies

$$\varphi(R) = \sum_{i=1}^{n} \alpha_i \hat{\varphi}(R_i).$$

By anonymity, one must have $\alpha_i = 1/n$ for all i.   □

It must be emphasized that sensitiveness, and the average compensation solution, do not represent the only way in which subjective assessments of handicaps by the whole population can be aggregated. For instance, a solution proposed by van Parijs [16], and refined by Iturbe and Nieto [6] and Fleurbaey [5], also uses other agents' preferences to assess any given agent's position. Van Parijs' (multi-valued) solution selects allocations such that for any pair of agents i, j, there is at least some agent k such that

$$(x_i, y_i) R_k(x_j, y_j).$$

One sees that this solution is only sensitive to whether, according to agent k's preferences, (x_i, y_i) is better or worse than (x_j, y_j). The average compensation solution is in a sense more sensitive to the agents' preferences.

Appendix: Proofs

The following lemma is useful in the proof of Proposition 3.

Lemma 1. *Any anonymous consistent solution is such that $\forall \mathcal{E} = (y; R; \omega)$, $\mathcal{E}' = (y; R : \omega'), \omega \neq \omega', \forall i$,*

$$\frac{\varphi_i(\mathcal{E}) - \varphi_i(\mathcal{E}')}{\omega - \omega'} \in [0, 1] \cup \mathbb{R} \backslash \mathbb{Q}.$$

Proof.   Suppose that $[(\varphi_i(\mathcal{E}) - \varphi_i(\mathcal{E}'))/(\omega - \omega')] = p/q$, with p and q integers.

First case: $p > q > 0$. Consider the vector k such that $k_i = p - q$, and for $j \neq i, k_j = p$. Expand the economies $\mathcal{E}$ and $\mathcal{E}'$ into $(y^{(k)}; R^{(k)}; p\omega - q\varphi_i(\mathcal{E}))$ and $(y^{(k)}; R^{(k)}; p\omega' - q\varphi_i(\mathcal{E}'))$, respectively. It is easily checked that these two expanded economies are identical. By expansion invariance and Proposition 2, one should have $\varphi_i(\mathcal{E}) = \varphi_i(\mathcal{E}')$, and hence a contradiction.

Second case: $p < 0 < q$. Consider the vector k such that $k_i = -p + q$, and for $j \neq i, k_j = -p$. Expand the economies $\mathcal{E}$, and $\mathcal{E}'$ into

$(y^{(k)}; R^{(k)}; -p\omega + q\varphi_i(\mathscr{E}))$ and $(y^{(k)}; R^{(K)}; -p\omega' + q\varphi_i(\mathscr{E}'))$, respectively. It is easily checked that these two expanded economies are identical. By expansion invariance and Proposition 2, one should have $\varphi_i(\mathscr{E}) = \varphi_i(\mathscr{E})$, and hence a contradiction. $\qquad\square$

Proof of Proposition 3. Fix n, y, and R, and let $f = \varphi(y; R; \cdot)$. Suppose that f is continuous on its domain. Choose any i and any x_0 in the domain of f_i. The assumption made in Section 2 entails that $[x_0, +\infty[$ belongs to this domain. By continuity the image set of $]x_0, +\infty[$ by $(f_i, (x) - f_i(x_0))/(x - x_0)$ is an interval J. But by Lemma 1, $J \subset [0,1] \cup \mathbb{R}\backslash\mathbb{Q}$. Therefore, if J is not a subset of $[0,1]$, J is a singleton $\{\mu\}$, with $\mu > 1$ or $\mu < 0$. Note that if $\mu > 1$ (resp. $\mu < 0$), then for x high enough. $f_i(x) > x$ (resp. $f_i(x) < 0$), which contradicts the feasibility of the solution φ. As a consequence $J \subset [0,1]$. Since this is true for any x_0 in the domain of f_i, and for any i, that implies that each f_i is Lipschitzian on its domain. Therefore φ is Lipschitzian.

Assume that, on the contrary, f has a discontinuity point x_0, and that f is continuous over $]x_0, x_0 + \varepsilon[$, for some ε. Then, for any i, the function $(f_i(x) - f_i(x_0))/(x - x_0)$ is continuous over $]x_0, x_0 + \varepsilon[$. By Lemma 1, the image of this interval by this function is an interval $J \subset [0,1] \cup \mathbb{R}\backslash\mathbb{Q}$. But this implies that f is Lipschitzian, and thus that $\lim_{x \to x_0^+} f_i(x) = f_i(x_0)$. Since this is true for any i, f is right-continuous at x_0. By similar reasoning, one can show that if f is continuous over $]x_0 - \varepsilon, x_0[$, then f is left continuous at x_0. As a consequence, if x_0, is a discontinuity point, then in any interval $]x_0 - \varepsilon, x_0 + \varepsilon[$, there is another discontinuity point. In other words, the set of discontinuity points of f has no isolated point. $\qquad\square$

Proof of Proposition 4. By Proposition 3 the solution is then continuous. In the proof of that proposition, it was in fact shown that in this case, for any pair (x, x'), and any i, $(f_i, (x) - f_i(x'))/(x - x') \in [0,1]$. This directly means resource monotonicity. $\qquad\square$

Proof of Proposition 7. Let the function $\tilde{u}$ represent $\tilde{R}$ over $\mathbb{R}_+ \times Y$ (and be continuous in x). Choose any economy $\mathscr{E}$ in $\mathscr{D}$. For any $x \in \mathbb{R}_+^n$ such that $\sum_{i=1}^n x_i = \omega$, define $f(x) = \min\{\tilde{u}(x_i, y_i) \mid 1 \leqslant i \leqslant n\}$. By continuity of $\tilde{u}$, the function f is continuous, over a compact, and therefore attains its maximum in some feasible allocation x^*. Consider an agent i for whom $x_i^* > 0$. If $\tilde{u}(x_i^*, y_i) > f(x^*)$, then a small transfer can be made from i to all agents with the minimum level of welfare $f(x^*)$. Since $\tilde{R}$ is monotonic, with the resulting allocation x one has $f(x) > f(x^*)$, but that is impossible. As a consequence, all agents i such that $x_i^* > 0$ are such that $\tilde{u}(x_i^*, y_i) = f(x^*)$, and all agents i for whom $\tilde{u}(x_i^*, y_i) > f(x^*)$ are such that $x^* = 0$. It is immediate to check that this fits the definition of conditional equality. This solution is therefore not empty for $\mathscr{E}$.

The rest of the proof is omitted here.   □

Proof of Proposition 8. Let $\mathscr{E} \in \mathscr{D}$. The set $K = \{x \in \mathbb{R}_+^n \mid \forall i, x_i \geqslant \gamma(y_i, R_i)$, and $\sum_{i=1}^n x_i = \omega\}$ is then non-empty. It is also compact.

By continuity of the representation of R_i, if $x_i \geqslant \gamma(y_i, R_i)$ then $(x_i, y_i)R_i(0, \tilde{y})$ and therefore the set $\{\tilde{x}_i \in \mathbb{R}_+ \mid (x_i, y_i)R_i(\tilde{x}, \tilde{y})\}$ is not empty. It is also bounded because R_i belongs to $\mathscr{R}$, and thus it is compact, too, due to the continuity of the representation of R_i. Let $g_i(x_i)$ denote its maximum. It is easy to check that the function g_i, is continuous and increasing over the interval $[\gamma(y_i, R_i), \omega]$.

Let $f(x) = \min\{g_i(x_i) \mid 1 \leqslant i \leqslant n\}$. This function is well defined and continuous over K. Therefore it attains its maximum at some feasible allocation x^*.

Consider an agent i such that $g_i(x_i^*) > f(x^*)$. If $x_i^* > \gamma(y_i, R_i)$, then a small transfer from i to the agents j such that $g_j(x_j^*) = f(x^*)$ would yield an allocation $x \in K$ such that $f(x) > f(x^*)$. But this is impossible. Now, if $x_i^* = \gamma(y_i, R_i)$ and $x_i^* > 0$, then, by continuity of the representation of R_i, $(x_i^*, y_i)I_i(0, \tilde{y})$, i.e., $g_i(x_i^*) = 0$. This is again impossible. Therefore one must have $x_i^* = 0$.

Therefore. if $x_i^* > 0$, then $g_i(x_i^*) = f(x^*)$, i.e., $(x_i^*, y_i)I_i(f(x^*), \tilde{y})$. And if $g_i(x_i^* > f(x^*)$, i.e., $(x_i^*, y_i)P_i(f(x^*), \tilde{y})$, then $x_i^* = 0$. In short, x^* satisfies the definition of the egalitarian-equivalent solution.

Conversely, assume that $\sum_i \gamma(y_i, R) > \omega$. Assume there is an allocation x and a number $\tilde{x}$ satisfying the definition of the egalitarian-equivalent solution. Necessarily, for all i, $(x_i, y_i)R_i(0, \tilde{y})R_i(0, \tilde{y})$, which implies $x_i \geqslant \gamma(y_i, R_i)$. But then x cannot be feasible.

The rest of the proof is omitted here.   □

References

1. J. Aczel, *A Short Course on Functional Equations*, Reidel, Dordrecht, 1987.
2. R. Aumann and M. Maschler, 'Game theoretic analysis of a bankruptcy problem from the Talmud', *Journal of Economic Theory* **36** (1985), 195–213.

3. Y. Chun, 'The proportional solution for rights problems', *Mathematical Social Sciences* **15** (1988), 231–246.

4. M. Fleurbaey, 'On fair compensation', *Theory and Decision* **36** (1994), 277–307.

5. M. Fleurbaey, 'The requisites of equal opportunity', *Advances in Social Choice Theory and Cooperative Games*, in W. Barnett, H. Moulin, M. Salles and N. Schofield (eds.), Cambridge: Cambridge University Press, in press.

6. I. Iturbe and J. Nieto, 'On fair allocations and monetary compensations', mimeo, 1992.

7. B. O'Neill, 'A problem of rights arbitration in the Talmud', *Mathematical Social Sciences* **2** (1982), 345–371.

8. E. Pazner and D. Schmeidler, 'Egalitarian-equivalent allocations: A new concept of economic equity', *Quarterly Journal of Economics* **92** (1978), 671–687.

9. J. E. Roemer, 'Equality of resources implies equality of welfare', *Quarterly Journal of Economics* **101** (1986), 751–784.

10. J. E. Roemer, 'The mismarriage of bargaining theory and distributive justice', *Ethics* **97** (1986), 88–110.

11. J. E. Roemer, 'A pragmatic theory of responsibility for the egalitarian planner', *Philosophy & Public Affairs* **22** (1993), 146–166.

12. A. K. Sen, *Commodities and Capabilities*, Amsterdam: North-Holland. 1985.

13. A. K Sen, Social choice theory, in *Handbook of Mathematical Economics* K. J. Arrow and M. D. lntriligator (eds.), Amsterdam: North-Holland. 1986.

14. W. Thomson, 'The fair division of a fixed supply among a growing population', *Mathematics of Operations Research* **8** (1983), 319–326.

15. W. Thomson, 'A study of choice correspondences in economies with a variable number of agents', *Journal of Economic Theory* **46** (1988), 237–254.

16. P. van Parijs, 'Equal endowments as undominated diversity', *Recherches Economiques de Louvain* **56** (1990), 237–355.

17. H. P. Young, 'On dividing an amount according to individual claims or liabilities', *Mathematics of Operations Research* **12** (1987), 398–414.

CHAPTER 3

On the Equivalence between Welfarism and Equality of Opportunity

François Maniquet

ABSTRACT. A welfarist way of allocating resources consists in (1) equipping individuals with comparable indices of their well-being and (2) applying a unique aggregation rule to individual well-being levels. An equality of opportunity way of allocating resources consists in (1) making the distinction between personal characteristics which are under and beyond individuals' control, and (2) decreasing inequalities due to differences in characteristics beyond individuals' control. We show that under the proviso that indifferent individuals should not influence social judgements, welfarist and equal opportunity judgements on resource allocation are equivalent.

1. Introduction

Two main ethical theories have the lead in welfare economics, welfarism and equality of opportunity. Welfarism is the view that individual utilities are all what matters for equitable decision making. Public decisions of resource allocation should all be driven by their impact on individual utilities. Once

This paper presents research results of the Belgian Program on Interuniversity Poles of Attraction initiated by the Belgian State, Prime Minister's Office, Science Policy Programming. I thank seminar participants at the Institute for Advanced Study and especially Eric Maskin for their comments, Louis Gevers and Yves Sprumont for stimulating discussions, and Walter Bossert, Marc Fleurbaey and two anonymous referees for detailed remarks and suggestions.

Soc Choice Welfare **23**: 127–147 (2004)
©Springer-Verlag 2004

impacts on utilities are determined, collective choices are made on the grounds of an aggegation rule of individual utilities. This aggregation rule does not depend on the specific choice to be made, nor on the specific utility functions of the agents. Utilitarianism, for instance, is the welfarist theory where aggregation is obtained by summing up individual utilities.

Welfarism is prevalent, for instance, in public economics, where optimal taxation theory is built under the assumption that the social planner tries to maximize a welfarist (usually utilitarian) social welfare function. There are two main criticisms addressed towards welfarism. First, political philosophers object that social justice cannot be stated in terms of individual utilities. Rawls, in particular, has forcefully argued that taking utilities into account conflicts with a view of human beings as autonomous moral agents (see Rawls [20]). Second, welfarism also suffers from the fact that there is no consensus among economists (nor among psychologists or any others) on how to measure utilities. Public economists circumvent the latter difficulty by stating that individual utilities should not necessarily reflect agents' happiness or satisfaction but, rather, they reflect the ethical choices of the planner, that is, how the planner views the agents' happiness or satisfaction.

Recently, theories of justice based on the idea that opportunities should be equalized have been applied to economic issues. There are several competing theories of equality of opportunity (see below, beginning of Section 3). All agree that differences in agents' outcomes come from differences in characteristics they should be responsible for (e.g., because they control the value taken by those characteristics) and differences in characteristics they should not be responsible for. Equalizing opportunities consists of allocating external, transferable resources in such a way that differences in the latter characteristics, and only those differences, are eliminated. Those theories differ in how they define outcomes, and in where they put the cut between characteristics that need to be counterbalanced, which we call here compensation parameters, and characteristics which do not justify any intervention, which we call responsibility parameters. Once outcomes are defined and the compensation/responsibility cut is chosen, theories also differ with respect to the way lists of (typically unequal) individual opportunity sets are compared, that is, how individual opportunities are aggregated (see, e.g., Roemer [22] and Bossert *et al.* [6], or Kranich [17], [18], and Kranich and Ok [19]).

In this paper, we show equivalence between these two ethical theories. More precisely, we prove that if a consistency condition is imposed then any social welfare judgement based on the idea that opportunities should be equalized is equivalent to building individual utility functions and applying a utility aggregation rule. Consistency means that removing indifferent agents does not influence the social preference over suballocations. Consistency properties have been extensively studied in game theory and the fair allocation literature (see Thomson [27]). They are also reminiscent to separability conditions which are common in welfare economics (see e.g., Fleming [11] and d'Aspremont and Gevers [8]). The major aggregation rules encountered in social choice theory satisfy consistency (like the utilitarian, leximin and Nash social welfare functions; see below, Section 3).

Let us give here some first intuition of our result. It is based on a representation theorem (drawn from Blackorby *et al.* [4]) according to which any allocation ordering in an economy where the profile of preferences is fixed can be represented as a social welfare ordering, that is, an ordering on vectors of individual utility levels. This is no more than a representation, and such a so-called single profile welfarism is radically different from welfarism, since the aggregation criterion is allowed to vary from one economy to another. The main part of the result consists in showing that our axioms allow us to extend that single profile welfarism into welfarism.

This extension can be illustrated as follows. Let us consider a two-agent economy $(\{1,2\},(\theta_{c1},\theta_{c2}),(\theta_{r1},\theta_{r2}))$ where 1 and 2 stand for the names of the agents, and θ_{ci},θ_{ri} stand for the compensation and responsibility parameters of agent i respectively, for $i \in \{1,2\}$. Let us assume that individual characteristics are different. As we will argue below when defining our requirements formally, we think that equality of opportunity does not have much bite on this economy. However, our social evaluation need to be consistent with, say, economy $(\{1,2,3\},(\theta_{c1},\theta_{c2},\theta_{c3}),(\theta_{r1},\theta_{r2},\theta_{r3}))$ where we assume that $\theta_{c3} = \theta_{c1}$ and $\theta_{r3} = \theta_{r2}$. As $\theta_{c3} = \theta_{c1}$ agents 3 and 1 are different only in terms of parameters for which they are held responsible, so that resources should not be used to eliminate any kind of inequality among those agents. As $\theta_{r3} = \theta_{r2}$, agents 3 and 2 are different only in terms of parameters for which they are not responsible so that resources should be allocated to eliminate inequalities among those agents. In that economy, therefore, a compensation property imposes restriction on the pair $\{2,3\}$, and a responsibility property on the pair $\{1,3\}$. Moreover, the social evaluation in the initial economy also needs to be consistent with that in economy $(\{1,2,4\},(\theta_{c1},\theta_{c2},\theta_{c4}),(\theta_{r1},\theta_{r2},\theta_{r4}))$ where $\theta_{c4} = \theta_{c2}$ and $\theta_{r4} = \theta_{r1}$. Now, compensation imposes a restriction on the pair $\{1,4\}$ and responsibility on the pair $\{2,4\}$. As it turns out, those cross economies restrictions are so severe that once the allocation ordering is fixed for one arbitrary profile in an economy, there is only one consistent ordering for any other profile for that economy, thereby extending single profile welfarism into welfarism.

A natural question raised by this result is that of the informational basis of those ethical theories. In particular, is it possible to construct utility functions in the way suggested here by relying only on ordinal noncomparable information on individual preferences, which is the only information revealed by deterministic individual choices? We prove it is, provided all what determines agents' utility function are part of the responsibility parameters, that is, parameters for which differences among individuals do not justify any compensation.

The main achievement of this paper is therefore that it opens a way for solving the problem faced by welfarist social observers as of how to construct utility functions in an ethically meaningful way. We show, indeed, that equal opportunity requirements can be used to perform this construction, even by sticking to traditional ordinal non-comparable preferences, consistent with revealed preferences.

The paper is organized as follows. We define the model in Section 2. We introduce and justify our properties in Section 3. We state the equivalence result in Section 4. We prove the compatibility between our approach and ordinalism non-comparability in Section 5. We give all the proofs in Section 6, and we conclude in Section 7.

2.   Model and Notations

We borrow the model from Fleurbaey [14]. It is the simplest model where both equality of opportunity and welfarism make sense. There are variable sets of agents drawn from the infinite population $\mathcal{N}$. For a set of agents $N \subset \mathcal{N}$, each agent $i \in N$ is characterized by two lists of parameters $(\theta_{ci}, \theta_{ri}) \in \Theta_c \times \Theta_r$. By convention, the list θ_{ci} refers to the parameters for which society would like to compensate the agent, whereas the list θ_{ri} refers to the parameters the value of which the agent should be held responsible for.

The characterization of agents through two sets of parameters is necessary to introduce equality of opportunity allocation ordering functions. Being able to vary the value of these characteristics is necessary to define welfarism, and we have chosen to vary those values by allowing the population to change, so that an agent can be replaced by another agent with other characteristics.

Agents are likely to obtain amounts of resources. The set of possible resource amounts is denoted X. An element $x_i \in X$ can be interpreted as a bundle of goods, or, preferably, as a budget (or opportunity) set. Given resources $x_i \in X$ and parameters $(\theta_{ci}\theta_{ri}) \in \Theta_c \times \Theta_r$, agent i reaches outcome $O(x_i, \theta_{ci}, \theta_{ri}) \in \mathcal{O}$. It is sufficient for our purpose to assume that $\mathcal{O}$ is a partially ordered set. On the other hand, let us observe that function $O : X \times \Theta_c \times \Theta_r \to \mathcal{O}$ is not parameterized by any $i \in \mathcal{N}$. This is consistent with the fact that any parameter determining the relevant characteristics of the agents are embodied in the θ's.

Let us give two examples. Assume first that we wish to equalize opportunities in the schooling system (such an analysis is carried out in Roemer [22]). We may consider that students are not responsible for their genes, nor for the socio-economic backgrounds of their parents, whereas they should be accountable for their schooling efforts. In this case, θ_{ci} represents student i's genes and her parents' characteristics, θ_{ri} represents her schooling effort, measured, say, in hours of work, x_i stands for the per student expenses of the government in student i's school, and $O(x_i, \theta_{ci}, \theta_{ri})$ stands for the wage rate, or the wage rate opportunity reached by i.

Assume, as a second example, that we study income taxation on the labor market (no reform of the schooling system is possible). We may consider that workers are not responsible for their wage opportunities, whereas they are free to choose their (yearly, or lifetime) labor time (see the analyses in Bossert [5], Fleurbaey and Maniquet [16] Bossert *et al.* [6] and Sprumont [25]). Then we would have θ_{ci} for the wage rate, θ_{ri} for the labor time, x_i for the tax paid or subsidy received, and $O(x_i, \theta_{ci}, \theta_{ri})$ for (an index of) the consumption level.

An *economy* is a set of agents $N \subset \mathcal{N}$, and a list of individual characteristics. We consider the set E of all economies $e = (N, \theta_c, \theta_r)$ such that $N \in \mathcal{N}, \theta_c \in \Theta_c^N$ and $\theta_r \in \Theta_r^N$. An *allocation for an economy* $e = (N, \theta_c, \theta_r) \in \mathcal{E}$ is a list $x \in X^N$ of individual resource bundles. For an economy $e = (N, \theta_c, \theta_r) \in \mathcal{E}$, the problem faced by the ethical planner is to order elements of X^N as a function of the characteristics of the agents. As the set of agents is variable, an ethical theory can be represented by a resource allocation ordering function $\bar{R}$ whose domain is the set of economies, $\mathcal{E}$, and such that for all $e \in \mathcal{E}, \bar{R}(e)$ is an ordering on X^N, (that is, a complete, reflexive and transitive binary relation).

We will restrict ourselves in this paper to problems where compensation is possible, that is, where the amount of resources needed to equalize opportunities is always finite.

Assumption A. For all $i \in \mathcal{N}$, all $\theta_{ci}, \theta'_{ci} \in \Theta_c, \theta_{ri} \in \Theta_r, x_i \in X$, there exists $x'_i \in X$ such that $O(x_i, \theta_{ci}, \theta_{ri}) = O(x'_i, \theta'_{ci}, \theta_{ri})$.

Even if this is a severe limitation (it is indeed likely that no finite amount of money would lead any human in good health agree to become severely handicapped), it is legitimate to raise the question of compensation only when nature does not exclude by itself the possibility of compensating (as it is the case, for instance, in the two examples above).

3. Properties

In this section, we give the formal definitions of the ethical theories we are interested in. Our definitions will be axiomatic. We will begin with equality of opportunity, which is not as well known among economists as welfarism.

"There is, in the notion of equality of opportunity, a 'before' and an 'after': before the competition starts, opportunities must be equalized, by social intervention if need be, but after it begins, individuals are on their own" (Roemer [22], p. 2). Let us call 'before' the principle of compensation, and 'after' the principle of responsibility.

There are three branches of economic literature on equality of opportunity. They differ in several respects. First, they do not all give the same emphasis on the responsibility principle. Second, they do not use the same method of justification to their proposals: some are axiomatic, some are not. Third, the extent to which they have led to applications varies.

The first branch of literature, initiated by Roemer [21], directly addresses the question of the definition of the social optimum, in the social welfare function tradition. Another key feature of the approach is that the part of an individual's outcome for which she is responsible is defined as her precise place in the statistical distribution of outcomes among agents of the same type (see [28]). This approach has led to various applications, studying for instance how to finance the schooling system or the health system (see Roemer [22]).

The second branch, initiated by Fleurbaey [12] and Bossert [5], tries to define the social optimum axiomatically, and focusses on the possible dilemma between the principles of compensation and responsibility. The approach has been applied to health care insurance system (see Schokkaert *et al.* [23]) and minimum income (see Fleurbaey *et al.* [15]).

In those first two branches, it is assumed that individuals draw their outcomes from opportunity sets, opportunities depend both on resources and individual parameters, and the objective is to evaluate distribution of resources. In the third branch, initiated by Kranich [17], the purpose is to evaluate distributions of opportunity sets directly, and optimal distributions are equal ones. How people derive outcomes from opportunity sets is no longer part of the picture. Also, and more importantly, how opportunity sets depend on the combination of resources and individual parameters is no longer an issue. Therefore, one can say that the approach concentrates on the compensation principle, and axiomatically develops ways to measure the degrees of achievement of the compensation objective (such a measure straightforwardly yields an ordering: a distribution of opportunity sets is at least as good as another if the equality measure is at least as high for the first distribution as for the other one). One key result in this approach is that inequality between opportunity sets should be evaluated on the basis of general advantage functions: inequality is measured on the grounds of differences in the advantage associated to each set. To the best of our knowledge, it has not yet given rise to empirical applications.

We begin by stating properties which allocation ordering functions should satisfy if they are to capture the equality of opportunity ethics. Given the different theoretical developments of these ideas in the economic literature, our strategy is to define weak properties which may be viewed as being somehow at the intersection of all three main branches of the literature. We briefly explain below the degree to which each branch is compatible with our own properties.

All those properties are inspired by the indifference version of Suppes' grading principles (Suppes [26]; Sen [24]), and, therefore, they are consistent with any degree of inequality aversion. The first property, called Compensation, requires that permuting the outcome levels of two agents having the same responsibility parameters but possibly different compensation parameters leads to two socially equivalent allocations. The justification is clear: as those agents have the same responsibility parameters, society should treat the outcomes of those two agents anonymously: if outcomes are permuted, then we obtain an equally good, or equally bad, allocation. Let us illustrate the principle by using the second example presented in Section 3. Let $\theta_{ci}, \theta_{ri}, x_i$ and $O(x_i, \theta_{ci}, \theta_{ri})$ denote the wage rate, labor time, tax paid (or subsidy received) and consumption of an agent $i \in \mathcal{N}$, that is, $O(x_i, \theta_{ci}, \theta_{ri}) = x_i + \theta_{ci}\theta_{ri}$. If two agents have the same labor time, $\theta_{rj} = \theta_{rk}$, then society should treat differences in their consumption independently of their wage rate, that is, tax profiles (x_j, x_k) and (x'_j, x'_k) such that $x_j + \theta_{cj}\theta_{rj} = x'_k + \theta_{ck}\theta_{rk}$ and $x'_j + \theta_{cj}\theta_{rj} = x_k + \theta_{ck}\theta_{rk}$ should be equivalent.

Compensation. For all $e = (N, \theta_c, \theta_r) \in \mathcal{E}, j, k \in N$ such that $\theta_{rj} = \theta_{rk}, x, x' \in X^N$ such that $x_i = x'_i$ for all $i \neq j, k$: if $O(x_j, \theta_{cj}, \theta_{rj}) = O(x'_k, \theta_{ck}, \theta_{rk})$ and $O(x'_j, \theta_{cj}, \theta_{rj}) = O(x_k, \theta_{ck}, \theta_{rk})$, then $x\bar{I}(e)x'$.

It will be sufficient in some cases below to focus on the following much weaker property. It offers a similar requirement as that above but restricted to the cases where the agents' responsibility parameters are equal to some reference parameter $\tilde{\theta}_r \in \Theta_r$.

Minimal Compensation. There exists $\tilde{\theta}_r \in \Theta_r$ such that for all $e = (N, \theta_c, \theta_r) \in \mathcal{E}, j, k \in N$ such that $\theta_{rj} = \theta_{rk} = \tilde{\theta}_r, x, x' \in X^N$ such that $x_i = x'_i$ for all $i \neq j, k$: if $O(x_j, \theta_{cj}, \theta_{rj}) = O(x'_k, \theta_{ck}, \theta_{rk})$ and $O(x'_j, \theta_{cj}, \theta_{rj}) = O(x_k, \theta_{ck}, \theta_{rk})$, then $x\bar{I}(e)x'$.

The next two properties are consistent with the idea that society should counterbalance differences in compensation parameters only. That is, if two agents differ only in terms of their responsibility parameters, society should treat them indifferently, so that their respective outcomes reflect the differences in the parameters they control. The third property, called Responsibility, requires that permuting the bundles of two agents having the same compensation parameters but possibly different responsibility parameters leads to two socially equivalent allocations. Again, the justification is clear: as those agents have the same compensation parameters, society should treat the resources allocated to those two agents anonymously. By permuting resource bundles, we obtain an equally good, or equally bad, allocation. Coming back to the example above, Responsibility requires that when two agents have the same wage rate $\theta_{cj} = \theta_{ck}$, differences in their taxes should be treated independently of their labor time, that is, tax profiles (x_j, x_k) and (x'_j, x_k) such that $x_j = x'_k$ and $x'_j = x_k$ should be equivalent.

Responsibility. For all $e = (N, \theta_c, \theta_r) \in \mathcal{E}, j, k \in N$ such that $\theta_{cj} = \theta_{ck}, x, x' \in X^N$ such that $x_i = x'_i$ for all $i \neq j, k$: if $x_j = x'_k$ and $x'_j = x_k$, then $x\bar{I}(e)x'$.

It will also prove sufficient in some cases below to focus on a weaker property, obtained by restricting the above requirement to the cases where the agents' compensation parameters are equal to some reference parameter $\tilde{\theta}_c \in \Theta_c$.

Minimal Responsibility. There exists $\tilde{\theta}_c \in \Theta_c$ such that for all $e = (N, \theta_c, \theta_r) \in \mathcal{E}, j, k \in N$ such that $\theta_{cj} = \theta_{ck} = \tilde{\theta}_c, x, x' \in X^N$ such that $x_i = x'_i$ for all $i \neq j, k$: if $x_j = x'_k$ and $x'_j = x_k$, then $x\bar{I}(e)x'$.

Let us now briefly comment on how Compensation and Responsibility articulate with the three approaches to equality of opportunity. Roemer's main proposal consists in maximizing a social objective which, under appropriate assumptions, can be stated as follows. Suppose that Θ_c contains a finite set of values, and that Θ_r is a completely ordered infinite set. Assume that the values taken by θ_c and θ_r are independent of the distribution of resources x. Let $F(\theta_r \mid \theta_c)$ denote the cumulative distribution function of the responsibility parameter θ_r in the infinite group of agents with compensation parameter θ_c. Two agents with different compensation parameters $\theta_c \neq \theta'_c$ are viewed to have equivalent responsibility parameters θ_r and θ'_r if $F(\theta_r \mid \theta_c) = F(\theta'_r \mid \theta'_c)$. Let us rewrite the outcome function as $Q(x, \theta_c, \pi) = O(x, \theta_c, \theta_r)$ if $F(\theta_r \mid \theta_c) = \pi$. The social objective is to allocate resources so as to maximize

$$\int_0^1 \min_{\Theta_c} Q(x(\theta_c, \theta_r), \theta_c, \pi) d\pi.$$

Provided that we replace θ_r with $F(\theta_r \mid \theta_c)$, this objective satisfies Compensation: permuting the outcomes of two agents having the same π does not affect the minimization operation. On the other hand, this objective does not satisfy even Minimal Responsibility.

In the Fleurbaey-Bossert approach, both compensation and responsibility principles play a crucial role. The traditional requirements in that literature are that outcomes be equalized among agents with the same responsibility parameters and that resources be equalized among agents with the same compensation parameters. Those requirements amount to imposing an infinite degree of inequality aversion, whereas Compensation and Responsibility as stated in this paper are compatible with any degree of inequality aversion. Some prominent solutions proposed in that literature typically satisfy one principle and the minimal version of the other.

In the Kranich approach, allocations of opportunity sets should be evaluated by using some advantage function, measuring how each set offers more or less advantages than the others. In the model of this paper, we may assume that the set of opportunities of an agent typically depends on her resources x and her compensation parameter θ_c. Let us assume that it is possible to construct a function S such that $S(x, \theta_c)$

denotes the opportunity set facing an agent with resources x and parameter θ_c. Under these assumptions, if two agents have the same compensation parameters, say θ_c, then their opportunity set only depends on the resource they get: $S(x_j, \theta_{cj}) = S(x_k, \theta_{ck})$ whenever $x_j = x_k$. Any opportunity set inequality measure, therefore, satisfies Responsibility. Moreover, let us assume that the outcome function O is real-valued. By defining an advantage function A as $A(S(x_i, \theta_{ci})) = O(x, \theta_{ci}, \tilde{\theta}_r)$ for some $\tilde{\theta}_r \in \Theta_r$, we obtain an opportunity set inequality measure satisfying Minimal Compensation.

Resources should be allocated to equalize opportunities. Consequently, resource bundles only matter inasmuch as they allow agents to reach high outcome levels. The crucial parameters which the planner should look at to compare allocations should not be the resource bundles as such but agents' outcomes. This is captured by the following Social Indifference property. It requires that two allocations leading to the same outcome to each agent should be deemed equivalent. It is reminiscent to the usual Pareto Indifference property. Recall that we did not introduce preferences explicitly in our setting.

Social Indifference. For all $e = (N, \theta_c, \theta_r) \in \mathscr{E}, x, x' \in X^N$, if $O(x_i, \theta_{ci}, \theta_{ri}) = O(x'_i, \theta_{ci}, \theta_{ri})$ for all $i \in N$, then $x \bar{I}(e) x'$.

We consider that the five axioms defined so far are the cornerstone of equality of opportunity. Any particular theory could, of course, be more demanding about either the compensation or the responsibility principle, but the ideas captured in those principles must be part of any specific theory. At the generality level of the model we study here, however, the existence of social ordering functions satisfying Compensation and Responsibility is not guaranteed (thereby illustrating the trade-off analysed in the second branch of the literature presented above), so that we will restrict ourselves to combining either principle with the minimal version of the other.

This paper is aimed at studying the relationship between recent theories of equality of opportunity and welfarism, the long since dominating theory in welfare economics. It is essential here to distinguish between two different traditions in welfarist ethics. Of course, all welfarists agree that collective choice should be a matter of welfare aggregation, but not all welfarists agree on what welfare refers to.

In the first tradition, welfare refers to some subjective appraisal of one's own well-being (see e.g., Blackorby *et al.* [3]). In the second tradition, welfare is not necessarily a subjective notion but can refer to any a priori comparable indices of individual well-being (see d'Aspremont and Gevers [9]). These indices are commonly interpreted as utility functions representing individual preferences, but may as well be summaries of individuals' doings and beings, or life expectancy, etc. That is, welfarism, in the latter tradition, is a flexible ethical theory, as it can be used to aggregate any kind of well-being indicators. But, as a consequence, it is an incomplete theory, as it does not tell the ethical observer how to construct those indicators. This paper is an attempt to complement this tradition with an ethically meaningful theory of how to construct welfare indicators.

We now proceed by recalling the definition of welfarism (see e.g., d' Aspremont and Gevers [9]).

A *utility function* is a function $U : X \to \mathbb{R}$. The set of all utility functions is denoted $\mathscr{U}$. A *utility representation of the outcome function* is a function $U : \Theta_c \times \Theta_r \to \mathscr{U}$ such that for all $(\theta_c, \theta_r) \in \Theta_c \times \Theta_r$, and $x, x' \in X$:

$$[O(x, \theta_c, \theta_r) \geq O(x', \theta_c, \theta_r)] \Leftrightarrow [U_{\theta_c, \theta_r}(x) \geq U_{\theta_c, \theta_r}(x')].$$

A *social welfare ordering* for $N \subset \mathscr{N}$ is an ordering on $\mathbb{R}^N$. A *social welfare ordering function*, denoted $\underline{R}$, associates to each $N \subset \mathscr{N}$ an ordering $\underline{R}(N)$ on $\mathbb{R}^N$.

Welfarism. There exist $U_{..}$ and a unique $\underline{R}$ such that for all $e = (N, \theta_c, \theta_r) \in \mathscr{E}$, $x, x' \in X^N$

$$x \bar{R}(e) x' \Leftrightarrow u \underline{R}(N) u'$$

where for all $i \in N, u_i = U_{\theta_{ci}, \theta_{ri}}(x_i)$ and $u'_i = U_{\theta_{ci}, \theta_{ri}}(x'_i)$ and $\underline{R}$ is said to be associated to $\bar{R}$.

We will restrict our attention to welfarist ordering functions that are minimally equitable in the sense of anonymity. It is clear that any defendable ethical theory satisfies this requirement. *Anonymity* requires that the identities of the agents do not matter in social judgements, that is, if two agents permute their utility levels, then the social welfare ranking remains unaffected. For $N \in \mathscr{N}$, let Π_N denote the set of all permutations of N.

Anonymity[W]. For all $N \in \mathscr{N}, u, u' \in \mathbb{R}^N$ and $\pi \in \Pi_N$: if $u \underline{R}(N) u'$ then $\pi(u) \underline{R}(N) \pi(u')$.

Our main result, stated in the following section, establishes the equivalence between the two theories we are interested in, provided they satisfy some cross-economy consistency requirement.[1] The next axiom is a natural adaptation in our framework of the consistency property which has been extensively studied in game theory and the fair allocation literature (see Thomson [27]). Consistency works like this. If an allocation is socially as good as another, and if a subset of agents are assigned exactly the same resource bundles in both allocations, then removing those agents with their resources should not change the social preference, that is, the suballocation obtained from the first allocation by removing those agents should still be as good for the subeconomy as the allocation obtained from the second allocation.

Consistency. For all $e = (N, \theta_c, \theta_r) \in \mathscr{E}, M \subset N, x, x' \in X^N$, if $x_i = x'_i$ for all $i \in N \backslash M$, then

$$x\bar{R}(e)x' \Rightarrow x_M \bar{R}(M, \theta_{cM}, \theta_{rM})x'_M,$$
$$x\bar{P}(e)x' \Rightarrow x_M \bar{P}(M, \theta_{cM}, \theta_{rM})x'_M.$$

Consistency properties in the same spirit as this property have been extensively studied in the equality of opportunity literature. Consistency, as we define it in this paper, is not compatible with the approach proposed by Roemer, as removing agents from an economy affects the relative place in the outcome distribution of others[2] (recall that in Roemer's approach, an agent is responsible for her place in the statistical distribution of outcomes among agents of the same type). On the other hand, there is no difficulty in combining Consistency with the other two approaches to equality of opportunity.[3]

---

[1]Readers may have noticed that all the equality of opportunity requirements are single profile requirements, whereas welfarism is multi-profile. A comparison is therefore possible only if some inter-profile requirement is added. Consistency is a cross-economy requirement, but, as shown in the proof below, applying it several times allows us to remove and add agents with same identities and different preferences, so that it has inter-profile consequences.

[2]As it does not satisfy Consistency, applying the Roemer proposal to the school funding system, for instance, will lead to different results if, say, the relative funding of schools A and B are computed as part of a City or a State policy. This may be viewed as a weakness of that approach.

[3]Regarding the second branch of literature, Consistency is studied in e.g., Fleurbaey [13]. As for the third branch, Consistency is compatible with e.g., the cardinality based approach of Ok and Kranich [19].

A welfarist social welfare ordering function satisfies Consistency if and only if the social welfare ordering function which is associated to it satisfies the following Consistency^W axiom.

Consistency^W. For all $N \in \mathcal{N}, M \subset N, u, u' \in \mathbb{R}^N$, if $u_i = u'_i$ for all $i \in N \backslash M$, then

$$u \underline{R}(N) u' \Rightarrow u_M \underline{R}(M) u'_M,$$

$$u \underline{P}(N) u' \Rightarrow u_M \underline{P}(M) u'_M.$$

If social welfare is defined as the sum (utilitarianism) or the leximin (the so-called Rawlsian social welfare function) of agents' utilities, then the resulting social welfare ordering function satisfies Consistency^W. If social welfare is defined as the product (the Nash social welfare function), then the ordering function also satisfies Consistency^W provided agents' utility levels are restricted to be strictly positive. Generalized Gini social welfare orderings, on the other hand, do not satisfy this property (see, e.g., Blackorby *et al.* [2]).

The consistency property defined above looks similar to separability conditions that are encountered in welfare economics and the theory of social choice (see Fleming [11] and d'Aspremont; Gevers [8]). The separability conditions, with some variations, state that agents who are indifferent over some alternatives should not influence social preferences over those alternatives. Our condition says that removing those agents from the economy should not alter social preferences.

4. The Result

We are now equipped to prove our main result. It is an equivalence result between two seemingly unrelated equity theories. If an allocation ordering function is consistent with the goal of equalizing opportunities in the sense of satisfying properties of compensation and responsibility as stated in the previous section and satisfies Consistency, then it is Welfarist. Conversely, given any Welfarist way of aggregating utilities, there exists a way of constructing utility functions such that the resulting ordering function equalizes opportunities in the sense above. Let us note that Consistency is not needed for that implication. Indeed, starting with some social welfare ordering function and building utility functions so that the resulting allocation orderings satisfy a list of properties (as it is done to prove Theorem 2) turns out to be much easier than the converse construction (developed in the proof of Theorem 1).

There are two ways of stating this result, depending on which of the equal opportunity requirements we emphasize (recall that the existence of allocation ordering functions satisfying Compensation and Responsibility is not guaranteed in our model). Indeed, we can either combine Compensation and Minimal Responsibility, or Minimal Compensation and Responsibility. This gives us the following theorems.

Theorem 1. *Under Assumption A, if an allocation ordering function $\bar{R}$ satisfies* Social Indifference, Compensation, Minimal Responsibility *and* Consistency, *then it is* Welfarist *and the social welfare ordering function $\underline{R}$ associated to it satisfies* Anonymity^{W} *and* Consistency^{W}.

Theorem 2. *For each social welfare ordering function $\underline{R}$ satisfying* Anonymity^{W}, *there exists a* Welfarist *allocation ordering function $\bar{R}$ satisfying* Social Indifference, Compensation *and* Minimal Responsibility.

We give the proof of those statements in Section 6. Let us, here, explain in words why equality of opportunity turns out to be equivalent to welfarism. Let us start with any given economy. It is well-known in this case that any allocation ordering satisfying Social Indifference can be represented as if agents were equipped with some utility function and the ordering followed a utility aggregation rule (see e.g., Blackorby *et al.* [4]). This is called in the literature single-profile welfarism. This first step is no more than a technical representation and it has nothing to do with the requirement that social welfare orderings be independent of the particular utility functions that create the utility levels.

But the key feature of the equality of opportunity properties is that they allow us to extend this single profile welfarism into welfarism. This comes from the fact that equality of opportunity combines two orthogonal requirements, one on compensation parameters and the other one on responsibility parameters. Moreover, Consistency imposes robustness across orderings in different economies, so that the restriction on the ordering in one society imposes restriction on the orderings in the others as well.

Let us recall the intuition of the result. Let us consider a two-agent economy $(\{1,2\}, (\theta_{c1}, \theta_{c2}), (\theta_{r1}, \theta_{r2}))$ where individual characteristics are different. None of our compensation and responsibility properties has any bite on this economy. Our social evaluation need to be consistent with an economy $(\{1,2,3\}, (\theta_{c1}, \theta_{c2}, \theta_{c3}), (\theta_{r1}, \theta_{r2}, \theta_{r3}))$ where we can assume that $\theta_{c3} = \theta_{c1}$

and $\theta_{r3} = \theta_{r2}$. In that economy, a compensation property imposes restriction on the pair $\{2,3\}$, and a responsibility property on the pair $\{1,3\}$. Moreover, the social evaluation in the initial economy also needs to be consistent with that in economy $(\{1,2,4\}, (\theta_{c1}, \theta_{c2}, \theta_{c4}), (\theta_{r1}, \theta_{r2}, \theta_{r4}))$ where $\theta_{c4} = \theta_{c2}$ and $\theta_{r4} = \theta_{r1}$. Now, compensation imposes a restriction on the pair $\{1,4\}$ and responsibility on the pair $\{2,4\}$. As it turns out, those cross economies restrictions are so severe that once the allocation ordering is fixed for one arbitrary economy, there is only one consistent ordering for any other economy, thereby extending single profile welfarism into welfarism. The two versions of the result simply state that combining Compensation and Minimal Responsibility or Minimal Compensation and Responsibility respectively is sufficient to determine the necessary restrictions on the initial allocation ordering in some specific economy.

Theorem 3. *Under Assumption A, if an allocation ordering function $\bar{R}$ satisfies* Social Indifference, Minimal Compensation, Responsibility *and* Consistency, *then it is* Welfarist *and the social welfare ordering function $\underline{R}$ associated to it satisfies* Anonymity^{W} *and* Consistency^{W}.

Theorem 4. *For each social welfare ordering function $\underline{R}$ satisfying* Anonymity^{W}, *there exists a* Welfarist *allocation ordering function $\bar{R}$ satisfying* Social Indifference, Minimal Compensation *and* Responsibility.

The proof of the last theorems parallels the proof of the previous ones and will be omitted.

The brief outline of the proof above allows us to make two comments on the model we use. First, the argument above can only be made because agents 3 and 4's parameters have the required value. This comes from the assumption that the domain is a product set (that is $\Theta_c \times \Theta_r$). Second, if the model is enriched so that an agent i is characterized by more parameters than θ_{ci} and θ_{ri} then it is a consequence of the axioms in Theorems 1 and 3 above that a change in those additional parameters does not affect the allocation orderings.

5. Ordinal Non-Comparability

We now turn to the question of the informational basis of the ethical theories we have been studying. Which measurability and comparability assumption do we have to impose on preferences to be able to construct equal opportunity or welfarist social ordering functions? We prove in this section that all the results that have been stated up to now are compatible with the weakest informational assumptions on preferences. Indeed, constructing utility functions in a way consistent with Theorems 1 and 3 is possible even with only ordinal non-comparable information on preferences, provided the parameters determining agents' utility functions are part of the responsibility parameters. The latter proviso is advocated by some political philosophers (see Rawls [20]; Dworkin [10]). They claim, indeed, that taking utility levels as the outcome society should be interested in would deny that individuals are autonomous moral agents.

Throughout this section, we consider that outcomes are actually utility levels. That is, we fix $\mathcal{O} \subseteq \mathbb{R}$ (recall that $\mathcal{O}$ is the image set of the outcome function) so that $O(x_i, \theta_{ci}, \theta_{ri})$ stands for the utility level reached by an agent i having parameters θ_{ci}, θ_{ri} and being assigned resources x_i. Society considers that agents are responsible for their utility function, that is, what determines agents' utility functions is part of their responsibility parameters. For the sake of simplicity, we will assume that the responsibility parameters gather all and only what makes utility functions differ from one agent to another. We will come back to this assumption at the end of the section.

A resource allocation ordering function satisfies *Ordinal Non-Comparability* whenever the rankings of the allocations only depend on the individual rankings and not on the utility levels they reach. That is, if the utility function of an agent changes so that her new function is simply obtained by a strictly increasing transformation of the original, then the social ranking should not change.

Ordinal Non-Comparability. For all $e = (N, \theta_c, \theta_r), \in \mathscr{E}, j \in N, \theta'_{rj} \in \Theta_r$ if there exists a strictly increasing function $g : \mathbb{R} \to \mathbb{R}$, such that for all $x_j \in X$,

$$O(x_j, \theta_{cj}, \theta_{rj}) = g(O(x_j, \theta_{cj}, \theta'_{rj}))$$

then

$$\bar{R}(e) = \bar{R}(N, \theta_c, (\theta_{rN \setminus \{j\}}, \theta'_{rj})).$$

Our second result is that the properties required in the previous section imply *Ordinal Non-Comparability*.

Theorem 5. *If an allocation ordering function $\bar{R}$ satisfies* Responsibility *and* Consistency, *then it satisfies* Ordinal Non-Comparability.

The intuition of that result goes as follows. Let us consider two-agent economies $(\{1,2\}, (\theta_{c1}, \theta_{c2}), (\theta_{r1}, \theta_{r2}))$ and $(\{1,2\}, (\theta_{c1}, \theta_{c2}), (\theta_{r1}, \theta'_{r2}))$ identical in all but agent 2's utility function associated to her preferences, that is, for all $x \in X, O(x, \theta_{c2}, \theta_{r2}) = g(O(x, \theta_{c2}, \theta'_{r2}))$. We need to show that the allocation orderings are the same in both economies. By consistency, those orderings need to be consistent with those in economies $(\{1,2,3\},$ $(\theta_{c1}, \theta_{c2}, \theta_{c3}), (\theta_{r1}, \theta_{r2}, \theta_{r3}))$ and $(\{1,2,3\}, (\theta_{c1}, \theta_{c2}, \theta_{c3}), (\theta_{r1}, \theta'_{r2}, \theta_{r3}))$ respectively, where we can assume that $\theta_{c3} = \theta_{c2}$. In either economy, Responsibility imposes restrictions on the pair $\{2,3\}$. But Consistency also requires that both orderings be consistent with economy $(\{1,3\}, (\theta_{c1}, \theta_{c3}),$ $(\theta_{r1}, \theta_{r3}))$, which can be obtained from either economy by removing agent 2. It turns out that all those restrictions can only be satisfied if the orderings we begin with are the same.

If *Responsibility* is replaced with *Minimal Responsibility*, then we would only obtain *Ordinal Non-Comparability* for agents having the reference parameter $\tilde{\theta}_r$. Nonetheless, if *Compensation* is added, then, by the same kind of argument as in the previous section, this result generalizes to all other responsibility parameters.

Let us come back to the assumption that the whole list of responsibility parameters determine agents' utility function. Let us now assume, instead, that there are two lists of parameters, respectively θ_r and θ_u whereas only θ_u enters the definition of the utility function. *Responsibility* would still be stated with the proviso that $\theta_{cj} = \theta_{ck}$, and *Ordinal Non-Comparability* would be adapted so that the utility transformation reads

$$O(x, \theta_{cj}, \theta_{rj}, \theta_{uj}) = g(O(x, \theta_{cj}, \theta_{rj}, \theta'_{uj})).$$

It is clear that the statement just proven would hold a fortiori. So it is sufficient that the parameters determining the utility function be part of what society would like to hold agents responsible for.

6. Proofs

We begin this proof section by stating and proving an important consequence of the *Consistency* property.

Lemma 1. *If a social ordering function $\bar{R}$ satisfies* Consistency, *then it satisfies the following property: for all $e = (N, \theta_c, \theta_r), e' = (M, \theta_{cM}, \theta_{rM}) \in \mathscr{E}$, such that $N \cap M = \emptyset$, $x, x' \in X^N$ and $y \in X^{|M|} : x\bar{R}(e)x'$ if and only if $(x, y)\bar{R}(e, e')(x', y)$.*

Proof. Suppose the claim is wrong, so that, for instance, $x\bar{R}(e)x'$ whereas $(x'y)\bar{P}(e,e')(x,y)$ (a similar argument works in the case $x\bar{P}e)x'$ whereas $(x',y)\bar{R}(e,e')(x,y)$). By *Consistency*, $(x',y)\bar{P}(e,e')(x,y)$ implies $x'\bar{P}(e)x$, a contradiction which proves the claim.

6.1.   *Theorem 1*

Proof.   Let $\bar{R}$ satisfy the axioms. Let $\tilde{\theta}_c$ be a compensation parameter value for which $\bar{R}$ satisfies *Minimal Responsibility*. Let us fix $N \in \mathcal{N}$. Let $\theta_r^* \in \Theta_r$ be any responsibility parameter value. Let us define the economy $\tilde{e} = (N,(\tilde{\theta}_c,\ldots,\tilde{\theta}_c),(\theta_r^*,\ldots,\theta_r^*)) \in \mathcal{N}$. By *Social Indifference*, we can use Propositions 1 and 2 in Blackorby, Donaldson and Weymark [4], so that there exist a social welfare ordering, say $\underline{R}$ on $\mathbb{R}^N$, and a utility function, say $U \in \mathcal{U}$ such that for all $x, x' \in X^N$,

$$x\bar{R}(\tilde{e})x' \Leftrightarrow u\underline{R}u'$$

where for all $i \in N, u_i = U(x_i)$ and $u_i' = U(x_i')$ and U represents O at $\tilde{\theta}_c, \theta_r^*$, that is,

$$[O(x,\tilde{\theta}_c,\theta_r^*) \geq O(x',\tilde{\theta}_c,\theta_r^*)] \Leftrightarrow [U(x) \geq U(x')].$$

By *Compensation*, for all $\pi \in \Pi_N, x\bar{I}(\tilde{e})\pi(x)$ and $x'\bar{I}(\tilde{e})\pi(x')$. Therefore, $u\underline{R}u' \Leftrightarrow \pi(u)\underline{R}\pi(u')$, and $\underline{R}$ satisfies *Anonymity*^{W}.

Step 1. Construction of $U_{..}$. For all $x \in X$, let $U_{\tilde{\theta}_c\theta_r^*}(x) \equiv U(x)$. For all $\theta_c \in \Theta_c$ and all $\tilde{x} \in X$, by Assumption A, there exists $x \in X$ such that $O(x,\theta_c,\theta_r^*) = O(\tilde{x},\tilde{\theta}_c,\theta_r^*)$. Let $U_{\theta_c\theta_r^*}$ be defined by: for all $x \in X$,

$$U_{\theta_c,\theta_r^*}(x) = U(\tilde{x}) \Leftrightarrow O(x,\theta_c,\theta_r^*) = O(\tilde{x},\tilde{\theta}_c,\theta_r^*).$$

Finally, for all $\theta_r' \in \Theta_r$, let $U_{\theta_c,\theta_r'}$ be defined by: for all $x \in X$,

$$U_{\theta_c,\theta_r'}(x) = U_{\theta_c,\theta_r^*}(x).$$

Step 2. $\bar{R}$ is *Welfarist*. Let $e = (N,\theta_{cN},\theta_{rN}) \in \mathcal{E}, x, x' \in X^N$. We have to show that

$$x\bar{R}(e)x' \Leftrightarrow u\underline{R}u'$$

where for all $i \in N, u_i = U_{\theta_{ci},\theta_{ri}}(x_i)$ and $u_i' = U_{\theta_{ci},\theta_{ri}}(x_i')$. Let $N' \in \mathcal{N}$ be such that $|N| = |N'|$ so that there exists a bijection $\beta : N \to N'$. Let $e' = (N',(\tilde{\theta}_c,\ldots,\tilde{\theta}_c),\theta_r') \in \mathcal{E}, y, y' \in X^{N'}$ be such that for all $i \in N, \theta_{ri} =$

$\theta'_{r\beta(i)}, U_{\tilde{\theta}_c,\theta'_{r\beta(i)}}(y_{\beta(i)}) = u_i$ and $U_{\tilde{\theta}_c,\theta'_{r\beta(i)}}(y'_{\beta(i)}) = u'_i$. By *Consistency* and Lemma 1,

$$x\bar{R}(e)x' \Leftrightarrow (x,y')\bar{R}(e,e')(x',y').$$

By *Compensation* applied to every pair of agents $i, \beta(i), (x,y')\bar{I}(e,e')(x',y)$. Therefore,

$$(x,y')\bar{R}(e,e')(x',y') \Leftrightarrow (x',y)\bar{R}(e,e')(x',y').$$

By *Consistency* and Lemma 1,

$$(x',y)\bar{R}(e,e')(x',y') \Leftrightarrow y\bar{R}(e')y'.$$

Recall that $\tilde{e} = (N, (\tilde{\theta}_c,\ldots,\tilde{\theta}_c), (\theta_r^*,\ldots,\theta_r^*))$. Let $\tilde{x}, \tilde{x}' \in X^N$ be defined by for all $i \in N, \tilde{x}_i = y_{\beta(i)}$ and $\tilde{x}'_i = y'_{\beta(i)}$. By *Consistency* and Lemma 1,

$$y\bar{R}(e')y' \Leftrightarrow (y,\tilde{x}')\bar{R}(e',\tilde{e})(y',\tilde{x}').$$

By *Minimal Responsibility*, $(y,\tilde{x}')\bar{I}(e',\tilde{e})(y',\tilde{x})$. Therefore,

$$(y,\tilde{x}')\bar{R}(e',\tilde{e})(y',\tilde{x}') \Leftrightarrow (y'\tilde{x})\bar{R}(e',\tilde{e})(y',\tilde{x}').$$

By *Consistency* and Lemma 1,

$$(y',\tilde{x})\bar{R}(e',\tilde{e})(y',\tilde{x}') \Leftrightarrow \tilde{x}\bar{R}(\tilde{e})\tilde{x}'.$$

To sum up,

$$x\bar{R}(e)x' \Leftrightarrow \tilde{x}\bar{R}(\tilde{e})\tilde{x}'.$$

Now, we know that

$$\tilde{x}\bar{R}(\tilde{e})\tilde{x}' \Leftrightarrow \tilde{u}\underline{R}\tilde{u}'.$$

where for all $i \in N, \tilde{u}_i = U_{\tilde{\theta}_{ci},\theta_{ri}^*}(\tilde{x}_i)$ and $\tilde{u}'_i = U_{\tilde{\theta}_{ci},\theta_{ri}^*}(\tilde{x}'_i)$. By construction, for all $i \in N, U_{\theta_{ci},\theta_{ri}}(x_i) = U_{\tilde{\theta}_{ci},\theta_{ri}^*}(\tilde{x}_i)$ and $U_{\theta_{ci},\theta_{ri}}(x'_i) = U_{\tilde{\theta}_{ci},\theta_{ri}^*}(\tilde{x}'_i)$. Therefore,

$$\tilde{u}\underline{R}\tilde{u}' \Leftrightarrow u\underline{R}u'.$$

Combining all the equivalences, we get, by transitivity,

$$x\bar{R}(e)x' \Leftrightarrow u\underline{R}u',$$

the desired outcome. $\qquad\square$

6.2. Theorem 2

Proof. Let us fix some $\tilde{\theta}_c \in \Theta_c$. Let U be some utility representation of O satisfying the following properties: for all $\theta_c \in \Theta_c, \theta_r \theta_r' \in \Theta_r, x, x' \in X$,

$$U_{\theta_c, \theta_r}(x) = U_{\theta_c, \theta_r'}(x)$$

$$U_{\theta_c, \theta_r}(x) = U_{\tilde{\theta}_c, \theta_r}(x') \Leftrightarrow O(x, \theta_c, \theta_r) = O(x', \tilde{\theta}_c, \theta_r).$$

Let $\bar{R}$ be defined by for all $e = (N, \theta_c, \theta_r) \in \mathcal{E}, x, x' \in X^N$

$$x\bar{R}(e)x' \Leftrightarrow u\underline{R}(e)u'$$

where for all $i \in N, u_i = U_{\theta_{ci}, \theta_{ri}}(x_i)$ and $u_i' = U_{\theta_{ci}, \theta_{ri}}(x_i')$. By construction, $\bar{R}$ is *Welfarist*. We prove that it satisfies the axioms.

(1) *Social Indifference.* It follows directly from the fact that, by *Welfarism*, $\bar{R}$ does not discriminate between allocations yielding the same utility vector.

(2) *Compensation.* Let us take any $e = (N, \theta_c, \theta_r) \in \mathcal{E}, j, k \in N$ such that $\theta_{rj} = \theta_{rk}, x, x', \in X^N$ such that $x_i = x_i'$ for all $i \neq j, k$ and $O(x_j, \theta_{cj}, \theta_{rj}) = O(x_k', \theta_{ck}, \theta_{rk})$ and $O(x_j', \theta_{cj}, \theta_{rj}) = O(x_k, \theta_{ck}, \theta_{rk})$. By *Anoymity*^{W},

$$u\underline{I}(N)u',$$

where for all $i \in N, u_i = U_{\theta_{ci}, \theta_{ri}}(x_i)$ and $u_i' = U_{\theta_{ci}, \theta_{ri}}(x_i')$. By construction of $\bar{R}$,

$$x\bar{I}(e)x'.$$

(3) *Minimal Responsibility.* Let us take any $e = (N, \theta_c, \theta_r) \in \mathcal{E}, j, k \in N$ such that $\theta_{ci} = \theta_{ck} = \tilde{\theta}_c$, and any $x, x' \in X^N$ such that $x_i = x_i'$ for all $i \neq j, k$ and $x_j = x_k'$ and $x_j' = x_k$. By construction of $U_{..}, U_{\tilde{\theta}_c, \theta_{ri}}(x) = U_{\tilde{\theta}_c, \theta_{rj}}(x)$ and $U_{\tilde{\theta}_c, \theta_{ri}}(x') = U_{\tilde{\theta}_c, \theta_{rj}}(x')$. By *Anonymity* of $\underline{R}$,

$$u\bar{I}(N)u'$$

where for all $i \in N, u_i = U_{\theta_{ci}, \theta_{ri}}(x_i)$ and $u_i' = U_{\theta_{ci}, \theta_{ri}}(x_i')$. By construction of $\bar{R}$,

$$x\bar{I}(e)x',$$

the desired outcome.   □

6.3.   *Theorem* 5

We first need an additional definition and a lemma. *Anonymity* requires that the identities of the agents do not matter in social judgements, that is, if two agents permute their parameters, then the social ranking remains unaffected provided the resources allocated to those agents are also permuted.

Anonymity. For all $e = (N, \theta_c, \theta_r), \in \mathscr{E}$, $j, k \in N$, $x, x' \in X^N$, $(\theta'_{cj}, \theta'_{rj})$, $(\theta'_{ck}, \theta'_{rk}) \in \Theta_c \times \Theta_r$ such that $(\theta'_{cj}, \theta'_{rj}) = (\theta_{ck}, \theta_{rk})$ and $(\theta'_{ck}, \theta'_{rk}) = (\theta_{cj}, \theta_{rj})$, and $x''_j, x''_k, x'''_j, x'''_k$ such that $x''_j = x_k, x''_k = x_j, x'''_j = x'_k$ and $x'''_k = x'_j$,

$$x \bar{R}(e) x' \Leftrightarrow (x_{N \setminus \{j,k\}}, x''_j, x''_k) \bar{R}(e')(x'_{N \setminus \{j,k\}}, x'''_j, x'''_k),$$

where $e' = (N, (\theta_{cN \setminus \{j,k\}}, \theta'_{cj}, \theta'_{ck}), (\theta_{rN \setminus \{j,k\}}, \theta'_{rj}, \theta'_{rk}))$.

Lemma 2.   *If an allocation ordering function $\bar{R}$ satisfies Responsibility and* Consistency, *then it satisfies Anonymity.*

Proof.   Let $e = (N, \theta_c, \theta_r), \in \mathscr{E}$, $x, x' \in X^N$ be such that

$$x \bar{R}(e) x'.$$

Let $j, k \in N$. Let $\{l, m\} \subset \mathscr{N} \setminus N$. Let $\theta'_j, \theta'_k, \theta_l, \theta_m \in \Theta_c \times \Theta_r$ and $x''_j, x''_k, x'''_j, x'''_k, x_l, x_m, x'_l, x'_m$ be defined by

$$\theta'_j = \theta_m \equiv \theta_k,$$

$$\theta'_k = \theta_l \equiv \theta_j,$$

$$x''_j = x_m \equiv x_k,$$

$$x''_k = x_l \equiv x_j,$$

$$x'''_j = x'_m \equiv x'_k, \quad \text{and}$$

$$x'''_k = x'_l \equiv x'_j.$$

For the sake of convenience, let us define $M = N \setminus \{j, k\}$, $N' = N \setminus \{j, k\} \cup \{l, m\}$, and $P = N \cup \{l, m\}$. By *Consistency* and Lemma 1,

$$(x, x'_l, x'_m) \bar{R}(P, (\theta_c, \theta_{cl}, \theta_{cm}), (\theta_r, \theta_{rl}, \theta_{rm}))(x', x'_l, x'_m).$$

By *Responsibility*,

$$(x_M, x'_j, x'_k, x_l, x_m) \bar{R}(P, (\theta_c, \theta_{cl}, \theta_{cm}), (\theta_r, \theta_{rl}, \theta_{rm}))(x', x'_l, x'_m).$$

By *Consistency*,

$$(x_M, x_l, x_m)\bar{R}(N', (\theta_{cM}, \theta_{cl}, \theta_{cm}), (\theta_{rM}, \theta_{rl}, \theta_{rm}))(x'_M, x'_l, x'_m).$$

Let $\theta^*_{cP} = (\theta_{cM}, \theta'_{cj}, \theta'_{ck}, \theta_{cl}, \theta_{cm})$ and $\theta^*_{rP} = (\theta_{rM}, \theta'_{rj}, \theta'_{rk}, \theta_{rl}, \theta_{rm})$. By *Consistency* and Lemma 1 again,

$$(x_M, x''_j, x''_k, x_l, x_m)\bar{R}(P, \theta^*_{cP}, \theta^*_{rP})(x'_M, x''_j, x''_k, x'_l, x'_m).$$

By *Responsibility*,

$$(x_M, x''_j, x''_k, x_l, x_m)\bar{R}(P, \theta^*_{cP}, \theta^*_{rP})(x'_M, x'''_j, x'''_k, x_l, x_m).$$

By *Consistency*,

$$(x_M, x''_j, x''_k)\bar{R}(N, (\theta_{cM}, \theta'_{cj}, \theta'_{ck}), (\theta_{rM}, \theta'_{rj}, \theta'_{rk}))(x'_M, x'''_j, x'''_k),$$

the desired outcome.   □

Proof. (of Theorem 5) By Lemma 2, $\bar{R}$ satisfies *Anonymity*. Let $e = (N, \theta_c, \theta_r), \in \mathscr{E}, j, \in N, \theta'_{rj} \in \Theta_r$, be such that there exists a strictly increasing function $g : \mathbb{R} \to \mathbb{R}$, such that for all $x \in X$,

$$O(x, \theta_{cj}, \theta_{rj}) = g(O(x, \theta_{cj}, \theta'_{rj})).$$

Let $x, x' \in X^N$ be such that

$$x\bar{R}(e)x'.$$

We need to prove that

$$x\bar{R}(N, \theta_c, (\theta_{rN\backslash\{j\}}, \theta'_{rj}))x'.$$

Let $k \notin N, \theta_{ck} \in \Theta_c, \theta_{rk}, \theta'_{rk} \in \Theta_r, x_k, x'_k \in X$ be such that $\theta_{ck} = \theta_{cj}, \theta_{rk} = \theta_{rj}, \theta'_{rk} = \theta_{rj}, x_k = x_j$ and $x'_k = x'_j$. By *Consistency* and Lemma 1,

$$(x, x'_k)\bar{R}(N \cup \{k\}, (\theta_c, \theta_{ck}), (\theta_r, \theta'_{rk}))(x', x'_k).$$

By *Anonymity*,

$$(x_{N\backslash\{j\}}, x'_j, x_k)\bar{R}(N \cup \{k\}, (\theta_c, \theta_{ck}), (\theta_{rN\backslash\{j\}}, \theta'_{rj}, \theta_{rk}))(x', x'_k).$$

Since $\theta_{ck} = \theta_{cj}$, by *Responsibility*,

$$(x_{N\backslash\{j\}}, x_j, x'_k)\bar{R}(N \cup \{k\}, (\theta_c, \theta_{ck}), (\theta_{rN\backslash\{j\}}, \theta'_{rj}, \theta_{rk}))(x', x'_k).$$

By *Consistency*,

$$x\bar{R}(N, \theta_c, (\theta_{rN\setminus\{j\}}, \theta'_{rj}))x',$$

the desired outcome.   □

7. Conclusion

We have shown in this paper that there is an equivalence between two seemingly unrelated, if not opposed, families of resource allocation ordering functions. The first family of functions, which we consider consistent with modern equal opportunity theories, satisfy properties of compensation and responsibility. The second family of functions are the welfarist functions. We have shown that among the ordering functions satisfying *Consistency*, each member of the first family was also a member of the second one, and vice versa.

We would like to emphasize again that allocation ordering functions as defined here can be constructed without making use of cardinal or comparable information on preferences. This comes from the fact that the welfarist ordering functions we deal with here, are not based on the assumption that utility functions are intrinsically related to the human nature. Instead, utility functions are assumed to be constructed by social observers, and, precisely, the observers we were interested in are equal opportunity advocates. This is why it is possible to be welfarist and still use only ordinal noncomparable information on individual preferences.

There are several consequences to draw from our results. May be the main lesson is that welfarism is far from being an obsolete ethical theory. Moreover, welfare economists can do more than letting the social planner construct the utility representation of agents' preferences. Indeed, the social planner should only be asked to choose the cut between compensation and responsibility parameters, and the aggregation process of individual opportunity indicators. Welfare economists should then be able to compute, for instance, optimal tax schemes, in a similar way as it is currently done in public economics. If, in addition, the social planner considers individual preferences as part of the responsibility parameters, then all the information needed to compute the optimal allocation can be extracted from agents' choices. The results presented here should therefore yield new approaches to the design of optimal social policies.

References

1. R. Arneson. 'Equality and equality of opportunity for welfare', *Philosophical Studies* **56** (1989), 77–93.
2. C. Blackorby, W. Bossert and D. Donaldson. 'Generalized Ginis and cooperative bargaining solutions', *Econometrica* **62** (1994), 1161–1178.
3. C. Blackorby, W. Bossert and D. Donaldson. 'In defense of welfarism', mimeo. 2002.
4. C. Blackorby, D. Donaldson and J. A. Weymark. 'A welfarist proof of Arrow's theorem', *Recherches Economiques de Louvain* **56**(3–4) (1990), 259–286.
5. W. Bossert. 'Redistribution mechanisms based on individual characteristics', *Mathematical Social Sciences* **29** (1995), 1–17.
6. W. Bossert, M. Fleurbaey and D. Van de gaer. 'Responsibility, talent, and compensation: A second-best analysis', *Review of Economic Design* **4** (1999), 35–55.
7. G. A. Cohen. 'On the currency of egalitarian justice', *Ethics* **99** (1989), 906–944.
8. C. d' Aspremont and L. Gevers. 'Equity and the informational basis of collective choice', *Review of Economic Studies* **44** (1977), 199–209.
9. C. d' Aspremont and L. Gevers. 'Social welfare functional and interpersonal comparability', in K. J. Arrow, A. K. Sen and K. Suzumura (eds.), *Handbook of Social Choice and Welfare*, Vol. 1, Cambridge: Cambridge University Press, pp. 459–541, 2002.
10. R. Dworkin. 'What is equality? Part 1: Equality of welfare; Part 2: Equality of resources', *Philosophy & Public Affairs* **10** (1981), 185–246 and 283–345.
11. M. Fleming. 'A cardinal concept of welfare', *Quarterly Journal of Economics* **66** (1952), 366–384.
12. M. Fleurbaey. 'On fair compensation', *Theory Decision* **36** (1994), 277–307.
13. M. Fleurbaey. 'Three solutions to the compensation problem', *Journal of Economic Theory* **65** (1995), 505–521.
14. M. Fleurbaey. 'Equality among responsible individuals', in M. Fleurbaey, J.-F. Laslier, N. Gravel and A. Trannoy (eds.), *Freedom in Economics: New Perspective in Normative Analysis*, London: Routledge. 1998.
15. M. Fleurbaey, C. Hagnere, M. Martinez and A. Trannoy. 'Les minima sociaux en France: Entre compensation et responsabilité', *Economie & Prévision* **138–139** (1999), 1–24.

16. M. Fleurbaey and F. Maniquet. 'Optimal income taxation: An ordinal approach', DP #9865, CORE, 1998.

17. L. J. Kranich. 'Equitable opportunities: An axiomatic approach', *Journal of Economic Theory* **71** (1996), 131–147.

18. L. J. Kranich. 'Equitable opportunities in economic environments', *Social Choice and Welfare* **14** (1997), 57–64.

19. E. A. Ok and L. J. Kranich. 'The measurement of opportunity inequality: A cardinality-based approach', *Social Choice and Welfare* **15** (1998), 263–288.

20. J. Rawls. *Theory of Justice*, Cambridge, MA: Harvard University Press. 1971.

21. J. E. Roemer. 'A pragmatic theory of responsibility for the egalitarian planner', *Philosophy & Public Affairs* **22** (1993), 146–166.

22. J. E. Roemer. *Equality of Opportunity*, Cambridge, MA: Harvard University Press. 1998.

23. E. Schokkaert, G. Dhaene and C. Van de Voorde. 'Risk adjustment and the trade-off between efficiency and risk selection: An application of the theory of fair compensation', *Health* **7** (1998), 465–480.

24. A. K. Sen. *Collective Choice and Social Welfare*, San Fransisco: Holden-Day. 1970.

25. Y. Sprumont. 'Balanced egalitarian redistribution of income', *Mathematical Social Sciences* **33** (1997), 185–201.

26. P. Suppes. 'Some formal models of grading principles', *Synthese* **6** (1966), 284–306.

27. W. Thomson. *Consistent Allocation Rules*, mimeo, University of Rochester, 1996.

28. D. Van de gaer. 'Some trade-offs in Roemer's mechanism', in M. Fleurbaey, J.-F. Laslier, N. Gravel and A. Trannoy (eds.), *Freedom in Economics: New Perspective in Normative Analysis*, London: Routledge. 1998.

PART 2
Unequal Earning Abilities and Income Redistribution

CHAPTER 4

Fair Allocation with Unequal Production Skills: The No Envy Approach to Compensation

Marc Fleurbaey and François Maniquet

ABSTRACT. We consider a simple production model and assume that the agents have unequal production skills that can in no way be considered their responsibility. We study how it is possible, if at all, to compensate for differential skills while holding agents responsible for their preferences towards consumption and leisure. Our main result is a characterization of a class of solutions, called the Reference Welfare Equivalent Budget. In this class, each solution is based on reference preferences, and selects allocations in which the agents' budget sets are deemed equivalent by these reference preferences.

1. Introduction

Consider a group of agents who share a technology that produces a consumption good with their labor. Suppose that these agents have unequal production skills, and that these differences are due to inherited physical or intellectual handicaps or abilities that can in no way be considered the agents' responsibility. It would then be unfair if handicaps entailed a low welfare for disadvantaged agents, and this raises the issue of devising an allocation rule that counterbalances handicaps.

Mathematical Social Sciences **32**: 71–93, 1996.

If the agents' utility levels are interpersonally comparable, then we may think that equalizing utilities adequately compensates handicap differentials. The problem is that this solution compensates not only skill handicaps, but also utility differences. An agent with a high skill but a low utility function will receive an indemnity just as a handicapped agent would. If we think that agents must bear some responsibility for their utility levels, this solution is not satisfying.

The idea that fairness does not consist in a pattern of utility levels because the agents must take some responsibility for their own utility, but rather consists in an equitable allocation of resources (taking handicaps into account) has been strongly advocated by several philosophers such as Rawls (1971, 1982), Dworkin (1981a, b) and, more recently, by Sen (1985), Arneson (1989), Cohen (1989) and Van Parijs (1990). This idea has been introduced into the economic literature on fair allocation by Roemer (1985, 1986, 1993) and Fleurbaey (1994, 1995), and a similar approach has been followed by Bossert (1995).

The general scheme is that agents are characterized by a set of variables, and that this set is partitioned into two subsets. Variables from the first subset are viewed as talents for which the agents are not held responsible, while variables from the second subset are viewed as choice or personality variables whose influence on well-being the agents must bear. In this paper we concentrate on production economies as described above, and we assume that the agents are absolutely not responsible for their production skills, whereas they are wholly responsible for their preferences and utility. This clearcut assumption may not be exactly congruent with some philosophers' approach,[1] but it is convenient for modelling purposes, and our results can be extended to the more general case with slight modification.

In this paper, we study how the axioms of compensation for handicaps that have been proposed by Fleurbaey (1994, 1995) in a pure exchange framework can be applied to the production model defined above. We focus on two kinds of requirements. A first requirement is that the agents' differentials in skills should be fully counterbalanced, and we take this to mean that agents who have the same utility functions should end up with the same utility level. Actually, since agents are held responsible for their utilities, it is enough to restrict attention to allocation rules based on ordinal

---

[1]In some cases, the agents may be deemed partly responsible for their skills, e.g. when they have made education choices in the past, and the agents may also be deemed partly non-responsible for their preferences, if these are influenced by their upbringing.

preferences; indeed, two agents with the same preferences but different utility functions have no reason to receive different indemnities. Therefore, the above requirement can be rephrased in the following way: agents with the same preferences should be put on the same indifference curve.[2]

The second kind of requirement we consider is that indemnity should be given for skill differences only, and not for differences in preferences. In the one-good model of Fleurbaey (1994, 1995), this is interpreted as meaning that equal handicap implies equal resource. In the present model there are two goods, labor and a consumption good, so that 'equal resource' no longer has an unambiguous meaning. It might be interpreted as an 'equal budget' requirement, but, assuming a market environment is often viewed as too restrictive, and we therefore resort to the 'No Envy' condition (Tinbergen, 1953; Foley, 1967). The No Envy condition is met if no agent strictly prefers another agent's bundle of goods to her own bundle.[3] No Envy is consistent with the idea of providing the same opportunity set to all agents: if agents maximize their welfare on an equal opportunity set, then they cannot end up envying one another. No Envy is thus a weaker requirement than equal budget, and is almost equivalent to equal budget in large economies, as shown by Varian (1976) and Champsaur and Laroque (1981). The requirement of compensation limited to skills then becomes that agents with equal skills should not envy each other.

The starting point of this paper is that, under Pareto Optimality, these two requirements are incompatible. We then proceed by weakening one axiom or the other in order to identify the frontier of possible combinations of axioms grounded on the idea of compensation and responsibility. Our main result is a characterization of a class of solutions, called Reference Welfare Equivalent Budget; in this class, each solution is based on reference preferences, and selects allocations in which the agents' budget sets are deemed equivalent by these reference preferences; that is, an agent with

---

[2]Notice an important difference between our model and the exchange model. In the latter, talents are an argument of preferences, whereas, in the production case, skills do not influence the agents' satisfaction directly.

[3]Observe that the 'Envy' terminology is not perfectly appropriate since the No Envy condition does not correspond to eliminating envy in the common sense. For instance, we do take account of the fact that an agent could envy the other's higher production skill, nor that she could wish to have the other's preferences. Moreover, reference to the envy feeling is dubious ethical justification for the No Envy condition. This condition finds better foundations in the idea of 'equal resource' or 'equal opportunity'. It might be appropriate to rename it 'permutation-proofness', as suggested by L. Gevers.

such preferences would be indifferent between her best choices in all budget sets. The performance of these solutions in terms of full compensation for equal preferences, however, is rather weak: actually, full compensation is carried out only for agents having the reference preferences.

It seems to us that this work sheds light on the difficulties encountered with the No Envy condition in the production model, which have been pointed out by Pazner and Schmeidler (1974) and Varian (1974).[4] These authors have shown that when agents differ in skills as well as in preferences, the No Envy axiom, which stipulates that each agent must weakly prefer her own consumption-leisure bundle to any other agent's bundle, cannot be met by any allocation rule under Pareto Optimality. This result has been viewed as a major setback for the No Envy approach. Now, one easily sees that No Envy implies that two agents with identical preferences must be on the same indifference curve, and obviously implies No Envy among equally skilled agents. In brief, No Envy implies the two compensation requirements stated above. Therefore, the incompatibility between these two requirements is at the heart of the non-existence result concerning No Envy, and is, in fact, a much stronger result.

Recall that, facing this difficulty, these authors have proposed two alternative solutions. Pazner and Schmeidler (1978b) proposed to equalize the agents' 'full incomes' (Becker, 1965), i.e., the income they can earn if they take no leisure. As criticized by Varian (1974) and Dworkin (1981b), this allocation rule treats the high-skill agents harshly, since they are heavily taxed, and may actually be forced to work in order to be able to pay for it ('slavery of the talented'). Varian has instead proposed the 'Wealth-Fair' allocation rule which selects the Walrasian allocations in which only endowments in external resources (profit shares in the model) are equalized. This allocation rule is very favorable to the high skill agents, and one can view it as performing no compensation at all for handicaps. This rule applies the envy test in the following dubious way: a (low-skill) agent may envy a (high-skill) agent only if she considers she is giving the same contribution of efficient labor (which may be very difficult for an agent with low skill).[5] The interesting upshot of our analysis is that these two allocations are just the two opposite extreme cases in the RWEB class. Therefore, this class can be resorted to if one looks for intermediate solutions between these two

---

[4]The literature on No Envy is surveyed in Arnsperger (1994).
[5]On these two solutions, see also Thomson and Varian (1985).

polar solutions so as to avoid their symmetrical drawbacks.[6] These results provide some greater generality to the analysis of fairness like No Envy in the production model.

Our work is also related to the literature on optimal taxation, and our model is similar to Mirrlees' one (see Mirrlees, 1971). But the optimal taxation literature usually considers the distribution of utilities, either in a utilitarian way (e.g. Mirrlees, 1971) or in an egalitarian way (e.g. Dasgupta and Hammond, 1980), and never addresses the responsibility issue. But since these authors assume identical utility functions among agents, we may consider that they restrict themselves to the case where all agents have exercised their responsibility with exactly the same degree. Our egalitarian approach (expressed by the Equal Welfare for Equal Preferences condition) is then closer to Dasgupta and Hammond's work, which is directly relevant to our problem. They show, in particular, that when skills are not known by the planner but are observable when used in production (an agent may choose a lower skill than her true one), then it is nonetheless possible to implement the equal utility first-best allocation rule. In the present paper we do not give further attention to the implementation issue, but study only the definition of first-best allocation rules.

The paper is organized as follows. Section 2 presents the main compensation axioms, and states the basic incompatibility result. Section 3 examines the consequences of restricting compensation to agents having some reference preferences, and the characterization of the RWEB class of allocation rules is then presented. Section 4 pursues the analysis of the trade-off between the requirements of full compensation and the requirements of responsibility for one's preferences.

2. Two Basic Requirements

First, we define the model. An *economy* e is a list $(a_1, \ldots, a_n, R_1, \ldots, R_n, f)$ $\in \mathbb{R}_+^n \times \boldsymbol{R}^n \times \boldsymbol{F}$, where n is the finite cardinality of a set $N = \{1, \ldots, n\}$

---

[6]We may not be satisfied with the fact that choosing between the RWEB allocation rules requires a reference preference ordering to be chosen. Our results do not give any clue as to how this choice should be made. To some extent, this problem is similar to that of choosing the reference bundles or sets of bundles for the Egalitarian-Equivalent solution proposed by Pazner and Schmeidler (1978a). At any rate, the reference preferences do not imply any paternalism over individual *preferences*, but simply reflect the social policy concerning differential *skills*.

of agents, a_i denotes agent i's production skill, $\boldsymbol{R}$ is the class of continuous and convex orderings on bundles $(x, y) \in [0, \bar{x}] \times \mathbb{R}_+$ with the property that, ceteris paribus, more of the first good is never strictly preferred to less (think of labor time) and more of the second good is always strictly preferred to less, and $\boldsymbol{F}$ is the set of strictly increasing and continuous production functions f from $\mathbb{R}_+$ to $\mathbb{R}_+$. We will often restrict our attention to the subdomain $\boldsymbol{F}^C$ of concave production functions. The class of economies (a, R, f) will be referred to as $\boldsymbol{E}$ if the domain of the production functions is $\boldsymbol{F}$, or as $\boldsymbol{E}^C$ if it is $\boldsymbol{F}^C$. Given $A \subseteq \mathbb{R}_+^2$, and $R_i \in \boldsymbol{R}$, let $m(R_i, A)$ denote the set of bundles (if any) that maximize agent i's preferences R_i over a set A of bundles; that is, $m(R_i, A) = \{z_i \in A \mid \forall z_i' \in A, z_i R_i z_i'\}$.

An *allocation* $z = (z_1, \ldots, z_n) \in ([0, \bar{x}] \times \mathbb{R}_+)^n$ is a list of bundles $z_i = (x_i, y_i), i \in N$, one bundle per agent, i.e., we assume that the input contribution of each agent is non-negative and bounded and the consumption is non-negative. An allocation z is *feasible* for the economy $e = (a, R, f) \in \boldsymbol{E}$ if and only if

$$\sum_{i=1}^n y_i \leq f\left(\sum_{i=1}^n a_i \cdot x_i\right).$$

The set of feasible allocations for an n-agent economy $e \in \boldsymbol{E}$ is denoted by $Z^n(e)$.

An *allocation rule* S, defined over a subset $\boldsymbol{D}^S$ of $\boldsymbol{E}$, is a correspondence that associates to every economy $e = (a, R, f) \in \boldsymbol{D}^S$ a non-empty subset $S(e)$ of the feasible allocations: $S(e) \subseteq Z^n(e)$.

Definition 1. An allocation rule S satisfies *Pareto Optimality* (PO) if and only if for every $e = (a, R, f) \in \boldsymbol{D}^S$, every $z \in S(a, R, f)$, and every $z' \in Z^n(e)$,

$$[z_i' R_i z_i, \ \forall i \in N] \Rightarrow [z_i' I_i z_i, \forall i \in N].$$

We denote the set of Pareto-optimal allocations of an economy (a, R, f) by $P(a, R, f)$.

We now formally define the two basic requirements that we introduced in Section 1. The first axiom, Equal Welfare for Equal Preferences, requires full compensation among agents having the same preferences. The second axiom, No Envy among Equally Skilled, is consistent with the idea that agents should receive compensation for their skill only, and not for their differences in preferences.

Definition 2. An allocation rule S satisfies *Equal Welfare for Equal Preferences* (EWEP) if and only if for every $e = (a, R, f) \in \boldsymbol{D}^S$, every $z \in S(a, R, f)$, and every $i, j \in N$ such that $R_i = R_j$:

$$z_i I_{i,j} z_j.$$

Definition 3. An allocation rule S satisfies *No Envy among Equally Skilled* (NEES) if and only if for every $e = (a, R, f) \in \boldsymbol{D}^S$, every $z \in S(a, R, f)$, and every $i, j \in N$ such that $a_i = a_j$:

$$z_i R_i z_j \quad \text{and} \quad Z_j R_j z_i.$$

The EWEP and NEES axioms are logically implied by the original axiom of No Envy. However, while No Envy is incompatible with PO, allocation rules exist that satisfy one of the two weaker axioms and PO over the appropriate domain of economies. Any egalitarian-equivalent allocation rule (cf. Pazner and Schmeidler, 1978a), for which the reference bundle does not depend on skills, satisfies EWEP and PO. The domain of economies over which this compatibility holds is, therefore, unrestricted. However, Varian's (1974) Wealth-Fair, and Pazner and Schmeidler's (1978b) Full-Income-Fair allocation rules, for instance, satisfy NEES and PO. Since NEES is equivalent to the traditional No Envy requirement in economies with equal skills, then the compatibility with PO holds over the domain $\boldsymbol{E}^C$ only, as was proven by Vohra (1992).

But Theorem 1 shows that under PO, EWEP is incompatible with NEES, and even with a much weaker axiom, namely No Domination among Equally Skilled (the requirement of No Domination was introduced in Thomson, 1983).

Definition 4. An allocation rule S satisfies *No Domination among Equally Skilled* (NDES) if and only if for every $e = (a, R, f) \in \boldsymbol{D}^S$, every $z \in S(a, R, f)$, every $i, j \in N$ such that $a_i = a_j$:

$$z_i > z_j, \quad \text{or} \quad z_j > z_i, \quad \text{or} \quad z_i = z_j,$$

where $z_i > z_j$ means that $x_i > x_j$ and $y_i > y_j$.

Theorem 1. *There is no allocation rule defined over the domain $\boldsymbol{E}^C$ that satisfies PO, EWEP and NDES.*

Proof. The proof is similar to that of Fleurbaey (1995, Proposition 1). Let $e = ((a_l, a_2, a_3, a_4), (R_1, R_2, R_3, R_4), f) \in \boldsymbol{E}^C$ be defined by: $a_1 = a_2 = 0, a_3 = a_4 = 1, R_1, R_2, R_3$ and R_4 have representations u_1, u_2, u_3

and u_4, where $u_1(x, y) = u_3(x, y) = y - (1 - \alpha) \cdot x$ and $u_2(x, y) = u_4(x, y) = y - \alpha x$, with $1/2 < \alpha < 1$, $f(x) = x$ and $\bar{x} = 1$. Let S satisfy the three axioms, and let $z = (z_1, z_2, z_3, z_4) \in S(e)$. By PO, $x_1 = x_2 = 0$ and $x_3 = x_4 = 1$; by EWEP, $y_1 = y_3 - (1 - \alpha)$ and $y_2 = y_4 - \alpha$. By NDES, $y_1 = y_2$ and $y_3 = y_4$, the desired impossibility. $\square$

Remark. In the above example, it is possible to eliminate the domination between the two low skill agents' bundles, by putting $y_1 = y_2$ and allowing a large domination by agent 4's bundle over agent 3's bundle. Symmetrically, we can eliminate the domination between the bundles of the latter agents, while making the ratio y_1/y_2 maximal. Besides these two extreme cases, one can try to minimize the maximal domination ratio, $\max\{y_1/y_2, y_4/y_3\}$. This is done when the equality $y_1/y_2 = y_4/y_3$ holds. If we take the feasibility and the PO constraints into account, then we come to this ratio: $y_1/y_2 = (1 + 2\alpha)/(3 - 2\alpha)$, which tends to 3 as α tends to its maximal value 1. This means that the maximal domination ratio is bounded in this four-agent economy. However, it is not bounded in general, so that EWEP is incompatible with NDES, even if the latter axiom requires only that no fraction ε of any selected bundle be strictly dominating another bundle (such a weakened version of the No Domination requirement is proposed in Moulin and Thomson, 1988). Indeed, add to the above economy n agents having the same characteristics as agent 2, and n agents having the same characteristics as agent 4. Let α be now defined by $\alpha = n/(1 + n)$. If n tends to infinity, then PO and EWEP together imply that y_2 tends to $1/(1 + 2n)$. Therefore, the ratio y_1/y_2 corresponding to the minimal domination tends to $\sqrt{1 + 2n}$, which, in turn, is not bounded.

In the remainder of the paper we propose two ways out of the impossibility result stated in Theorem 1. First, we insist on the responsibility for one's preferences, while strongly weakening the EWEP requirement. Second, we weaken both EWEP and NEES.

3. Introducing Reference Preferences

In this section we propose to fix some reference preferences, and to weaken EWEP in the following way: the welfare of agents having the same preferences is to be equalized only if they have the reference preferences. Formally.

Definition 6. Let $\tilde{R} \in \boldsymbol{R}$ denote the reference preferences. An allocation rule S satisfies *Equal Welfare for $\tilde{R}$-Reference Preferences* (EWRP) if and only if for every $e = (a, R, f) \in \mathscr{D}^S$, if for every $i \in N, R_i = \tilde{R}$, then for every $z \in S(a, R, f)$, every $i, j \in N$:

$$z_i \tilde{I} z_j.$$

This (rather weak) axiom is not only compatible with NEES, but also proves compatible with the stronger requirement of Monotonicity, according to which an allocation rule should be independent of changes in preferences that extend agents' lower contour sets at their assigned bundles.

Definition 7 (Maskin, 1977). *An allocation rule S satisfies Monotonicity[7] (M) if and only if for every $e = (a, R, f) \in \boldsymbol{D}^S$, every $z = ((x_i, y_i)_{i \in N}) \in S(a, R, f)$, every $R' \in \boldsymbol{R}^n$:*

$$[\{(x, y) \in Z_i^n(e) | z_i R_i(x, y)\} \subseteq \{(x, y) \in Z_i^n(e) | z_i R_i'(x, y)\},$$

$$\forall i \in N] \Rightarrow [z \in S(a, R', f)],$$

where $Z_i^n(e)$ denotes the projection of $Z^n(e)$ on i's consumption set.

This axiom is usually motivated from a viewpoint of incentive compatibility rather than equity. In our model, indeed, an allocation rule can be implemented in Nash equilibrium if and only if it satisfies Monotonicity (cf. Maskin, 1977). It is a consequence of a result obtained in Fleurbaey and Maniquet (1995b), however, that if we limit ourselves to horizontally equitable allocation rules (i.e., rules that provide the same welfare to agents having both the same skill and the same preferences), then NEES is a logical consequence of Monotonicity. This is consistent with the following equity justification of Monotonicity. Philosophers like Rawls and Dworkin argue that if individuals are held responsible for their preferences, and if society is neutral as regards preferences, ideally the individuals' endowment of comprehensive resources (including talent, for Dworkin) should be equal, and, in particular, should not depend on their preferences (for instance, expensive tastes elicit neither a tax penalty nor a compensatory subsidy). In the current model, an individual's comprehensive endowment can be viewed as a profit share in the 'firm' plus the personal productivity parameter. A direct application of this view would then require the (shadow) profit shares of the agents to depend only on their talents (in some compensatory

---

[7] Gevers (1986) uses a slightly modified version of Maskin's axiom of Monotonicity to characterize the Walrasian Rule. But this distinction is not relevant here.

way, presumably), and not on their preferences. This is a rather strong
requirement for an allocation rule. But Monotonicity and NEES are more
reasonable, successive weakenings[8] of such a requirement. That No Envy
is not too weak and still carries an idea of responsibility for one's preferences, as well as an idea of social neutrality w.r.t. preferences is obvious
if one recalls that in large economies it tends to equalize budgets. Monotonicity even more directly retains the idea of a partial independence of the
allocation rule w.r.t, preferences.[9]

The RWEB rule, defined below, is an example of a rule satisfying PO,
EWRP and Monotonicity, as proven in Proposition 1. In words, at a RWEB
allocation, the budget line of every agent is tangential to the same reference
indifference curve, or, in other words, a reference agent would be indifferent
between all the budget sets. We first define the following terminology: given
$(x, y) \in [0, \bar{x}] \times \mathbb{R}_+, a_o \in \mathbb{R}_+$, and $w \in \mathbb{R}_+$, let $B((x, y), a_o, w)$ denote the
budget set that has the property that (x, y) lies on its frontier and the slope
of the frontier is worth $a_o \cdot w$.

Definition 8. Let $\tilde{R} \in \boldsymbol{R}$ denote the reference preferences. The $\tilde{R}$-
Reference Welfare Equivalent Budget (RWEB) is defined by: for every
$(a, R, f) \in \boldsymbol{D}^{\text{RWEB}}$

$$z \in \text{RWEB}(a, R, f) \Leftrightarrow \exists \, w \in \mathbb{R}_+, \quad \text{s.t. } w \text{ supports } z \quad \text{and}$$

$$m(\tilde{R}, B(z_i, a_i, w)) \tilde{I}_m (\tilde{R}, B(z_j, a_j, w)), \quad \forall i, \; j \in N.$$

A RWEB allocation is illustrated in Figure 1 for a two-agent economy
$((a_1, a_2), (R_1, R_2), f)$. Preferences R_1, R_2, and $\tilde{R}$ are drawn in the labor
time–consumption space, the production function f is represented by the
function f_2 defined by: $f_2(x) = f(a_2 \cdot x)$, and the skill ratio is indicated
on the x axis. The slopes of agents' budget lines are proportional to their
skills. We claim that $z = (z_1, z_2) \in \text{RWEB}((a_1, a_2), (R_1, R_2), f)$. Clearly, w
supports both the firm at $(a_1/a_2 \cdot x_1 + x_2, y_1 + y_2)$ and agents 1 and 2 at

---

[8]To be rigorous, that Monotonicity is a weakening of the requirement is true under,
for instance, the additional condition that the allocation rule selects are competitive
equilibria for the chosen endowments.

[9]If the individuals' endowment were interpreted as their (shadow) budget set or simply
their bundle, then the requirement that the endowment should not depend on preferences
would be incompatible with PO and, again, Monotonicity can be viewed as a reasonable
weakening that preserves the idea of independence while being compatible with PO.

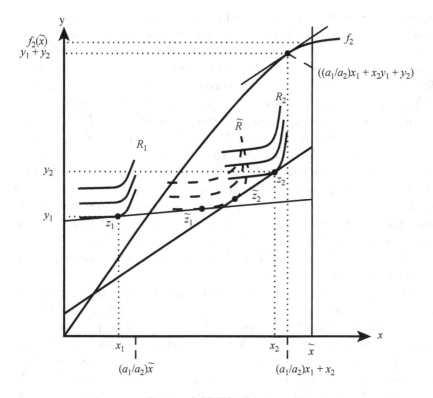

Fig. 1. A RWEB allocation.

z_1 and z_2, respectively. Secondly, the reference agent is indifferent between the two budget sets since the points $\tilde{z}_1$ and $\tilde{z}_2$, corresponding to her best choice in $B(z_1, a_1, w)$ and $B(z_2, a_2, w)$ lie on the same indifference curve.

Proposition 1. *Let $\tilde{R} \in R$ denote the reference preferences. Over the domain $\mathbf{E}^C$, the RWEB rule satisfies PO, EWRP, and Monotonicity.*

The straightforward proof of the properties is omitted. The proof of non-emptiness is sketched in the appendix.

We thus have a class of attractive allocation rules. Each particular allocation rule is parameterized by the corresponding reference preferences. It is worth identifying some special cases of the general class. First of all, let us consider the case where $\tilde{R}$ is defined as follows: $(x, y)\tilde{R}(x', y')$ if and only if $y \geqslant y'$; that is, the reference agent is not made worse off when working longer. As a consequence, all the budget lines cross at a point $(\bar{x}, y^*)$, which implies that $\pi_i + w \cdot a_i \cdot \bar{x} = y^*$, for all $i \in N$, where $\pi_i = y_i - w \cdot a_i \cdot x_i$. This corresponds to Pazner and Schmeidler's Full-Income-Fair allocation rule (cf. Pazner and Schmeidler, 1978b). Alternatively, let the reference preferences $\tilde{R}$ be defined as follows: $(x, y)\tilde{R}(x', y')$ if and only if $y - \alpha \cdot x \leqslant y' - \alpha \cdot x'$ for some $\alpha \in \mathbb{R}_+$. Then, for every economy $e = (a, R, f)$, we can choose a sufficiently large α so that we obtain an allocation rule that satisfies the following property: for every selected allocation $z \in RWEB(a, R, f), \pi_i = \pi^*$, for all $i \in N$, which gives us Varian's Wealth-Fair allocation rule (cf. Varian, 1974). Nonetheless, the definition of the RWEB rules does not allow us to choose the reference preferences as a function of the economy. If we include the lexicographic preferences R^L (defined by $(x, y)R^L(x', y') \Leftrightarrow x < x'$, or $(x = x'$ and $y \geqslant y'))$ in the set of admissible reference preferences, however, then the Wealth-Fair rule becomes an element of the RWEB class of rules, with reference preferences R^L. Therefore, it will be convenient to consider the domain $\boldsymbol{R^*} = \boldsymbol{R} \cup \{\boldsymbol{R^L}\}$ as the appropriate domain of admissible reference preferences.

The choice of particular reference preferences has the following meaning from a compensation point of view. Let us recall first that any RWEB rule violates EWEP. Therefore, if two agents have the same preferences but different skills, then one of them is likely to envy the other. At a Wealth-Fair allocation, it is always the case that the low skill agent envies the high skill agent. At a Full-Income-Fair allocation, the converse is always true. At any other RWEB allocation, the envy relation can go in either direction, depending on the agents' preferences. In the special case where preferences satisfy the single crossing property vis-à-vis the reference preferences (i.e., any reference indifference curve crosses an indifference curve of an agent at most once), the direction is clear: if an agent maximizes her welfare given her assigned budget by working longer (respectively, less) than the reference agent, then she never envies an agent who has the same preferences but a lower (respectively, higher) skill.

Theorem 2 proves that the RWEB rules are the most appealing solutions that satisfy PO, EWRP, and Monotonicity. Firstly, we require two additional minor properties.

Definition 9 (Thomson, 1983). An allocation rule S satisfies *Non-Discrimination* (ND) between Pareto-indifferent allocations if and only if for every $e = (a, R, f) \in \boldsymbol{D^S}$, every $z \in S(a, R, f)$, every $z' \in Z(e)$:

$$[z_i' I_i z_i, \ \forall i \in N] \Rightarrow [z' \in S(a, R, f)].$$

The next axiom was introduced by Moulin (1990).[10] This axiom refers to a particular contraction of the technology: if a selected allocation remains feasible after the contraction, then Contraction Independence requires that it remains selected for the contracted economy.

Definition 10 (Moulin, 1990). An allocation rule S satisfies *Contraction Independence* (CI) if and only if for every $e = (a, R, f) \in D^S$ and every $g \in F$ such that $g(x) \leqslant f(x)$ for all $x \in \mathbb{R}_+$:

$$[z \in S(a, R, f) \text{ and } z \in Z(a, R, g)] \Rightarrow [z \in S(a, R, g)].$$

Theorem 2.[11] *Let $\tilde{R} \in R^*$ denote the reference preferences. Over the domain E^C, the RWEB is the smallest allocation rule, with respect to inclusion, which satisfies PO, EWRP, Monotonicity, ND and CI.*

Proof. We omit the proof that RWEB satisfies ND and CI. Let S satisfy the five axioms. We show that for every $e = (a, R, f) \in E^C$, $S(a, R, f) \supseteq$ RWEB(a, R, f). Let $z^* \in$ RWEB(a, R, f). Let $w^* \in \mathbb{R}_+$ be the corresponding input price. Let the economy $e^1 = (a, R', g)$ be defined by: $(x, y)R'_i(x', y') \Leftrightarrow y - w^* \cdot a_i \cdot x \geqslant y' - w^* \cdot a_i \cdot x'$, for every $i \in N$, and

$$g(x) = \Sigma_i(y_i^* - w^* \cdot a_i \cdot x_i^*) + w^* \cdot x.$$

---

[10]This axiom was firstly termed Independence of Irrelevant Alternatives by Moulin, given the similarity to Nash's axiom. However, we find Thomson's (1994) term of CI more appropriate, since the changes in the feasibility set from which the solution should be independent are due to changes in the production possibilities only and not to changes in preferences.

[11]Monotonicity can be replaced by NDES in this characterization result, provided an additional axiom is added. This axiom, called Stability under Division, is inspired by an axiom introduced by Thomson (1988) in the context of fair division. It says that if the set of agents in an economy can be decomposed into the number K of subsets having the property that the list of production skills is identical between subsets and if a selected allocation for this economy has the property that the sum of the bundles assigned to the agents in any subset could be produced with a technology worth precisely $1/K$th of the actual technology, then any suballocation of the bundles assigned to the agents in one of the subsets must also be selected for the economy defined by these agents with their preferences and their skills, and the production function worth $1/K$th of the original production function. This axiom, however, is mainly justified from an informational simplicity point of view (cf. Thompson, 1988) rather than from an equity point of view. Therefore, we do not consider that this second characterization result is as important as Theorem 2, and we do not give it. The proof is available from the authors.

Let $z^1 \in S(e^1)$. By PO of S, z^1 is supported by w^*. For every $i \in N$, let $z_i' \in m(\tilde{R}, B(z_i^1, a_i, w^*))$. By ND, $z' = (z_i')_{i \in N} \in S(e^1)$. Suppose that $z^1 \notin \text{RWEB}(e^1)$. Then $z' \notin \text{RWEB}(e^1)$. Therefore, there exist j and $k \in N$ such that $z_j' \tilde{P} z_k'$. By M, $z' \in S(a, \tilde{R}, g)$, which violates EWRP. As a consequence, $z^1 \in RWEB(e^1)$. Now, by construction, $z^* \in RWEB(e^1)$ also. Since z^* and z^1 are supported by the same input price, then for every $i \in N$, $B(z_i^1, a_i, w^*) = B(z_i^*, a_i, w^*)$. Indeed, if it were not the case, then we would have

$$m(\tilde{R}, B(z_i^1, a_i, w^*)) \tilde{P} m(\tilde{R}, B(z_i^*, a_i, w^*)), \quad \text{for all } i \in N,$$

or the converse relation, which conflicts with PO of z^* and z^1. As a result, $z_i^1 I_i' z_i^*$, for all $i \in N$, so that by ND, $z^* \in S(e^1)$. By Monotonicity, $z^* \in S(a, R, g)$, and finally by CI, $z^* \in S(a, R, f)$. $\qquad\square$

As we noted in the introduction, Pazner and Schmeidler's Full-Income-Fair rule has been criticized by Varian (1974) and Dworkin (1981b), on the basis that this allocation rule is very hard for the skill agents, since they are heavily taxed, and may actually be forced to work in order to be able to pay it ('slavery of the talented'). Let us, indeed, define the profit π_i of agent i by $\pi_i = y_i - w \cdot a_i \cdot x_i$. By the concavity of f, the sum of the individual profits is always positive. Moreover, by the convexity of the reference preferences, we have $a_i < a_j$ implies $\pi_i \geqslant \pi_j$. As a result, the share of profit of the agent with the lowest skill is always positive. Thus, the Full-Income-Fair rule has the property that the share of profit of any other agent may be strictly negative. This feature has a bad consequence on the welfare of high skill agents, as shown in Theorem 3, but the most striking fact is that this criticism can be addressed equivalently to almost all RWEB rules. Theorem 3 makes use of the following axiom, which is even less demanding than a requirement of positive profit for all.

Definition 11. An allocation rule S induces *Participation* (P) if and only if for every $e = (a, R, f) \in D^S$, every $z \in S(a, R, f)$, every $i \in N$:

$$z_i R_i(0, 0).$$

Theorem 3. *The Wealth-Fair rule is the only member of the RWEB class of rules that satisfies Participation.*

Proof. That Wealth-Fair satisfies Participation follows, for instance, from Moulin (1990, Theorem 1). Let $\tilde{R} \in \boldsymbol{R}$ denote the reference preferences. Let $\pi_0 > 0$ be given, and $\tilde{I}_0$ denote the reference indifference curve through the bundle $(0, \pi_0)$. Let $(x_0, y_0) \neq (0, \pi_0)$ satisfy $(0, \pi_0) \tilde{I}(x_0, y_0)$ and their exists w_0 such that $(x_0, y_0) \in m(\tilde{R}, B((0, -\pi_0), 1, w_0))$. Such a point (x_0, y_0) exists since $\tilde{R} \neq R^L$. Let $e = ((0, 1), (R_1, R_1), f) \in \boldsymbol{E}^C$ be such that $z R_1 z' \Leftrightarrow y - w_0 \cdot x \geqslant y' - w_0 \cdot x'$ and $f(x) = w_0 \cdot x$. Then $\text{RWEB}_1(e) = (0, \pi_0)$ while $\text{RWEB}_2(e)$ is any non-negative point on the line $y = -\pi_0 + w_0 \cdot x$, to which agent $(1, R_1)$ strictly prefers $(0,0)$. □

4. Weakening the Basic Requirements

Theorems 2 and 3 are somehow disappointing. The trade-off between correcting for differential skills and guaranteeing a sufficiently high minimal welfare to all agents, however, can be partially fulfilled if we drop Monotonicity. This is the topic of this section. It will allow us to clarify further the trade-off between axioms of responsibility for one's preferences and axioms of full compensation.

Let us consider the following welfare lower bound, called the Work-Alone lower bound, which guarantees to each agent at least as much welfare as the highest welfare she could reach if all the other agents had the same preferences as she but a zero skill (so that they will end up with a bundle of the form $(0, y^*)$), and if she were not allowed to enjoy a higher welfare level than the other agents. The Work-Alone lower bound guarantees to positively skilled agents a minimum welfare that is higher than their participation level.

Definition 12. An allocation rule S satisfies the Work-Alone lower bound if and only if for every $e = (a, R, f) \in \boldsymbol{D}^S$, every $z \in S(a, R, f)$:

$$z_i R_i m(R_i, Y),$$

where $Y = \{(x, y) | y \leqslant f(a_i \cdot x) - (n - 1) \cdot y^*, \text{ where } (0, y^*) R_i(x, y)\}$.

The Wealth-Fair rule satisfies the Work-Alone lower bound (this is a consequence of Moulin, 1990, Theorem 1).

Finally, we introduce a full compensation requirement that is stronger than $\widetilde{\text{EWRP}}$ but still weaker than EWEP and a requirement of non-discrimination among preferences that is weaker than NEES. The first one, called Equal Welfare for Uniform Preferences, equalizes welfare only if all the agents have the same preferences. The second one, called No Envy among Uniformly Skilled, eliminates envy only if all the agents have the same skill. Parallel weakenings are proposed in Fleurbaey (1994).[12]

Definition 13. An allocation rule S satisfies *Equal Welfare for Uniform Preferences* (EWUP) if and only if for every $e = (a, R, f) \in \boldsymbol{D}^S$, every $z \in S(a, R, f)$:

$$[R_i = R_j \text{ for every } i, j \in N] \Rightarrow [z_i I_i z_j \text{ for every } i, j \in N].$$

Definition 14. An allocation rule S satisfies *No Envy among Uniformly Skilled* (NEUS) if and only if for every $e = (a, R, f) \in \boldsymbol{D}^S$, every $z \in S(a, R, f)$,

$$[a_i = a_j \text{ for every } i, j \in N] \Rightarrow [z_i R_i z_j \text{ for every } i, j \in N].$$

Let us observe that if a welfare lower bound guarantees to an agent (a_i, R_i) a minimal welfare level that is strictly superior to her Work-Alone welfare level and that does not depend on the other agent's characteristics, then this welfare lower bound is incompatible with EWUP. Let us consider, indeed, the economy $((0, \ldots, a_i, \ldots, 0), (R_i, \ldots, R_i), f)$ and let us note that the EWUP axiom precisely requires that this agent be at most at her Work-Alone welfare level). In other words, the Work-Alone lower bound is the highest lower bound compatible with EWUP.

Theorem 4. (i) *There is a rule defined over the Domain $\boldsymbol{E}^C$ which satisfies PO, NEES, EWUP and the Work-Alone lower bound.* (ii) *The same as* (i), *except that NEES is replaced by NEUS, and EWUP is replaced by EWEP.*

Proof. First, we introduce the following terminology. For every $e = (a, R, f) \in \boldsymbol{E}^C$, every $z \in P(a, R, f)$, let $w(z, e) \in \mathbb{R}_+$ denote a supporting input price of z, and $\pi_i(z, e) = y_i - w(z, e) \cdot a_i \cdot x_i$. Moreover, for every $z_i \in \mathbb{R}_+^2, R_i \in \boldsymbol{R}$, let $y^0(z_i, R_i) \in \mathbb{R}_+$ be defined by $(-y^0(z_i, R_i), 0) I_i z_i$ if $(0, 0) P_i z_i$, and $(0, y^0(z_i, R_i)) I_i z_i$ if $z_i R_i (0, 0)$. We now construct two allocation rules satisfying the requirements of the claims. For every $e = (a, R, f) \in \boldsymbol{E}^C$, let the preferences $\hat{R}(R)$ be represented by the

---

[12]It is noticeable that Van Parijs' solution, defined for every pair i, j, there exists $k \in N$, such that $z_i R_k z_j$ (cf. Van Parijs, 1990), satisfies EWUP and only No Envy among Uniformly Skilled, whereas it satisfies the axioms corresponding to EWUP and NEES in the simple exchange model studied in Fleurbaey (1994).

following utility function: $\hat{u}(x,y) = \min_i y^0((x,y), R_i)$. Then, we define the allocation rule S^X:

$$z \in S^X(a, R, f) \Leftrightarrow z \in P(a, R, f) \quad \text{and} \quad \forall i, \ j \in N,$$

$$m(\hat{R}, \{(x,y)|y - w(z,e) \cdot a_i \cdot x \leqslant \pi_i(z,e)\})\hat{I}$$

$$m(\hat{R}, \{(x,y)|y - w(z,e) \cdot a_j \cdot x \leqslant \pi_j(z,e)\}),$$

i.e., a reference agent, who by construction is lazier[13] than all the agents at bundles in a neighborhood of the y-axis, would be indifferent between all the budget sets. In a somewhat dual fashion, let agent k be such that $a_k = \min_i(a_1, \ldots, a_n)$. Then, we define the allocation rule S^Y:

$$z \in S^Y(a, R, f) \Leftrightarrow z \in P(a, R, f) \quad \text{and}$$

$$z_i I_i m(R_i, \{(x,y)|y - w \cdot a_k \cdot x \leqslant \pi_k(z,e)\}), \quad \forall i \in N,$$

i.e., each agent is indifferent between receiving her bundle or having access to the budget set of the agent having the lowest skill. Non-emptiness of S^X follows from the non-emptiness of RWEB. The proof that S^Y is also non-empty is sketched in the appendix. The straightforward proof that S^X satisfies PO, NEES, EWUP, and that S^Y satisfies PO, NEUS and EWEP is omitted. We now prove that both S^X and S^Y satisfy the Work-Alone lower bound. Let us first prove that for every (a, R, f) and every $z \in S^X(a, R, f) \cup S^Y(a, R, f)$,

$$\min_i y^0(z_i, R_i) \geqslant \max_i \pi_i(z,e).$$

By definition of S^X, $\pi_i(z,e) \leqslant y^0(\hat{z}, \hat{R})$ for all $i \in N$, where $\hat{z}$ is any point on the reference indifference curve corresponding to z. We prove now that $y^0(z_i, R_i) \geqslant y^0(\hat{z}, \hat{R})$ for all $i \in N$. Suppose $y^0(z_i, R_i) < y^0(\hat{z}, \hat{R})$ for some $i \in N$, and let z^* be defined by $z_i I_i z^*$ and $\hat{z} \hat{I} z^*$. Such a z^* exists since the indifference curves through z_i and $\hat{z}$ are tangential to the same budget line. We then have $y^0(z^*, R_i) < y^0(z^*, \hat{R})$, which contradicts the way $\hat{R}$ was defined. Conversely, by the definition of S^Y, $\pi_k(z, a, R, f) \leqslant y^0(z_i, R_i)$, for all $i \in N$. We now prove that $\pi_i(z,e) \geqslant \pi_k(z,e)$. But it directly follows from $a_i \geqslant a_k$ and $m(R_i, \{(x,y)|y - w \cdot a_k \cdot x \leqslant \pi_k(z,e)\})I_i m(R_i, \{(x,y)|y - w \cdot a_i \cdot x \leqslant \pi_i(z,e)\})$ for all $i \in N$. Then the proof of Theorem 4 is completed by the following lemma. $\square$

---

[13]Agent with preferences R_i is lazier than agent with preferences R_j if and only if for every w and every $\pi, m(R_i, \{(x,y)|y - w \cdot x \leqslant \pi\}) \leqslant m(R_i, \{(x,y)|y - w \cdot x \leqslant \pi\})$.

Lemma 1. *If a Pareto-optimal allocation rule S satisfies the property that for every (a, R, f) and every $z \in S(a, R, f)$, $\min_i y^0(z_i, R_i) \geq \max_j \pi_j(z, a, R, f)$, then S satisfies the Work-Alone lower bound.*

Proof. First, we require the following notation. Let the function EWUP be defined by: for every $(a_1, \ldots, a_n) \in \mathbb{R}^n_+$, every $R^* \in \mathbf{R}$, and every $f \in \mathbf{F}$.

$$\mathrm{EWUP}((a_1, \ldots, a_n), R^*, f)$$

$$= (0, y^0) \Leftrightarrow \exists z \in P((a_1, \ldots, a_n), (R^*, \ldots, R^*), f) | z_i I^*(0, y^0) \quad \forall i.$$

Now, let $e = (a, R, f) \in \mathbf{E}^C$, $z \in S(a, R, f)$ be given. Let $g \in \mathbf{F}$ be defined by $g(x) = \Sigma_i \pi_i(z, e) + w(z, e) \cdot x$, so that for all x, $f(x) \leq g(x)$. Let us observe that $z_i \in m(R_i, \{(x, y) \in [0, \bar{x}] \times \mathbb{R}_+ \mid y \leq g(a_i \cdot x) - \Sigma_{j \neq i} \pi_i(z, e)\})$ for all $i \in N$. As a consequence of the property stated in the claim, $y^0(z_i, R_i) \geq 1/(n-1)(\Sigma_{j \neq i} \pi_j(z, e))$ for all $i \in N$. Therefore,

$$z_i R_i m(R_i, \{(x, y) \mid y \leq g(a_i \cdot x) - (n-1) \cdot y^0((x, y), R_i)\}) \quad \text{for all } i \in N,$$

so that $z_i R_i \mathrm{EWUP}((0, \ldots, a_i, \ldots, 0), R_i, g)$ for all $i \in N$, which implies $z_i R_i \mathrm{EWUP}((0, \ldots, a_i, \ldots, 0), R_i, f)$ for all $i \in N$, the desired outcome. $\square$

Remarks. (1) Let us note some properties satisfied by the rules S^X and S^Y defined in the proof above. First, S^X and S^Y satisfy ND and CI. Secondly, they are both continuous with respect to changes in production skills and changes in preferences. Thirdly, the axioms of No Envy in the claims could even be replaced with corresponding axioms of Equal Budget. Finally, at an S^X allocation, the laziest agent (if any) does not envy any other agent. Conversely, at an S^Y allocation, no agent envies the agent having the lowest skill.

(2) In the same way as Monotonicity and Horizontal Equity imply NEES, we can prove that Monotonicity and EWEP together imply Pazner and Schmeidler's (1974) axiom of No Envy, which they prove incompatible with PO, even in two-agent economies. This is sufficient to prove that no allocation rule can simultaneously satisfy PO, Monotonicity and EWUP.

5. Concluding Remarks

Through Theorems 2, 3, and 4, we have identified the trade-off between axioms of full compensation and axioms of responsibility for one's preferences. Moreover, we have shown how these axioms can be combined with

Table 1.1. The trade-off between axioms of full compensation and axioms of responsibility for one's preferences.

	EWEP	EWUP	EWRP
Monotonicity	Incompatible	Incompatible	EW satisfies WALB,
	under PO	under PO	Otherwise,
			RWEB violates P
NEES	Incompatible	S^X satisfies	
	under PO	WALB	
NEUS	S^Y satisfies		
	WALB		

individual welfare lower bounds in order to avoid the 'slavery of the talented'. These results are summarized in Table 1.1.

All the solutions discussed in this paper (the RWEB solutions as well as S^X and S^Y) boil down to the Equal Profit Walrasian rule in the equal skill environment. This is a consequence of holding agents responsible for their preferences, through applying (at least) No Envy among Uniformly Skilled. The Equal Profit Walrasian rule is indeed the most prominent rule that satisfies No Envy when all agents have the same production skill. In a related paper, however, we analyse the same model by emphasizing the value of full compensation for equal preferences, and we even introduce a stronger requirement than Equal Welfare for Equal Preferences (cf. Fleurbaey and Maniquet, 1995a). As a result, we axiomatize some rules that do not coincide with the Equal Profit Walrasian rule in uniform skill economies.

Therefore, one can view the results of this paper as justifying several ways to generalize the Equal Profit Walrasian solution to the case of unequal production skills.

Finally, we note that in Section 3 we have been able to define a weaker axiom than Equal Welfare for Uniform Preferences by choosing some reference preferences. This strategy, however, would not be fruitful if we were to weaken No Envy among Uniformly Skilled. Let us assume indeed that a level $\tilde{a}$ of skill has been chosen as reference skill. Given a preferences profile R and a production function f, then for any uniform skill level $a \neq \tilde{a}$, it is always possible to find a production function g such that the projection of the feasible allocations onto the leisure-consumption space is exactly the same for the problem (a, R, g) as for the problem $(\tilde{a}, R, f)$. In other words, the economies (a, R, g) and $(\tilde{a}, R, f)$ differ only with respect to the unit in which skills are measured. But it is dubious that skill units can be meaningfully distinguished from units of (efficient) input contribution. Therefore, if we want to be neutral with respect to skill units, then any axiom of No Envy among agents having the reference skill would be equivalent to No Envy among Uniformly Skilled. This is a major difference with the pure exchange model studied in Fleurbaey (1995).

Acknowledgments

This paper was prepared while M. Fleurbaey was at INSEE, Paris, France, and F. Maniquet was visiting INSEE, July 1993. The authors wish to thank Guy Laroque and Philippe Michel for their helpful suggestions, and Louis Gevers, Peter Hammond, Hervé Moulin, William Thomson, two anonymous referees and an anonymous associate editor for valuable comments on an earlier draft.

Appendix

In this appendix we sketch the proof that Reference Welfare Equivalent Budget allocations and S^Y-allocations always exist in a convex economy. The more technical lemmas are left to the reader.

A.1. *Non-emptiness of RWEB*

Let the economy $e = (a, R, f) \in \boldsymbol{E}^C$ be given. If $\tilde{R} = R^L$, then we should prove the well-known non-emptiness of the Equal Income Walrasian rule. Therefore, we assume $\tilde{R} \neq R^L$. Let u_i and $\tilde{u}$ denote the utility representations of R_i and $\tilde{R}$, respectively. The functions u_i are normalized so that $u_i(\hat{x}_i, 0) = 0$, where

$$\hat{x}_i = \begin{cases} 0, & \text{if } a_i = 0, \\ \bar{x}, & \text{if } a_i > 0, \end{cases}$$

that is, $\hat{x}_i$ represents the maximal contribution level provided by agent i at a Pareto-optimal allocation when $a_i > 0$, and a contribution level to which agent i does not strictly prefer any other contribution level when $a_i = 0$. Let $U \subset \mathbb{R}^n$ be defined by

$$U = \{u \in \mathbb{R}^n | \exists z \in P(a, R, f) \quad \text{and} \quad u_i = u_i(z_i)\}.$$

The case in which $U = \{(0, \ldots, 0)\}$ is easily handled; RWEB is obviously non-empty. From now on, we consider the other cases.

Lemma A.1. *The set U is homeomorphic to the closed simplex Δ^{n-1}.*

Proof. First we prove that $P(a, R, f)$ is closed. Given $e = (a, R, f) \in \mathbf{E}^C$, let $WP(a, R, f)$ be the set of weak Pareto-optimal allocations of e, and $Z_0^n(e)$ the set of feasible allocations where agents with zero skill do not work at all, i.e.,

$$WP(a, R, f) = \{z \in Z^n(e) | \forall \, z' \in Z_n(e), \, \sim[z_i' P_i z_i, \text{ for all } i \in N]\},$$

$$Z_0^n(e) = \{z \in Z^n(e) | a_i = 0 \Rightarrow x_i = 0\}.$$

Since n is finite and f varies over $\mathbb{R}_+$, both $WP(a, R, f)$ and $Z_o^n(e)$ are closed. Let $e = (a, R, f) \in \mathbf{E}^C$ be given, and let $z \in WP(a, R, f)$, but $z \notin P(a, R, f)$. If $\Sigma_i y_i < f(\Sigma_i a_i \cdot x_i)$, then we can define $d > 0$ and $z' \in Z^n(e)$ by

$$d = \frac{f(\Sigma_i a_i \cdot x_i) - \Sigma_i y_i}{n}$$

and $z_i' = (x_i, y_i + d)$ for all $i \in N$, so that $z_i' P_i z_i$, for all $i \in N$, a contradiction. As a result, $\Sigma_i y_i = f(\Sigma_i a_i \cdot x_i)$. Now, by assumption, f is strictly increasing. Therefore, if there exist $w \in \mathbb{R}_{++}$ and $j \in N$ such that w supports the firm at $(\Sigma_i a_i \cdot x_i, \Sigma_i y_i)$ but $z_j \notin m(R_j, B(z_j, a_j, w))$, then either $a_j = 0$ or there exists $z_j'' \in \text{int}(B(z_j, a_j, w))$ such that $z_j'' I_j z_j$ and $\Sigma_{i \neq j} y_i + y_j'' < f(\Sigma_{i \neq j} a_i \cdot x_i + a_j \cdot x_j'')$, which contradicts $z \in WP(a, R, f)$ (the sets $B(\cdot)$ have been defined above and $\text{int}(\cdot)$ denotes the interior). Consequently, $a_j = 0$. This proves that $P(a, R, f) = WP(a, R, f) \cap Z_0^n(e)$, and then $P(a, R, f)$ is closed.

Now let us consider the function $p: U \rightarrow \Delta^{n-1}$ defined by (recall that $\Sigma_i u_i > 0$ because $(0, \dots, 0)$ is excluded)

$$p(u) = \frac{1}{\Sigma_i u_i} u.$$

Since U represents the Pareto-optimal allocations, p is a one-to-one function. By the continuity assumptions, the functions p and p^{-1} are continuous. $\square$

Part 1. Let us assume that f is continuously differentiable. Let us define the function $W: U \rightarrow \mathbb{R}_+$ by

$$W(\bar{u}) = w(z, a, R, f), \quad \text{where for all } i \in N, \quad \bar{u}_i = u_i(z_i).$$

Note that the assumption on f guarantees that any Pareto-optimal allocation has a unique supporting price, which in turn supports all allocations which are Pareto indifferent to this allocation (i.e., to any point in Δ^{n-1} corresponds only one supporting price).

Lemma A.2. *The function W is continuous.*

The proof is omitted.

Let us define the functions $\Pi_i : U \to \mathbb{R}$ as follows:

$$\Pi_i(\bar{u}) = \pi_i(z, e)$$

where $\bar{u}_i = u_i(z_i)$, and $\pi_i(z, e)$ is defined as in the proof of Proposition 4.

Lemma A.3. *The functions Π_i are continuous.*

The proof is omitted.

Let us define the correspondences $B_i : \mathbb{R}_+ \times \mathbb{R}_+ \to [0, \bar{x}] \times \mathbb{R}_+$ as follows:

$$B_i(\bar{u}, w) = \{(x, y) \in [0, \bar{x}] \times \mathbb{R}_+ \mid y - w \cdot a_i \cdot x \leqslant \Pi_i(\bar{u})\}$$

i.e., $B_i(\bar{u}, w)$ denotes the budget set defined by the input price w and the profit level corresponding to $\Pi_i(\bar{u})$.

Lemma A.4. *The correspondences B_i are continuous and compact valued.*

The proof is omitted.

Let us now define the function $\mu : \Delta^{n-1} \to \mathbb{R}^n$ as follows:

$$\mu_i(\lambda) = \max\{\tilde{u}(x, y) \mid (x, y) \in B_i(p^{-1}(\lambda), \, W(p^{-1}(\lambda)))\},$$

i.e., $\mu_i(\lambda)$ denotes the utility level which can be reached by a reference agent maximizing over the budget set $B_i(p^{-1}(\lambda), W(p^{-1}(\lambda)))$.

Lemma A.5. *The function μ is continuous.*

Proof. Given the continuity of $\tilde{u}, B_i$ and W, and given the compactness of Δ^{n-1}, the result is obtained by applying the maximum theorem. $\square$

Let the sets E_i be defined as follows:

$$E_i = \{\lambda \in \Delta^{n-1} \mid \mu_i(\lambda) \geqslant \mu_j(\lambda), \, \forall j \neq i\},$$

i.e., a element of E_i is the representation in the closed simplex Δ^{n-1} of a Pareto-optimal allocation where the budget set of agent i would be (weakly) preferred by the reference agent to all the other agents' budget sets.

Lemma A.6. *All the sets E_i are closed and non-empty.*

The proof is omitted.

Lemma A.7. *For every subset of agents $I \subseteq N$ and for every vector $\lambda \in \Delta^{n-1}$ such that for all $j \notin I, \lambda_j = 0$, we have $\lambda \in \cup_{i \in I} E_i$.*

Proof. Let us assume, by way of contradiction, that there exists a subset of agents, say I, and a vector, say λ, such that for all $j \notin I, \lambda_j = 0$ and $\lambda \notin \cup_{i \in I} E_i$, i.e., there exists an agent, say j_0, who does not belong to the subset I, such that $\lambda_{j0} = 0$, whereas $\mu_{j0}(\lambda) > \mu_i(\lambda)$, for all $i \in I$. By the construction of Π_i, and by the concavity of f, we have

$$\forall \bar{u} \in U, \quad \bar{u}_i = 0 \Rightarrow \Pi_i(\bar{u}) \leqslant 0$$

and

$$\forall \bar{u} \in U, \quad \sum_{i \in N} \Pi_i(\bar{u}) \geqslant 0.$$

However, since $\lambda_{j0} = 0$ we also have $\bar{u}_{j0} = 0$. Therefore, $\Pi_{j0}(\bar{u}_{j0}, W(\bar{u})) \leqslant 0$. We now investigate two cases.

Case 1: Either $a_{j0} = 0$, or $W(\bar{u}) = 0$, i.e., the reference agent's choice set over agent j_0's budget set necessarily includes the bundle $(0,0)$. In this case there is at least one agent of I, say i, such that $\Pi_i(\bar{u}_i, W(\bar{u})) \geqslant 0$, so that even if $a_i = 0$, we have $\mu_{j0}(\lambda) \leqslant \mu_i(\lambda)$, the desired contradiction.

Case 2: $a_{j0} \cdot W(\bar{u}) > 0$. In this case the agent receives the bundle $(\bar{x}, 0)$ and at least one agent of I, say i, has a strictly positive consumption, so that $u_{j0}(\lambda) < \mu_i(\lambda)$, the desired contradiction. $\qquad\square$

Proposition A.1. *If f is continuously differentiable, then a RWEB allocation exists.*

Proof. By the preceding lemma and the Knuster–Kuratowsky–Mazurkiewicz theorem, we obtain:

$$\bigcap_{i \in N} E_i \neq \varnothing,$$

i.e., there exists a vector λ^* such that $\mu_i(\lambda_i^*) = \mu_j(\lambda_j^*), \forall i, j \in N$. As a result, the allocation z^* such that $u_i(z_i^*) = p^{-1}(\lambda_i^*) \forall i \in N$, is a RWEB allocation. □

Part 2. The production function f is not continuously differentiable.

The key point in this part is that we can find a sequence f^k of continuously differentiable production functions which converges to f. The sequence of allocations z^k corresponding to λ^{*k}, defined at the end of Part 1, varies in a compact subset of $\mathbb{R}^{2n}$ and therefore has a cluster point z^*, which in turn defines a RWEB allocation.

A.2. *Non-emptiness of S^Y*

This proof is essentially similar to the previous one. The production function is first assumed to be continuously differentiable, and the non-differentiable case is treated as above. The sets E_i are now defined by

$$E_i = \left\{ \lambda \in \Delta^{n-1} \mid \pi_k^i(z,e) \geqslant \pi_k^j(z,e), \ \forall j \neq i, \text{ where } \lambda_i = \frac{1}{\Sigma_i u_i} u_i(z_i) \right\},$$

where $\pi_k^i(z,e)$ satisfies $z_i I_i m(R_i, \{(x,y) \mid y - w \cdot a_k \cdot x \leqslant \pi_k^i(z,e)\})$. That is to say, an element of E_i is the representation in the closed simplex Δ^{n-1} of the Pareto-optimal allocation where the budget set which would leave agent i indifferent to z_i if she had the same skill as agent k, contains all the budget sets which would leave any other agent j indifferent to z_j, had she the same skill as agent k.

The proof that E_i are closed and non-empty follows the same way as in the preceding proof and is thus omitted.

Lemma A.8. *For every subset of agents $I \subseteq N$ and for every vector $\lambda \in \Delta^{n-1}$ such that for all $j \notin I, \lambda_j = 0$, we have $\lambda \in \cup_{i \in I} E_i$.*

Here again we can reproduce the proof of Lemma A.7, by using the fact that

$$\text{if } a_i = 0, \quad \text{then } \pi_k^i(z,e) = \Pi_i(u(z)),$$
$$\text{if } a_i > 0, \quad \text{then } \pi_k^i(z,e) \geqslant \Pi_i(u(z)).$$

The non-emptiness of S^Y follows from the same fixed point argument as in Proposition A.1.

References

1. R. J. Arneson. 'Equality and equal opportunity for welfare', *Philosophical Studies* **56** (1989), 77–93.
2. Ch. Arnsperger. 'Envy-freeness and distributive justice: A survey of the literature', *Journal of Economic Surveys* **8** (1994), 155–186.
3. G. S. Becker. 'A theory of the allocation of time', *Journal of Economic Surveys* **75** (1965), 493–517.
4. W. Bossert. 'Redistribution mechanisms based on individuals characteristics', *Mathematical Social Sciences* **29** (1995), 1–17.
5. P. Champsaur and G. Laroque. 'Fair allocations in large economies', *Journal of Economic Theory* **25** (1981), 269–282.
6. G. A. Cohen. 'On the currency of egalitarian justice', *Ethics* **99** (1989), 906–944.
7. P. Dasgupta and P. Hammond. 'Fully progressive taxation', *Journal of Public Economics* **33** (1980), 141–154.
8. R. Dworkin. 'What is equality? Part 1: Equality of welfare', *Philosophy & Public Affairs* **10**(3) (1981a), 185–246.
9. R. Dworkin. 'What is equality? Part 2: Equality of resources', *Philosophy & Public Affairs* **10**(4) (1981b), 283–345.
10. M. Fleurbaey. 'Three solutions to the compensation problem', *Journal of Economic Theory* **65** (1995), 505–521.
11. M. Fleurbaey. 'On fair compensation', *Theory and Decision* **36** (1994), 277–307.
12. M. Fleurbaey and F. Maniquet. 'Fair allocation with unequal production skills: The solidarity approach to compensation', University of Cergy-Pontoise Discussion Paper, 1995a.
13. M. Fleurbaey and F. Maniquet. Implementability and horizontal equity require no-envy, mimeo, 1995b.
14. D. Foley. 'Resource allocation and the public sector', *Yale Economic Essays* **7**(1) (1967), 45–98.
15. L. Gevers. 'Walrasian social choice: Some simple axiomatic approaches', in W. Heller *et al.* (eds.), *Social Choice and Public Decision Making, Essays in Honor of K.J. Arrow*, Cambridge: Cambridge University Press. 1986.

16. E. Maskin. 'Nash equilibrium and welfare optimality', mimeo, 1977.

17. J. A. Mirrlees. 'An exploration in the theory of optimal income taxation', *Review of Economic Studies* **38** (1971), 175–208.

18. H. Moulin. 'Joint ownership of a convex technology: Comparison of three solutions', *Review of Economic Studies* **57** (1990), 439–452.

19. H. Moulin and W. Thomson. 'Can everyone benefit from growth? Two difficulties', *Journal of Mathematical Economics* **17** (1988), 339–345.

20. E. Pazner and D. Schmeidler. 'A difficulty in the concept of fairness', *Review of Economic Studies* **41** (1974), 441–443.

21. E. Pazner and D. Schmeidler. 'Egalitarian equivalent allocations: A new concept of economic equity', *Quarterly Journal of Economics* **92** (1978a), 671–687.

22. E. Pazner and D. Scbmeidler. 'Decentralization and income distribution in socialist economies', *Economic Inquiry* **16** (1978b), 257–264.

23. J. Rawls. *A Theory of Justice*, Cambridge, MA: Harvard University Press. 1971.

24. J. Rawls. 'Social unity and primary goods', in A. K. Sen and B. Williams (eds.), *Utilitarianism and Beyond*, Cambridge: Cambridge University Press. 1982.

25. J. E. Roemer. 'Equality of talent', *Economics and Philosophy* **1** (1985), 151–187.

26. J. E. Roemer. 'Equality of resources implies equality of welfare', *Quarterly Journal of Economics* **101** (1986), 751–784.

27. J. E. Roemer. 'A pragmatic theory of responsibility for the egalitarian planner', *Philosophy & Public Affairs* **22** (1993), 146–166.

28. A. K. Sen. *Commodities and Capabilities*, Amsterdam: North-Holland. 1985.

29. W. Thomson. 'Equity in exchange economies', *Journal of Economic Theory* **29** (1983), 217–244.

30. W. Thomson. 'A study of choice correspondences in economics with a variable number of agents', *Journal of Economic Theory* **46** (1988), 237–254.

31. W. Thomson. *Bargaining Theory: The Axiomatic Approach*, San Diego: Academic Press. 1994.

32. W. Thomson and H. Varian. 'Theories of justice based on symmetry', in L. Hurwicz *et al.* (eds.), *Social Goals and Social Organization*, Cambridge: Cambridge University Press. 1985.

33. J. Tinbergen. *Redelijke Inkomensverdeling*, 2nd edn., Haarlem: N. DeGuiden Pers. 1953.

34. P. van Parijs. 'Equal endowments as undominated diversity', *Recherches Economique de Louvain* **56** (1990), 327–355.

35. H. Varian. 'Equity, envy, and efficiency', *Journal of Economic Theory* **9** (1974), 63–91.

36. H. Varian. 'Two problems in the theory of fairness', *Journal of Public Economics* **5** (1976), 249–260.

37. R. Vohra. 'Equity and efficiency in non-convex economies', *Social Choice and Welfare* **9** (1992), 185–202.

CHAPTER 5

Cooperative Production with Unequal Skills: The Solidarity Approach to Compensation

Marc Fleurbaey and François Maniquet

ABSTRACT. We consider a simple production model and we assume that agents have unequal production skills which can in no way be attributed to their responsibility. We study how it is possible, if at all, to compensate for differential skills by applying Rawls's idea of a collective sharing in the benefits of skills. For this purpose, we introduce an axiom of solidarity, according to which agents should all be affected in the same direction if the profile of personal skills changes. We show that particular allocation rules are characterized be combining this axiom with a requirement of non-discrimination among preferences, or with a property capturing Nozick's idea of guaranteeing a minimal benefit from one's own skill.

1. Introduction

'No one deserves his place in the distribution of natural endowments, any more than one deserves one's initial starting place in society' (Rawls 1971, p. 74). On the basis of this rather obvious observation, Rawls made the much more controversial proposal 'to regard the distribution of natural talents as a common asset and to share in the benefits of this distribution whatever it turns out to be' (p. 101). This idea has triggered a fierceful opposition by Nozick (1974), who alleged that it amounts to a denial of

We thank seminar participants in Osnabrück and Cergy, an Associate Editor and three referees for their comments on previous drafts. The usual *caveat* applies.

Soc Choice Welfare **16**: 569–583 (1999)

©Springer-Verlag 2004

individuals' basic self-ownership, and a violation of the Kantian principle that no one should be used as a means for others' purposes.

Nozick's argument goes a little too far, because it fails to acknowledge that personal talents can be used by their owner only in a set of social conventions and institutions. There is no natural system of self-ownership which exclusively respects integrity of the person and of the personal talents. As noted by Waldron (1988), what is a talent and what is a handicap is even partly endo-geneously determined by the surrounding institutions (the talents of a good apparatchik and those of an entrepreneur do not flourish in the same institutional setting). Now, the very problem addressed by Rawls and others is precisely to design an appropriate set of institutions, which would respect the integrity of the moral agent while neutralizing morally arbitrary inequalities.

Nonetheless, even if it is excessive to consider that respect of self-ownership and collective sharing in talents are incompatible, one must admit that the various ways of enforcing such sharing may be more or less favorable to the talented and less talented agents. In this paper, we study the consequences of a particular concept of collective sharing. This concept has now become familiar in the literature on equity and fair division, and is based on the idea of solidarity: if agents collectively share in the benefits of a resource, they should all be affected in the same direction when the total amount of this resource varies (Thomson, 1983; Roemer, 1986; Thomson, 1990). This can be applied to personal talents. If the profile of personal talents changes, and if all agents are supposed to share 'in the distribution whatever it turns out to be', their welfare should uniformly increase or decrease.

More specifically, we study a simple one-input-one-output production model, in which agents are assumed to have unequal production skills. They may also have different preferences over input-output bundles. Our approach is axiomatic, and we examine whether allocation rules (i.e. correspondences which select a subset of feasible allocations for each possible economy) exist that satisfy properties reflecting the idea of solidarity, as well as other appealing properties.

Section 2 below presents the model and analyzes variants of the solidarity concept. In particular, solidarity with respect to skills essentially implies that two agents with identical preferences must be given bundles on the same indifference curve, a basic axiom of compensation for skill inequalities that has been introduced in related work (Fleurbaey, and Maniquet, 1996b).

Since allocation rules satisfying the solidarity requirement may nonetheless have unattractive features in other respects, we examine whether such features can be avoided. The first idea is that an allocation rule should not discriminate among various preferences. In the absence of any moral judgement about various kinds of preferences, there is indeed no reason to give preferential treatment to some agents on the basis of their preferences. We examine in Section 3 two ways in which this idea can be formalized. Both refer to the idea of equal opportunity. It turns out that it is not easy to satisfy the solidarity requirement without favoring some preferences. This trade-off between solidarity and non-discrimination between preferences enables us to single out an allocation rule called Equal Wage Equivalent, which is characterized by axioms embodying these two principles and other minor requirements. This rule selects the Pareto optimal allocations having the property that each agent derives from her bundle the level of welfare she would enjoy if she could choose her labor time given a constant wage rate, which is the same for all agents.

In Section 4, we turn to Nozick's concern, and examine how the solidarity requirement can be counter-balanced by requiring that an agent should be guaranteed a minimal benefit from her own skill. Some allocation rules may give excessive bonus to the low-skill agents, at the expense of high-skill agents. To represent the idea of minimal benefit from one's own skills, we propose the axiom of Work Alone lower bound, according to which each agent must be at least as well off as if she worked alone and gave the others a bundle to which she is indifferent. This is a rather weak requirement, but it turns out that we cannot guarantee more under the solidarity requirement, as we already obtain a characterization of an allocation rule, namely, the Egalitarian Equivalent rule. This rule selects the Pareto optimal allocations in which each agent is indifferent between her assigned bundle and a reference bundle with zero input contribution.

This paper is closely related to Moulin and Roemer's (1989) article. They studied the combination of private ownership of personal talents and public ownership of external resources, and showed that the degree of welfare inequality compatible with such a combination may be very low. Our focus is very different, since we study the idea of collective sharing in the talents, as opposed to private ownership. But it turns out that a simplified version of their main theorem is a corollary of our results. And therefore it seems that our work sheds some light on their result. This is discussed in Section 3.

The present work is part of a larger research project (Fleurbaey, 1994, 1995; Fleurbaey and Maniquet, 1994; Maniquet, 1998), which examines how inequalities in talents, when deemed undesirable, can be alleviated by appropriate allocation rules. Our general assumption is that, in contrast, agents are responsible for their preferences and utility level, which implies in particular that we can restrict ourselves to a purely ordinal analysis (we let the agents bear the full consequences of their utility function, given their preferences; we are, however, obliged to take preferences into account, for Pareto optimality in particular).

2. Skill Solidarity

Firstly, we define the model. There is a set N of n agents. There are two goods and agent i's consumption bundle is denoted $z_i = (x_i, y_i)$, where x_i, is interpreted as labor time, y_i as consumption. The agents' consumption sets are identical: $[0, \bar{x}] \times \mathbb{R}_+$. Our results can be extended to the case of unequal consumption sets. Agent i's preferences over this consumption set are defined by an ordering R_i (with indifference and strict preference denoted I_i and P_i, respectively). The ordering R_i is continuous and convex, and is such that more of the first good is never strictly preferred, and more of the second good is always strictly preferred. Let $\boldsymbol{R}$ denote the set of such orderings.

Agent i also has a skill parameter a_i, which measures how efficient her labor time is in the production process. That is, the total output of the production process is equal to $f(\sum_{i=1}^{n} a_i \cdot x_i)$, where $f : \mathbb{R}_+ \to \mathbb{R}_+$ is the production function representing the available technology. The parameter a_i is non-negative for all i in N, and f is increasing and continuous. The assumption that efficient labor $a_i \cdot x_i$ is proportional to labor time is made for simplicity, and is commonplace in this kind of model, although it is sometimes introduced as an assumption about preferences. The general case when efficient labor is not proportional to labor time is more difficult to analyze, even though some of our results could easily be extended, and we leave it to future research. When $f(0)$ is positive, it is simply the amount of the second good which is already available before production takes place. Let $\boldsymbol{F}$ denote the set of such functions.

An *economy* is a list $(a_1, \ldots, a_n, R_1, \ldots, R_n, f) \in \boldsymbol{E} = \mathbb{R}_+^n \times \boldsymbol{R}^n \times \boldsymbol{F}$, and we shall usually adopt a more compact notation: $e = (a, R, f)$, with $a = (a_1, \ldots, a_n)$, and $R = (R_1, \ldots, R_n)$. We will often restrict our attention to a particular subdomain of $\boldsymbol{F}$, for instance the subdomain $\boldsymbol{F}^C$ of concave production functions, the subdomain $\boldsymbol{F}^D$ of decreasing returns to scale production functions and the subdomain $\boldsymbol{F}^I$ of increasing returns to scale production functions. The class of economies (a, R, f) will be referred to as $\boldsymbol{E}$ if the domain of the production functions is $\boldsymbol{F}$, or as $\boldsymbol{E}^C, \boldsymbol{E}^D$ or $\boldsymbol{E}^I$ if the domain of the production functions is restricted in the corresponding way.

An *allocation* is a vector $z = (z_1, \dots, z_n) \in ([0, \bar{x}] \times \mathbb{R}_+)^n$ of bundles $z_i = (x_i, y_i)$. An allocation z is *feasible* for the economy $e = (a, R, f) \in \boldsymbol{E}$ if and only if

$$y_N = \sum_{i=1}^n y_i \le f\left(\sum_{i=1}^n a_i \cdot x_i\right).$$

We denote by $Z(e)$ the set of feasible allocations for an economy $e \in \boldsymbol{E}$.

An *allocation rule* S, defined over a subset $\boldsymbol{D}^S$ of $\boldsymbol{E}$, is a correspondence which associates to every economy $e = (a, R, f)$ in its domain $\boldsymbol{D}^S$ a nonempty set $S(e) \subseteq Z(e)$. Moreover, we restrict our attention to allocation rules which satisfy the two following properties.

Definition 1. An allocation rule S satisfies **Anonymity** (A) if and only if for every $e = (a, R, f) \in \boldsymbol{D}^S$, every $z \in S(a, R, f)$, and every permutation π over N,

$$(z_{\pi(1)}, \dots, z_{\pi(n)}) \in S((a_{\pi(1)}, \dots, a_{\pi(n)}), (R_{\pi(n)}, \dots, R_{\pi(n)}), f).$$

Definition 2. An allocation rule S satisfies **Pareto Optimality** (PO) if and only if for every $e = (a, R, f) \in \boldsymbol{D}^S$, every $z \in S(a, R, f)$, and every $z' \in Z(e)$,

$$[z_i' R_i z_i, \ \forall i \in N] \Rightarrow [z_i' I_i z_i, \ \forall i \in N].$$

The set of Pareto Optimal allocations for an economy $(a, R, f) \in \boldsymbol{E}$ is denoted by $P(a, R, f)$. We now define the requirement of Skill Solidarity, which is intended to capture the idea of collective ownership of skills. It says that all agents should be affected in the same direction, in terms of welfare, when the profile of skill parameters changes. This kind of solidarity requirement has already been introduced in the literature in relation to other changes, such as changes in the available resources or technology, or in the population size (see e.g., Thomson, 1983; Moulin and Thomson, 1988). The collective ownership interpretation of solidarity requirements has been defended in particular by Moulin and Roemer (1989).

Definition 3.   An allocation rule S satisfies **Skill Solidarity** (SS) if and only if for every $e = (a, R, f) \in D^S$, every $a' \in \mathbb{R}^n_+$ such that $(a', R, f) \in D^S$, and every $z \in S(a, R, f)$ and $z' \in S(a', R, f)$,

$$\text{either} \quad z_i R_i z'_i, \quad \forall i \in N,$$

$$\text{or} \quad z'_i R_i z_i, \quad \forall i \in N.$$

Notice that this kind of axiom would make sense equally well in a more general context in which skill parameters would not be linearly combined with labor times in the production function.

We begin our analysis by noting some implications of Skill Solidarity. Firstly, we can characterize the allocation rules which satisfy Skill Solidarity and Pareto Optimality. Namely, all such allocations are of the Monotone Welfare Path type (see Roemer and Silvestre 1989). That is, for a given profile R and a given production function f, there is a monotone path in the n-individual welfare space such that the welfare representation of the selected allocations for any economy (a, R, f) lies at the intersection of this monotone path and the Pareto frontier of (a, R, f). This is obvious because any violation of monotonicity of the welfare path would imply a violation of Skill Solidarity.

Secondly, we define three requirements which are logically related to Skill Solidarity: Skill Monotonicity, Essential Single-Valuedness, and Equal Welfare for Equal Preferences. The first one, Skill Monotonicity, combines ideas of solidarity and Pareto Optimality, by stating that an increase in agents' skills cannot entail any loss in welfare for anyone.

Definition 4.   An allocation rule S satisfies **Skill Monotonicity** (SM) if and only if for every $e = (a, R, f) \in D^S$, every $j \in N$, every $a'_j \in \mathbb{R}_+$ such that $((a, \ldots, a'_j, \ldots, a_n), R, f) \in D^S$, and every $z \in S(a, R, f)$ and $z' \in S((a_1, \ldots, a'_j, \ldots, a_n), R, f)$,

$$[a'_j \geq a_j] \Rightarrow [z'_i R_i z_i, \forall i \in N].$$

Obviously, if an allocation rule satisfies Skill Solidarity and Pareto Optimality, then it satisfies Skill Monotonicity. The second requirement, Essential Single-Valuedness, is a consequence of Skill Solidarity and Pareto Optimality, too, and it is also a direct consequence of Skill Monotonicity (by considering the case $a'_j = a_j$).

Definition 5.   An allocation rule S satisfies **Essential Single-Valuedness** (ESV) if and only if for every $e = (a, R, f) \in D^S$, and every

$z, z' \in S(a, R, f),$

$$z_i I_i z_i', \quad \forall i \in N.$$

The third requirement, Equal Welfare for Equal Preferences, says that agents with identical preferences must be given bundles on a common one of their indifference curves. This intuitively reflects the idea of compensation for unequal skills, and turns out to be a direct consequence of the idea of collective ownership of skills, as stated in the lemma below.

Definition 6. An allocation rule S satisfies **Equal Welfare for Equal Preferences** (EWEP) if and only if for every $e = (a, R, f) \in \boldsymbol{D}^S$, every $z \in S(a, R, f)$, and every $i, j \in N$ such that $R_i = R_j$,

$$z_i I_i z_j.$$

Lemma 1. *If an allocation rule satisfies Skill Solidarity and Anonymity, then it also satisfies Equal Welfare for Equal Preferences.*

Proof. Let $(a, R, f) \in \boldsymbol{D}^S$, $z \in S(a, R, f)$, and i, j such that $R_i = R_j$, be given. Let a' be obtained by permuting a_i with a_j. By Anonymity, $z' \in S(a', R, f)$ where z' is obtained by permuting z_i, with z_j. By SS, $z_i R_j z_i$ and $z_j R_i z_i$, so that $z_i I_i z_i$. Q.E.D.

3. Non-Discrimination Among Preferences

In this section, we study two requirements which partly capture the intuition of non-discrimination among preferences. The first one is called No-Envy among Uniformly Skilled. This requirement, to some extent, guarantees that we compensate for lower skill only, and not for preferences, given the equal opportunity justification of the No-Envy condition (see Kolm, 1993).

Definition 7. An allocation rule S satisfies **No-Envy among Uniformly Skilled** (NEUS) if and only if for every $e = (a, R, f) \in \boldsymbol{D}^S$ such that $a_i = a_j$ for all $i, j \in N$, and for every $z \in S(a, R, f)$,

$$z_i R_i z_j \quad \forall i, \ j \in N.$$

Fleurbaey and Maniquet (1994) proved that it is compatible with Equal Welfare for Equal Preferences, and provided examples of rules satisfying both axioms. But it is not compatible with our stronger conditions of collective sharing in skills, as stated in our first result. Since No-Envy is incompatible with Pareto Optimality on the domains studied here that are larger than E^C (see Vohra, 1992), we restrict our attention to convex economies for this proposition.

Proposition 1. *There is no allocation rule defined over E^C which satisfies Pareto Optimality, Skill Monotonicity and No-Envy among Uniformly Skilled.*

Proof. Let $e = ((a_1, a_2, a_3), (R_1, R_2, R_3), f)$ be defined by: $a_1 = a_2 = a_3 = 1$, $f(x) = x$, for $x \leq 2$ and $f(x) = 2$, for $x \geq 2$, and

$$(x, y) R_1(x', y') \Leftrightarrow y - \frac{1}{10} \cdot x \geq y' - \frac{1}{10} \cdot x'$$

$$(x, y) R_2(x', y') \Leftrightarrow y - \frac{9}{10} \cdot x \geq y' - \frac{9}{10} \cdot x'$$

$$(x, y) R_3(x', y') \Leftrightarrow y - x \geq y' - x'$$

with $\bar{x} = 1$. Let S be any rule satisfying PO and NEUS and let $z = (z_1, z_2, z_3) \in S(e)$. By PO, $x_1 = x_2 = 1$, $x_3 = 0$ and $y_1 + y_2 + y_3 = 2$. Therefore, by NEUS, $y_1 = y_2$, and $y_2 - 1 \leq y_3 \leq y_2 - \frac{9}{10}$. Combining the restrictions, we have $\frac{29}{30} \leq y_1 \leq 1$. The allocation satisfying these properties which is worst for agent 1 is $((1, \frac{29}{30}), (1, \frac{29}{30}), (0, \frac{29}{30}))$.

Now let $e' = ((a_1', a_2', a_3'), (R_1, R_2, R_3), f)$ be such that $a_1' = a_2' = a_3' = 20$. Let $z' = (z_1', z_2', z_3') \in S(e')$. By PO, $x_2 = x_3 = 0$, $x_1 = \frac{1}{10}$, and $y_1 + y_2 + y_3 = 2$. Therefore, by NEUS, $y_2 = y_3$, and $y_2 + \frac{1}{100} \leq y_1 \leq y_2 + \frac{9}{100}$. Combining the restrictions, we have $\frac{202}{300} \leq y_1 \leq \frac{218}{300}$. The allocation satisfying these properties which is preferred by agent 1 is:

$$\left(\left(\frac{1}{10}, \frac{218}{300} \right), \left(0, \frac{191}{300} \right), \left(0, \frac{191}{300} \right) \right).$$

However, we have $(1, \frac{29}{30}) P_1(\frac{1}{10}, \frac{218}{300})$, so that SM is violated.   Q.E.D.

A second plausible interpretation of the idea of non-discriminating among preferences consists of guaranteeing to each agent a minimal welfare level which is defined by an opportunity set which satisfies the following property: whatever the agents' best choices over this set may be, the corresponding welfare level vector is feasible. The minimal welfare level works as follows: each agent is required to be at least as well off at every selected allocation as at her best choice over this opportunity set. Since the opportunity set is identical among agents, this approach is akin to the

No-Envy requirement although it works only as a lower bound. Moreover, such a lower bound carries some idea of compensation for skill differentials since the opportunity sets of two differently skilled agents are identical.

Several minimal welfare functions have been analysed in Maniquet (1998). We now concentrate on a minimal welfare requirement which has been studied, in the case of equally skilled agents, by Fleurbaey and Maniquet (1996a). This requirement refers to the appealing value of proportionality. Proportionality is a widely accepted value of equity in situations involving private contributions to a collective surplus, as exemplified by the cost-sharing literature. In our setting, an allocation is said to be proportional when the output consumption/input contribution ratio is identical among agents and when each and every agent is maximizing her welfare over the opportunity set composed of all bundles having this output/input ratio. The Constant Returns lower bound works as follows. Every agent is required to be at least as well off as at the proportional allocation whose corresponding fixed ratio satisfies the following property: whatever the agents' total input may be, the corresponding proportional output is feasible for the actual technology. Before stating the axiom formally, we need the following notation. Let $m(R_i, A)$ denote the set of bundles that maximize agent i's preferences R_i over a set A of bundles, that is

$$m(R_i, A) = \{z_i \in A | \forall z_i' \in A, z_i R_i z_i'\}.$$

Since agent i is indifferent between all of the bundles of $m(R_i, A)$, we sometimes use $m(Ri, A)$ to denote any bundle in $m(Ri, A)$.

Definition 8. An allocation rule S satisfies the **Constant Returns lower bound** (CRLB) if and only if for every $(a, R, f) \in \boldsymbol{D}^S$, and every $z \in S(a, R, f)$,

$$z_i R_i m(R_i, \{(x, y) \in [0, \bar{x}] \times \mathbb{R}_+ | y \leq h \cdot x\}),$$

where h is the highest scalar satisfying: $\forall x$ such that $x \leq n \cdot \bar{x}$, $h.x \leq f(\tilde{a} \cdot x)$, where $\tilde{a} = \min_i \{a_i\}$.

There exist Pareto Optimal allocation rules that satisfy the Constant Returns lower bound and Skill Solidarity, as exemplified by the following allocation rule, called the Equal Wage Equivalent rule. This rule selects all the Pareto Optimal allocations which have the following property: each agent is as well off at her assigned bundle as if she maximized her welfare by choosing her labor time given a wage rate which is the same for all agents.

Definition 9. The **Equal Wage Equivalent** rule is the allocation rule EWE such that for every (a, R, f), there exists $w \in \mathbb{R}_+$,

$$[z \in EWE(a, R, f)] \Leftrightarrow [z \in P(a, R, f) \quad \text{and}$$

$$z_i I_i m(R_i, \{(x, y) \in X | y \leq w \cdot x\}), \ \forall i \in N].$$

Let us note that the Equal Wage Equivalent rule is non-empty over the entire domain $\boldsymbol{E}$. In the case of equal production skills, the Equal Wage Equivalent corresponds to the Constant Returns Equivalent, introduced by Mas-Colell (1980).

We now define two additional axioms, which are mild requirements satisfied by most rules. The first axiom, called Contraction Independence, was introduced in Moulin (1990), and takes its inspiration from Nash's Independence of Irrelevant Alternatives. It is satisfied by all major allocation rules which are studied in this framework (see Moulin, 1990; Fleurbaey and Maniquet, 1996a,b). This axiom refers to contraction of the technology: if a selected allocation remains feasible after the contraction, then Contraction Independence requires that it still be selected in the contracted economy. The second axiom, called Non-Discrimination, was introduced by Thomson (1983) and Gevers (1986). It simply says that if an allocation is selected, then any allocation which is Pareto indifferent to it (namely, every agent is indifferent between the two) should also be selected.

Definition 10. An allocation rule S satisfies **Contraction Independence** (CI) if and only if for every $(a, R, f) \in \boldsymbol{D}^S$, and every $g \in \boldsymbol{F}$ such that $(a, R, g) \in \boldsymbol{D}^S$ and $g(x) \leq f(x)$ for all $x \in \mathbb{R}_+$, we have,

$$[z \in S(a, R, f) \text{ and } z \in Z(a, R, g)] \Rightarrow [z \in S(a, R, g)].$$

Definition 11. An allocation rule S satisfies **Non-Discrimination** (ND) if and only if for every $e = (a, R, f) \in \boldsymbol{D}^S$, every $z \in S(a, R, f)$, and every $z' \in Z(e)$,

$$[z'_i I_i z_i, \ \forall i \in N] \Rightarrow [z' \in S(a, R, f)].$$

Proposition 2. *On E^D, E^I or E, the Equal Wage Equivalent rule is the only allocation rule which satisfies Pareto Optimality, Skill Solidarity, the Constant Returns lower bound, Contraction Independence and Non-Discrimination.*

Proof. We omit the proof that EWE satisfies the axioms. Let us show that if S satisfies the axioms, then $S = EWE$. Let $(a, R, f) \in \boldsymbol{E}$ and $z \in$

$EWE(a, R, f)$ with corresponding parameter w be given. Let $\tilde{a} \in \mathbb{R}_+$ and z' be defined by: $z_i I_i z_i'$ for every $i \in N$, and $z' \in EWE((\tilde{a}, \ldots, \tilde{a}), R, f)$. Such $\tilde{a}$ and z' always exist by continuity of the preferences and given that the range of a production skill is $\mathbb{R}_+$. Let $g \in \boldsymbol{F}$ be defined by: $g(x) = \max\{f(x), \frac{w}{\tilde{a}} \cdot x\}$. Note that if $f \in \boldsymbol{F}^D$ or F^I, then $g \in \boldsymbol{F}^D$ or F^I as well. By construction, $z' \in P((\tilde{a}, \ldots, \tilde{a}), R, g)$. By CRLB, any $z'' \in S((\tilde{a}, \ldots, \tilde{a}), R, g)$ is such that $z_i'' R_i z_i'$ for every $i \in N$. Hence, $z_i'' I_i z_i$ for every $i \in N$. By ND, $z' \in S((\tilde{a}, \ldots, \tilde{a}), R, g)$. By CI, $z' \in S((\tilde{a}, \ldots, \tilde{a}), R, f)$. By SS, any allocation $z'' \in S(a, R, f)$ is such that for all $i \in N$, $z_i'' R_i z_i'$, or for all $i \in N$, $z_i' R_i z_i''$. By PO, z'' must be efficient in (a, R, f). Since z is also efficient in (a, R, f) and is Pareto-indifferent to z', z'' must be Pareto-indifferent to z and z'. By ND, $z \in S(a, R, f)$, so that $S(a, R, f) \supseteq EWE(a, R, f)$. Now, since S is essentially single-valued and satisfies ND, $S(a, R, f) = EWE(a, R, f)$.

Q.E.D.

We then explore the following question: Does this result still hold if Skill Solidarity is weakened to Skill Monotonicity, or to Essential Single-Valuedness and Equal Welfare for Equal Preferences? Propositions 3 and 4 state that Skill Solidarity can be replaced with Skill Monotonicity if Technological Monotonicity (defined below) is added, or with Essential Single-Valuedness and Equal Welfare for Equal Preferences if Consistency (defined below) is added.

Definition 12 (Roemer, 1986). An allocation rule S satisfies **Technological Monotonicity** (TM) if and only if for every $e = (a, R, f) \in \boldsymbol{D}^S$, for every $g \in \boldsymbol{F}$ such that $(a, R, g) \in \boldsymbol{D}^S$ and $g(x) \geq f(x)$ for every $x \in \mathbb{R}_+$, for every $z \in S(a, R, f)$ and every $z' \in S(a, R, g)$,

$$z_i' R_i z_i, \quad \forall i \in N.$$

Definition 13 (Thomson, 1988; Moulin and Shenker, 1992). An allocation rule S satisfies **Consistency** (CONS) if and only if for every $e = (a, R, f) \in \boldsymbol{D}^S$, every $z \in S(a, R, f)$, and every $M \subseteq N$,

$$z_M \in S(a_M, R_M, g_M^z),$$

provided $(a_M, R_M, g_M^z) \in \boldsymbol{D}^S$, where $g_M^z(x) = \max\{0, f(x + \sum_{j \notin M} a_j \cdot x_j,) - \sum_{j \notin M} y_j\}$, and $z_M = (z_i)_{i \in M}, a_M = (a_i)_{i \in M}$.

Proposition 3. *On E^D or E, the Equal Wage Equivalent rule is the only allocation rule which satisfies Pareto Optimality, Skill Monotonicity,* *the Constant Returns lower bound, Technological Monotonicity and Non-Discrimination.*

Proof. First of all, we note that CI is a consequence of PO and TM. Therefore, Proposition 3 can be deduced from Proposition 2 and the following lemma.

Lemma 2. *On E^D or E, if an allocation rule satisfies Pareto Optimality, Skill Monotonicity and Technological Monotonicity, then it also satisfies Skill Solidarity.*

Proof. Let S satisfy PO, SM and TM. Let $(a, R, f) \in E$, $z \in S(a, R, f)$, $(a', R, f) \in E$ and $z' \in S(a', R, f)$ be given. First we note that if S satisfies PO and SM, then it also satisfies the property: $z_i R_i(0, 0)$, for all $i \in N$. Indeed, if $a_i = 0$ for all $i \in N$, then by PO, $z_i R_i(0, 0)$. If $a_i \geq 0$ for all $i \in N$, then by SM and transitivity of preferences, it remains true that $z_i R_i(0, 0)$. Now, let $y_i^0 \in \mathbb{R}_+$, $g \in F$ and $h \in F$ be defined by $(0, y_i^0) I_i z_i$ for every $i \in N$, $g(x) = \sum_i y_i^0$, and $h(x) = \max\{f(x), g(x)\}$ for every x. Observe that if $f \in F^D$, then $h \in F^D$. Since $z \in P(a, R, h)$, then by PO and TM, z is Pareto-indifferent to any allocation in $S(a, R, h)$. By PO and TM again, $((0, y_i^0)_{i \in N})$ is Pareto-indifferent to any allocation in $S(a, R, g)$. Since g is constant, then by applying PO and SM n times, we have $((0, y_i^0)_{i \in N})$ is Pareto-indifferent to any allocation in $S(a', R, g)$. Let $z'' \in S(a', R, h)$. By TM, either (i) $z_i'' I_i(0, y_i^0)$ for every $i \in N$, or (ii) $z_i'' R_i(0, y_i^0)$ for every $i \in N$, with a strict preference for at least one agent. If (i) holds, then by TM $z_i'' R_i z_i'$ for every $i \in N$, although we may have n indifference relations, which implies $z_i R_i z_i'$ for every $i \in N$, the desired outcome. If (ii) holds, then $\sum_i y_i'' > \sum_i y_i^0$, so that by TM and PO, $z_i'' I_i z_i'$ for every $i \in N$, which also implies $z_i' R_i z_i$ for every $i \in N$, the desired outcome.   Q.E.D.

Moulin and Roemer (1989) proved that in two-agent economies where agents have identical preferences and the production function is convex and satisfies $f(0) = 0$, any solution satisfying Pareto Optimality, Technological Monotonicity, Limited Self-Ownership (defined below) and Protection of Low Skill (defined below) equalizes welfares. Limited Self-Ownership requires that the talented agent be at least as well-off as the non-talented one. In Moulin and Roemer's proof, this axiom is used only to require that if the agents have the same skill, they will end up enjoying the same welfare level. But observe that this symmetry property is also a consequence of our Anonymity and Essential Single-Valuedness axioms.

Protection of Low Skill requires that the non-talented agent be better off than if both were non-talented. Now, it directly follows from our Lemmas 1 and 2 that, allowing $f(0) > 0$ as we do, but assuming identical preferences as they do, any solution satisfying Pareto Optimality, Anonymity, Technological Monotonicity and Skill Monotonicity equalizes welfares. Again, observe that in the case of two agents, Skill Monotonicity can be replaced in the above Lemma 2 by Protection of Low Skill and Limited Self-Ownership. Moulin and Roemer's (1989) theorem is therefore almost a corollary of Lemmas 1 and 2, the difference stemming from the assumptions on the technology.

Proposition 4. *On E, the Equal Wage Equivalent rule is the only allocation rule which satisfies Pareto-Optimality, Essential Single-Valuedness, Equal Welfare for Equal Preferences, the Constant Returns lower bound, Contraction Independence, Consistency and Non-Discrimination.*

Proof. Let S be any allocation rule satisfying the axioms. First, we show that $S \supseteq EWE$. Let $(a, R, f) \in E$, $z \in EWE(a, R, f)$ be given. Let the $2n-1$ agent economy $(a', R', g) \in E$, and the allocation $z' \in ([0, \bar{x}] \times \mathbb{R}_+)^{2n-1}$, be such that for all $i \leq n$, $a'_i = a_i$, $R'_i = R_i$, $z'_i = z_i$, and for all $i \leq n-1$, $a'_{n+i} = a_i$, $R'_{n+i} = R_{i+1}$, $z'_{n+i} I'_{n+i} z_{i+1}$, and $z' \in P(a', R', g)$ where

$$
g(x) = \begin{cases} \dfrac{\sum_{i \leq n-1} y_{n+1}}{\sum_{i \leq n-1} a'_{n+i} \cdot x_{n+i}} \cdot x & \text{for } x \leq \sum_{i \leq n-1} a'_{n+i} \cdot x_{n+i} \\[4ex] \sum_{i \leq n-1} y_{n+i} + f\left(x - \sum_{i \leq n-1} a'_{n+i} \cdot x_{n+i} \right) & \text{for } x \geq \sum_{i \leq n-1} a'_{n+i} \cdot x_{n+i} \end{cases}
$$

By construction, $z' \in EWE(a', R', g)$. Let $z'' \in S(a', R', g)$. By CONS, $(z''_i, z''_{n+i}) \in S((a_i, a'_{n+i}), (R_i, R'_{n+i}), g^{z''}_{\{i,n+i\}})$, for every $i \leq n - 1$. However, in uniformly skilled economies, EWE is the only allocation rule which satisfies ESV, CRLB, CI, and ND (see Fleurbaey and Maniquet, 1996a). Therefore, there exists w_i for every $i \leq n-1$, such that $z''_i I_i m(R_i, \{(x, y) \in [0, \bar{x}] \times \mathbb{R}_+ | y \leq w_i \cdot x\})$ and $z''_{n+i} I'_{n+i} m(R'_{n+i}, \{(x, y) \in [0, \bar{x}] \times R_+ | y \leq w_i \cdot x\})$. Now, recall that $R'_{n+i} = R_{i+1}$. By EWEP, $z''_{n+i} I_{i+1} z''_{i+1}$, for every $i \leq n-1$, which amounts to $w_i = w_{i+1}$, for every $i \leq n-1$. Therefore, by PO, $z'' \in EWE(a', R', g)$. By ND, $z' \in S(a', R', g)$, and by CONS, $z \in S(a, R, f)$, the desired outcome. Finally, since EWE is essentially single-valued and S satisfies ESV and ND, we have $S = EWE$. Q.E.D.

If the production function f is differentiable, Pareto-Optimality is not needed in this result because, in the proof, Pareto-optimality of z'' is then entailed by Pareto-Optimality of all $(z_i'', z_{n+i}'') \in EWE((a_i, a_{n+i}'),$ $(R_i, R_{n+i}'), g_{\{i,n+i\}}^{z''})$. We do not know whether the axiom CI is independent of the others.

Notice that in Propositions 2 through 4, the axiom CRLB is used only in the context of uniformly skilled economies.

4.   Limited Self-Ownership of Skill

In this section, we turn to Nozick's concern, and examine how the solidarity requirement can be counter-balanced by imposing the requirement that an agent should be guaranteed a minimal benefit from her own skill. An agent's minimal benefit from her skill must be defined as a welfare level which depends at least on her own characteristics (skill and preferences). Moreover, it seems natural to make it also depend on the production possibilities. Indeed, let us consider the case when the production possibilities increase (although this increase cannot be credited to any particular agent). Then, the benefit from one's own skill should increase, too. There are several ways to define the minimal benefit from one's skill along these lines. Here, we propose to define the welfare level corresponding to an agent's minimal benefit in the following way: let this agent maximize her welfare by freely operating the technology, provided she guarantees to all other agents a minimal consumption. This minimal consumption is determined under the proviso that the considered agent does not strictly prefer her position to the position of the others. Guaranteeing a limited self-ownership of skill consists of requiring the minimal benefit from skill as a welfare lower bound. We call it the Work Alone lower bound.

Definition 14.   An allocation rule S satisfies the **Work Alone lower bound** (WALB) if and only if for every $e = (a, R, f) \in \boldsymbol{D}^S$, and every $z \in S(a, R, f)$,

$$z_i R_i m(R_i, W_i), \quad \forall \in N,$$

where $W_i = \{(x, y) \in [0, \bar{x}] \times \mathbb{R}_+ | \exists y_0 \in \mathbb{R}_+ \text{ s. t. (i) } y + (n-1). \, y_0 \leq f(a_i x),$ and (ii) $(0, y_0) R_i(x, y)\}$.

There exist Pareto Optimal allocation rules that satisfy the Work Alone lower bound and Skill Solidarity, as exemplified by the Egalitarian

Equivalent rule. We now define this rule, which belongs to the family of rules proposed by Pazner and Schmeidler (1978).

Definition 15. The **Egalitarian Equivalent** rule is the allocation rule EE such that for every economy (a, R, f), there exists $y_0 \in \mathbb{R}_+$,

$$[z \in EE(a, R, f)] \Leftrightarrow [z \in P(a, R, f) \text{ and } z_i I_i(0, y_0)), \ \forall i \in N].$$

Proposition 5. *On any subdomain of E, the Egalitarian Equivalent rule is the only allocation rule which satisfies Pareto Optimality, Skill Solidarity, the Work Alone lower bound, and Non-Discrimination.*

Proof. We omit the proof that EE satisfies SS and WALB. We simply show that if S satisfies the four axioms, then $S = EE$. Let us assume that $S \nsubseteq EE$, i.e. there exist $(a, R, f) \in E$ and $z \in S(a, R, f)$ such that $z \notin EE(a, R, f)$. For any $i \in N$, let y_{0i} is $\mathbb{R}_+$ be defined by $z_i I_i(0, y_{0i})$. This is well defined, because WALB implies $z_i R_i(0, 0)$, for all i. Since $z \notin EE(a, R, f)$, there must be an agent j such for all $i \in N, y_{0i} \geq y_{0j}$, with at least one strict inequality. Let a'_j and z' be defined by: $z_i I_i x'_i$ for all i, and $z' \in P((0, \ldots, a'_j, \ldots, 0), R, f)$. Such a'_j and z' always exist by continuity of the preferences and given that the range of a production skill is $\mathbb{R}_+$. Let z'' be such that $z'' \in S((0, \ldots, a'_j, \ldots, 0), R, f)$. By PO and SS, we have $z_i I_i z''_i$ for all i. But by WALB one must have $z''_j R_j z^*_j$ for any $z^* \in EE((0, \ldots, a'_j, \ldots, 0), R, f)$. This implies $y_{0i} \leq y_{0j}$ for all $i \in N$, hence a contradiction. Therefore, $S(a, R, f) \subseteq EE(a, R, f)$. Now, since S satisfies ND, and since all allocations in $EE(a, R, f)$ are Pareto indifferent, $S(a, R, f) = EE(a, R, f)$. Q.E.D.

As with Proposition 2 above, we examine what happens when Skill Solidarity is weakened to Skill Monotonicity, or to Essential single-Valuedness and Equal Welfare for Equal Preferences. We obtain "parallel" results.

Proposition 6. *On E^D or E, the Egalitarian Equivalent rule is the only allocation rule which satisfies Skill Monotonicity, Contraction Independence, the Work Alone lower bound, and Non-Discrimination.*

Proof. This is a direct application of Fleurbaey and Maniquet (1996a), Proposition 3. Q.E.D.

Actually, Skill Monotonicity could be weakened into Essential single-Valuedness in this Proposition. Notice that Pareto-Optimality is not necessary in this result, as well as in the following one.

Proposition 7. *On E^C, E^D or E, the Egalitarian Equivalent rule is the only allocation rule which satisfies Essential Single-Valuedness, Equal Welfare for Equal Preferences, Consistency, the Work Alone lower bound and Non-Discrimination.*

Proof. Let S be any allocation rule satisfying the axioms. First, we show that $S \supseteq EE$. Let $(a, R, f) \in \boldsymbol{E}, z \in EE(a, R, f)$ be given. Let the $2n$ agent economy $(a', R', g) \in \boldsymbol{E}$, and the allocation $z' \in ([0, \bar{x}] \times \mathbb{R}_+)^{2n}$, be such that $a'_i = a_i, R'_i = R_i, z'_i = z_i, a'_{n+i} = 0$, $R'_{n+i} = R_i, x'_{n+i} = 0$, and $z'_{n+i} I_i z_i$, for all $i \leq n$, and $g(x) = \sum_{i \leq n} y'_{n+i} + f(x)$. By construction, $z' \in EE(a', R', g)$. Note that if $f \in \boldsymbol{F}^C$ or $\boldsymbol{F}^D$, then $g \in \boldsymbol{F}^C$ or F^D as well. By ND, there exists $z'' \in S(a', R', g)$ such that $x''_{n+i} = 0$, for all $i \leq n$. By CONS, $(z''_{n+i})_{i \leq n} \in S((0, \ldots, 0), \boldsymbol{R}, g^{z''}_{\{n+1, \ldots, 2n\}})$. By WALB $y''_{n+j} \geq \frac{1}{n} \cdot \sum_{i \leq n} y''_{n+i}$, for all $j \leq n$. Therefore, there exists y''_0 such that $y''_{n+j} = y''_{n+k} = y''_0$, for all $j, k \leq n$. Moreover, we claim $S(a', R', g) \subseteq P(a', R', g)$. Suppose not. By ND there then exists $z^* \in S(a', R', g)$ such that $\sum_{i \leq 2n} y^*_i < g(\sum_{i \leq 2n} a_i x^*_i)$ and such that $x^*_{n+i} = 0$ for all $i \leq n$. But this implies, by CONS, that $(z^*_{n+i})_{i \leq n} \in S((0, \ldots, 0), \boldsymbol{R}, g^{z^*}_{\{n+1, \ldots, 2n\}})$ with $\sum_{i \leq n} y^*_{n+i} < g^{z^*}_{\{n+1, \ldots, 2n\}}(0)$. The latter inequality is incompatible with WALB, hence a contradiction. Now, by EWEP, $z''_i I_i(0, y''_0)$, for every $i \leq n$, so that in view of the Pareto-Optimality of $S(a', R', g), z'' \in EE(a', R', g)$. By ND, $z' \in S(a', R', g)$, and by CONS, $z \in S(a, R, f)$, the desired outcome. Finally, since EE satisfies ESV and S satisfies ESV and ND, we have $S = EE$.   Q.E.D.

We do not know if EWEP is independent of the other axioms when the domain is E or E^D.

5. Conclusion

In this paper we analyze the idea of neutralizing the inequalities in skill endowments, by referring to the principle of collective sharing in the benefits of the population's profile of skills, a principle which can be formally embodied in axioms of solidarity with respect to changes in the profile. The results emphasize the relevance of allocation rules based on the egalitarian-equivalence criterion, and we characterized two rules of this kind by combining solidarity axioms with axioms representing either a concern for social neutrality about individual preferences, or a requirement of minimal protection of self-ownership.

This work suffers from several limitations that call for further research. First of all, the allocation rules are studied in a first-best context and their implementation is not studied. We tend to think that the most relevant extension to a second best framework is a taxation model á la Mirrlees. Second, we chose to put individuals' responsibility entirely and solely on their preferences, whereas other approaches could certainly allow for some partial responsibility for skills and some lack of responsibility for preferences. To some extent, the current formal framework could accommodate such refinements, by appropriate redefinitions of the variables, but only under rather special specifications of preferences and technology. A related issue is the analysis of the process of endogeneous formation of skills.

References

1. M. Fleurbaey. 'On fair compensation', *Theory and Decision* **36** (1994), 277–307.
2. M. Fleurbaey. 'Three solutions for the compensation problem', *Journal of Economic Theory* **65** (1995), 505–521.
3. M. Fleurbaey and F. Maniquet. 'The cooperative production problem: A comparison of welfare bounds', *Games and Economic Behavior* **17** (1996a), 200–208.
4. M. Fleurbaey and F. Maniquet. 'Fair allocation with unequal production skills: The no-envy approach to compensation', *Mathematical Social Sciences* **32** (1996b), 71–93.
5. L. Gevers. Walrasian social choice: Some simple axiomatic approaches. in W. Heller *et al.* (eds.), *Social Choice and Public Decision Making, Essays in Honor of K. J. Arrow*, Vol. 1, pp. 97–114. Cambridge: Cambridge University Press. 1986.
6. S. C. Kolm. 'Equal freedom'. C.G.P.C. 1993.
7. F. Maniquet. 'Allocation rules for a commonly owned technology: The average cost lower bound', *Journal of Economic Theory* **69** (1996), 490–507.
8. F. Maniquet, 'An equal right solution to the compensation-responsibility dilemma,' *Mathematical Social Sciences* **35** (1998), 185–202.
9. A. Mas-Colell. 'Remarks on the game-theoretic analysis of a simple distribution of surplus problem', *International Journal of Game Theory* **9** (1980), 125–140.

10. H. Moulin. 'Joint ownership of a convex technology: Comparison of three solutions', *Review of Economic Studies* **57** (1990), 439–452.

11. H. Moulin and J. E. Roemer. 'Public ownership of the external world and private ownership of self', *Journal of Political Economics* **97** (1989), 347–367.

12. H. Moulin and S. Shenker. 'Average cost pricing vs serial cost pricing: An axiomatic approach', *Journal of Economic Theory* **64** (1994), 178–201.

13. R. Nozick. *Anarchy, State, and Utopia*. New York: Basic Books. 1974.

14. E. Pazner and D. Schmeidler. 'Egalitarian equivalent allocations: A new concept of economic equity', *Quarterly Journal of Economics* **92** (1978), 671–687.

15. J. Rawls. *A Theory of Justice*. Cambridge, MA: Harvard University Press. 1971.

16. J. E. Roemer. 'Equality of resources implies equality of welfare', *Quarterly Journal of Economics* **101** (1986), 751–784.

17. J. E. Roemer and J. Silvestre. 'Public ownership: Three proposals for resource allocation'. University of California, Davis, mimeo, 1989.

18. W. Thomson. 'Equity in exchange economies', *Journal of Economic Theory* **29** (1983), 217–244.

19. W. Thomson. 'A study of choice correspondences in economies with a variable number of agents', *Journal of Economic Theory* **46** (1988), 237–254.

20. W. Thomson. 'A replacement principle'. University of Rochester, mimeo, 1990.

21. P. Van Parijs. 'Equal endowments as undominated diversity', *Recherches Economiques de Louvain* **56** (1990), 327–355.

22. R. Vohra. 'Equity and efficiency in non-convex economies', *Social Choice and Welfare* **9** (1992), 185–202.

23. J. Waldron. *The Right to Private Property*. Oxford: Clarendon Press. 1988.

CHAPTER 6

An Equal Right Solution to the Compensation–Responsibility Dilemma

François Maniquet

ABSTRACT. In a simple production model where skills may differ among agents, we consider that skills are common resources, and we propose to give all agents an equal property right to both the technology and the skills. A class of welfare lower bounds is derived from this idea. We argue that the conflicting objectives of unequal skill compensation and preferences responsibility are partially achieved by allocation rules satisfying these welfare bounds. Combining them with other compensation or responsibility properties allows us to characterize two classes of allocation rules in a parallel fashion. ©1998 Elsevier Science B.V.

Keywords: Skill compensation; Preferences responsibility; Egalitarian equivalence; Budget equality.

1. Introduction

We consider simple production economies in which finite sets of agents are characterized by their preferences over output consumption–labor time bundles and by their production skills. We search for equitable rules determining each agent's labor time and share of the output as a function of the production possibilities, the number of agents, the list of production skills and the list of preferences.

Our starting point is that equity must be defined in these economies with respect to the values of compensation and responsibility (the same starting point is adopted in Bossert [1], Bossert and Fleurbaey [2], Bossert,

Mathematical Social Sciences **35** 185–202 (1998).

Fleurbaey and Van de gaer [3], Fleurbaey [5–8], Fleurbaey and Maniquet [9, 10], Iturbe and Nieto [12], Roemer [22–24], Sprumont [25]). The story behind this assumption is that skills are internal resources which agents do not control, whereas preferences are the domain of responsibility of individuals because individuals must assume responsibility for their ends. As a consequence, we consider that an equitable organization of these economies should compensate low skill agents for their low skill, and should not discriminate among agents on the basis of differences in their preferences towards output consumption–labor time bundles.

Skill compensation is achieved when the differences in final outcomes obtained by the agents can not be attributed to differences in skills but only to differences in preferences. The final outcomes we are interested in here are the agents' assigned welfare levels. Preferences responsibility is achieved when the differences in social resources which an agent can use to implement her view of the good life can not be attributed to differences in preferences but only to differences in skills. Social resources are interpreted here as the access to the production possibilities. The axioms which have been proposed in Fleurbaey and Maniquet [9] to capture these two notions in the simple production model have proved incompatible, under Pareto efficiency (we will recall these results below). Actually, the existence of a dilemma between properties of compensation and responsibility is shared by the models studied in Bossert [1], Bossert and Fleurbaey [2], Bossert, Fleurbaey and Van de gaer [3], Fleurbaey [5–8], Fleurbaey and Maniquet [9], Iturbe and Nieto [12].

In this paper, we explore the idea of giving each agent an equal right to the resources, when resources consist not only of technological possibilities but also of the skill profile. An equal right is defined as a virtual consumption–labor time opportunity set, which satisfies the following property: the vector of the agents' best choice over this opportunity set is always feasible for the real economy, whatever preferences may be. An allocation rule guarantees an equal right if it satisfies the particular welfare lower bound where the minimal welfare level is defined with respect to each agent's best choice over this equal right. The equal right notion is therefore clearly related to the welfare bounds approach to equity developed in recent papers (see in particular Moulin [18]).

Since an equal right is by definition identical among agents, two agents having the same preferences are given the same minimal welfare level. Therefore, low skill agents are clearly compensated. They are not fully compensated, however, since the equal right only defines a minimal welfare level, which can be much lower than the final welfare obtained by the agents. This is the reason why we define and study properties capturing the idea that larger equal rights allow us to better compensate low skill agents.

On the other hand, two agents having the same skill are given access to the same resources since they are free to choose their best bundle in the same opportunity set. They are thus held responsible for their preferences. They are not fully responsible, however, since the resources to which they are given free access only define a minimal opportunity set so that the resources which the agents will end up with may still vary among equally skilled agents. Here again we can say that the objective of holding agents responsible for their preferences is better achieved with larger equal rights.

The paper has two parts. In the first part, we study the notion of an equal right, and we show that there are severe constraints on having it very large. As a conclusion to this first part, we define a family of equal rights, called x^*-equal right, where x^* denotes a reference labor time. An allocation rule guarantees an x^*-equal right if it always selects allocations which all agents deem at least as good as a reference allocation where all agents supply the reference labor time and the resulting output is divided equally.

In the second part, we try to combine the x^*-equal rights with other compensation or responsibility requirements studied in Fleurbaey and Maniquet [9, 10]. Our main result is a parallel characterization of two classes of solutions.

The first class generalizes an egalitarian equivalent allocation rule proposed in Fleurbaey and Maniquet [9].[1] This allocation rule was justified on grounds of a strong compensation axiom. Our result shows that it also satisfies a nontrivial responsibility requirement, that is, it guarantees an x^*-equal right.

The second class of allocation rules has also been defined and analysed by Kolm [13] and is a subset of the equivalent budget rules proposed in Fleurbaey and Maniquet [9]. The two extreme members of our class are the equal wealth rule and the equal full income rule, introduced by Varian [27] and Pazner and Schmeidler [21] respectively. These two rules were

---

[1] It is worth recalling that egalitarian equivalence was introduced by Pazner and Schmeidler [20] as a solution to the incompatibility between Pareto efficiency and the celebrated no-envy requirement in the unequal skill production environment we are considering in this paper.

considered until recently as the main solutions for production economies with unequal individual skills.

In conclusion, this shows that the equal right approach to the responsibility/compensation dilemma allows us to define new solutions and to shed some light on results previously obtained in the literature. This should be an incentive to apply this approach to other models as well.

The paper is organized as follows. In Section 2, we define the model and introduce the basic definitions. In Section 3, we define and justify the notion of an x^*-equal right. In Section 4, we combine x^*-equal rights with other requirements of compensation or responsibility. In Section 5, we characterize the two polar classes of rules satisfying x^*-equal rights.

2.   Model and Basic Definitions

Firstly, we define the model. An economy is defined as a list $d = (\bar{s}, \bar{R}, \bar{f}) = ((s_1, \ldots, s_n), (R_1, \ldots, R_n), f) \in \mathbb{R}_{++}^n \times \mathscr{R}^n \times \mathscr{F}$ where $n \geq 2$ is the finite cardinality of a variable set N of agents, s_i denotes agent i's production skill, $i \in N$, R_i denotes agent i's continuous and convex ordering on bundles $(x, y) \in X = [0; \bar{x}] \times \mathbb{R}_+$ which are strictly decreasing in the first argument (labor time) and strictly increasing in the second argument (a desirable consumption good), and $f \in \mathscr{F}: \mathbb{R}_+ \to \mathbb{R}_+$ is an one input–one output strictly increasing and concave production function. The domain of all such economies $(\bar{s}, \bar{R}, f)$ is denoted by $\mathscr{D} = \cup_{n \geq 2}(\mathbb{R}_{++}^n \times \mathscr{R}^n \times \mathscr{F})$. By the assumptions of a strictly increasing production function and strictly positive production skills, we are guaranteed that any change in any agent's labor time has an influence on the quantity of output which has been produced. As a consequence, the agents' labor time and consumption will never be trivially fixed at $(0, 0)$ by requiring Pareto efficiency.

An **allocation** $\bar{z} \in X^n$ is a n-dimensional vector $(z_1, \ldots, z_n)$ of bundles $z_i = (x_i, y_i)$, $i \in N$, one bundle per agent. An allocation $\bar{z}$ is **feasible** for the economy $d = (\bar{s}, \bar{R}, f) \in \mathscr{D}$ if and only if

$$\sum_{i=1}^n y_i \leq f\left(\sum_{i=1}^n s_i x_i\right).$$

We denote by $Z(d)$ the set of feasible allocations for an economy $d \in \mathscr{D}$, and by $Z_i(d)$ the projection of $Z(d)$ on i's consumption set X. An **allocation rule** S is a correspondence which associates to every economy $d \in \mathscr{D}$ a nonempty subset of feasible allocations $S(d) \subset Z(d)$.

We now introduce the basic definitions. Let E be a correspondence: $\cup_{n \geq 2}(\mathbb{R}^n_{++} \times \mathscr{F}) \to X$, such that for all $n \geq 2$, $\bar{s} \in \mathbb{R}^n_{++}$, $f \in \mathscr{F}$, $E(\bar{s}, f)$ is a closed subset of X satisfying free-disposal in X (that is, a larger labor time is always possible, provided it remains smaller than $\bar{x}$, and a smaller consumption is always possible, provided it remains positive). We use $\partial E(\bar{s}, f)$ to denote the north-west frontier of $E(\bar{s}, f)$ Before defining an equal right, we require the following notation. For $R \in \mathscr{R}$, and $A \subset X$, let $m(R, A)$ denote the set of bundles (if any) which maximize preferences R over a set A of bundles, that is

$$m(R, A) = \{z \in A \text{ s.t. } \forall z' \in A, zRz'\}$$

Let $m_x(R, A)$(resp. $m_y(R, A)$) denote the set of first (resp. second) coordinates of the elements of $m(R, A)$. Since all bundles in $m(R, A)$ are indifferent for R, we sometimes use $m(R, A)$ to denote any of its bundles.

Definition 1.   The correspondence E defines an **equal right** if and only if for every $d = (\bar{s}, \bar{R}, f) \in \mathscr{D}$,

$$m(R_1, E(\bar{s}, f)) \times \cdots \times m(R_n, E(\bar{s}, f)) \subset Z(d).$$

Definition 2.   An allocation rule S **guarantees the equal right**[2] E if and only if for every $d = (\bar{s}, \bar{R}, f) \in \mathscr{D}$, $\bar{z} \in S(d)$,

$$z_i R_i m(R_i, E(\bar{s}, f)), \forall i \in N$$

Definition 3.   An allocation rule S is **Pareto efficient** if and only if for every $d = (\bar{s}, \bar{R}, f) \in \mathscr{D}$, $\bar{z} \in S(d)$, $\bar{z}' \in Z(d)$

$$[z_i' R_i z_i, \forall_i] \Rightarrow [z_i' I_i z_i, \forall_i].$$

3.   The x^*-Equal Right

An equal right is compensating low skill agents by itself, since the minimal welfare levels obtained by two agents having the same preferences are the same, and moreover it lets the agents be responsible for their choice over the opportunity set, so that the difference between the minimal welfare levels guaranteed to two agents having the same skill only reflects their different preferences. The compensation it carries out, however, may be rather low, if the equal right itself is small.

---

[2]Let us note that if a correspondence E does not satisfy the feasibility constraint of definition 1, then it can not be guaranteed by any allocation rule.

In this section, we study the idea that rights should be large. We will quickly observe, however, that some large equal rights may also be unsatisfactory. Our objective is to design simple equal rights satisfying some acceptable largeness property. We will therefore proceed by defining properties capturing the intuition of largeness and simplicity. As a result of the discussion, we will define and justify a family of equal rights.

The first property one may think of is a participation requirement.[3]

Definition 4.   An equal right E **induces participation** if for all $n \in \mathbb{N}$, $(\bar{s}, f) \in \mathbb{R}^n_{++} \times \mathscr{F}$, we have $(0, (f(0)/n)) \in E(\bar{s}, f)$.

We will argue, however, that this participation property is NOT necessarily a desirable property for an equal right, as far as we are interested in skill compensation. Let us, indeed, consider an economy $(\bar{s}, \bar{R}, f) \in \mathscr{D}$ satisfying the property that the allocation $\bar{z} = ((0, (f(0)/n)), \ldots, (0, (f(0)/n)))$ is Pareto efficient and no other allocation is Pareto equivalent to $\bar{z}$. If an allocation rule S guarantees an equal right E which induces participation, then the allocation $\bar{z}$ must be selected because by assumption all preferences R_i, $i \in N$, satisfy the property $m_x(R_i, E(\bar{s}, f)) = \{0\}$, that is, all agents maximize their welfare over $E(\bar{s}, f)$ by choosing a labor time equal to 0. As a consequence, two agents having the same preferences enjoy the same welfare level, and we can say that compensation is fully achieved among these agents. If, by contrast, preferences are such that $m_x(R_i, E(\bar{s}, f)) = \{\bar{x}\}$ but $(f(\Sigma_i s_i \bar{x})/n)$ is much larger than $f(s_{\min}\bar{x})$, then, even if the allocation $\bar{z} = ((\bar{x}, (f(\Sigma_i s_i \bar{x})/n)), \ldots, (\bar{x}, (f(\Sigma_i s_i \bar{x})/n)))$ is Pareto efficient, it may be the case that $\bar{z}$ is not selected, and, moreover, that there is a huge difference between the consumption level of two agents having the same preferences. In this sense, we can say that an equal right inducing participation is maximal at the contribution level $x = 0$ but not at $x = \bar{x}$.

In conclusion, an equal right which induces participation discriminates among preferences in the sense that the compensation which this right achieves is always larger among agents choosing a smaller labor time. Therefore, we weaken the participation requirement and we define the following largeness property.

---

[3]This property also captures the idea of protecting high skill agents in the sense that the low skill agent compensation should not be carried out by imposing on the former agents so long a labor time that they end up worse off than if they withdrew from the economy. This idea was defended by Varian [27] and Dworkin [4] and was later formally studied by Fleurbaey and Maniquet [9]. In our case, it amounts to allowing each agent, including low skill agents, to choose not to work at all.

Definition 5.   Let m be a strictly positive integer. An equal right E is **maximal at m points in** $[0, \bar{x}]$ if for all $n \geq 2$, all $(\bar{s}, f) \in \mathbb{R}^n_{++} \times \mathscr{F}$, there exists a list $x_1, \ldots, x_m \in [0, \bar{x}]$ such that for all $j, k \in \{1, \ldots, m\}, x_j \neq x_k$ and

$$\left(x_j, \frac{f\left(\sum_{i=1}^n s_i x_j\right)}{n}\right) \in \partial E(\bar{s}, f). \tag{1}$$

Let us note that if for some $(\bar{s}^*, f^*) \in \mathbb{R}^n_{++} \times \mathscr{F}$, there exist several points at which equation (maximal) holds, whereas for the other $(\bar{s}, f) \in \mathbb{R}^n_{++} \times \mathscr{F}$, there is only one point at which Eq. (1) holds, then this equal right is said maximal at one point only.

Given the idea that an equal right should be large, we may wish to have equal rights maximal at as many points as possible. The following lemma tells us that an equal right cannot be maximal at two points. This shows that there are severe constraints on having large equal rights.

Lemma 1.   *If an equal right E is maximal at m points, then $m = 1$.*

Proof.   We simply show that there are economies where equation (Eq. (1)) cannot hold at two different points. Let us consider a two agent economy (s_1, s_2, R_1, R_2, f) where $s_1 < s_2$, and for all $x \in \mathbb{R}_+, f(x) = x$. Suppose E is maximal at, say, x_1 and x_2, with $x_1 < x_2$. Let us assume that R_1 and R_2 are such that $m_x(R_1, E(\bar{s}, f)) = \{x_2\}$ and $m_x(R_2, E(\bar{s}, f)) = \{x_1\}$. Definition 1 commands that the allocation $((x_2, \frac{1}{2}f(s_1x_2+s_2x_2)), ((x_1, \frac{1}{2}f(s_1x_1+s_2x_1)))$ be feasible. This requires $\frac{1}{2}f(s_1x_2 + s_2x_2) + \frac{1}{2}f(s_1x_1 + s_2x_1) \leq f(s_1x_2 + s_2x_1)$. By $f(x) = x$ and $s_1x_2 + s_2x_1 < s_1x_1 + s_2x_2$, the inequality becomes

$$\frac{1}{2}(s_1x_1 + s_2x_1) + \frac{1}{2}(s_1x_2 + s_2x_2) \leq (s_1x_2 + s_2x_1) \Leftrightarrow \frac{1}{2}(s_1x_1 + s_2x_2)$$

$$\leq \frac{1}{2}(s_1x_2 + s_2x_1) \Leftrightarrow (s_2 - s_1)x_2$$

$$\leq (s_2 - s_1)x_1$$

$$\Leftrightarrow x_2 \leq x_1$$

the desired impossibility.   □

As a consequence of the above lemma, we keep the maximality at one point requirement, as a good largeness property.

To this largeness property, we would like to add simplicity properties. First of all, we may require that the points at which an equal right is maximal do not depend on the economy, so that the equal right is always maximal at the same point. But we may also impose the following property, which we call monotonicity. An equal right is monotonic if all agents always agree upon the fact that an opportunity set $E(\bar{s}, f)$ is preferable to another opportunity set $E(\bar{s}', f')$.

Definition 6. An equal right E is **monotonic** if whenever there exist $R \in \mathcal{R}$, $n, n' \geq 2$, $(\bar{s}, f) \in \mathbb{R}^n_{++} \times \mathcal{F}$, $(\bar{s}', f') \in \mathbb{R}^{n'}_{++} \times \mathcal{F}$ such that $m(R, E(\bar{s}, f)) P m(R, E(\bar{s}', f'))$, then

$$m(R', E(\bar{s}, f)) P' m(R', E(\bar{s}', f')), \quad \forall R' \in \mathcal{R}.$$

Let us note that this property is equivalent to having all opportunity sets $E(\cdot, \cdot)$ completely ordered by the inclusion operation. This justifies the monotonicity terminology, and makes clear that monotonic equal rights are simple objects.

As we will prove in our first theorem, equal rights exist which are both monotonic and maximal at a point. Here is an example. An x^*-equal right guarantees to each agent at least as much welfare as if every agent was asked to spend a specified level x^* of contribution and if the resulting output was divided equally. In fact, this defines a family of rights, each of which is parameterized by the reference contribution level.

Definition 7. Let $x^* \in [0; \bar{x}]$ be given. The x^*-**equal right** E_{x^*} is defined by: for all $n \geq 2$, $(\bar{s}, f) \in \mathbb{R}^n_{++} \times \mathcal{F}$, $E_{x^*}(\bar{s}, f) =$

$$\left\{ (x, y) \in X \mid x \geq x^*, y \leq \frac{f\left(\sum_i s_i . x^*\right)}{n} \right\}.$$

An x^*-equal right is illustrated in Figure 1.

The following theorem is a strong justification of the x^*-equal right.[4]

Theorem 1. *An x^*-equal right is monotonic and maximal at a point. Conversely if an equal right is monotonic and always maximal at the same point x^*, then it is an x^*-equal right.*

Proof. The proof of the first part of the theorem is left to the reader. Let us suppose that E is always maximal at the point x^*, E is monotonic, and $E \neq E_{x^*}$. Then there exist $n \in \mathbb{N}$, $(\bar{s}, f) \in \mathbb{R}^n_{++} \times \mathcal{F}$ and either $x^\circ < x^*, y^\circ \geq 0$, such that $(x^\circ, y^\circ) \in \partial E(\bar{s}, f)$, or $x^\circ > x^*$, $y^\circ > (f(\Sigma_{i=1}^n s_i x^*)/n)$ such that $(x^\circ, y^\circ) \in \partial E(\bar{s}, f)$. Let $y^* \in \mathbb{R}_{++}$ be defined by $y^* = (f(\Sigma_{i=1}^n s_i x^*)/n)$. We derive a contradiction in either case.

---

[4]Frédéric Gaspart put me on the track of this theorem.

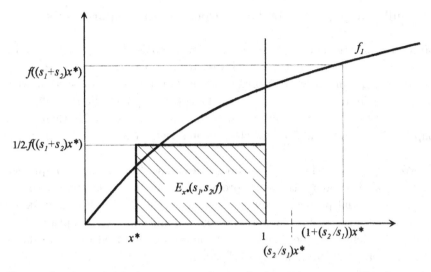

Fig. 1. An x^*-equal right for parameters (s_1, s_2, f) where f is represented by the graph of f_1 defined by: $f_1(x) = f(s_1x)$, and the relative value of s_1 and s_2 is illustrated by the abscissa $(s_2/s_1)x^*$ compared with x^*.

Case 1. Let $n' \in \mathbb{N}$, $\varepsilon \in \mathbb{R}_{++}$ be such that $x^\circ < ((n' - 1 - \varepsilon)/n')x^*$. Let $(\bar{s}', f') \in \mathbb{R}_{++}^{n'} \times \mathbb{F}$ be defined by $s'_1 = 1$, $s'_2 = \cdots = s'_{n'} = (\varepsilon/(n' - 1))$, $f'(x) = (n'y^*/x^*)x$. By maximality at x^*, $(x^*, (1 + \varepsilon)y^*) \in \partial E(\bar{s}', f')$, as $f'(\Sigma_{i=1}^{n'} s'_i x^*) = (1 + \varepsilon)n'y^*$. By monotonicity, $E(\bar{s}', f') \supset E(\bar{s}, f)$. Let $\bar{R} \in \mathscr{R}^{n'}$ be such that $m_x(R_1, E(\bar{s}', f')) = \{x^\circ\}$ whereas $m_x(R_i, E(\bar{s}', f')) = \{x^*\}, i \in \{2, \ldots, n'\}$. The contradiction is derived from $f'(x^\circ + \varepsilon x^*) - (n' - 1)(1 + \varepsilon)y^* = (x^\circ - ((n' - 1 - \varepsilon)/n')x^*)(n'y^*/x^*) < 0$, which implies that $(x^\circ, y^\circ) \notin E(\bar{s}', f')$, and therefore $(x^\circ, y^\circ) \notin E(\bar{s}, f)$.

Case 2. Let $n' \in \mathbb{N}$, $\varepsilon \in \mathbb{R}_{++}$ be such that

$$\frac{(n' - 1 - \varepsilon)x^*y^* + \varepsilon n'x^\circ y^*}{(n' - 1)x^*} < y^\circ. \tag{2}$$

Let $(\bar{s}', f') \in \mathbb{R}_{++}^{n'} \times \mathscr{F}$ be defined as above. Let $\bar{R} \in \mathscr{R}^{n'}$ be such that $m_x(R_i, E(\bar{s}', f')) = \{x^*\}, i \in \{1, \ldots, n - 1\}$ whereas $m_x(R_n, E(\bar{s}', f')) = \{x^\circ\}$. By Eq. (2), $f'((1 + (n' - 2)\varepsilon)x^* + (\varepsilon/(n' - 1))x^\circ) < (n' - 1)(1 + \varepsilon)y^* + y^\circ$ which implies that $(x^\circ, y^\circ) \notin E(\bar{s}', f')$, and therefore $(x^\circ, y^\circ) \notin E(\bar{s}, f)$. □

The above theorem is the main result of the first part of this paper. We stop here our analysis of equal rights. In the following two sections, we will study allocation rules satisfying an x^*-equal right.

4. Full Compensation or Full Responsibility Requirements

Since an equal right only meets the conflicting goals of compensation and responsibility partially, one may still want to combine it with other requirements of skill compensation or preferences responsibility. In this section, we recall the definition of properties studied in Fleurbaey and Maniquet [9, 10] (the motivation for the properties defined below was developed in these two papers). Then, we establish how the x^*-equal rights can be combined with such properties.

We begin with the two key properties. The first property requires that two agents having the same preferences end up at the same welfare level. The second property requires that two agents having the same skill receive the same amount of external resources, and this idea is captured by the requirement that they do not envy the bundle received by each other (see Fleurbaey and Maniquet [10]). Formally,

Definition 8. An allocation rule S satisfies **equal welfare for equal preferences** if and only if for every $n \in \mathbb{N}$, $d = (\bar{s}, \bar{R}, f) \in \mathcal{D}$, $\bar{z} \in S(\bar{s}, \bar{R}, f)$, and $i, j \in N$,

$$[R_i = R_j] \Rightarrow [z_i I_i z_j].$$

Definition 9. An allocation rule S satisfies **no-envy among equally skilled** if and only if for every $n \in \mathbb{N}$, $d = (\bar{s}, \bar{R}, f) \in \mathcal{D}$, $\bar{z} \in S(\bar{s}, \bar{R}, f)$, and $i, j \in N$,

$$[s_i = s_j] \Rightarrow [z_i R_i z_j \quad \text{and} \quad z_j R_j z_i].$$

Each of these two requirements can be weakened by requiring equal welfare (resp. no-envy) only when all agents have the same preferences (resp. skill). Formally,

Definition 10. An allocation rule S satisfies **equal welfare for uniform preferences** if and only if for every $n \in \mathbb{N}$, $d = (\bar{s}, \bar{R}, f) \in \mathcal{D}$, $\bar{z} \in S(\bar{s}, \bar{R}, f)$,

$$[R_i = R_j \forall i, j \in N] \Rightarrow [z_i I_i z_j].$$

Definition 11. An allocation rule S satisfies **no-envy among uniformly skilled** if and only if for every $n \in \mathbb{N}$, $d = (\bar{s}, \bar{R}, f) \in \mathcal{D}$,

$\bar{z} \in S(\bar{s}, \bar{R}, f)$,

$$[s_i = s_j \forall i, j \in N] \Rightarrow [z_i R_i z_j \forall i, j \in N].$$

If we add the weak horizontal equity requirement that two agents having the same preferences and the same skill should end up with the same welfare, then we can also strengthen the two basic requirements in the following way. The property of skill solidarity, stronger than equal welfare for equal preferences, requires that any change in the skill profile affects agents' final welfare in the same way, that is, either all gain or all loose. Preferences monotonicity (introduced by Maskin [16]), stronger than no-envy among equally skilled, requires that the selection operated by a rule be independent from changes in preferences which extend agents' lower contour sets at their assigned bundles. Formally,

Definition 12. An allocation rule S satisfies **skill solidarity** if and only if for every $d = (\bar{s}, \bar{R}, f), d' = (\bar{s}', \bar{R}, f) \in \mathcal{D}, \bar{z}' \in S(\bar{s}', \bar{R}, f), \bar{z}' \in S(\bar{s}'\bar{R}, f)$,

$$z_i R_i z_i', \forall i \in N, \quad \text{or} \quad z_i' R_i z_i, \forall i \in N.$$

Definition 13. An allocation rule S satisfies **preferences monotonicity** if and only if for every $d = (\bar{s}, \bar{R}, f) \in \mathcal{D}, \bar{z} \in S(\bar{s}, \bar{R}, f), i \in N$ and $R_i' \in \mathcal{R}$

$$[z_i R_i(x, y) \Rightarrow z_i R_i'(x, y) \forall (x, y) \in z_i(d)] \Rightarrow [\bar{z} \in S(s, (R_{-i}, R_i'))].$$

The following table summarizes the logical relationship among these axioms. Two axioms on the same line are compatible with each other even if we add Pareto efficiency.

Compensation requirements	Responsibility requirements
Skill solidarity	
$\Downarrow^5$	
Equal welfare for equal preferences	No-envy among uniformly skilled
$\Downarrow$	$\Uparrow$
Equal welfare for uniform preferences	No-envy among equally skilled
	$\Uparrow^6$.
	Preferences monotonicity

---

[5] This logical implication holds only if the additional requirement of equal treatment of equals is also imposed (agents are equal if both their skills and their preferences are identical).

[6] Here again, equal treatment of equals need to be added.

The following theorem states the general possibility of combining an x^*-equal right with other compensation or responsibility requirements. Before stating the theorem, we define the subdomain $\mathscr{D}^{\equiv}$ by: $\mathscr{D}^{\equiv} \cup_{n \geq 2}$ $(\mathbb{R}^n_{++} \times \mathscr{R}^{\equiv n} \times \mathscr{F}\})$ where $R \in \mathscr{R}^{\equiv} \Leftrightarrow R \in \mathscr{R}$ and for every $(x, y) \in X$, there exists $y' \in \mathbb{R}_+$ such that $(\bar{x}, y')I(x, y)$, that is, the welfare level an agent can reach when working $\bar{x}$ is not bounded above.

Theorem 2. *Let $x^* \in [0, \bar{x}]$ be given. There exists (at least) one allocation rule guaranteeing the x^*-equal right which satisfies Pareto efficiency and each one of the following axioms or lists of axioms:*

1. *skill solidarity over $\mathscr{D}^{\equiv}$,*
2. *equal welfare for equal preferences and no-envy among uniformly skilled,*
3. *equal welfare for uniform preferences and no-envy among equally skilled over $\mathscr{D}^{\equiv}$,*
4. *preferences monotonicity.*

The compatibility between the x^*-equal right and skill solidarity is exemplified by the x^*-egalitarian equivalent rules which can be defined as follows. Given a reference contribution x^*, the x^*-egalitarian equivalent allocations are the Pareto efficient allocations which satisfy the property that each agent is indifferent between receiving her bundle or contributing x^* and consuming an amount y_0 which is the same for all agents. The concept of egalitarian equivalence was introduced by Pazner and Schmeidler [20].

Definition 14. The x^*-**egalitarian equivalent** rule $E_{x^*}^{\equiv}$ associates to every $d = (\bar{s}, \bar{R}, f) \in \mathscr{D}$ the set of all Pareto efficient allocations $\bar{z}$ such that there exists $y_0 \in \mathbb{R}_+$ and

$$z_i I_i(x^*, y_0), \quad \forall i \in N.$$

An x^*-egalitarian equivalent allocation is illustrated in Figure 2.

The compatibility between the x^*-equal right and preferences monotonicity is exemplified by the x^*-equal budget rule. This rule selects all Pareto efficient allocations having the property that all budget lines cross each other at a point of abscissa x^*. Before defining this allocation rule, we introduce the following notation. For $s \in \mathbb{R}_{++}$, $w \in \mathbb{R}_{++}$, and $\pi \in \mathbb{R}$, let the budget $B(s, w, \pi) \subset X$ be defined by

$$B(s, w, \pi) = \{(x, y) \in X \mid y \leq \pi + swx\}.$$

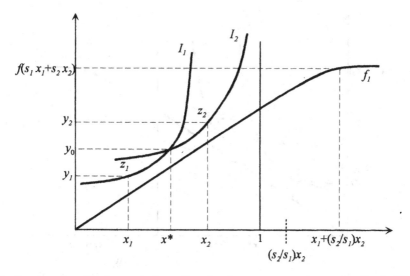

Fig. 2. An x^*-egalitarian equivalent allocation for an economy (s_1, s_2, R_1, R_2, f). The conventions are the same as in Fig. 1, and R_1 and R_2 are illustrated by indifference curves I_1 and I_2 respectively.

Definition 15. Let x^* denote the reference contribution. The x^*-**equal budget** $B_{x^*}^=$ is the Pareto efficient rule such that for every $d = (\bar{s}, \bar{R}, f) \in \mathscr{D}$, $\bar{z} \in B_{x^*}^=(\bar{s}, \bar{R}, f)$, there exist $w \in \mathbb{R}+$, $\pi \in \mathbb{R}^n$, and $y_0 \in \mathbb{R}_+$, such that for all $i \in N$

$$z_i \in m(R_i, B(S_i, w, \pi_i)),$$

$$(x^*, y_0) \in \partial B(s_i, w, \pi_i).$$

An x^*-equal budget allocation is illustrated in Figure 3.

This family of allocation rules is a subclass of an other family, called the reference welfare equivalent budget family of rules, introduced by Fleurbaey and Maniquet [9]. Moreover, the family of x^*-equal budget rules coincides with Kolm's [13] class of solutions, although the latter is derived in a very different way.

The reference contribution parameter x^* can take two extreme values, that is, 0 and $\bar{x}$. In the former case, all budget lines cross each other at a point of abscissa 0, which implies that all profit shares are identical. In this case, the x^*-equal budget coincides with the equal share Walrasian rule, called the wealth-fair rule by Varian [27]. In the other extreme case, all the budget lines cross each other at a point of abscissa $\bar{x}$ and we obtain Pazner and Schmeidler's [21] full-income-fair rule.

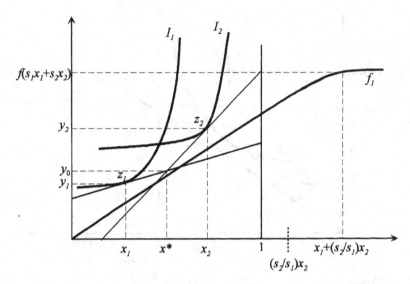

Fig. 3.   An x^*-equal budget allocation for an economy (s_1, s_2, R_1, R_2, f). The conventions are the same as in Fig. 2.

Following Pazner and Schmeidler [21], we may consider the following process of decentralization of a x^*-equal budget: each agent gets a coupon entitling her to $(1/n)$ of a part $(x^*/\bar{x})$ of each agent's labor time in addition to $(1/n)$ of the property of the firm. The x^*-equal budget allocations are obtained at the corresponding Walrasian equilibria. This also reminds us that the Walrasian allocation process is more easily defended with respect to the value of preferences responsibility than the value of compensation.

As a matter of fact, there is no equivalent way of decentralizing the x^*-egalitarian equivalent rules, since the rights which must be given to each agent in the property of either the firm or other agents' labor time depend on the skill as well as the preferences profiles. The way of solving the preferences revelation problem which the planner faces in this case is described by the implementation literature, and requires that agents be much better informed about each other than in the decentralization process described above.[7] It was proven by Bossert, Fleurbaey and Van de gaer [3], however, that monotone welfare paths can be easily used to define ordinal

---

[7] For instance, every x^*-egalitarian equivalent rule can be subgame perfect Nash implemented by a generalized Divide-and-Choose mechanism (see Maniquet [15]).

social welfare functions to guide second best public policies.[8] In the case of an x^*-egalitarian equivalent rule, the social welfare function must be defined by: $\bar{z} = (z_1, \ldots, z_n)$ is socially preferred to $\bar{z}' = (z', \ldots, z'_n)$ in the economy $d = (\bar{s}, \bar{R}, f)$, if and only if

$$\min_i\{y_{0i}\} \geq \min_i\{y'_{0i}\},$$

where y_{0i} and y'_{0i} are defined by

$$(x^*, y_{0i})I_i z_i, \quad \forall_i \in N,$$

$$(x^*, y'_{0i})I_i z'_i, \quad \forall_i \in N.$$

The problem then becomes that of maximizing the social welfare function under the usual incentive constraints, which only requires that the planner be informed about the preferences distribution, assuming skills can be observed.

We are now ready for the rest of the proof of theorem 2.

Proof. First, we introduce the following terminology. For $d \in \mathcal{D}$, let $P(d)$ denote the set of Pareto efficient allocations. For $d = (\bar{s}, \bar{R}, f)$, $\bar{z} = (z_1, \ldots, z_n) \in P(d)$, let $w(\bar{z}, d) \in \mathbb{R}_{++}$ denote a supporting input price of $\bar{z}$, and $\pi_i(\bar{z}, d) \in \mathbb{R}$ be defined by $\pi_i(\bar{z}, d) = y_i - s_i w(\bar{z}, d)x_i$. For $n \in \mathbb{N}$, $\bar{s} \in R_{++}^n$, let $s_{\min}(\bar{s}) = \min_{i \in N}\{s_i\}$ and $s_{\max}(\bar{s}) = \max_{i \in N}\{S_i\}$.

(1) The proof that the x^*-egalitarian equivalent rules satisfy Pareto efficiency, the corresponding x^*-equal rights and skill solidarity over $\mathcal{D}^{\equiv}$ is left to the reader.

(2) Let the allocation rules $S_{x^*}^X$, be defined by:

$$\bar{z} \in S_{x^*}^X(\bar{s}, \bar{R}, f) \Leftrightarrow \bar{z} \in P(\bar{s}, \bar{R}, f) \quad \text{and} \quad \exists y^* \in \mathbb{R}_{++}, \text{ s.t.}$$

$$z_i I_i m(R_i, B_{\max} \cap B_{\min}),$$

where $B_{\max} = \{(x, y) \in X \mid y - s_{\max}(\bar{s})w(\bar{z}, d)x \leq y^* - s_{\max}(\bar{s})w(\bar{z}, d)x^*\}$ and $B_{\min} = \{(x, y) \in X \mid y - s_{\min}(\bar{s})w(\bar{z}, d)x \leq y^* - s_{\min}(\bar{s})w(\bar{z}, d)x^*\}$. The proof, omitted here, that $S_{x^*}^X$ is nonempty over $\mathcal{D}$ parallels Fleurbaey and Maniquet's [9] proof of the nonemptiness of allocation rule S^X defined in that paper. The proof that $S_{x^*}^X$ satisfies equal welfare for equal preferences and no-envy among uniformly skilled is left to the reader. We now prove that $S_{x^*}^X$ satisfies the

---

[8]Social welfare functions based on monotone welfare paths also appeared in Maniquet [14].

x^*-equal right, Let $d = (\bar{s}, \bar{R}, f) \in \mathcal{D}$ and $\bar{z} \in S^X_{x^*}(d)$ with associated y^* be given. By concavity of f,

$$\sum_{i=1}^{n} (\pi_i(\bar{z}, d) + s_i w(\bar{z}, d) x^*) \geq f\left(\sum_{i=1}^{n} s_i x^*\right). \tag{3}$$

By construction,

$$\pi_i(\bar{z}, d) + s_i w(\bar{z}, d) x^* \leq y^*, \quad \forall i \in N. \tag{4}$$

By putting Eqs. (3) and (4) together, $y^* \geq (f(\sum_{i=1}^{n} s_i x^*)/n)$. By construction again, $z_i R_i(x^*, y^*)$, which completes the proof.

(3) Let the allocation rule $S^Y_{x^*}$ be defined in the following way. For $(x, y) \in X$, $R \in \mathcal{R}^{\equiv}$, let $y^*((x, y), R) \in \mathbb{R}$ be defined by $(x^* - y^*((x, y), R), 0) I(x, y)$ if $(x^*, 0) P(x, y)$, and $(x^*, y^*((x, y), R)) I(x, y)$ if $(x, y) R(x^*, 0)$. For $d \in \mathcal{D}^{\equiv}$, let preferences $\hat{R}(\bar{R})$ be represented by the following function: $\hat{u}(x, y) = \min_i y^*((x, y), R_i)$.

$$\bar{z} \in S^Y_{x^*}(\bar{s}, \bar{R}, f) \Leftrightarrow \bar{z} \in P(\bar{s}, \bar{R}, f) \quad \text{and} \quad \forall i, j \in N,$$
$$m(\hat{R}(\bar{R}), B(s_i, w(\bar{z}, d), \pi_i(\bar{z}, d))) \hat{I}(\bar{R}) m(\hat{R}(\bar{R}), B(s_j, w(\bar{z}, d), \pi_j(\bar{z}, d))).$$

The nonemptiness of $S^Y_{x^*}$ over $\mathcal{D}^{\equiv}$ can be deduced from Fleurbaey and Maniquet's [9] proof of the nonemptiness of allocation rules *RWEB* defined in that paper. The proof that $S^Y_{x^*}$ satisfies equal welfare for uniform preferences and no-envy among equally skilled is left to the reader. We now prove that $S^Y_{x^*}$ satisfies the x^*-equal right. Let $d = (\bar{s}, \bar{R}, f) \in \mathcal{D}$ and $\bar{z} \in S^Y_{x^*}(d)$ with associated $u^* = \hat{u}(m(\hat{R}(\bar{R}), B(S_i, w(\bar{z}, d), \pi_i(\bar{z}, d))))$, be given, for all $i \in N$. By concavity of f, Eq. (3) still holds. By construction of $S^Y_{x^*}$ and $\hat{u}$,

$$u^* \geq \pi_i(\bar{z}, d) + s_i w(\bar{z}, d) x^*, \forall i \in N.$$

As a consequence,

$$(x^*, u^*) \hat{R}(\bar{R}) \left(x^*, \frac{f\left(\sum_{i=1}^{n} s_i x^*\right)}{n}\right).$$

Therefore, by construction of $S^Y_{x^*}$ and $\hat{u}, z_i R_i(x^*, u^*)$, $i \in N$, which completes the proof.

(4) The proof that the x^*-equal budget rules satisfy Pareto efficiency, the corresponding x^*-equal rights and preferences monotonicity is left to the reader. $\square$

5. Two Polar Classes of Simple Rules

We finish this paper by showing that the two classes of rules which we have defined at the end of the previous section are the most simple rules guaranteeing x^*-equal rights. Indeed, we add three weak properties of informational simplicity to the already defined properties, and we obtain complete characterizations of all the members of the two classes. These three properties are satisfied by a very large range of already known solutions to the production problem (e.g., rules studied in Moulin [17], Fleurbaey and Maniquet [9, 10]).

First, the consistency requirement is adapted from Moulin and Shenker [19] (see also Thomson [26]). It requires that a suballocation of a selected allocation be also selected in the subproblem defined by the corresponding subset of agents equipped with their initial skill and preferences and a reduced production function, obtained by fixing the bundles assigned to agents outside of this subset. Before stating the axiom formally, we introduce the following notation. For $d = (\bar{s}, \bar{R}, f) \in \mathscr{D}$, $C \subset N$, and $\bar{z} \in Z(d)$, let the function $g[d, C, z] \colon \mathbb{R}_+ \to \mathbb{R}_+$ be defined by:

$$g[d, C, z](x) = \max \left\{ 0, f \left(x + \sum_{i \notin C} s_i x_i \right) - \sum_{i \notin C} y_i \right\}.$$

Definition 16. An allocation rule S satisfies **consistency** if and only if for every $d = (\bar{s}, \bar{R}, f) \in \mathscr{D}, C \subseteq N, \bar{z} \in S(\bar{s}, \bar{R}, f)$, if

$$(\langle s_i \rangle_{i \in C}, \langle R_i \rangle_{i \in C}, g[d, C, z]) \in \mathscr{D},$$

then

$$\langle z_i \rangle_{i \in C} \in S(\langle s_i \rangle_{i \in C}, \langle R_i \rangle_{i \in C}, g[d, C, z]).$$

A reduced production function may fail to be concave. The x^*-equal budget rules, however, are only well defined in convex economies. The x^*-egalitarian equivalent rules, on the other hand, are well defined independently of the shape of the production function, provided the class of admissible preferences profiles is restricted to $\mathscr{R}^=$. We will take this fact into account in the following theorem, where we will enlarge the domain to $\mathscr{D}_{x^*}^{E=}$, defined by the restriction that preferences are drawn from $\mathscr{R}^=$, but without the concavity restriction on the production function.

Second, the replication invariance requirement requires that the replica of a selected allocation be also selected for the problem defined by replicating the initial problem (see Thomson [26]). Before stating the axiom formally, we introduce the following notation. For $\nu \in \mathbb{N}$, let νA mean that the object A is replicated ν times, and for $f \in \mathscr{F}$, let $f^\nu \in \mathscr{F}$ be defined by:

$$f^\nu(x) = \nu f\left(\frac{x}{y}\right).$$

Definition 17. An allocation rule S satisfies **replication invariance** if and only if for every $d = (\bar{s}, \bar{R}, f) \in \mathscr{D}$, $\bar{z} \in S(\bar{s}, \bar{R}, f)$, $\nu \in \mathbb{N}$,

$$\nu\bar{z} \in S(\nu\bar{s}, \nu\bar{R}, f^\nu).$$

The last axiom simply requires that if an allocation is selected, then all the allocations which are Pareto indifferent to this allocation be also selected (see Gevers [11]).

Definition 18. An allocation rule S satisfies **nondiscrimination** between Pareto indifferent allocations if and only if for every $d = (\bar{s}, \bar{R}, f) \in \mathscr{D}$, $\bar{z} \in S(\bar{s}, \bar{R}, f), \bar{z}' \in Z(\bar{s}, \bar{R}, f)$,

$$[z_i' I_i, \quad \forall i] \Leftrightarrow [\bar{z}' \in S(\bar{s}, \bar{R}, f)].$$

We are now able to characterize our two families of rules in a perfectly parallel way.

Theorem 3. *Let x^* denote the reference contribution. The x^*-egalitarian equivalent rule is the only Pareto efficient allocation rule which satisfies skill solidarity, consistency, replication invariance, nondiscrimination and guarantees the x^*-equal right over $\mathscr{D}_{x^*}^{E\equiv}$.*

Proof. The proof that the x^*-egalitarian equivalent rules satisfy consistency, replication invariance and nondiscrimination is left to the reader.

(1) $S \subseteq E_{x^*}^{\equiv}$. First, we introduce some notation. For $d = (\bar{s}, \bar{R}, f) \in \mathscr{D}^{\equiv}$, $\bar{z} \in P(d)$, let $\Sigma(\bar{z}, d) \subset \mathbb{R}_{++}^n$ be defined by

$$\Sigma(\bar{z}, d) = \{\bar{s}|\, \exists \bar{z}' \in P(\bar{s}', \bar{R}, f) \text{ s.t. } z_i I_i z_i', \quad \forall i \in N\}.$$

Let S satisfy the axioms. Let $d = (\bar{s}, \bar{R}, f)$, $\bar{z} \in S(d)$ be given. Let us suppose that $\bar{z} \notin E_{x^*}^{\equiv}(d)$. Let $j, k \in N$, and $y_{0j}, y_{0k} \in \mathbb{R}_{++}$ be such that

$$(x^*, y_{0j})I_j z_j, (x^*, y_{0k})I_k z_k \quad \text{and} \quad y_{0j} < y_{0k}$$

and

$$z_j P_j (0,0) \quad \text{or} \quad z_k P_k(0,0). \tag{5}$$

The key point of this proof is that in a large enough replication of d, it is possible, by rescaling skills, to find an efficient allocation Pareto indifferent to the replication of $\bar{z}$ with agents j and k working exactly x^*. Let w_j, $w_k \in \mathbb{R}_{++}$ be such that there exist $\pi_j, \pi_k \in \mathbb{R}$ satisfying

$$(x^*, y_{0j}) \in m(R_j, B(1, w_j, \pi_j)),$$

$$(x^*, y_{0k}) \in m(R_k, B(1, w_k, \pi_k)).$$

Let $\sigma_{jk}(\bar{z}, d) \subset \mathbb{R}_{++}$ be defined by

$$\sigma_{jk}(\bar{z}, d) = \left\{ s \in \mathbb{R}_+ | \exists \bar{s}' \in \Sigma(\bar{z}, d) \text{s.t.} \frac{s'_j}{s'_k} = \frac{w_j}{w_k} \quad \text{and} \quad s = \max\{s'_j, s'_k\} \right\}.$$

We have the crucial properties that for all $\nu, \nu' \in \mathbb{N}$,

$$[\nu < \nu'] \Rightarrow [\sigma_{jk}(\nu\bar{z}, \nu d) \subset \sigma_{jk}(\nu'\bar{z}, \nu'd)],$$

and $\sigma_{jk}(\nu'\bar{z}, \nu'd)$ is unbounded so that for all $s \in \mathbb{R}_{++}$, there exists $\nu \in \mathbb{N}$ such that

$$s \in \sigma_{jk}(\nu\bar{z}, \nu d).$$

Therefore, we can fix ν sufficiently large so that there exist $\bar{z}' \in P(\nu d)$, $\bar{s}'' \in \Sigma(\bar{z}', \nu d)$, $\bar{z}'' \in P(\bar{s}'', \nu\bar{R}, f^\nu)$ such that $\bar{z}' = \nu\bar{z}$ and

$$z'_i I_i z''_i, \quad \forall i \in \{1, \ldots, \nu n\},$$

$$z''_j = (x^*, y_{0j}),$$

$$z''_k = (x^*, y_{0k}).$$

By replication invariance,

$$\bar{z}' \in S(\nu d).$$

By Pareto efficiency, skill solidarity, and nondiscrimination,

$$\bar{z}'' \in S(\bar{s}'', \nu\bar{R}, f^\nu).$$

By consistency and Eq. (5),

$$(Z''_j, z''_k) \in S((s''_j, s''_k), (R_j, R_k), g[(\bar{s}'', \nu\bar{R}, f^\nu), \{j, k\}, z'']),$$

which violates E_{x^*} since $y_{0j} < ((y_{0j} + y_{0k})/2)$. Therefore, $\bar{z} \in E_{x^*}^{\equiv} = (d)$.

(2) $S = E_{x^*}^{\equiv}$. Let us observe that $E_{x^*}^{\equiv}$ is single-valued, that is, all selected allocations are Pareto indifferent. Therefore, the claim follows from nondiscrimination and $S \subseteq E_{x^*}^{\equiv}$. $\qquad\square$

Our last result is also stated under a weak domain restriction. Let $\mathscr{F}^d$ denote the set of differentiable production functions, and $\mathscr{D}^d$ the set of economies $d = (\bar{s}, \bar{R}, f)$ where $f \in \mathscr{F}^d$.

Theorem 4. *Let x^* denote the reference contribution. The x^*-equal budget rule is the smallest Pareto efficient allocation rule, with respect to inclusion, which satisfies preferences monotonicity, consistency, replication invariance, nondiscrimination and guarantees the x^*-equal right over $\mathscr{D}^d$.*

Proof.   The proof that the x^*-equal budget rules satisfy consistency, replication invariance and nondiscrimination is left to the reader. Let S satisfy the axioms. Let $d = (\bar{s}, \bar{R}, f)$, $\bar{z} \in B_{x^*}^=(d)$ be given. We have to prove that $\bar{z} \in S(d)$. Let $w \in \mathbb{R}_+$, and $\bar{\pi} \in \mathbb{R}^n$ be associated to $\bar{z}$. Let us consider $d^l = (\bar{s}, \bar{R}^l, f) \in \mathscr{D}$ defined by: for all $i \in N$

$$(x, y) R_i^l (x', y') \Leftrightarrow y - w s_i x \geq y' - w s_i x'.$$

Let $\bar{z}^l \in S(d^l)$ be given, and let us assume that $\bar{z}^l \notin B_{x^*}^=(d^l)$. Let $w^l \in \mathbb{R}_+$, and $\bar{\pi}^l \in \mathbb{R}^n$ be associated to $\bar{z}^l$. By Pareto efficiency, $w^l = w$. Let $j, k \in N$ be such that

$$\pi_j^l + w s_j x^* < \pi_k^l + w s_k x^*$$

and either $\pi_j^l > 0$ or $\pi_k^l > 0$. Let $\nu_\iota, \nu_\kappa \in \mathbb{N}$ be such that

$$\nu_\iota \pi_\iota^l + \nu_\kappa \pi_\kappa^l > 0, \iota, \kappa \in \{j, k\}.$$

By differentiability of

$$\sup_{\nu \in \mathbb{N}} \{ g[\nu d^l, (\nu_\iota \iota, \nu_\kappa \kappa), \nu \bar{z}^l](0) \} = \nu_\iota \pi_\iota^l + \nu_\kappa \pi_\kappa^l,$$

$$\sup_{\nu \in \mathbb{N}} \{ g[\nu d^l, (\nu_\iota \iota, \nu_\kappa \kappa), \nu \bar{z}^l] = \nu_\iota s_\iota x^* + \nu_\kappa s_\kappa x^*) \}$$

$$= \nu_\iota (\pi_\iota^l + w s_\iota x^*) + \nu_\kappa (\pi_\kappa^l + w s_\kappa x^*).$$

We can fix ν sufficiently large so that

$$g[\nu d^l, (\nu_\iota \iota, \nu_\kappa \kappa), \nu \bar{z}^l](0) \geq 0,$$

$$g[\nu d^l, (\nu_\iota \iota, \nu_\kappa \kappa), \nu \bar{z}^l](\nu_\iota s_\iota x^* + \nu_\kappa s_\kappa x^*) \geq (\nu_\iota + \nu_\kappa)(\pi_j^l + w s_j x^*).$$

Note that the concavity of $g[\nu d^l, (\nu_\iota \iota, \nu_\kappa \kappa), \nu \bar{z}^l]$ is guaranteed by Eq. (6). By replication invariance,

$$\nu \bar{z}^l \in S(\nu d^l).$$

By consistency,

$$(\nu_\iota z_\iota, \nu_\kappa z_\kappa) \in S((\nu_\iota s_\iota, \nu_\kappa s_\kappa), (\nu_\iota R_\iota, \nu_\kappa R_\kappa), g[\nu d^l, (\nu_\iota \iota, \nu_\kappa \kappa), \nu \bar{z}^l]),$$

violating E_{x^*}. Therefore, $\bar{z}^l \in B_{x^*}^{=}(d^l)$. By nondiscrimination, $\bar{z} \in S(d^l)$. By preferences monotonicity, $\bar{z} \in S(d)$. $\qquad\qquad\square$

Acknowledgments

I would like to thank Frédéric Gaspart, Louis Gevers and especially Marc Fleurbaey for stimulating discussions, and Bart Capéau and two anonymous referees for their comments on an earlier version. I also benefited during the preparation of this paper from the excellent research atmosphere at the Department of Economics, Universitat Autónoma de Barcelona. Partial financial support from HCM grant ERBCHBGCT940699 is gratefully acknowledged.

References

1. W. Bossert. 'Redistribution mechanisms based on individual characteristics', *Mathematical Social Sciences* **29** (1995), 1–17.
2. W. Bossert and M. Fleurbaey. 'Redistribution and compensation', *Social Choice and Welfare* **13** (1996), 343–355.
3. W. Bossert, M. Fleurbaey and D. Van de gaer. 'On second best compensation', mimeo, 1996.
4. R. Dworkin. 'What is equality? Part 2: Equality of resources', *Philosophy and Public Affairs* **10** (1981), 283–345.
5. M. Fleurbaey. 'Equal opportunity or equal social outcome', *Economics and Philosophy* **11** (1995), 25–55.
6. M. Fleurbaey. 'Three solutions to the compensation problem', *Journal of Economic Theory* **65** (1995), 505–521.
7. M. Fleurbaey. 'On fair compensation', *Theory and Decision* **36** (1994), 277–307.
8. M. Fleurbaey. 'Equality and responsibility', *European Economic Review* **39** (1995), 683–689.
9. M. Fleurbaey and F. Maniquet. 'Fair allocation with unequal production skills: The no-envy approach to compensation', *Mathematical Social Sciences* **32** (1996), 71–93.

10. M. Fleurbaey and F. Maniquet. 'Fair allocation with unequal production skills: The solidarity approach to compensation', University of Cergy-Pontoise, mimeo, 1994.

11. L. Gevers. 'Walrasian social choice: Some simple axiomatic approaches', in W. Heller *et al.* (eds.), *Social Choice and Public Decision Making*, vol. 1, Cambridge: Cambridge University Press. 1986, pp. 97–114.

12. I. Iturbe and J. Nieto. 'On fair allocations and monetary compensations', *Economic Theory* **7** (1996), 125–138.

13. S. C. Kolm. 'Macrojustice', CG-PC, Paris, 1997.

14. F. Maniquet. 'Distribution rules for a commonly owned technology: The average cost lower bound', F.U.N.D.P. (Namur) Cahier de Recherche #**123**, 1993.

15. F. Maniquet. 'A generalized divide-and-choose mechanism for the implementation of allocation functions', F.U.N.D.P. (Namur) mimeo, 1995.

16. E. Maskin. 'Nash equilibrium and welfare optimality', *Review of Economic Studies* **66** (1999), 23–38.

17. H. Moulin. 'Joint ownership of a convex technology: Comparison of three solutions', *Review of Economic Studies* **57** (1990), 439–452.

18. H. Moulin. 'Welfare bounds in the cooperative production problem', *Games and Economic Behavior* **4** (1992), 373–401.

19. H. Moulin and S. Shenker. 'Average cost pricing vs. serial cost sharing: An axiomatic comparison', *Journal of Economic Theory* **64** (1994), 178–201.

20. E. Pazner and D. Schmeidler. 'Egalitarian equivalent allocations: A new concept of economic equity', *Quarterly Journal of Economics* **92** (1978), 671–687.

21. E. Pazner and D. Schmeidler. 'Decentralization and income distribution in socialist economies', *Economic Inquiry* **16** (1978), 257–264.

22. J. E. Roemer. 'Equality of talent', *Economics and Philosophy* **1** (1985), 151–187.

23. J. E. Roemer. 'Equality of resources implies equality of welfare', *Quarterly Journal of Economics* **101** (1986), 751–784.

24. J. E. Roemer. 'A pragmatic theory of responsibility for an egalitarian planner', *Philosophy & Public Affairs* **22** (1993), 146–166.

25. Y. Sprumont. 'Balanced egalitarian redistribution of income', *Mathematical Social Sciences* **33** (1997), 185–202.

26. W. Thomson. 'A study of choice correspondences in economies with a variable number of agents', *Journal of Economic Theory* **46** (1988), 237–254.

27. H. Varian. 'Equity, envy, and efficiency', *Journal of Economic Theory* **9** (1974), 63–91.

CHAPTER 7

Fair Social Orderings When Agents Have Unequal Production Skills

Marc Fleurbaey and François Maniquet

ABSTRACT. We develop an approach which escapes Arrow's impossibility by relying on information about agents' indifference curves instead of utilities. In a model where agents have unequal production skills and different preferences, we characterize social ordering functions which rely only on ordinal non-comparable information about individual preferences. These social welfare functions are required to satisfy properties of compensation for inequalities in skills, and equal access to resources for all preferences.

1. Introduction

Since Arrow's celebrated theorem on social choice (Arrow 1950, 1951), the theory of social choice has been replete with negative results taking the shape of impossibilities. It is now widely believed that: (1) the only escape from Arrow's impossibility is by resorting to interpersonal comparisons of utility, and (2) interpersonal comparisons of utility have no sound empirical basis. From these two statements it is almost inevitable

We thank participants of the SCW conference in Vancouver (July 1998), of workshops at Cergy and Osnabrück, and of seminars at Tokyo (Hitotsubashi U.) and Caen. We are also grateful to an Associate Editor and two referees for their very helpful comments. Financial Support from European TMR Network FMRX-CT96-0055 is gratefully acknowledged.

Soc Choice Welfare **24**: 93–127, 2005.

©Springer-Verlag 2005

DOI: 10.1007/s00355-003-0294-y

to conclude that welfare economics is caught in a dilemma. It can either restrict its attention to minimal notions like Pareto-optimality, or obtain results which depend on unknown utility functions.

Over several decades, Sen[1] has brilliantly fought this pessimistic mood by proposing to make interpersonal comparisons of *capabilities* instead of utilities, a concept which includes utility ingredients but also objective notions of well-being which might supposedly be easier to observe and measure (the capability to move, for instance, can be compared between healthy and handicapped persons).

We share Sen's optimism, but propose a different way out. Contrary to the first of the above statements, we think it is not true that the only escape from Arrow's impossibility is by resorting to interpersonal comparisons of utility, or capability, or any direct measure of individual well-being. There does exist another interesting, albeit usually overlooked, escape from Arrow's impossibility, which does not introduce any other informational input than individual preferences. In brief, it consists in *weakening Arrow's axiom of independence of irrelevant alternatives so as to take account of information about individual indifference curves.* In this paper we develop this idea and show how this approach to social choice can be fruitful, through the construction of social preferences which rely on the shape of individual indifference curves. The relationship between our approach and Arrow's axioms, and more generally the social choice literature, is analyzed more formally at the end of the paper.[2]

In this introduction, however, we can at least provide an intuition of why knowing indifference curves is enough to construct consistent social preferences. Figure 1 depicts an allocation (z_1, z_2) in a two-agent production economy similar to the model studied in this paper. There are two goods, labor time and a consumption good, and agents 1 and 2 have individual production skill levels denoted s_1 and s_2 respectively. Production skills must be interpreted as the (constant) amount of consumption good one agent is able to produce per unit of labor time.

Let us say, for instance, that an allocation of labor time and consumption levels among agents is socially preferred to a second one if the "social value" of the former is larger than that of the latter.[3] On the basis of agents'

---

[1]For a summary of his work on this point, see Sen (1999).

[2]A more general introduction of this approach was made in Fleurbaey and Maniquet (1996b).

[3]The reference to a numerical social value is not essential to our approach, but in this example it makes things simple and guarantees that social preferences are transitive.

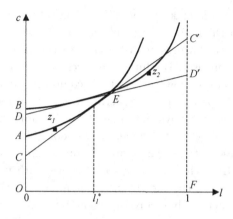

Fig. 1.

indifference curves through their consumption bundles, there are a myriad of ways of computing the social value of (z_1, z_2). Let us consider just a few, based on the construction of points A, B, C, C', D, D', E and F on the figure. Point A is such that having the quantity of good OA and a labor time equal to zero is as good for agent 1 as consuming z_1. The line CC' has slope s_1 and is such that agent 1 is indifferent between consuming z_1 or freely choosing a labor-consumption bundle on this line (in which case she would choose l_1^*). Point B and line DD' are constructed for agent 2 in a similar way (DD' has slope $s_2 < s_1$). Point E is the intersection between CC' and DD', and point F is simply the $(1, 0)$ point in the labor-consumption space. The social value of (z_1, z_2) can be, for instance, the sum of OA and OB, the minimum of OC and OD, the sum $OC + CE + ED' + D'F$, the area $OCED'F$, the area $ODEC'F$, etc.[4]

It is easy to check that social preferences based on the above examples of social valuation are anonymous (the agents' names do not matter) so that there is no Arrovian dictator, and that they all satisfy the Weak Pareto property (if all individual bundles lie on higher indifference curves, then the social value is larger). Moreover, none of these social preferences uses information other than indifference curves (and productivities). These examples of social preferences should convince the reader that relying on indifference curves opens a host of possibilities, and offers, actually, too many. But this

---

[4]These definitions do not apply directly to all allocations, but they can easily be extended to cover all cases.

is good news, because it makes it possible to introduce additional ethical requirements, other than anonymity and Pareto, and based for instance on principles of equality or fairness, in order to select ethically appealing social preferences. This is precisely the line of research we pursue here.

One likely objection, however, is that computing distance OA, for instance, can be interpreted as constructing a numerical representation of agent 1's preferences, and plays the same role as a traditional utility function. The first example of social value, above, looks like a utilitarian sum of such utility representations. Therefore, the objection goes, this approach is not so different from the theory of social choice with utility functions. This objection overlooks the fact that in our approach, the initial input is not this utility function, but only the agent's preferences. In the theory of social choice with utilities, social preferences over allocations are sensitive to exogenous individual utility functions, so that social preferences may change when utility functions change, even if individual preferences do not change. This cannot occur in our approach, where social preferences depend only, deep down, on individual preferences. Moreover, if the social value that is obtained in our analysis happens to rely on numerical representations of the agents' preferences, this has to be justified by ethical properties of the *social preferences* themselves, and cannot be based on an arbitrarily chosen profile of utility functions.

In addition, and this is the most important point, the objection does not apply to all of the examples provided above. For instance, there is no way to relate the social value computed as the area $ODEC'F$ to a traditional kind of social welfare function with individual utilities. Therefore, our approach is quite different from the theory of social choice with utilities. It covers a different, and formally broader, spectrum of social preferences, and does not introduce utility functions except when ethical arguments about social preferences make it appropriate to rely on endogenous representations of exogenous preferences.

The model of the above example is essentially the model studied in this paper. The problem under consideration here is the definition of social preferences in a model with one-input-one-output production, where agents can differ in their productivity as well as in their consumption-leisure preferences. We define several "social ordering functions", namely, functions which, for every economy in a domain, determine a ranking of all allocations in this economy. They are given axiomatic justifications on the basis of ethical considerations. Apart from efficiency and separability conditions (with some variants, separability conditions state that indifferent agents should not matter in the social evaluation of two alternatives), the main ethical principles retained here are that (1) inequalities due to differences in productivity should be reduced, (2) differences in preferences should not lead to unequal access to resources. It is explained below how it is possible to embody these general principles into a variety of specific, precise axioms.

It is on purpose that we consider a particular economic model. Although it is possible to apply our approach to the abstract social choice framework in which Arrow's theory of social choice is often presented,[5] it is in economic models only, with enough information about resources and preferences, that it is possible to define, and rely on, interesting principles of equity in order to define valuable social preferences. And one should realize that many ethical principles really do make sense only in particular economic contexts. For instance, consider the principle that it is unjust if among two equally talented agents, one works less and consumes more than the other one. This principle cannot be easily relied upon in an abstract model where the allocation of resources is not explicitly described, and would not make sense in a different context with, say, pure public goods. Moreover, the model we study here is a particularly relevant one for welfare economics and public economics. This model has been introduced in the literature a long time ago, from different viewpoints, by Mirrlees (1971), and Pazner and Schmeidler (1974). In a companion paper (Fleurbaey and Maniquet 1998), we study the application of the social orderings defined here to the problem of optimal income taxation, and show that new insights in the issue of optimal taxation are indeed obtained along this way. For instance, we find justifications to a tax scheme characterized by exemption until an income threshold, followed by taxation at increasing marginal rates.[6]

It is usually thought that there is a third option in the above dilemma for welfare economics, namely, to study allocation rules that do not rank all options but only select a first-best subset. This is the topic of the

---

[5] In the abstract setting, there are no "indifference curves", but one can rely on upper contour sets instead. Actually, weakenings of the independence axiom in the abstract social choice model have already been studied by Hansson (1973) and Campbell and Kelly (2000). Nonetheless, recall that Arrow's (1950, 1951) initial presentation dealt with an economic model. And since then, an important literature has proved that Arrow's theorem applies to most economic contexts (see Le Breton 1997 for a survey).

[6] See also Bossert, Fleurbaey for a similar study of linear taxation (1999). For a different approach to optimal tax with responsibility-sensitive social goals, see Schokkaert *et al.* (2001), Roemer *et al.* (2000).

(purely ordinal) literature on fair allocations.[7] Although we think that this approach is very useful, it is also commonly acknowledged that only fine-grained orderings of allocations can help in decisions about reforms (going from an "imperfect" allocation to another "imperfect" allocation), and that the theory of optimal taxation is more easily constructed in terms of maximizing a social ordering over possible tax schemes (or, more precisely, over the set of incentive compatible allocations). Therefore it is important to construct orderings over all allocations, and not only to construct allocation rules. More fundamentally, it should be emphasized that it is not much more difficult to construct orderings than allocation rules. Actually, both approaches rely on the same departure from Arrow's impossibility setting, namely, weakening the axiom of independence of irrelevant alternatives. This is explained in more detail in Section 5.

Although we think that the part of welfare economics dealing with utilities is useful in many respects, we do think that depending on a purely ordinal information, without any interpersonal comparisons, is certainly a practical advantage for a social ordering or social welfare function, an advantage that has to be reckoned against possible losses in other dimensions. And we hope that the social orderings proposed in this paper are appealing because they combine their pure ordinalism with significant equity requirements. Moreover, ordinalism may itself be a reasonable ethical requirement in some contexts, as argued for instance by Rawls (1971, 1982) and Dworkin (1981) in the field of social justice, on the basis of the principle that autonomous moral agents should be held responsible for their goals, their utility functions. It turns out that in this paper we adopt the related ethical principle that access to resources should not be unequal due to different preferences. It is immediate to see that ordinalism itself can be viewed as an application of this principle, because saying that differences in utilities should not elicit a differential treatment is equivalent to endorsing ordinalism and rejecting interpersonal comparisons of utilities.

The paper is organized as follows. In Section 2 below the model is presented and notations are introduced. In Section 3 the ethical principles are discussed in more detail and the related axioms are proposed. In Section 4 the main axiomatic results are stated and proved. Section 5 is devoted to a discussion of the results and their relationship to the

---

[7]For a survey see e.g. Moulin and Thomson (1997). Allocation rules in the same model as here are studied in Fleurbaey and Maniquet (1996a, 1999a).

literature. Section 6 concludes. The appendix gathers the proofs of the theorems and shows the logical independence of the axioms referred to in the theorems.

2. Model and Basic Definitions

The main mathematical notations and conventions are the following ones. The set of real numbers (resp. non-negative, positive real numbers) is $\mathbb{R}$ (resp. $\mathbb{R}_+, \mathbb{R}_{++}$), the set of positive integers is $\mathbb{N}_{++}$. The cardinal of any set A is denoted $|A|$. A vector $(x_a)_{a \in A}$ whose components $x_a \in B$ are indexed on a set A is denoted x_A and is considered to belong to the set of functions from A to B, which is denoted B^A. An ordering is a complete reflexive and transitive binary relation. Set inclusion is denoted $\subseteq$, and strict inclusion $\subset$.

The economic model can now be presented. There are two goods, labor time (l) and consumption (c). The population is finite and the set of agents is denoted N. Any agent $i \in N$ has a *production skill* $s_i \geq 0$ enabling him/her to produce the quantity $s_i l_i$ of consumption good with labor time l_i. Agent i also has *preferences* defined by an ordering R_i over bundles $z_i = (l_i, c_i)$ such that $0 \leq l_i \leq 1$ and $c_i \geq 0$. Let $X = [0,1] \times \mathbb{R}_+$ denote the agent's consumption set.

We will actually study a whole domain $\mathcal{E}$ of economies. Let $\mathcal{N}$ denote the set of non-empty subsets of $\mathbb{N}_{++}$, and $\mathcal{R}$ the set of continuous, convex and strictly monotonic (negatively in labor, positively in consumption) orderings over X. An *economy* is defined as a list $e = (s_N, R_N)$, and such an economy is said to belong to the domain $\mathcal{E}$ if $N \in \mathcal{N}, s_N \in \mathbb{R}_+^N$, and $R_N \in \mathcal{R}^N$. In other words, one has:

$$\mathcal{E} = \bigcup_{N \in \mathcal{N}} (\mathbb{R}_+^N \times \mathcal{R}^N).$$

An *allocation* is a vector $z_N = (z_i)_{i \in N} \in X^N$. It is *feasible* for $e = (s_N, R_N) \in \mathcal{E}$ if

$$\sum_{i \in N} c_i \leq \sum_{i \in N} s_i l_i.$$

Let $Z(e)$ denote the set of feasible allocations for an economy $e \in \mathcal{E}$, and $Z_i(e)$ denote the projection of $Z(e)$ over the ith subspace of X^N:

$$Z_i(e) = \{z \in X | \exists z_N \in Z(e), \ z = z_i\}.$$

An allocation $z_N \in Z(e)$ is *Pareto-optimal* in e if:

$$\forall z'_N \in Z(e), \quad [\forall i \in N, z'_i R_i z_i] \Rightarrow [\forall i \in N, z'_i I_i z_i].$$

For $R \in \mathcal{R}$, and $A \subset X$, let $m(R, A) \subseteq A$ denote the set of bundles (if any) which maximize preferences R over A, that is

$$m(R, A) = \{z \in A | \forall z' \in A, z R z'\}.$$

Since all bundles in $m(R, A)$ are indifferent for R, we sometimes use $m(R, A)$ to denote any of its bundles.

For $s \in \mathbb{R}_+$ and $z = (l, c) \in X$, let $B(s, z) \subset X$ denote the *budget set* obtained with skill s and such that z is on the budget frontier:

$$B(s, z) = \{(l', c') \in X \mid c' - sl' \leq c - sl\}.$$

In the special case where $s = 0$ and $c = 0$, we adopt the convention that

$$B(s, z) = \{(l', c') \in X \mid c' = 0, l' \geq l\}.$$

For $s \in \mathbb{R}_+, R \in \mathcal{R}$ and $z = (l, c) \in X$, let $I\!B(s, R, z) \subset X$ denote the *implicit budget* at bundle z for any agent with characteristics (s, R), that is, the budget set with slope s having the property that z is indifferent for R to the preferred bundle in the budget set:

$$I\!B(s, R, z) = B(s, z') \text{ for any } z' \text{ such that } z'Iz \text{ and } z' \in m(R, B(s, z')).$$

By strict monotonicity of preferences, this definition is unambiguous. Notice that bundle z need not belong to the implicit budget. Figure 2 illustrates these definitions.

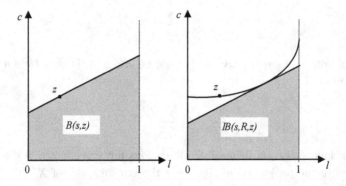

Fig. 2.

In this paper, we are interested in devising social preferences over the set of allocations, for all economies in the domain. A *social ordering* on economy $e = (s_N, R_N)$ is an ordering over the set X^N. A *social ordering function* is a function $\bar{R}$ associating every $e \in \mathcal{E}$ with a social ordering $\bar{R}(e)$ on e (strict social preference and social indifference are denoted $\bar{P}(e)$ and $\bar{I}(e)$ respectively).[8] It is also useful, for later discussions, to define an *allocation rule*. It is a correspondence S associating every $e \in \mathcal{E}$ with a subset of feasible allocations $S(e) \subset Z(e)$.

3. Ethical Principles

As it is standard in social choice, the selection of a good social ordering function will not be arbitrary, but will have to be justified on grounds of desirable properties satisfied by the social ordering function. We will first rely on standard social choice conditions, such as efficiency, separability and continuity. Efficiency is embodied in the following Pareto conditions.

Weak Pareto. *For all* $e = (s_N, R_N) \in \mathcal{E}, z_N, z'_N \in X^N$, *if for all* $i \in N, z'_i P_i z_i$, *then* $z'_N \bar{P}(e) z_N$.

Strong Pareto. *For all* $e = (s_N, R_N) \in \mathcal{E}, z_N, z'_N \in X^N$, *if for all* $i \in N, z'_i R_i z_i$, *then* $z'_N \bar{R}(e) z_n$. *If in addition, for some* $j \in N, z'_j P_j z_j$, *then* $z'_N \bar{P}(e) z_N$.

A well-known consequence of the latter requirement is that $z'_N \bar{I}(e) z_N$ whenever $z'_i I_i z_i$ for all $i \in N$. In this case we say that z_N and z'_N are Pareto-indifferent.

The next axiom is a natural strengthening of separability conditions that are encountered in welfare economics[9] and the theory of social choice.[10] The separability conditions, with some variations, state that agents who are indifferent over some alternatives should not influence social preferences over those alternatives. Our condition deals only with agents whose bundles are unchanged, but says that removing those agents from the economy

---

[8]Notice that the ordering is defined over X^N, and not only over $Z(e)$. Indeed, there is no reason to restrict the definition of the ordering to the feasible set, because all orderings that we know are straightforwardly extended from $Z(e)$ to X^N.

[9]See e.g., Fleming (1952).

[10]See d'Aspremont and Gevers (1977).

would not alter social preferences. It is therefore a cross-economy robustness property and is actually an adaptation to this framework of the consistency condition commonly used in the literature on fair allocation rules.[11]

Consistency. *For all* $e = (s_N, R_N) \in \mathcal{E}$, *all* $G \subset N$, *all* $z_N, z'_N \in X^N$ *such that* $z_{N \setminus G} = z'_{N \setminus G}$,

$$z_N \bar{R}(e) z'_N \Leftrightarrow z_G \bar{R}(e_G) z'_G,$$

where $e_G = (s_G, R_G)$.

The next axiom simply requires continuity of the social ordering.

Continuity. *For all* $e = (s_N, R_N) \in \mathcal{E}$, *all* $z_N \in X^N$, *the sets* $\{z'_N \in X^N \mid z'_N \bar{R}(e) z_N\}$ *and* $\{z'_N \in X^N \mid z_N \bar{R}(e) z'_N\}$ *are closed.*

In addition to these basic conditions, we will be interested in redistributive principles. The (Pareto-optimal) laisser-faire allocations of these economies are such that every agent $i \in N$ chooses her preferred bundle in her budget set $B(s_i, (0,0))$. One can argue that although these allocations permit a free expression of consumption-leisure preferences, they are inequitable, in particular if differences in skills come from inherited features which cannot be attributed to the agents' responsibility, or if s_i is interpreted as the wage rate associated with the job assigned to agent i and agents could be more productive but are constrained by the unavailability of jobs with higher wage rates. It may be, however, that agents' skills are also partly the outcome of previous personal choices about investment in human capital. Symmetrically, one may argue that agents are only partially responsible for their preferences over consumption and leisure. But in order to have a simpler analysis, here we will adopt the clear-cut convention that, in this model, one would like: (1) to *neutralize the consequences of differential skills*, and (2) to be *neutral with respect to choices* due to different preferences. To some extent, it is always possible to apply our analysis to different contexts by re-interpreting one parameter (s_i) as whatever should be neutralized and the other parameter (R_i) as whatever is irrelevant with respect to inequalities.

Let us consider the two above ethical goals in turn. We propose two ways of capturing the idea that differential skills should not entail unequal individual outcomes. The first way is inspired by Hammond's equity axiom (Hammond 1976). Consider two agents who have the same preferences but

---

[11] See Thomson (1996) for a survey on the consistency condition.

different skills. If one agent has a bundle on a higher indifference curve, one can argue that the above ethical goal is not fully satisfied and that, other things equal, it would be better to assign them bundles on indifference curves closer to each other. More generally, any gap between the agents' indifference curves may be considered as going against this goal. Therefore, replacing the bundle of the agent on a higher indifference curve with a worse bundle, and the bundle of the other agent with a better bundle should be a social improvement. This leads to the following axiom, which, as in the Hammond equity axiom, features an infinite inequality aversion.[12]

Hammond Compensation. *For all* $e = (s_N, R_N) \in \mathcal{E}, z_N, z'_N \in X^N$, *if there exist* $j, k \in N$ *such that* $R_j = R_k$, *and for all* $i \in N$ *such that* $i \neq j, k, z_i = z'_i$, *then*

$$[z_j P_j z'_j P_j z'_k P_k z_k] \Rightarrow [z'_N \bar{P}(e) z_N].$$

The second way is inspired by Suppes' grading principles (Suppes 1966, Sen 1970). It requires that permuting the bundles of two agents having the same preferences but possibly different skills does not affect the position of the allocation in the social ranking.[13] Recall that, contrary to Hammond equity, this is consistent with any degree of inequality aversion (including negative inequality aversion).

Suppes Compensation. *For all* $e = (s_N, R_N) \in \mathcal{E}, z_N, z'_N \in X^N$, *if there exist* $j, k \in N$ *such that* $R_j = R_k$, *and for all* $i \in N$ *such that* $i \neq j, k, z_i = z'_i$, *then*

$$[z_j = z'_k \text{ and } z_k = z'_j] \Rightarrow [z'_N \bar{I}(e) z_N].$$

It will soon turn out that those axioms need to be sharply weakened. Therefore, we will consider the following Minimal Hammond Compensation and Minimal Suppes Compensation axioms, where the above requirements are imposed only among agents having some reference preferences, which do not depend on the types of actual agents but can be fixed arbitrarily.

---

[12]Notice that no interpersonal comparison of utility is involved in such notions, although the Hammond equity axiom was traditionally applied to interpersonally comparable levels of welfare.

[13]The traditional formulation of the grading principle is in terms of welfare, but we adopt here a weaker condition, although under Strong Pareto the two formulations (permuting indifference curves or permuting bundles) are equivalent.

Minimal Hammond Compensation. *For at least one $\tilde{R} \in \mathcal{R}$ it holds true that for all $e = (s_N, R_N) \in \mathcal{E}, z_N, z'_N \in X^N$, if there exist $j, k \in N$ such that $R_j = R_k = \tilde{R}$, and for all $i \in N$ such that $i \neq j, k, z_i = z'_i$, then*

$$[z_j \tilde{P} z'_j \tilde{P} z'_k \tilde{P} z_k] \Rightarrow [z'_N \bar{P}(e) z_N].$$

Minimal Suppes Compensation. *For at least one $\tilde{R} \in \mathcal{R}$ it holds true that for all $e = (s_N, R_N) \in \mathcal{E}, z_N, z'_N \in X^N$, if there exist $j, k \in N$ such that $R_j = R_k = \tilde{R}$, and for all $i \in N$ such that $i \neq j, k, z_i = z'_i$, then*

$$[z_j = z'_k \text{ and } z_k = z'_j] \Rightarrow [z'_N \bar{I}(e) z_N].$$

We will also consider the requirement that in economies where *all* the agents have the same preferences, an allocation which is socially weakly preferred to all other feasible allocations must be such that all agents are on the same indifference curve. This requirement is logically implied by Hammond Compensation.

Equal Welfare in Equal-Preference Economies. *For all $e = (s_N, R_N) \in \mathcal{E}, z_N \in Z(e)$, if for all $i, j \in N, R_i = R_j$ and for all $z'_N \in Z(e), z_N \bar{R}(e) z'_N$, then for all $i, j \in N, z_i I_i z_j$.*

Let us now turn to the second ethical goal introduced above. It implies that the various preferences displayed in the population should not be treated differently, that is, the agents should not receive any differential amount of resources on the pure basis that they have "good" or "bad" preferences. Therefore, agents with identical skills should ideally be free to choose their preferred bundle in the same opportunity set.

Since we want to rank all allocations, without considering how they might be generated by particular economic institutions, it is not obvious how to define a relevant notion of "access to resources" or "opportunity set" here. As a consequence we adopt a very limited notion, compatible with Pareto-optimality. We say that the ideal situation for two agents with identical skills would be to have the same linear budget set with a slope equal to their skill. And, minimally, we consider that there is a problematic inequality in access to resources only for agents whose bundles could have been chosen in unequal budget sets whose slope is equal to their skill.

Again, we propose two ways of defining the distributional requirements. The first way is in line with the Hammond equity axiom, and reflects an infinite inequality aversion for budgets among agents having the same skill and choosing their preferred bundle in their budgets.

Hammond Equal Access. *For all* $e = (s_N, R_N) \in \mathcal{E}, z_N, z'_N \in X^N$, *if there exist* $j, k \in N$ *such that* $s_j = s_k$, *and for all* $i \in N, i \neq j, k, z_i = z'_i$, *then*

$$[\forall\, h \in \{j, k\}, z_h \in m(R_h, B(s_h, z_h)) \text{ and } z'_h \in m(R_h, B(s_h, z'_h)), \text{ and}$$

$$B(s_j, z_j) \supset B(s_j, z'_j) \supset B(s_k, z'_k) \supset B(s_k, z_k)] \Rightarrow [z'_N \bar{P}(e) z_N].$$

The second way is again inspired by the Suppes grading principles. It requires that permuting the budgets of two agents having the same skill but possibly different preferences (and maximizing over these budgets) does not alter the value of the allocation in the social ranking.

Suppes Equal Access. *For all* $e = (s_N, R_N) \in \mathcal{E}, z_N, z'_N \in X^N$, *if there exist* $j, k \in N$ *such that* $s_j = s_k$, *and for all* $i \in N, i \neq j, k, z_i = z'_i$, *then*

$$[\forall\, h \in \{j, k\}, z_h \in m(R_h, B(s_h, z_h)) \text{ and } z'_h \in m(R_h, B(s_h, z'_h)), \text{ and}$$

$$B(s_j, z_j) = B(s_k, z'_k) \text{ and } B(s_j, z'_j) = B(s_k, z_k)] \Rightarrow [z'_N \bar{I}(e) z_N].$$

And again it will be useful to have weak versions of these conditions.

Minimal Hammond Equal Access. *For at least one* $\tilde{s} \in \mathbb{R}_+$ *it holds true that for all* $e = (s_N, R_N) \in \mathcal{E}, z_N, z'_N \in X^N$, *if there exist* $j, k \in N$ *such that* $s_j = s_k = \tilde{s}$, *and for all* $i \in N, i \neq j, k, z_i = z'_i$, *then*

$$[\forall\, h \in \{j, k\}, z_h \in m(R_h, B(\tilde{s}, z_h)) \text{ and } z'_h \in m(R_h, B(\tilde{s}, z'_h)), \text{ and}$$

$$B(\tilde{s}, z_j) \supset B(\tilde{s}, z'_j) \supset B(\tilde{s}, z'_k) \supset B(\tilde{s}, z_k)] \Rightarrow [z'_N \bar{P}(e) z_N].$$

Minimal Suppes Equal Access. *For at least one* $\tilde{s} \in \mathbb{R}_+$ *it holds true that for all* $e = (s_N, R_N) \in \mathcal{E}, z_N, z'_N \in X^N$, *if there exist* $j, k \in N$ *such that* $s_j = s_k = \tilde{s}$, *and for all* $i \in N, i \neq j, k, z_i = z'_i$, *then*

$$[\forall\, h \in \{j, k\}, z_h \in m(R_h, B(\tilde{s}, z_h)) \text{ and } z'_h \in m(R_h, B(\tilde{s}, z'_h)), \text{ and}$$

$$B(\tilde{s}, z_j) = B(\tilde{s}, z'_j) \text{ and } B(\tilde{s}, z'_k) = B(\tilde{s}, z_k)] \Rightarrow [z'_N \bar{I}(e) z_N].$$

We define another logical weakening of Hammond Equal Access by noting that, in economies where all agents have the same skill, it implies that there should be no redistribution, that is, the laisser-faire allocations are the best ones.

Laisser-Faire in Equal Skill Economies. *For all* $e = (s_N, R_N) \in \mathcal{E}$, $z_N \in Z(e)$, *if for all* $i, j \in N, s_i = s_j$ *and for all* $z'_N \in Z(e), z_N \bar{R}(e) z'_N$, *then for all* $i \in N, z_i \in m(R_i, B(s_i, (0, 0)))$.

4. Fair Social Ordering Functions

In this section, we study how to combine the conditions presented in the previous section in order to construct social ordering functions. Here is a summary of the results.

We begin by showing that it is impossible to combine compensation and equal access requirements in their strong versions (Theorems 1 and 2). This impossibility is, however, not one that makes social choice a deadlock, but, rather, it forces us to make an ethical choice as to which of these two incompatible principles should have priority over the other. And after this negative but purely introductory result, we show that by combining a strong version of one principle with a weak version of the other principle, we are able to define and characterize several social ordering functions, which nicely reflect the ethical values embodied in the various axioms (Theorems 3, 4 and 5).

One may not, however, be fully satisfied with the social ordering functions obtained in this way, as they are extremely egalitarian and rely on the leximin criterion. We then show how it is possible to obtain less extreme social ordering functions (Theorems 7 and 8).

4.1. *The Compensation-Equal Access dilemma*

Theorem 1. *No social ordering function satisfies* Hammond Compensation *and* Hammond Equal Access.

Theorem 2. *No social ordering function satisfies* Weak Pareto, Suppes Compensation *and* Suppes Equal Access.

These impossibilities are similar to results by Fleurbaey (1994) and Fleurbaey and Maniquet (1996a) which bear on allocation rules, but Theorem 2 above displays the additional feature that no inequality aversion is embodied in the axioms, and therefore reveals that the conflict between the ethical principles of compensation and equal access has nothing to do with egalitarianism.

4.2. *Social ordering functions of the leximin type*

As mentioned above, the Hammond versions of the equity properties imply an infinite inequality aversion. Not surprisingly, those properties will lead us to social ordering functions of the leximin type. But the novelty of this work is that the way in which the relative positions of the agents are compared, according to the leximin criterion, is not a priori given but is properly constructed in order to satisfy the axioms.

Defining these social ordering functions requires the following terminology. For $R \in \mathcal{R}$, and $(z_i)_{i \in N}, (z_i')_{i \in N} \in X^N$, we write

$$(z_i)_{i \in N} R_{\text{lex}} (z_i')_{i \in N}$$

to denote that the first list is weakly preferred to the second list according to the lexicographic maximin criterion applied with respect to satisfaction of preferences R (that is, the least preferred element of the first list is strictly preferred, according to R, to the least preferred element of the second list, or they are deemed equivalent but the second least preferred element of the first list is strictly preferred to the second least preferred element of the second list, and so on). Similarly, for two lists of subsets of X, say $(B_i)_{i \in N}$ and $(B_i')_{i \in N}$ belonging to a family of sets ordered by set inclusion, we write

$$(B_i)_{i \in N} \supseteq_{\text{lex}} (B_i')_{i \in N}$$

to denote that the first list is weakly preferred to the second list according to the lexicographic maximin criterion applied with respect to set inclusion.

The first ordering function we introduce is based on the following idea. If all agents had the same talent, say $\tilde{s}$, it would be nice to reduce inequalities in implicit budgets and inequalities are easily measured because all such budget sets are nested (i.e. ordered by the inclusion operation). Now, from the standpoint of compensation, whether an agent has talent $\tilde{s}$ or not is, in essence, irrelevant, and what matters is her level of satisfaction. Therefore, it makes sense to assess her relative satisfaction by measuring her implicit budget in terms of $\tilde{s}$, and to try and equalize all these budgets. Of course, this approach requires choosing one reference parameter $\tilde{s}$, because it is impossible to seek equality of implicit budgets with respect to different skill parameters at the same time, as implied by Theorem 1.

$\tilde{s}$-implicit-budget leximin function. *For all $e \in \mathcal{E}, z_N, z_N' \in X^N$,*

$$z_N \bar{R}(e) z_N' \Leftrightarrow (I\!B(\tilde{s}, R_i, z_i))_{i \in N} \supseteq_{\text{lex}} (I\!B(\tilde{s}, R_i, z_i'))_{i \in N}.$$

The preferred allocations for this social ordering function, among feasible allocations, are such that all agents' implicit budgets $I\!B(\tilde{s}, R_i, z_i)$ are equal. In the particular case $\tilde{s} = 0$, this corresponds to the Egalitarian Equivalent allocation rule studied in Fleurbaey and Maniquet (1999a).

The following theorem provides a characterization of this family of social ordering functions.

Theorem 3. *A social ordering function satisfies* Strong Pareto, Hammond Compensation, Suppes Compensation, Minimal Suppes Equal Access *and* Consistency *if and only if it is a $\tilde{s}$-implicit-budget leximin function for some $\tilde{s}$. In addition, for any $\tilde{s}$, the $\tilde{s}$-implicit-budget leximin function satisfies* Minimal Hammond Equal Access.

A corollary of the above theorem is that the axioms imply that Minimal Suppes Equal Access will be satisfied by the social ordering function in a minimal way, that is, for a unique $\tilde{s}$. Also observe that Minimal Hammond Equal Access is not needed in the characterization result: it is implied by the other axioms.

A clear ethical drawback of any $\tilde{s}$-implicit-budget leximin is that it does not always select laisser-faire allocations in economies where agents have the same skill. This raises the question of the possibility to combine compensation requirements with the axiom of Laisser Faire in Equal Skill Economies.

The following result answers this question. It pinpoints another social ordering function, evaluating bundles by reference to the budget set that would, for some skill and in the absence of any transfer (that is, in a laisser-faire allocation), give the agent the same satisfaction as the current bundle. Formally, let $\mathcal{W}$ be the class containing all sets $B(s, (0, 0))$ for some $s \geq 0$ and all sets $B(0, (0, l))$ for some $l \in [0, 1]$. Let us note that all budget sets in $\mathcal{W}$ are nested (that is, for any pair $B, B' \in \mathcal{W}$, either $B \subseteq B'$ or $B' \subseteq B$). For $z \in X, R \in \mathcal{R}$, let $W(z, R) \in \mathcal{W}$ be defined by

$$W(z, R) = \max\{A \in \mathcal{W} | zIm(\mathcal{R}, \mathcal{A})\},$$

where the maximum is taken with respect to set inclusion.

Wage-equivalent leximin function. *For all $e \in \mathcal{E}, z_N, z_N' \in X^N$,*

$$z_N \bar{R}(e) z_N' \Leftrightarrow (W(z_i, R_i))_{i \in N} \supseteq_{\text{lex}} (W(z_i', R_i))_{i \in N}.$$

The preferred allocations for this social ordering function, among feasible allocations, are such that all agents' equivalent wages $W(z_i, R_i)$ are equal. This corresponds to the Equal Wage Equivalent allocation rule studied in Fleurbaey and Maniquet (1999a).

Theorem 4. *The* wage-equivalent leximin function *satisfies* Strong Pareto, Hammond Compensation, Suppes Compensation, Laisser-Faire in Equal-Skill Economies *and* Consistency.

There are other social ordering functions satisfying the five axioms listed above. With the same kind of proof as in steps 1 and 4 of Theorem 3, however, it is possible to show that any social ordering function $\bar{R}$ satisfying these axioms also satisfies: for all $e = (s_N, R_N)$, all z_N, z'_N,

$$(0,0) \in \min\{W(z'_i, R_i)|i \in N\} \subset \min\{W(z_i, R_i)|i \in N\} \Rightarrow z_N \bar{P}(e)z'_N,$$

where the minimum is taken with respect to set inclusion.

The $\tilde{s}$-implicit-budget and wage-equivalent leximin functions satisfy the strong versions of the compensation requirements, and we now turn to a family of social ordering functions which, at the other end of the spectrum, satisfy Hammond and Suppes Equal Access.

Each ordering in the following family is parameterized by some reference preferences $\tilde{R} \in \mathcal{R}$. The comparison between two allocations, according to one such ordering, works as follows. The bundle of each agent is evaluated by the reference preferences applied to the agent's implicit budget computed on the basis of her actual skill. Then, the leximin criterion is applied to these evaluations.

$\tilde{R}$-implicit-budget leximin function. *For all* $e \in \mathcal{E}, z_N, z'_N \in X^N$,

$$[z_N \tilde{R}(e)z'_N] \Leftrightarrow (m(\tilde{R}, I\!B(s_i, R_i, z_i)))_{i \in N} \tilde{R}_{\text{lex}}(m(\tilde{R}, I\!B(s_i, R_i, z'_i)))_{i \in N}.$$

The preferred allocations for this social ordering function, among feasible allocations, are such that all agents' implicit budgets $I\!B(s_i, R_i, z_i)$ are deemed equivalent by the reference preferences $\tilde{R}$. This corresponds to the Reference Welfare Equivalent Budget allocation rules studied in Fleurbaey and Maniquet (1996a). This shows that, at least in this particular framework, the theory of equity focussing on allocation rules and the present study of social ordering functions lead to consistent results.

Theorem 5. *A social ordering function satisfies* Strong Pareto, Minimal Suppes Compensation, Hammond Equal Access, Suppes Equal Access, *and* Consistency *if and only if it is a* $\tilde{R}$-implicit-budget leximin function *for some* $\tilde{R}$. *In addition, for any* $\tilde{R} \in \mathcal{R}$, *the* $\tilde{R}$-implicit-budget leximin function *satisfies* Minimal Hammond Compensation.

Exactly as we criticized $\tilde{s}$-implicit-budget social orderings for failing to select the laisser-faire allocations in equal-skill economies, we can criticize

$\tilde{R}$-implicit-budget social orderings for failing to select the equal satisfaction allocations in equal-preference economies. Unfortunately, in this case the argument does not provide another interesting social ordering function, as stated in the next theorem.

Theorem 6. *No social ordering function satisfies* Strong Pareto, Hammond Equal Access, Equal Welfare in Equal-Preference Economies, *and* Consistency.

A similar impossibility would be reached if *Hammond Equal Access* were replaced with *Suppes Equal Access*.

4.3. *Social ordering functions of the utilitarian type*

As already mentioned above, one may prefer the Suppes versions of the properties, as they are compatible with any degree of inequality aversion. On the other hand, none of the leximin functions satisfies Continuity. The following results meet both criticisms, as they replace the Hammond type axioms with Continuity. This leads us to additive social ordering functions bearing some similarity to generalized utilitarianism. If we focus on compensation, we obtain the following family of functions. In order to define it, however, we have to introduce a few notions. We call a *valuation function* a real-valued mapping on the set $\mathcal{B} = \{B(s, z) | s \in \mathbb{R}_+, z \in X\}$. Such a function, say g, will be said to be *increasing* if for all $A, B \in \mathcal{B}, g(A) < g(B)$ whenever $A \subset B$. Its *continuity* is defined with respect to the Hausdorff distance.

$\tilde{s}$-implicit-budget generalized utilitarian function. *There exists some increasing and continuous valuation function g defined on $\mathcal{B}$ such that for all $e \in \mathcal{E}, z_N, z'_N \in X^N$,*

$$z_N \bar{R}(e) z'_N \Leftrightarrow \sum_{i \in N} g(I\!B(\tilde{s}, R_i, z_i)) \geq \sum_{i \in N} g(I\!B(\tilde{s}, R_i, z'_i)).$$

Theorem 7. *A social ordering function satisfies* Strong Pareto, Suppes Compensation, Minimal Suppes Equal Access, Consistency *and* Continuity *if and only if it is a $\tilde{s}$-implicit-budget generalized utilitarian function for some $\tilde{s}$.*

We now turn to social ordering functions that give priority to the equal access condition.

R̃-implicit-budget generalized utilitarian function. *There exists some real-valued, continuous function $\tilde{u}$ representing $\tilde{R}$ such that for all $e \in \mathcal{E}, z_N, z'_N \in X^N$,*

$$z_N \tilde{R}(e) z'_N \Leftrightarrow \sum_{i \in N} \tilde{u}(m(\tilde{R}, I\!B(s_i, R_i, z_i))) \geq \sum_{i \subset N} \tilde{u}(m(\tilde{R}, I\!B(s_i, R_i, z'_i))).$$

Theorem 8. *A social ordering function satisfies* Strong Pareto, Minimal Suppes Compensation, Suppes Equal Access, Consistency *and* Continuity *if and only if it is a $\tilde{R}$-implicit-budget generalized utilitarian function for some $\tilde{R}$.*

5. Relationship with the Literature

To the best of our knowledge, this model has not been studied in the theory of social choice in economic environments,[14] although it has a long history in the theory of fair allocation (starting with Pazner and Schmeidler (1974) at least). But it is clear that the negative results so common in the theory of social choice would essentially be preserved in this model if the same kind of approach was retained.

What makes our positive results possible is dropping the axiom of Independence of Irrelevant Alternatives (defined below). We would like to argue here that: (1) this axiom is appealing but not compelling; (2) an economic framework is especially fit to weakening this axiom; (3) the social ordering functions studied here satisfy interesting weakenings of it. Beforehand, let us recall the definition of this axiom in the current framework.

Independence of Irrelevant Alternatives. *For all $e = (s_N, R_N), e' = (s_N, R'_N) \in \mathcal{E}, z_N, z'_N \in X^N$, if for all $i \in N, z_i R_i z'_i \Leftrightarrow z_i R'_i z'_i$ and $z'_i R_i z_i \Leftrightarrow z'_i R'_i z_i$, then*

$$z_N \tilde{R}(e) z'_N \Leftrightarrow z_N \tilde{R}(e') z'_N.$$

This axiom is appealing because it makes the social comparison of two allocations depend only on how these two allocations are ranked by the agents, and this amount of information is minimal, in particular one immediately sees that with less information it would not be possible to satisfy a Pareto condition. In addition to this informational argument, which has

---

[14]See Le Breton (1997).

been widely developed in the social choice literature, this independence axiom, because it makes the social judgment depend little on the shape of individual preferences, fits well in a setting where differences in preferences are deemed irrelevant in the allocation of (access to) resources. Actually, this axiom can be shown to have a strong kinship with Equal Access. Consider the following axioms. The first one is satisfied by all leximin social ordering functions studied in this paper, and the second one by all social ordering functions.

Hammond Equal Treatment of Equals. *For all* $e = (s_N, R_N) \in \mathcal{E}, z_N,$ $z'_N \in X^N$, *if there exist* $j, k \in N$ *such that* $s_j = s_k$, *and* $R_j = R_k$, *and for all* $i \in N$ *such that* $i \neq j, k, z_i = z'_i$, *then*

$$z_j P_j z'_j P_j z'_k P_k z_k \Rightarrow z'_N \bar{P}(e) z_N.$$

Suppes Equal Treatment of Equals. *For all* $e = (s_N, R_N) \in \mathcal{E}, z_N, z'_N$ $\in X^N$, *if there exist* $j, k \in N$ *such that* $s_j = s_k$, *and* $R_j = R_k$, *and for all* $i \in N$ *such that* $i \neq j, k, z_i = z'_i$, *then*

$$z_j I_j z'_k \quad and \quad z'_j I_j z_k \Rightarrow z'_N \bar{I}(e) z_N.$$

Theorem 9. *If a social ordering function satisfies* Hammond (*resp.* Suppes) Equal Treatment of Equals and Independence of Irrelevant Alternatives, *then it satisfies* Hammond (*resp.* Suppes) Equal Access.

But, as shown above, there is a conflict between the ethical principle of equal access and the ideal of compensation, and it is not obvious that the former should always have the lead over other ethical principles, which shows that one should be cautious when endorsing the independence axiom. Moreover, if, as it turns out to be the case from Arrow's impossibility, the independence axiom is incompatible with Weak Pareto and a basic equity requirement such as anonymity,[15] then clearly one should admit that the independence axiom has to be weakened.

Weakening Independence of Irrelevant Alternatives means accepting to make use of more information about preferences than the ranking of the two options under consideration. In particular, in an economic model like ours, individuals can be compared in a meaningful way in terms of preferred labor-consumption mix, elasticity of substitution, relative size of the income/substitution effects, and so on. It seems easy to argue that such

---

[15]Anonymity means that permuting the names of the agents does not change the social ordering.

features of individual preferences are prima facie relevant to the allocation of resources.

Now, if one still endorses a view that the allocation of resources should be as little sensitive on individual preferences as compatible with other important requirements (like anonymity, compensation, etc.), one may ask for determining the minimal amount of information that is required about individual preferences. One can easily check that all social orderings analyzed in the previous section satisfy the following independence axiom, saying that indifference curves are all that matters in the comparison of two allocations.[16] For $x \in X, R \in \mathcal{R}$, let $I(x, R)$ denote the indifference hypersurface of x for preferences $R : I(x, R) = \{z \in X | x I z\}$.

Independence of Non-Indifferent Alternatives. *For all* $e = (s_N, R_N)$, $e' = (s_N, R'_N) \in \mathcal{E}, z_N, z'_N \in X^N$, *if for all* $i \in N, I(z_i, R_i) = I(z_i, R'_i)$ *and* $I(z'_i, R_i) = I(z'_i, R'_i)$, *then*

$$z_N \bar{R}(e) z'_N \Leftrightarrow z_N \bar{R}(e') z'_N.$$

In the literature, the axiom of Independence of Irrelevant Alternatives has also been given a justification in terms of feasible agenda, namely, social comparisons over a subset of alternatives (supposedly the feasible alternatives at the moment) should depend only on preferences over this subset. Of course the above criticism of the independence axiom is robust to this new interpretation. The taxonomy of individual types should not necessarily be based on their preferences on arbitrarily small subsets of alternatives. But in our framework the subset of feasible alternatives $Z(e)$ is not arbitrarily small, and, as suggested in Le Breton (1997), one can think of reformulating a weakened version of the independence axiom that refers only to this subset.

Independence of Unfeasible Bundles. *For all* $e = (s_N, R_N), e' = (s_N, R'_N) \in \mathcal{E}$, *if for all* $i \in N$, *and* $x, x' \in Z_i(e), x R_i x' \Leftrightarrow x R'_i x'$, *then for all* $z_N, z'_N \in Z(e)$,

$$z_N \bar{R}(e) z'_N \Leftrightarrow z_N \bar{R}(e') z'_N.$$

This axiom does not fit well with the idea of compensation, because the latter depends on knowing whether two agents have fully identical

---

[16]In the abstract model of social choice, this condition has been proposed by Hansson (1973), and shown to be satisfied by the Borda rule among others. In the fair division model, this condition has been introduced by Pazner (1979).

preferences, and it can be argued that when an agent is close to the boundary of $Z_i(e)$, it is reasonable to examine his or her preferences beyond $Z_i(e)$ to infer how well-off he or she is. Among the social orderings studied above, only the $\tilde{R}$-implicit budget orderings satisfy it.[17] The following theorem summarizes these results.

Theorem 10. *The $\tilde{s}$-implicit-budget leximin functions, the wage-equivalent leximin function, the $\tilde{R}$-implicit-budget leximin functions, the $\tilde{s}$-implicit-budget generalized utilitarian functions and the $\tilde{R}$-implicit-budget generalized utilitarian functions all satisfy Independence of Non-Indifferent Alternatives, but not Independence of Irrelevant Alternatives. Among them, only the $\tilde{R}$-implicit-budget leximin functions and the $\tilde{R}$-implicit-budget generalized utilitarian functions satisfy Independence of Unfeasible Bundles.*

Previous attempts to devise social orderings embodying equity principles have been made by Varian (1976), Suzumura (1981a, b, 1983) and Tadenuma (1998). But the two orderings proposed by Varian rely on utility functions, while the results obtained by Suzumura and Tadenuma are essentially negative and based on the interesting problem that no-envy (namely, for all $i, j, z_i R_i z_j$) is a property of allocations that is not preserved by Pareto-indifference, that is, one can find Pareto-indifferent allocations such that one is envy-free whereas the other has a lot of envy (for instance, everyone envies someone). Notice that our $\tilde{R}$-implicit budget leximin orderings, in every economy, select allocations that satisfy no-envy among agents having the same skill, while the other leximin orderings select allocations in which all agents with identical preferences have indifferent bundles. Both features of allocations are logical consequences of no-envy, and it is suggested in Fleurbaey and Maniquet (1996a) that they are relevant weakenings of no-envy in this model.[18]

---

[17]They even satisfy a stronger condition, namely, that one need only know agent i's preferences over bundles that are feasible for i given what the others receive.

[18]It is well known (Pazner and Schmeidler 1974) that in this model envy-free efficient allocations do not exist in general. It is shown in Fleurbaey and Maniquet (1996a) that this difficulty can be interpreted as a consequence of the conflict between compensation and equal access, and that interesting weakenings of no-envy can be proposed along these lines. We should also mention that this difficulty with no-envy has triggered a small literature on orderings of allocations based on the "quantity" of envy (Feldman and Kirman 1974, Daniel 1975, Chaudhuri 1986, Diamantaras and Thomson 1991). But the purpose of this literature is not to rank all allocations (the proposed orderings do not satisfy Weak Pareto), but only to rank Pareto-optimal allocations so as to define allocation rules that select allocations with the least "quantity" of no-envy.

It would be possible to present all of our results in a framework involving fully comparable utility functions in the definition of an economy, $e = (s_N, u_N)$, and reformulating the compensation axioms for pairs of agents having not only the same preferences, but also the same utility function ($u_j = u_k$). Hammond Compensation, in particular, would then mean that reducing inequality in *utilities* is a good thing. In this alternative presentation, therefore, ordinalism and non-comparability would not be assumed from the beginning. But it is not difficult to check that all the results would go through, and the same purely ordinal social ordering functions would be characterized.[19] This is because Equal Access axioms, not by themselves but in combination with the others, prevent the social ordering functions from making use of the available information about utilities.[20]

In conclusion to this section, we show why social ordering functions that rank all allocations are not really more difficult to construct than allocation rules that only select a first-best subset of allocations. Defining interesting allocation rules actually requires the same kind of departure from Arrow's approach, namely, weakening the independence condition.[21] Let us reformulate the independence condition in order to have an axiom that applies to allocation rules. This condition says that when individual preferences over two allocations are unchanged, it cannot be that only the first one is selected beforehand whereas only the second one is selected afterward.

Independence of Irrelevant Alternatives for allocation rules. *For all $e = (s_N, R_N), e' = (s_N, R'_N) \in \mathcal{E}, z_N \in S(e), z'_N \in Z(e)\backslash S(e)$, if for all $i \in N, z_i R_i z'_i \Leftrightarrow z_i R'_i z'_i$ and $z'_i R_i z_i \Leftrightarrow z'_i R'_i z_i$, then either $z_N \in S(e')$ or $z'_N \in Z(e')\backslash S(e')$.*

It is easy to check that essentially all of the allocation rules of the literature of fair allocation fail to satisfy this condition. For instance, the allocation rules derived from the social ordering functions studied in this paper (by selecting the first-best allocations in every economy) all violate this condition.

---

[19]This alternative presentation with utility functions is fully developed, for a different but related framework, in Fleurbaey and Maniquet (1999b).

[20]As it is well known, a similar presentation with utilities is possible for Arrow's theorem, and Arrow's Independence of Irrelevant Alternatives alone then implies ordinalism and non-comparability.

[21]This was already noticed in Fleurbaey (1996) and Roemer (1996).

6. Conclusion

The following table lists, for each social ordering function studied in this paper, the axioms it satisfies.

Several lessons can be drawn from this analysis. The first one is that it is possible to construct ethically appealing social orderings based only on ordinal, non comparable, information about preferences. Such a construction is possible because we accept to take into account the shape of individual indifference curves, as explained in the previous section.

The one-input-one-output production model we studied is an example, and fair social orderings could (and, to our opinion, should) also be studied in other economic models, such as the canonical models of fair division, public good provision, assignments, etc. Moreover, the ethical values of compensation and equal access analyzed here are examples, and other equity notions could be studied in this model and other models as

Table 7.1. Summary of solutions and the axioms they satisfy.

	$\tilde{s}$-IBLF	EWLF	$\tilde{R}$-IBLF	$\tilde{s}$-IBGUF	$\tilde{R}$-IBGUF
Weak Pareto	+	+	+	+	+
Strong Pareto	+	+	+	+	+
Hammond Compensation	+	+	−	−	−
Suppes Compensation	+	+	−	+	−
Min. Hammond Comp.	+	+	+	−	−
Min. Suppes Comp.	+	+	+	+	+
Eq. Welf. Eq. Pref. Econ.	+	+	−	−	−
Hammond Eq. Access	−	−	+	−	−
Suppes Eq. Access	−	−	+	−	+
Min. Hammond Eq. Access	+	−	+	−	−
Min. Suppes Eq. Access	+	−	+	+	+
Lais.-Faire Eq. Skill Econ.	−	+	+	−	−
Consistency	+	+	+	+	+
Continuity	−	−	−	+	+
Ind. Irr. Alternatives	−	−	−	−	−
Ind. Non-Ind. Alternatives	+	+	+	+	+
Ind. Unfeasible Bundles	−	−	+	−	+

well. Nonetheless, we consider that the social ordering functions proposed here may serve as benchmarks for ethical discussions in this particular context.

The main families of social ordering functions characterized in this paper involve reference parameters ($\tilde{s}$ or $\tilde{R}$). We have not discussed how to select those parameters, but we would like to emphasize that the presence of such parameters is not a characteristic feature of the approach. For instance, the Wage Equivalent leximin function discussed in Theorem 4 does not involve any reference parameter. In addition, the introduction of additional axioms in Theorems 3 and 5 could impose a particular choice of $\tilde{s}$ or $\tilde{R}$.

One restriction of our model is that returns to scale are assumed to be constant. This restriction may be justified for instance if one interprets the skill parameters s_i as wage rates on the labor market of a small open economy. But one may ask how our analysis would extend to the case on non constant returns to scale (or endogenous wages). The main consequence for our analysis would be that the implicit budgets would no longer have exogenous or even constant slope, and the ethical analysis of the equal access principle developed here would no longer be valid, and would have to be properly adapted.

To end up, we would like to emphasize again an important consequence of the general possibility results presented here. The theory of second best allocations and optimal taxation usually relies on the assumption that the planner has a complete ranking of allocations, representing the social objective. Our results, therefore, prove that it is possible to develop a theory of second best allocations by building social orderings based on explicit ethical values, without relying on cardinal or comparable notions of utility, and also without limiting oneself to efficiency considerations. We hope that this approach will make the theory of social choice more suitable to applications in public economics than it has been so far.

Appendix: Proofs and Independence of the Axioms

We give in this appendix the proof of the results and we show that the axioms involved in our four characterization results are independent. That is, we provide examples of ordering functions satisfying all but one axioms, for each axiom in each characterization.

Theorem 1

Proof.

Let us consider $e = ((s, s', s', s), (R, R, R', R')) \in \mathcal{E}$ and $z^a, z^b, z^c, z^d,$ $\bar{z}^a, \bar{z}^b, \bar{z}^c, \bar{z}^d \in X$ satisfying the following conditions: $s < s'$, and

$$z^a P z^b P z^c P z^d, \tag{1}$$

$$\bar{z}^a P' \bar{z}^b P' \bar{z}^c P' \bar{z}^d, \tag{2}$$

$$B(s, \bar{z}^c) \supset B(s, \bar{z}^d) \supset B(s, z^a) \supset B(s, z^b), \tag{3}$$

$$B(s', z^c) \supset B(s', z^d) \supset B(s', \bar{z}^a) \supset B(s', \bar{z}^b), \tag{4}$$

$$\forall t \in \{a, b\}, \quad z^t \in m(R, B(s, z^t)) \quad \text{and} \quad \bar{z}^t \in m(R', B(s', \bar{z}^t)), \tag{5}$$

$$\forall t \in \{c, d\}, \quad z^t \in m(R, B(s', z^t)) \quad \text{and} \quad \bar{z}^t \in m(R', B(s, \bar{z}^t)). \tag{6}$$

Such an economy exists, as exemplified by Figure 3.

By *Hammond Compensation* and condition (1), $(z^b, z^c, \bar{z}^b, \bar{z}^d) \bar{P}(e)(z^a,$ $z^d, \bar{z}^b, \bar{z}^d)$. By *Hammond Equal Access* and conditions (4), (5) and (6),

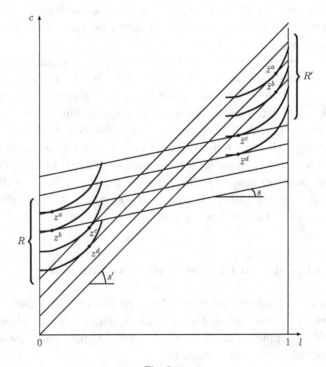

Fig. 3.

$(z^b, z^d, \bar{z}^a, \bar{z}^d)\bar{P}(e)(z^b, z^c, \bar{z}^b, \bar{z}^d)$. By *Hammond Compensation* and condition (2), $(z^b, z^d, \bar{z}^b, \bar{z}^c)\bar{P}(e)(z^b, z^d, \bar{z}^a, \bar{z}^d)$. By *Hammond Equal Access* and conditions (3), (5) and (6), $(z^a, z^d, \bar{z}^b, \bar{z}^d)\bar{P}(e)(z^b, z^d, \bar{z}^b, \bar{z}^c)$. By transitivity, $(z^a, z^d, \bar{z}^b, \bar{z}^d)\bar{P}(e)(z^a, z^d, \bar{z}^b, \bar{z}^d)$, the desired contradiction. $\square$

By a similar proof, one can show that no social ordering function satisfies *Hammond Compensation* and *Suppes Equal Access,* or *Suppes Compensation* and *Hammond Equal Access.*

Theorem 2

Proof.
Let us consider $e = ((s, s', s', s), (R, R, R', R')) \in \mathcal{E}$ and z^a, z^d, z^c, z^d, $z^e, z^f, \bar{z}^a, \bar{z}^b, \bar{z}^c, \bar{z}^d, \bar{z}^e, \bar{z}^f \in X$, satisfying the following conditions: $s < s'$, and

$$z^a P z^b P z^c P z^d P z^e P z^f, \tag{7}$$

$$\bar{z}^a P' \bar{z}^b P' \bar{z}^c P' \bar{z}^d P' \bar{z}^e P' \bar{z}^f, \tag{8}$$

$$B(s, z^b) = B(s, \bar{z}^a) \quad \text{and} \quad B(s, z^c) = B(s, \bar{z}^f), \tag{9}$$

$$B(s', z^f) = B(s', \bar{z}^c) \quad \text{and} \quad B(s', z^a) = B(s', \bar{z}^b), \tag{10}$$

$$\forall t \in \{a, f\}, \quad z^t \in m(R, B(s', z^t)) \quad \text{and} \quad \bar{z}^t \in m(R', B(s, \bar{z}^t)), \tag{11}$$

$$\forall t \in \{b, c\}, \quad z^t \in m(R, B(s, z^t)) \quad \text{and} \quad \bar{z}^t \in m(R', B(s', \bar{z}^t)). \tag{12}$$

Such an economy exists, as exemplified by Figure 4.

By *Weak Pareto* and conditions (7) and (8), $(z^a, z^d, \bar{z}^c, \bar{z}^e)\bar{P}(e)(z^b, z^e, \bar{z}^d, \bar{z}^f)$. By *Suppes Compensation,* $(z^d, z^a, \bar{z}^c, \bar{z}^e)\bar{I}(e)(z^a, z^d, \bar{z}^c, \bar{z}^e)$. By *Suppes Equal Access* and conditions (10), (11) and (12), $(z^d, z^f, \bar{z}^b, \bar{z}^e)\bar{I}(e)$ $(z^d, z^a, \bar{z}^c, \bar{z}^e)$. By *Suppes Compensation,* $(z^d, z^f, \bar{z}^e, \bar{z}^b)\bar{I}(e)(z^d, z^f, \bar{z}^b, \bar{z}^e)$. By *Weak Pareto* and conditions (7) and (8), $(z^c, z^e, \bar{z}^d, \bar{z}^a)\bar{P}(e)(z^d, z^f, \bar{z}^e, \bar{z}^b)$. By *Suppes Equal Access* and conditions (9), (11) and (12), $(z^b, z^e, \bar{z}^d, \bar{z}^f)\bar{I}(e)(z^c, z^e, \bar{z}^d, \bar{z}^a)$. By transitivity, $(z^b, z^e, \bar{z}^d, \bar{z}^f)\bar{P}(e)(z^b, z^e, \bar{z}^d, \bar{z}^f)$, the desired contradiction. $\square$

Notice that Figures 3 and 4 are constructed (for the sake of clarity) in such a way that some allocations involved in the proofs are not feasible. It should be clear, however, that the impossibility does not rest on considering alternatives out of the feasible set. Bundles and indifference curves in those examples could all be translated downwards so that all allocations become feasible.

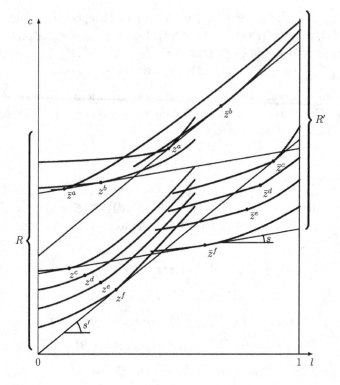

Fig. 4.

Theorem 3

Proof. We omit the straightforward proof that this social ordering function satisfies the axioms listed, and focus on the characterization part. Let $\bar{R}$ be a social ordering function satisfying the axioms, and choose any $\tilde{s} \in \mathbb{R}_+$ with respect to which $\bar{R}$ satisfies Minimal Suppes Equal Access.

Step 1. Consider two allocations z_N, z'_N and two agents j and k such that for all $i \neq j, k, z_i = z'_i$. Let

$$B_m = \min\{I\!\!B(\tilde{s}, R_j, z_j), I\!\!B(\tilde{s}, R_j, z'_j), I\!\!B(\tilde{s}, R_k, z'_k)\},$$

where the minimum is taken with respect to set inclusion. Let us assume, moreover, that $I\!\!B(\tilde{s}, R_k, z_k) \subset B_m$. If $z'_j R_j z_j$, then, by *Strong Pareto*, $z'_N \bar{P}(e) z_N$. Consider now the case $z_j P_j z'_j$, and assume that $z_N \bar{R}(e) z'_N$. We will derive a contradiction.

Let $e' = (s_{\{j,k,a,b\}}, R_{\{j,k,a,b\}}) \in \mathcal{E}$ and $z_a, z_b, z'_a, z'_b \in X$ be such that $s_a = s_b = \tilde{s}, R_a = R_j, R_b = R_k$, and

$$B(\tilde{s}, z_a) = B(\tilde{s}, z'_b) \quad \text{and} \quad B(\tilde{s}, z'_a) = B(\tilde{s}, z_b), \tag{13}$$

$$\mathbb{B}(\tilde{s}, R_k, z_k) \subset B(\tilde{s}, z_a) \subset B(\tilde{s}, z_b) \subset B_m, \tag{14}$$

$$\forall i \in \{a, b\}, \quad z_i \in m(R_i, B(\tilde{s}, z_i)) \quad \text{and} \quad z'_i \in m(R_i, B(\tilde{s}, z'_i)). \tag{15}$$

As $z_N \bar{R}(e) z'_N$, by *Consistency*, $(z_j, z_k) \bar{R}(s_{\{j,k\}}, R_{\{j,k\}})(z'_j, z'_k)$. By *Consistency* again, $(z_j, z_k, z_a, z_b) \bar{R}(e')(z'_j, z'_k, z_a, z_b)$. By *Hammond Compensation*, and conditions (14) and (15), $(z'_j, z_k, z'_a, z_b) \bar{P}(e')(z_j, z_k, z_a, z_b)$. By *Hammond Compensation* and *Strong Pareto*,[22] and conditions (14) and (15), $(z'_j, z'_k, z'_a, z'_b) \bar{P}(e')$ (z'_j, z_k, z'_a, z_b). By transitivity, $(z'_j, z'_k, z'_a, z'_b) \bar{P}(e')$ (z'_j, z'_k, z'_a, z_b). By transitivity, $(z'_j, z'_k, z'_a, z_b) \bar{P}(e')(z'_j, z'_k, z_a, z_b)$, which violates *Minimal Suppes Equal Access*, in view of conditions (13) and (15). This proves that $z'_N \bar{P}(e) z_N$.

Step 2. Consider two allocations z_N, z'_N and two agents j and k such that for all $i \neq j, k, z_i = z'_i$. Assume moreover that

$$\mathbb{B}(\tilde{s}, R_j, z_j) = \mathbb{B}(\tilde{s}, R_k, z'_k) \supset \mathbb{B}(\tilde{s}, R_j, z'_j) = \mathbb{B}(\tilde{s}, R_k, z_k). \tag{16}$$

Assume that $z_N \bar{P}(e) z'_N$. Then by *Consistency*, $(z_j, z_k) \bar{P}(s_{\{j,k\}}, R_{\{j,k\}})$ (z'_j, z'_k). Let $e' = (s_{\{j,k,a,b\}}, R_{\{j,k,a,b\}}) \in \mathcal{E}$ and $z_a, z'_a, z_b, z'_b \in X$, be such that $s_a = s_b = \tilde{s}, R_a = R_j, R_b = R_k$, and

$$\forall i \in \{a, b\}, \quad z_i \in m(R_i, B(\tilde{s}, z_i)) \quad \text{and} \quad z'_i \in m(R_i B(\tilde{s}, z'_i)), \tag{17}$$

$$z_a I_j z_j, \quad z'_a I_j z'_j, \quad z_b I_k z_k, \quad z'_b I_k z'_k. \tag{18}$$

By *Consistency*, $(z_j, z_k, z'_a, z'_b) \bar{P}(e')(z'_j, z'_k, z'_a, z'_b)$. By *Strong Pareto* and condition (18), $(z_a, z_b, z'_a, z'_b) \bar{I}(e')(z_j, z_k, z'_a, z'_b)$. By *Suppes Compensation*, $(z'_a, z_b, z_a, z'_b) \bar{I}(e')(z_a, z_b, z'_a, z'_b)$, and $(z'_a, z'_b, z_a, z_b) \bar{I}(e')(z'_a, z_b, z_a, z'_b)$, and by *Strong Pareto* and condition (18), $(z'_j, z'_k, z_a, z_b) \bar{I}(e')(z'_a, z'_b, z_a, z_b)$. By transitivity, $(z'_j, z'_k, z_a, z_b) \bar{P}(e')(z'_j, z'_k, z'_a, z'_b)$, violating *Minimal Suppes Equal Access*, in view of (16), (17) and (18). Therefore $z'_N \bar{R}(e) z_N$, and by symmetry of the argument in j and k, $z'_N \bar{I}(e) z_N$.

---

[22]This argument could be divided in two subarguments, as *Hammond Compensation* is used first to go from (z'_j, z_k, z'_a, z_b) to $(z'_j, z''_k, z'_a, z'_b)$ for some z''_k having the property that $z'_b P_k z''_k P_k z_k$, and *Strong Pareto* is then used to go from $(z'_j, z''_k, z'_a, z'_b)$ to (z'_j, z'_k, z'_a, z'_b). We combine those two simple subarguments to avoid additional notation. The same combination is used in the proof of Theorem 5.

Step 3. Consider two allocations z_N, z'_N such that $(I\!B(\tilde{s}, R_i, z_i))_{i \in N} = \text{lex}(I\!B(\tilde{s}, R_i, z_i))_{i \in N}$. There exists a permutation π on N such that for all $i \in N$, $I\!B(\tilde{s}, R_i, z_{\pi(i)}) = I\!B(\tilde{s}, R_i, z_i)$. Since a permutation can be decomposed into a finite number of transpositions, by repeated application of Step 2, one has $z'_N \bar{I}(e) z_N$.

Step 4. The rest of the proof parallels that of Hammond (1976). Consider two allocations $z_N, \bar{z}'_N$ such that $(I\!B(\tilde{s}, R_i, z_i))_{i \in N} \supset_{\text{lex}} (I\!B(\tilde{s}, R_i, z'_i))_{i \in N}$. Take $\bar{z}_N, \bar{z}'_N \in X^N$ such that

$$(I\!B(\tilde{s}, R_i, \bar{z}_i))_{i \in N} =_{\text{lex}} (I\!B(\tilde{s}, R_i, z_i))_{i \in N}$$

$$(I\!B(\tilde{s}, R_i, \bar{z}_i))_{i \in N} =_{\text{lex}} (I\!B(\tilde{s}, R_i, z'_i))_{i \in N},$$

and such that for all $i, j \in N$ with $i < j$,

$$I\!B(\tilde{s}, R_i, \bar{z}_i) \subseteq I\!B(\tilde{s}, R_i, \bar{z}_j) \quad \text{and} \quad I\!B(\tilde{s}, R_i, \bar{z}'_i) \subseteq I\!B(\tilde{s}, R_i, \bar{z}'_j).$$

Since $(I\!B(\tilde{s}, R_i, \bar{z}_i))_{i \in N} \supset_{\text{lex}} (I\!B(\tilde{s}, R_i, \bar{z}'_i))_{i \in N}$, there is $k \in N$ such that:

[1] $\bar{z}_k P_k \bar{z}'_k$;
[2] $\forall i < k, I\!B(\tilde{s}, R_i, \bar{z}_i) = I\!B(\tilde{s}, R_i, \bar{z}'_i)$ (and therefore $\bar{z}_i I_i \bar{z}'_i$);
[3] $\forall j > k, I\!B(\tilde{s}, R_k, \bar{z}'_k) \subset I\!B(\tilde{s}, R_j, \bar{z}_j)$.

By appropriately choosing $\bar{z}_N, \bar{z}'_N$, one can moreover have $\bar{z}_i = \bar{z}'_i$ for all $i < k$. We now have two allocations such that, among the agents who are not indifferent, agent k has an implicit budget in $\bar{z}'_N$ which is strictly lower than the other agents' implicit budgets in both allocations. The rest of the proof consists in applying Step 1 repeatedly by slightly moving up agent k's implicit budget and pulling down the other agents' budgets. After that, all agents have an implicit budget lower than or equal to theirs in $\bar{z}_N$.

Let $L = \{j \in N | \bar{z}'_j P_j \bar{z}_j\}$. If $L = \emptyset$, then $\bar{z}_N \bar{P}(e) \bar{z}'_N$ by *Strong Pareto*. If not, give a number from 1 to $|L|$ to agents in L, denoted $v(j)$, and choose $|L|$ allocations $z_N^{(n)}$, for $n = 1, \ldots, |L|$, defined by: for all $j \in N \backslash (L \cup \{k\})$, $z_j^{(n)} = \bar{z}'_j$; for all $j \in L, z_j^{(n)} = \bar{z}_j$ if $v(j) \le n$, and $z_j^{(n)} = \bar{z}'_j$ otherwise; and

$$\min\{I\!B(\tilde{s}, R_i, z_i) | i \in L \cup \{k\}\} \supset I\!B(\tilde{s}, R_k, z_k^{(|L|)})$$

$$\supset \cdots \supset I\!B(\tilde{s}, R_k, z_k^{(1)}) \supset I\!B(\tilde{s}, R_k, \bar{z}'_k).$$

By repeated application of Step 1, $z_N^{(|L|)} \bar{R}(e) z_N^{(|L|-1)} \bar{R}(e) \ldots \bar{R}(e) z_N^{(1)}$ $\bar{R}(e) \bar{z}'_N$. By *Strong Pareto*, $\bar{z}_N \bar{P}(e) z_N^{(|L|)}$. By transitivity, $\bar{z}_N \bar{P}(e) \bar{z}'_N$, so that, by step 3, $z_N \bar{P}(e) z'_N$. $\qquad \square$

Examples of social ordering functions satisfying all the axioms but:

1. (a) *Strong Pareto*. Replace the leximin criterion with the lexicographic minimax, which says that a distribution is at least as good as another one if its maximum is lower, or they are equal and the second highest value is lower, or ... or they are all equal.

   (b) *Hammond Compensation*. Any $\tilde{s}$-implicit-budget generalized utilitarian ordering function.

   (c) *Suppes Compensation*. Let $\bar{R}$ be defined by: for all $e \in \mathcal{E}, z_N, z'_N \in X^N, z_N \bar{P}(e) z'_N$ if

   $$(I\!B(\tilde{s}, R_i, z_i))_{i \in N} \supset_{\text{lex}} (I\!B(\tilde{s}, R_i, z'_i))_{i \in N},$$

   or if

   $$(I\!B(\tilde{s}, R_i, z_i))_{i \in N} =_{\text{lex}} (I\!B(\tilde{s}, R_i, z'_i))_{i \in N}$$

   and there exist $k, k' \in N$ with $s_k < s_{k'}$ such that

   $$\forall i \neq k, \quad I\!B(\tilde{s}, R_k, z_k) \subset I\!B(\tilde{s}, R_i, z_i),$$
   $$\forall i \neq k', \quad I\!B(\tilde{s}, R_{k'}, z'_{k'}) \subset I\!B(\tilde{s}, R_i, z'_i).$$

   In all other cases $z'_N \bar{I}(e) z_N$.

   (d) *Minimal Suppes Equal Access*. Let $\bar{R}$ be defined by: for all $e \in \mathcal{E}, z_N, z'_N \in X^N, z_N \bar{P}(e) z'_N$ if

   $$(I\!B(\tilde{s}, R_i, z_i))_{i \in N} \supset_{\text{lex}} (I\!B(\tilde{s}, R_i, z'_i))_{i \in N},$$

   or if

   $$(I\!B(\tilde{s}, R_i, z_i))_{i \in N} =_{\text{lex}} (I\!B(\tilde{s}, R_i, z'_i))_{i \in N},$$

   and there exist $k, k' \in N$ with $R_k \succ R_{k'}$ such that

   $$\forall i \neq k, \quad I\!B(\tilde{s}, R_k, z_k) \subset I\!B(\tilde{s}, R_i, z_i),$$
   $$\forall i \neq k', \quad I\!B(\tilde{s}, R_{k'}, z'_{k'}) \subset I\!B(\tilde{s}, R_i, z'_i).$$

   where $\succ$ is an asymmetric ordering on $\mathcal{R}$. In all other cases $z'_N \bar{I}(e) z_N$.

   (e) *Consistency*. Let $\bar{R}$ coincide with some $\tilde{s}$-implicit-budget leximin function on any economy $e = (s_N, R_N)$ such that there is i with $s_i = \tilde{s}$ and with some $\tilde{s}'$-implicit-budget leximin function, with $\tilde{s}' \neq \tilde{s}$ in all other economies.

Theorem 5

Proof. We omit the proof that the axioms are satisfied by the social ordering function. Let $\bar{R}$ be a social ordering function satisfying the axioms, and choose any $\tilde{R} \in \mathcal{R}$ with respect to which $\bar{R}$ satisfies *Minimal Suppes Compensation.*

Step 1. Consider $e \in \mathcal{E}, z_N, z_N' \in X^N$ and $j, k \in N$ such that for all $i \neq j, k, z_i = z_i'$. Let

$$\tilde{Z} = m(\tilde{R}, I\!\!B(s_j, R_j, z_j)) \cup m(\tilde{R}, I\!\!B(s_j, R_j, z_j')) \cup m(\tilde{R}, I\!\!B(s_k, R_k, z_k'))$$

and $\tilde{z} \in \tilde{Z}$ be such that for all $\tilde{z} \in \tilde{Z}, z\tilde{R}\tilde{z}$. In words, $\tilde{Z}$ is the union of the best bundles for $\tilde{R}$ in the three budgets, and $\tilde{z}$ is one the least preferred in these. Assume that

$$\tilde{z}\tilde{P}m(\tilde{R}, I\!\!B(s_k, R_k, z_k)). \tag{19}$$

If $z_j' R_j z_j$, then, by *Strong Pareto*, $z_N' \bar{P}(e) z_N$. Assume that $z_j P_j z_j'$ whereas $z_N \tilde{R}(e) z_N'$. Then by *Consistency*, $(z_j, z_k)\bar{P}(s_{\{j,k\}}, R_{\{j,k\}})(z_j', z_k')$.

Let $e' = (s_{\{j,k,a,b\}}, R_{\{j,k,a,b\}})$ be such that $R_a = R_b = \tilde{R}$, and $s_a = s_j, s_b = s_k$. Let $z_a, z_b, z_a', z_b' \in X$ be such that:

$$\tilde{z}\tilde{P}z_b\tilde{I}z_a'\tilde{P}z_a\tilde{I}z_b'\tilde{P}m(\tilde{R}, I\!\!B(s_k, R_k, z_k)), \tag{20}$$

$$\forall i \in \{a, b\}, \quad z_i \in m(R_i, B(s_i, z_i)) \quad \text{and} \quad z_i' \in m(R_i, B(s_i, z_i')). \tag{21}$$

By *Consistency*, $(z_j, z_k, z_a, z_b)\bar{P}(e')(z_j', z_k', z_a, z_b)$. By conditions (19) and (20), $m(\tilde{R}, I, B(s_j, R_j, z_j'))\tilde{R}\tilde{z}\tilde{P}z_a'$, so that $I\!\!B(s_j, R_j, z_j') \supset I\!\!B(s_a, R_a, z_a')$. Therefore, by *Hammond Equal Access* and (21), $(z_j', z_k, z_a', z_b)\bar{P}(e') (z_j, z_k, z_a, z_b)$. Similarly by *Hammond Equal Access* and *Strong Pareto,*[23] $(z_j', z_k', z_a', z_b')\bar{P}(e')(z_j', z_k, z_a', z_b')$. By *Strong Pareto* and condition (20), $(z_j', z_k', z_b, z_a)\bar{I}(e')(z_j', z_k', z_a', z_b')$. By transitivity, $(z_j', z_k', z_b, z_a)\bar{P} (e')(z_j', z_k', z_a, z_b)$, which violates *Minimal Suppes Compensation.* Therefore $z_N' \bar{P}(e) z_N$.

Step 2. Consider $z_N, z_N' \in X^N$ and $j, k \in N$ such that for all $i \neq j, k, z_i = z_i'$. Assume moreover that

$$m(\tilde{R}, I\!\!B(s_j, R_j, z_j))\tilde{I}m(\tilde{R}, I\!\!B(s_k, R_k, z_k'))$$

$$\tilde{P}m(\tilde{R}, I\!\!B(s_k, R_k, z_k))\tilde{I}m(\tilde{R}, I\!\!B(s_j, R_j, z_j')),$$

---

[23]There is an intermediary step, similar to the one explained in the preceding footnote.

whereas $z_N \bar{P}(e) z'_N$. Then by *Consistency*, $(z_j, z_k) \bar{P}(s_{\{j,k\}}, R_{\{j,k\}})(z'_j, z'_k)$. Let $z_j^*, z_k^*, z_j'^*, z_k'^* \in X$ satisfy

$$\forall i \in \{j, k\}, \quad z_i^* \in m(R_i, I\!\!B(s_i, R_i, z_i)),$$

$$\forall i \in \{j, k\}, \quad z_i'^* \in m(R_i, I\!\!B(s_i, R_i, z'_i)).$$

Let $e' = (s_{\{j,k,a,b\}}, R_{\{j,k,a,b\}}) \in \mathcal{E}$ be defined by $R_a = R_b = \tilde{R}$, and $s_a = s_j$, $s_b = s_k$. Let $z_a, z_b, z'_a, z'_b \in X$ be such that:

$$z_a \in m(\tilde{R}, B(s_j, z_j^*)), \tag{22}$$

$$z'_a \in m(\tilde{R}, B(s_j, z_j'^*)), \tag{23}$$

$$z_b \in m(\tilde{R}, B(s_k, z_k^*)), \tag{24}$$

$$z'_b \in m(\tilde{R}, B(s_k, z_k'^*)), \tag{25}$$

Note that, by construction, $z_a \tilde{I} z'_b$ and $z'_a \tilde{I} z_b$. By *Consistency*, $(z_j, z_k, z'_a, z'_b) \bar{P}(e')(z'_j, z'_k, z'_a, z'_b)$. By *Strong Pareto*, $(z_j^*, z_k^*, z'_a, z'_b) \bar{P}(e')(z_j'^*, z_k'^*, z'_a, z'_b)$. By *Suppes Equal Access* and conditions (4) and (5), $(z_j'^*, z_k^*, z_a, z'_b) \bar{I}(e')$ $(z_j^*, z_k^*, z'_a, z'_b)$. By *Suppes Equal Access* and conditions (24) and (25), $(z_j'^*, z_k'^*, z_a, z_b) \bar{I}(e')(z_j'^*, z_k^*, z_a, z'_b)$. By *Strong Pareto*, $(z_j'^*, z_k'^*, z'_b, z'_a) \bar{I}(e')$ $(z_j'^*, z_k'^*, z_a, z_b)$. By transitivity, $(z_j^*, z_k^*, z'_b, z'_a) \bar{P}(e')(z_j'^*, z_k'^*, z'_a, z'_b)$, violating *Minimal Suppes Compensation*. Therefore $z'_N \bar{R}(e) z_N$. By symmetry of the argument, $z'_N \bar{I}(e) z_N$.

The rest of the proof is similar to Steps 3 and 4 in the proof of Theorem 3. □

Examples of social ordering functions satisfying all the axioms but:

2. (a) *Strong Pareto*. A similar example as in 1(a) above.
   (b) *Minimal Suppes Compensation*: Let $\bar{R}$ be defined by: for all $e \in \mathcal{E}, z_N, z'_N \in X^N, z_N \bar{P}(e) z'_N$ if

$$(m(\tilde{R}, I\!\!B(s_i, R_i, z_i)))_{i \in N} \tilde{P}_{\text{lex}}(m(\tilde{R}, I\!\!B(s_i, R_i, z'_i)))_{i \in N}$$

   or if

$$(m(\tilde{R}, I\!\!B(s_i, R_i, z_i)))_{i \in N} \tilde{R}_{\text{lex}}(m(\tilde{R}, I\!\!B(s_i, R_i, z'_i)))_{i \in N}$$

and there exist $k, k' \in N$ with $s_k < s_{k'}$ such that

$$\forall i \neq k, \quad m(\tilde{R}, \mathbb{B}(s_i, R_i, z_i))\tilde{P}m(\tilde{R}, \mathbb{B}(s_i, R_i, z_i)),$$
$$\forall i \neq k', \quad m(\tilde{R}, \mathbb{B}(s_i, R_i, z_i'))\tilde{P}m(\tilde{R}, \mathbb{B}(s_i, R_i, z_i')).$$

In all other cases $z_N' \tilde{I}(e) z_N$.

(c) *Hammond Equal Access.* Any $\tilde{R}$-implicit-budget generalized utilitarian function.

(d) *Suppes Equal Access.* A similar example as in 1(d) and 2(b) above.

(e) *Consistency.* A similar example as in 1(e) above.

Theorem 6

Proof. Consider $e = ((s, s', s, s'), (R, R, R', R')) \in \mathcal{E}, z_i, z_i' \in X$, for $i \in \{1, \ldots, 4\}$, and $c, c', \varepsilon \in \mathbb{R}_{++}$ such that

$$z_1 \in m(R, B(s, (0, c))), \tag{26}$$

$$z_1' \in m(R, B(s, (0, c + \varepsilon))), \tag{27}$$

$$z_2 \in m(R, B(s', (0, \neg c))), \tag{28}$$

$$z_2' \in m(R, B(s', (0, -c - \varepsilon))), \tag{29}$$

$$z_3 \in m(R', B(s', (0, c'))), \tag{30}$$

$$z_3' \in m(R', B(s', (0, c' - \varepsilon))), \tag{31}$$

$$z_4 \in m(R', B(s', (0, -c'))), \tag{32}$$

$$z_4' \in m(R', B(s', (0, -c' + \varepsilon))), \tag{33}$$

$$z_1 I z_2 \quad \text{and} \quad z_3 I' z_4. \tag{34}$$

Assume also that preferences R and R' are quasi-linear with respect to consumption. Such an economy exists, as exemplified in Figure 5.

By (26) and (28), (z_1, z_2) is Pareto-optimal in the subeconomy $((s_1, s_2), (R_1, R_2))$, and, by (34), it equalizes satisfaction. In a similar way, by (30) and (32), (z_3, z_4) is Pareto-optimal in the subeconomy $((s_3, s_4), (R_3, R_4))$, and, by (34), it equalizes satisfaction. Since, by (27) and (29) (resp. by (31) and (33)), (z_1', z_2') (resp. (z_3', z_4') is feasible in economy $((s_1, s_2), (R_1, R_2))$ (resp. $((s_3, s_4), (R_3, R_4))$, by *Equal Welfare in Equal Preference Economies, Strong Pareto* and *Consistency,* $(z_1, z_2, z_3', z_4')\bar{R}(e)$ (z_1', z_2', z_3', z_4') and $(z_1, z_2, z_3, z_4)\bar{R}(e)(z_1, z_2, z_3', z_4')$. By *Hammond Equal*

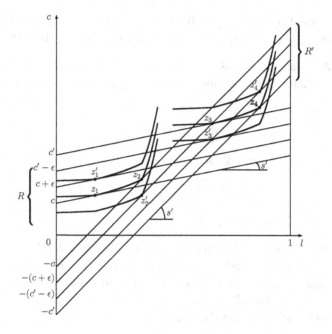

Fig. 5.

Access and Equations (28), (29), (32) and (33), $(z_1, z_2', z_3, z_4')\bar{P}(e)$ (z_1, z_2, z_3, z_4). By *Hammond Equal Access* and Equations (26), (27), (30) and (31), $(z_1', z_2', z_3', z_4')\bar{P}(e)(z_1, z_2', z_3, z_4')$. By transitivity, $(z_1', z_2', z_3', z_4')\bar{P}(e)(z_1', z_2', z_3', z_4')$, the desired contradiction. $\square$

Theorem 7

Proof. We omit the straightforward proof of the "if" part, and focus on the "only if" part. We begin with the following lemmas.

Lemma 1. *If a social ordering function $\bar{R}$ satisfies Strong Pareto, Consistency and Continuity, then for all $e = (s_N, R_n) \in \mathcal{E}$, there are $|N|$ continuous functions $g_i^e : X \to \mathbb{R}$ for $i \in N$, such that for all $z_N, z_N' \in X^N$,*

$$z_N \bar{R}(e) z_N' \Leftrightarrow \sum_{i \in N} g_i^e(z_i) \geq \sum_{i \in N} g_i^e(z_i').$$

Proof. This is a direct application of Debreu (1959)'s Theorem 3 on additive representation of separable preferences. By *Consistency*, all the arguments of $\bar{R}$ are independent. By *Strong Pareto* and our assumptions on $\mathcal{R}$, the arguments of $\bar{R}$ are essential. By *Consistency*, we can drop the requirement on the number of arguments. By *Continuity*, we get the result. □

Lemma 2. *For any $R \in \mathcal{R}$, and any continuous function u representing R, there is exactly one valuation function h defined on $\mathcal{B}$ which satisfies the condition*

$$h(\mathbb{B}(s, R, z)) = u(z)$$

for all $s \in \mathbb{R}_+$ and all $z \in X$. It is defined by

$$h(B) = \max\{u(x)|x \in B\}$$

and is continuous and increasing.

Proof. Let h be a valuation function satisfying $h(\mathbb{B}(s, R, z)) = u(z)$. For any $B \in \mathcal{B}$, Let $s \in \mathbb{R}_+$ and $z \in X$ be such that $B = B(s, z)$. Take $z' \in X$ such that $u(z') = \max\{u(x)|x \in B\}$. One has $\mathbb{B}(s, R, z') = B(s, z)$, and therefore $h(B) = h(\mathbb{B}(s, R, z')) = u(z') = \max\{u(x)|x \in B\}$.

Since preferences are strictly monotonic,

$$\max\{u(x)|x \in B(s, z)\} < \max\{u(x)|x \in B(s, z')\}$$

whenever $B(s, z) \subset B(s, z')$, so that h is increasing.

Consider a sequence (z^k) such that $B(s, z^k)$ tends to $B(s, z)$ for the Hausdorff distance. Since these sets are compact, by continuity of u, necessarily $\max\{u(x)|x \in B(s, z^k)\}$ tends to $\max\{u(x)|x \in B(s, z)\}$. Therefore h is continuous. □

We now continue the proof of the theorem. Let $e = (s_N, R_N) \in \mathcal{E}$. Let $e' = (s_{N'}, R_{N'}) \in \mathcal{E}$ be defined by $|N| = |N'|, R_N = R_{N'},$[24] and for all $i \in N', s_i = \tilde{s}$, where $\tilde{s}$ is chosen so that $\bar{R}$ satisfies *Minimal Suppes Equal Access* with respect to it.

Let $N'' = N \cup N'$ and $e'' = (s_{N''}, R_{N''})$. One has $e'' \in \mathcal{E}$. By Lemma 3, there exist continuous functions $g_i^{e''} : X \to \mathbb{R}$, for $i \in N''$, such that for all $z_{N''}, z'_{N''} \in X^{N''}$,

$$z_{N''} \bar{R}(e'') z'_{N''} \Leftrightarrow \sum_{i \in N''} g_i^{e''}(z_i) \geq \sum_{i \in N''} g_i^{e''}(z'_i).$$

---

[24]With an abuse of notation, this equality means that the distribution of preferences is identical.

By *Strong Pareto*, $g_i^{e''}(z_i) \geq g_i^{e''}(z_i') \Leftrightarrow z_i R_i z_i'$, for all $i \in N''$. Therefore, by Lemma 2 the valuation functions h_i defined over $\mathcal{B}$ by $h_i(B) = \max\{g_i^{e''}(z) \mid z \in B\}$ are continuous and increasing. By *Minimal Suppes Equal Access*, for all $z, z' \in X, i, j \in N'$ (remember that both i and j have skills equal to $\tilde{s}$),

$$h_i(B(\tilde{s}, z)) + h_j(B(\tilde{s}, z')) = h_i(B(\tilde{s}, z')) + h_j(B(\tilde{s}, z)).$$

Therefore, there is a real-valued, continuous and increasing function h defined over $\mathcal{B}$ and $\alpha_{N'} \in \mathbb{R}^{N'}$ such that for all $z \in X, i \in N', h_i(B(\tilde{s}, z)) = \alpha_i + h(B(\tilde{s}, z))$. For all $i \in N$, there is $j \in N'$ such that $R_i = R_j$. Therefore, by *Suppes Compensation*, for all $z, z' \in X$,

$$g_i^{e''}(z) + h(\mathbb{B}(\tilde{s}, R_j, z')) = g_i^{e''}(z') + h(\mathbb{B}(\tilde{s}, R_j, z)).$$

Therefore, there exist $\beta_N \in \mathbb{R}^N$ such that for all $i \in N, g_i^{e''}(z) = \beta_i + h(\mathbb{B}(\tilde{s}, R_j, z))$. Consequently, for all $z_{N''}, z_{N''}' \in X^{N''}$,

$$z_{N''} \bar{R}(e'') z_{N''}' \Leftrightarrow \sum_{i \in N''} h(\mathbb{B}(\tilde{s}, R_j, z_i)) \geq \sum_{i \in N''} h(\mathbb{B}(\tilde{s}, R_j, z_i')).$$

By *Consistency*, for all $z_N, z_N' \in X^N$,

$$z_N \bar{R}(e) z_N' \Leftrightarrow \sum_{i \in N} h(\mathbb{B}(\tilde{s}, R_i, z_i)) \geq \sum_{i \in N} h(\mathbb{B}(\tilde{s}, R_j, z_i')),$$

the desired outcome. $\qquad\square$

Examples of social ordering functions satisfying all the axioms but:

3. (a) *Strong Pareto*. Just reverse the ordering.
   (b) *Suppes Compensation*. Any $\tilde{R}$-implicit-budget generalized utilitarian function.
   (c) *Minimal Suppes Equal Access*. Let $\bar{R}$ be defined by for all $e \in \mathcal{E}, z_N, z_N' \in X^N$,

   $$z_N \bar{R}(e) z_N' \Leftrightarrow \sum_{i \in N} g(\mathbb{B}(s, (R_i), R_i, z_i)) \geq \sum_{i \in N} g(\mathbb{B}(s, (R_i), R_i, z_i')),$$

   where $s(\cdot)$ is a real-valued function defined on $\mathcal{R}$, such that $s(\mathcal{R})$ contains at least two elements.
   (d) *Consistency*. A similar example as in 1(e).
   (e) *Continuity*. Any $\tilde{s}$-implicit-budget leximin function.

Theorem 8

Proof. Let $e = (s_N, R_N) \in \mathcal{E}$. Let $e' = (s_{N'}, R_{N'}) \in \mathcal{E}$ be defined by $|N| = |N'|, s_N = s_{N'},$[25] and for all $i \in N', R_i = \tilde{R}$, where $\tilde{R}$ is chosen so that $\tilde{R}$ satisfies *Minimal Suppes Compensation* with respect to it. Then the proof mimics that of the previous theorem. □

Examples of social ordering functions satisfying all the axioms but:

4. (a) *Strong Pareto.* Just reverse the ordering.
   (b) *Minimal Suppes Compensation.* Let $\tilde{R}$ be defined by for all $e \in \mathcal{E}, z_N, z'_N \in X^N,$

$$z_N \bar{R}(e) z'_N \Leftrightarrow \sum_{i \in N} \tilde{u}_{s_i}(m(\tilde{R}_i, \mathbb{B}(s_i, R_i, z_i)))$$

$$\geq \sum_{i \in N} \tilde{u}_{s_i}(m(\tilde{R}_i, \mathbb{B}(s_i, R_i, z'_i))),$$

   where $\tilde{u}_{s_i}$ is a different representation of $\tilde{R}$ for different s_i.
   (c) *Suppes Equal Access*: any $\tilde{s}$-implicit-budget generalized utilitarian ordering function.
   (d) *Consistency*: a similar example as in 1(e).
   (e) *Continuity*: any $\tilde{R}$-implicit-budget leximin function.

Theorem 9

Proof. Let $e = (s_N, R_N) \in \mathcal{E}, z_N, z'_N \in X^N$ be such that there exist $j, k \in N$ with $s_j = s_k$, for all $i \in N, i \neq j, k, z_i = z'_i$, and

$$[\forall l \in \{j, k\}, \ z_l \in m(R_l, B(s_l, z_l)) \text{ and } z'_l \in m(R_l, B(s_l, z'_l)), \text{ and}$$

$$B(s_j, z_j) \supset B(s_j, z'_j) \supset B(s_k, z'_k) \supset B(s_k, z_k)].$$

Let $R_0 \in \mathcal{R}$ be chosen so that:

$$\forall l \in \{j, k\}, \ z_l \in m(R_0, B(s_l, z_l)) \quad \text{and} \quad z'_l \in m(R_0, B(s_l, z'_l)).$$

Let $e' = (s_N, R'_N)$ be defined by $R'_j = R'_k = R_0$, and $R'_i = R_i$ for all $i \in N, i \neq j, k$. By Hammond Equal Treatment of Equals, $z'_N \bar{P}(e') z_N$. By Independence of Irrelevant Alternatives, $z'_N \bar{P}(e) z_N$, as Hammond Equal Access would require.

The proof about the Suppes versions of the axioms is similar. □

---

[25] Again this means that the distributions are identical.

References

1. K. J. Arrow. 'A difficulty in the concept of social welfare', *Journal of Political Economics* **58** (1950), 328–346.
2. K. J. Arrow. *Social Choice and Individual Values*, New York: Wiley. 1951.
3. C. Blackorby, D. Primont and R. R. Russell. *Duality, Separability, and Functional Structure: Theory and Economic Applications*, New York: North Holland. 1978.
4. W. Bossert, M. Fleurbaey and D. Van de Gaer. 'Responsibility, talent, and compensation: A second-best analysis', *Review of Economic Design* **4** (1999), 35–55.
5. D. E. Campbell and J. S. Kelly. 'Information and preference aggregation', *Social Choice and Welfare* **17** (2000), 3–24.
6. A. Chaudhuri. 'Some implications of an intensity measure of envy', *Social Choice and Welfare* **3** (1986), 255–270.
7. T. Daniel. 'A revised concept of distributional equity', *Journal of Economic Theory* **11** (1975), 94–109.
8. C. d'Aspremont and L. Gevers. 'Equity and the informational basis of collective choice', *Review of Economic Studies* **44** (1977), 199–209.
9. G. Debreu. 'Topological methods in cardinal utility theory', in K. J. Arrow, S. Karlin and P. Suppes (eds.), *Mathematical Methods in the Social Sciences*, Stanford: Stanford University Press. 1959, pp. 16–26.
10. E. Diamantaras and W. Thomson. 'A refinement and extension of the no-envy concept', *Economic Letters* **33** (1991), 217–222.
11. R. Dworkin. 'What is equality? Part 1: Equality of welfare; Part 2: Equality of resources', *Philosophy & Public Affairs* **10** (1981), 185–246 and 283–345.
12. A. Feldman and A. Kirman. 'Fairness and envy', *American Economic Review* **64** (1974), 995–1005.
13. M. Fleming. 'A cardinal concept of welfare', *Quarterly Journal of Economics* **66** (1952), 366–384.
14. M. Fleurbaey. 'On fair compensation', *Theory and Decision* **36** (1994), 277–307.
15. M. Fleurbaey. *Théories Economiques de la Justice*, Economica, Paris, 1996.
16. M. Fleurbaey and F. Maniquet. 'Fair allocation with unequal production skills: The no-envy approach to compensation', *Mathematical Social Sciences* **32** (1996a), 71–93.

17. M. Fleurbaey and F. Maniquet. 'Utilitarianism versus fairness in welfare economics', in M. Fleurbaey, M. Salles and J. A. Weymark (eds.), *Justice, Political Liberalism and Utilitarianism: Themes from Harsanyi and Rawls*, Cambridge: Cambridge University Press. 2008, pp. 263–280.

18. M. Fleurbaey and F. Maniquet. 'Optimal income taxation: An ordinal approach'. DP #9865, CORE, 1998.

19. M. Fleurbaey and F. Maniquet. 'Fair allocation with unequal production skills: The solidarity approach to compensation', *Social Choice and Welfare* **16** (1999a), 569–583.

20. M. Fleurbaey and F. Maniquet. 'Compensation and responsibility', in K. J. Arrow, A. Sen and K. Suzumura (eds.), *Handbook of Social Choice and Welfare*, 1999b.

21. P. J. Hammond. 'Equity, Arrow's conditions and Rawls' difference principle', *Econometrica* **44** (1976), 793–804.

22. B. Hansson. 'The independence condition in the theory of social choice', *Theory and Decision* **4** (1973), 25–49.

23. M. Le Breton. 'Arrovian social choice on economic domains', in K. J. Arrow, A. Sen and K. Suzumura (eds.), *Social Choice Re-examined*, Vol. 1, New York: Macmillan, London St. Martin's Press. 1997.

24. J. Mirrlees. 'An exploration in the theory of optimum income taxation', *Review of Economic Studies* **38** (1971), 175–208.

25. H. Moulin and W. Thomson. 'Axiomatic analysis of resource allocation problems', in K. J. Arrow, A. Sen and K. Suzumura (eds.), *Social Choice Re-examined*, Vol. 1, New York: Macmillan, London St. Martin's Press. 1997.

26. E. Pazner. 'Equity, nonfeasible alternatives and social choice: A reconsideration of the concept of social welfare', in J. J. Laffont (ed.), *Aggregation and Revelation of Preferences*, Amsterdam: North Holland. 1979.

27. E. Pazner and D. Schmeidler. 'A difficulty in the concept of fairness', *Review of Economic Studies* **41** (1974), 991–993.

28. E. Pazner and D. Schmeidler. 'Decentralization and income distribution in socialist economies', *Economic Inquiry* **16** (1978), 257–264.

29. J. Rawls. *Theory of Justice*, Cambridge, MA: Harvard University Press. 1971.

30. J. Rawls. 'Social unity and primary goods', in A. Sen and B. Williams (eds.), *Utilitarianism and Beyond*, Cambridge: Cambridge University Press. 1982.

31. J. E. Roemer. *Theories of Distributive Justice*, Cambridge, MA: Harvard University Press. 1996.

32. J. E. Roemer *et al.* 'To what extent do fiscal regimes equalize opportunities for income acquisition among citizens?', *Journal of Public Economics* **87** (2003), 539–565.

33. E. Schokkaert, D. Van de Gaer and F. Vandenbroucke. 'Responsibility-sensitive egalitarianism and optimal linear income taxation'. Mimeo, 2001.

34. A. K. Sen. 'The possibility of social choice', *American Economic Review* **89** (1999), 349–378.

35. P. Suppes. 'Some formal models of grading principles', *Synthese* **16** (1966), 284–306.

36. K. Suzumura. 'On pareto-efficiency and the no-envy concept of equity', *Journal of Economic Theory* **25** (1981a), 367–379.

37. K. Suzumura. 'On the possibility of fair collective choice rule', *International Economic Review* **22** (1981b), 351–364.

38. K. Suzumura. *Rational Choice, Collective Decisions, and Social Welfare*, Cambridge: Cambridge University Press. 1983.

39. K. Tadenuma. 'Efficiency first or equity first? Two principles and rationality of social choice', DP #1998-01, Hitotsubashi University, 1998.

40. W. Thomson. *Consistent Allocation Rules*, University of Rochester. mimeo, 1996.

41. H. Varian. 'Equity, envy, and efficiency', *Journal of Economic Theory* **9** (1974), 63–91.

42. H. Varian. 'Two problems in the theory of fairness', *Journal of Public Economics* **5** (1976), 249–260.

CHAPTER 8

Fair Income Tax

Marc Fleurbaey and François Maniquet

ABSTRACT. In a model where agents have unequal skills and heterogeneous preferences over consumption and leisure, we look for the optimal tax on the basis of efficiency and fairness principles and under incentive-compatibility constraints. The fairness principles considered here are: (1) a weak version of the Pigou–Dalton transfer principle; (2) a condition precluding redistribution when all agents have the same skills. With such principles we construct and justify specific social preferences and derive a simple criterion for the evaluation of income tax schedules. Namely, the lower the greatest average tax rate over the range of low incomes, the better. We show that, as a consequence, the optimal tax should give the greatest subsidies to the working poor (the agents having the lowest skill and choosing the largest labour time).

1. Introduction

Fairness is a key concept in redistribution issues. In this paper, we study how particular requirements of fairness can shed light on the design of the optimal income tax schedule.

We consider a population of heterogeneous individuals (or households), who differ in two respects. First, they have unequal skills and, therefore, unequal earning abilities. Second, they differ in terms of their preferences about consumption and leisure and, as a consequence, typically make different labour time choices. Both kinds of differences generate income

Review of Economic Studies **73**: 55–83, 2006.

inequalities. We study how to justify and compute a redistribution income tax in this context.

Redistribution through an income tax usually entails distortions of incentives, but the resulting efficiency loss has to be weighed against potential improvements in the fairness of the distribution of resources. We address this efficiency–equity trade-off here by constructing social preferences which obey the standard Pareto principle in addition to fairness conditions.

Two fairness requirements are introduced below. Briefly, the first requirement, a qualification of the Pigou–Dalton principle, states that transfers reducing income inequalities are acceptable, *provided* they are performed between agents having identical preferences and identical labour time. Thanks to this proviso, this requirement (contrary to the usual Pigou–Dalton transfer principle which applies to all income inequalities) is still justified if we consider that incomes should not necessarily be equalized among agents having different labour time or, more generally, different willingness to work. The second fairness requirement is that the laisser-faire (that is, the absence of redistribution) should be the social optimum in the hypothetical case when all agents have equal earning abilities. The underlying idea is that income inequalities would then reflect free choices from different preferences on an identical budget set, and that such choices ought to be respected.

These two requirements, together with the Pareto principle and ancillary conditions of informational parsimony and separability (the idea that indifferent agents should not influence social preferences), lead us to single out a particular kind of social preferences. These social preferences measure individual well-being in terms of what we call "equivalent wage" (see Section 2). For any given individual, her equivalent wage, relative to a particular indifference curve, is the hypothetical wage rate which would enable her to reach this indifference curve if she could freely choose her labour time at this wage rate. This particular measure of well-being, which is induced by the fairness conditions, does not require any other information about individuals than their ordinal non-comparable preferences about their own consumption–leisure bundles.

It is then shown that, under some richness assumptions about the distribution of characteristics in the population, such social preferences yield a very simple criterion for the welfare comparison of tax schedules. This criterion is the maximal average tax rate over low incomes (i.e. incomes below the minimum wage). This criterion can be used for the comparison of any pair of tax schedules, no matter how far from the optimum, but it can also be used to seek the optimal tax schedule. As far as the optimal tax is concerned, the main result is that those individuals who have the lowest earning ability but work full time, namely, the *hardworking poor*, will be granted the greatest subsidy (i.e. the smallest tax) of the whole population.

The literature on optimal taxation has focused mostly on social objectives defined in terms of welfarist (typically, utilitarian) social welfare functions, based on interpersonal comparisons of utility. It has obtained valuable insights into the likely shape of the optimal tax, as can be grasped from the outstanding works of Mirrlees (1971), Atkinson (1973, 1995), Sadka (1976), Seade (1977) Tuomala (1990), Ebert (1992), and Diamond (1998), among many others. Many results depend on the particular choice of individual utility function and social welfare function. The social marginal utility of an individual's income may thus reflect various personal characteristics (individual utility) and ethical values embodied in the social welfare function, including, potentially, fairness requirements. But, apart from the important relationship between inequality aversion and (Schur-)concavity of the social welfare function, the link between fairness requirements and features of the social welfare function are not usually made explicit. In contrast, our approach starts from requirements of fairness, and derives social preferences on this basis.

This literature has traditionally assumed that agents differ only in one dimension (typically, their earning ability). Several authors (Choné and Laroque, 2001, Boadway, Marchand, Pestieau and Racionero, 2002) have recently examined optimal taxation under the assumption that agents may be heterogeneous in two dimensions, their consumption–leisure preferences and their earning ability, or skill. They immediately face a conceptual difficulty: there is no clear way to define the objective of a utilitarian planner, as summing utility levels of agents having different preferences requires a particular choice of utility functions. It seems therefore necessary to impose what Choné and Laroque (2001) appropriately call an ethical assumption. Boadway *et al.* (2002) consider a whole span of possible weights for various utility functions. In this paper we show that the relative weight of agents having different preferences does not need to be determined by assumption, but can be derived from fairness conditions. An additional notorious difficulty of multi-dimensional screening is the impossibility to derive simple solutions due to widespread bunching.[1] We are however able to describe some basic features of the optimal tax and to obtain a simple criterion for the comparison of taxes.

---

[1]See, e.g., Armstrong (1996) or Rochet and Choné (1998).

This recent literature suggests that, with double heterogeneity, negative marginal income tax rates are more likely to be obtained than if agents differ with respect to one parameter only. Our results go in the same direction. In Choné and Laroque (2001), however, the focus is on labour participation, so that agents work either zero or one unit, whereas we consider the whole interval. In addition, their social objective gives absolute priority to agents with the smallest income, so that negative tax rates may obtain for high incomes (and only for special distributions), whereas our social objective gives priority to the working poor, and non-positive tax rates are obtained on low incomes (for all distributions). In Boadway *et al.* (2002), negative marginal rates are obtained on low incomes and in a closer way to ours, since they arise in the case when the weights assigned to agents with a high aversion to work are lower than those assigned to agents with a low aversion to work. But their framework has only four types of agents, whereas our result is obtained for an unlimited domain.[2]

Our work also builds on previous studies of the same model (with unequal earning abilities and heterogeneous preferences) which dealt with first-best allocations (Fleurbaey and Maniquet, 1996a, 1999) or with linear tax (Bossert, Fleurbaey and Van de Gaer, 1999), or focused on different fairness concepts (Fleurbaey and Maniquet, 2005).

The paper is organized as follows. Section 2 introduces the model and the concept of social preferences. Section 3 contains the axiomatic analysis and derives social preferences. Section 4 develops the analysis of taxation. Concluding remarks are offered in the last section.

2. The Model

There are two goods, labour and consumption.[3] A *bundle* for agent i is a pair $z_i = (\ell_i, c_i)$, where ℓ_i is labour and c_i consumption. The agents' *consumption set* X is defined by the conditions $0 \leq \ell_i \leq 1$ and $c_i \geq 0$.

---

[2]Another branch of the literature sometimes obtains similar results by studying social objectives disregarding individual leisure–consumption preferences and focusing on income maintenance. See Besley and Coate (1995) for a synthesis. Here we retain a concern for efficiency via the Pareto principle, so that the social preferences obtained respect individual preferences.

[3]Introducing several consumption goods would not change the analysis much if prices were assumed to be fixed. The case of variable consumption prices would require a specific analysis. See Fleurbaey and Maniquet (1996b, 2001) for explorations of the problem of fair division of consumption goods.

The population contains $n \geq 2$ agents. Agents have two characteristics, their personal preferences over the consumption set and their personal skill. For any agent $i = 1, \ldots, n$, *personal preferences* are denoted R_i, and $z_i R_i z_i'$ (resp. $z_i P_i z_i'$, $z_i I_i z_i'$) means that bundle z_i is weakly preferred (resp. strictly preferred, indifferent) to bundle z_i'. We assume that individual preferences are continuous, convex and monotonic.[4]

The marginal productivity of labour is assumed to be fixed, as in a constant returns to scale technology. Agent i's earning ability is measured by her productivity or *wage rate*, denoted w_i, and is measured in consumption units, so that $w_i \geq 0$ is agent i's production when working $\ell_i = 1$ and, for any ℓ_i, $w_i \ell_i$ is the agent's pre-tax income (earnings). Figure 1 displays the consumption set, with typical indifference curves, and earnings as a function of labour time. As illustrated on the figure, an agent's consumption c_i may differ from her earnings $w_i \ell_i$. This is a typical consequence of redistribution.

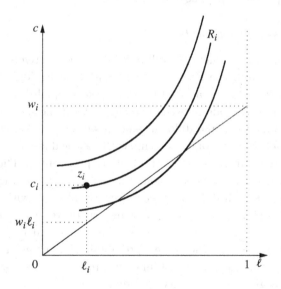

Fig. 1.

[4]Preferences are monotonic if $\ell_i \leq \ell_i'$ and $c_i > c_i'$ implies that $(\ell_i, c_i) P_i (\ell_i', c_i')$. Our analysis could be easily extended to the larger domain of preferences which are strictly monotonic in c, but not necessarily monotonic in ℓ. Assuming only local non-satiation, on the other hand, would require a more radical revision of the analysis (see footnote 5 below).

An allocation is a collection $z = (z_1, \ldots, z_n)$. Social preferences will allow us to compare allocations in terms of fairness and efficiency. Social preferences will be formalized as a complete ordering over all allocations in X^n, and will be denoted R, with asymmetric and symmetric components P and I, respectively. In other words, $z \, R \, z'$ means that z is at least as good as z', $z \, P \, z'$ means that it is strictly better, and $z \, I \, z'$ that they are equivalent.

Social preferences may depend on the population profile of characteristics $(R_1, \ldots, R_n)$ and $(w_1, \ldots, w_n)$. Formally, they are a *mapping* from the set of population profiles to the set of complete orderings over allocations. For the sake of simplicity, we do not introduce additional notations for these notions. The domain of economies for which we want social preferences to be defined contains all economies obeying the above conditions.

3. Fair Social Preferences

3.1. *Fairness requirements*

The main ethical requirement we will impose on social preferences, in this paper, is derived from the Pigou–Dalton transfer principle. Traditionally, however, this principle was applied to all income inequalities. This entails that no distinction is made between two agents with the same income but very different wage rates and different amounts of labour. We will be more cautious here, and apply it only to agents with identical labour. In addition, we will also restrict it to agents with identical preferences. There are two reasons for this additional restriction. First, applying the Pigou–Dalton principle to agents with different preferences would clash with the Pareto principle (to be defined more precisely below), as proved by Fleurbaey and Trannoy (2003). Second, when two agents have identical preferences one can more easily argue that they deserve to obtain similar incomes, whereas this is much less clear in the case of different preferences, as work disutility may differ. This gives us the following requirement:[5]

Transfer principle. If z and z' are two allocations, and i and j are two agents with identical preferences, such that $\ell_i = \ell_j = \ell'_i = \ell'_j$, and for

---

[5]The transfer principle makes sense only when preferences are strictly monotonic in c. Otherwise, a transfer might fail to increase the receiver's satisfaction.

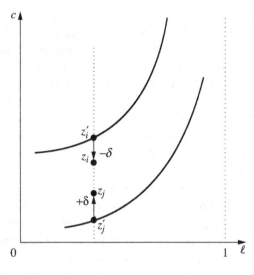

Fig. 2.

some $\delta > 0$,

$$c_i' - \delta = c_i > c_j = c_j' + \delta,$$

whereas for all other agents k, $z_k = z_k'$, then $z R z'$.

Figure 2 illustrates the transfer. The axiom may sound too weak with the restriction $\ell_i = \ell_j$ if one thinks that an agent with higher skill and identical preferences is likely to work more in ordinary circumstances (like those of taxation described in the next section). But recall that, at the stage of the construction of social preferences, we are only trying to find simple cases where our moral intuition is strong about how to improve the allocation. And we are not restricted to consider allocations that are likely to occur under specific institutions, since social preferences must rank all allocations. What this axiom says is simply that if, by whatever means, two agents with identical preferences and the same labour time happened to have different consumptions, then reducing this inequality would be socially acceptable. Independently of whether such a situation is likely or unlikely to occur (it is actually very common, in real life, for people who work full time), it is quite useful to consider it in order to put minimal constraints on social preferences.

Another possible objection is that if two agents have the same preferences, same labour but different productivity, it may seem normal that the more productive consumes more, whereas Pigou–Dalton transfers tend to eliminate inequality. In effect, the above axiom is justified only when agents cannot be held responsible for their differential productivity. This raises in particular the issue of whether the low-skilled may be considered to have responsibly chosen their lower productivity, or instead have suffered from various handicaps which have prevented them from acquiring higher skills. The Transfer Principle axiom is consistent with the latter view. We leave for future research the study of a richer model in which agents could be held partially responsible for their wage rate, via their educational or occupational choices.

The second fairness requirement we introduce has to do with providing opportunities and respecting individual preferences. Although reducing income inequalities is a generous goal, it is not obvious how to deal with agents who "choose" poverty out of a budget set which contains better income opportunities. In particular, when all agents have the same wage rate, it can be argued that there is no need for redistribution, as they all have access to the same labour–consumption bundles (Dworkin, 1981). Any income difference is then a matter of personal preferences. A laisser-faire allocation z^* is such that for every agent i, z_i^* is the best for R_i over the budget set defined by $c_i \leq w_i \ell_i$. The following requirement says that a laisser-faire allocation,[6] in this particular case of uniform earning ability, is (one of) the best among all feasible allocations.

Laisser-faire. If all agents have the same wage rate w, then for any laisser-faire allocation z^* and any allocation z' such that $\sum_i c_i' \leq w \sum_i \ell_i'$, one has $z^* R z'$.

A laisser-faire allocation in a two-agent equal-skill economy is illustrated in Figure 3. Both agents have the same budget. Agent i, on the figure, may choose to have more leisure and less consumption, and the axiom of Laisser-Faire declares this to be unproblematic. One sees that this principle is acceptable if individual preferences are fully respectable, but should be treated with caution if some individual preferences are influenced by questionable social factors (e.g., apparent laziness may be due to discouragement and social stigma; workaholism may be due to social pressure).

The other requirements are basic conditions derived from the theory of social choice. First, we want social preferences to obey the standard Pareto

---

[6]There may be several laisser-faire allocations if preferences are not strictly convex. But all laisser-faire allocations, in a given economy, give agents the same satisfaction.

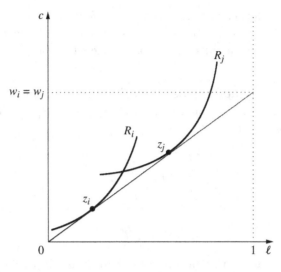

Fig. 3.

condition. This condition is essential in order to take account of efficiency considerations. Social preferences satisfying the Pareto condition will never lead to the selection of inefficient allocations. In this way we are preserved against excessive consequences of fairness requirements, such as equality obtained through levelling-down devices.

Weak pareto. If z and z' are such that for all i, $z_i \, P_i \, z'_i$, then $z \, P \, z'$.

Second, we want our social preferences to use minimal information about individual preferences, in the spirit of Arrow's (1951) condition of independence of irrelevant alternatives. Arrow's condition is, however, much too restrictive, and leads to the unpalatable results of his impossibility theorem. Arrow's independence of irrelevant alternatives requires social preferences over two allocations to depend only on individual preferences over these two allocations. This condition makes it impossible, for instance, to check that two agents have the same preferences, or that an allocation is a laisser-faire allocation, etc. For extensive discussions of how excessive Arrow's independence is, see Fleurbaey and Maniquet (1996b, 2001) and Fleurbaey, Suzumura and Tadenuma (2003). We will instead follow Hansson (1973) and Pazner (1979) who have proposed a weaker condition still consistent with the idea that information needed to make social choices should be as parsimonious as possible. That condition requires social preferences over two allocations to depend only on individual *indifference curves* at these two allocations. More formally, it requires social preferences over two allocations to be the same in two different profiles of preferences when agents' indifference curves through the bundles they are assigned in these allocations are the same.

Hansson independence. Let z and z' be two allocations, and R, R' be the social orderings for two profiles $(R_1, \ldots, R_n)$ and $(R'_1, \ldots, R'_n)$, respectively. If for all i, and all $q \in X$,

$$z_i \, I_i \, q \Leftrightarrow z_i \, I'_i \, q$$
$$z'_i \, I_i \, q \Leftrightarrow z'_i \, I'_i \, q,$$

then

$$z \, R \, z' \Leftrightarrow z \, R' \, z'.$$

Finally, we want our social preferences to have a separable structure, as is usual in the literature on social index numbers. The intuition for separability requirements is that agents who are not concerned by a social decision need not be given any say in it. This is not only appealing because it simplifies the structure of social preferences, but also because it can be related to a standard conception of democracy, implying that unconcerned populations need not intervene in social decisions. This is often called the subsidiarity principle. We retain the following condition, requiring social preferences over two allocations to be unchanged if an agent receiving the same bundle in both allocations is removed from the economy.

Separability. Let z and z' be two allocations, and i an agent such that $z_i = z'_i$. Then

$$z \, R \, z' \Rightarrow z_{-i} R_{-i} z'_{-i},$$

where $z_{-i} = (z_1, \ldots, z_{i-1}, z_{i+1}, \ldots, z_n)$, and R_{-i} is the social preference ordering for the economy with reduced population $\{1, \ldots, i-1, i+1, \ldots, n\}$.

3.2. *Social preferences*

The fairness conditions introduced above do not convey a strong aversion to inequality. Actually, the only redistributive condition here is the Transfer Principle, which, in the above weak formulation, is compatible with any degree of inequality aversion, including zero. Nonetheless, the combination of all the properties entails an infinite aversion to inequality, and forces social preferences to rely on the maximin criterion. Moreover, the maximin criterion needs to be applied to a precise evaluation of individual situations, as stated in the following theorem.

Theorem 1. *Let social preferences satisfy Transfer Principle, Laisser-Faire, Weak Pareto, Hansson Independence and Separability. For any allocations z, z', one has $z\,P\,z'$ if one of the following conditions holds:*

(i) $z_i\,P_i(0,0)$ *and* $z_i'\,R_i(0,0)$ *for all i, and*

$$\min_i W_i(z_i) > \min_i W_i(z_i'),$$

where $W_i(z_i) = \max\{w \in \mathbb{R}_+ \mid \forall \ell, z_i R_i(\ell, w\ell)\}$;
(ii) $z_i\,P_i(0,0)$ *for all i and* $(0,0)\,P_i\,z_i'$ *for some i.*

When $z_i\,R_i(0,0)$, the set $\{W \in \mathbb{R}_+ \mid \forall \ell, z_i R_i(\ell, w\ell)\}$ is not empty (it contains at least 0), and by monotonicity and continuity of preferences, it is compact, so that its maximum is well defined. The computation of $W_i(z_i)$ is illustrated in Figure 4. Concretely, $W_i(z_i)$ is the wage rate which would enable agent i to reach the same satisfaction as in z_i, if she were allowed to choose her labour time freely, at this wage rate: "What wage rate would give you the same satisfaction as your current situation?" Of course, we cannot think of using this question as a practical device for assessing

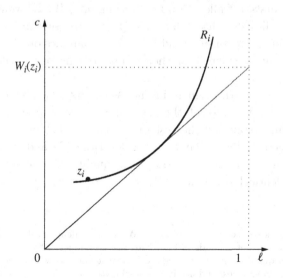

Fig. 4.

individuals' situations. First, they may have a hard time working out what the true answer is. Second, they would have incentives to misrepresent their situation. The next section will examine how this kind of measure can be practically implemented.

Another interpretation of $W_i(z_i)$ relates it more directly to the axiom of Laisser-Faire. Consider an agent i who is indifferent between z_i and the bundle z_i^* she would choose in a laisser-faire allocation that would be socially optimal if all agents had an equal wage rate w^*. Then $W_i(z_i) = w^*$. In other words, $W_i(z_i)$ is the hypothetical common wage rate which would render this agent indifferent between z_i and an optimal allocation.[7]

The function $W_i(z_i)$ is a particular utility representation of agent i's preferences (for a part of the consumption set). It makes it possible to compare the situations of individuals who have identical or different preferences, on the basis of their current indifference curves. In addition, the social preferences described in Theorem 1 give absolute priority to agents with the lowest $W_i(z_i)$. In this way, this result suggests a solution to the problem of weighting different utility functions, mentioned in the introduction. By giving priority to the worst-off, such social preferences also escape Mirrlees' criticism of utilitarian social welfare functions. Mirrlees (1974), indeed, proved that utilitarian first-best allocations had to display the property that high-skilled agents envy low-skilled agents, that is, the former are assigned bundles on lower indifference curves than the latter.[8] In contrast, a first-best allocation maximizing $\min_i W_i(z_i)$ would have the property that all agents have the same $W_i(z_i)$. Consequently, two agents having the same preferences would be assigned bundles on the same indifference curve, independently of their skills, and no one would envy the other.

The proof of the theorem is in the Appendix. We provide the intuition for it here (the rest of this section may be skipped without any problem for understanding the rest of the paper). Let us first show how the combination of Weak Pareto, Transfer Principle and Hansson Independence entails an infinite aversion to inequality. Consider two agents i and j with identical preferences R_0, and two allocations z and z' such

---

[7]This concept is closely related to the Equal Wage Equivalent first-best allocation rule characterized on different grounds in Fleurbaey and Maniquet (1999).

[8]Choné and Laroque (2001) generalize the criticism to the case where agents also differ in terms of their preferences, and use it as a justification for adopting social preferences of the maximin kind.

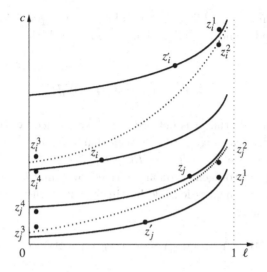

Fig. 5.

that

$$z_i' \, P_0 \, z_i \, P_0 \, z_j \, P_0 \, z_j'.$$

The related indifference curves are shown in Figure 5, and one sees in this particular example that the axiom of Transfer Principle cannot directly entail that z is preferable to z', because agent i's loss of consumption between z' and z is much greater than agent j's gain, and also because their labour times differ. By Hansson Independence, social preferences over z and z' can only depend on the indifference curves through those allocations, so that they must coincide with what they would be if the dotted indifference curves represented in Figure 5 were also part of agents i and j's preferences.

In this particular case, one can construct intermediate allocations such as z^1, z^2, z^3, z^4 in the figure. By Weak Pareto, $z^1 \, P \, z'$. By Transfer Principle, $z^2 \, R \, z^1$. By Weak Pareto again, $z^3 \, P \, z^2$. By Transfer Principle again, $z^4 \, R \, z^3$. Finally, Weak Pareto implies $z \, P \, z^4$, so, by transitivity, one can conclude that $z \, P \, z'$. Since this kind of construction can be done even when the gain is very small for j while i's loss is huge, one then obtains an infinite inequality aversion regarding indifference curves of agents with identical preferences.

The second central part of the argument consists in proving that the maximin has to be applied to $W_i(z_i)$. The crucial axioms are now

Laisser-Faire and Separability. Let us illustrate the proof in the case of two agents i and j and two allocations z and z' such that $z_k = z'_k$ for all $k \neq i, j$, and

$$W_i(z'_i) > W_i(z_i) > W_j(z_j) > W_j(z'_j).$$

We need to conclude that z is better than z'. Introduce two new agents, a and b, whose identical wage rate w is such that $W_i(z_i) > w > W_j(z_j)$, and whose preferences are $R_a = R_i$ and $R_b = R_j$. Let z^* denote a laisser-faire allocation for the two-agent economy formed by a and b, and (z_a, z_b) be another allocation which is feasible but inefficient in this two-agent economy, and such that

$$W_i(z_i) > W_a(z_a) > w > W_b(z_b) > W_j(z_j).$$

Figure 6 illustrates these allocations.

Let $R_{\{a,b\}}, R_{\{a,b,i,j\}}$ and $R_{\{i,j\}}$ denote the social preferences for the economies with population $\{a, b\}$, $\{a, b, i, j\}$ and $\{i, j\}$, respectively. By Laisser-Faire and Weak Pareto, a laisser-faire allocation is strictly better than any inefficient feasible allocation, so $z^* P_{\{a,b\}}(z_a, z_b)$. Therefore, by

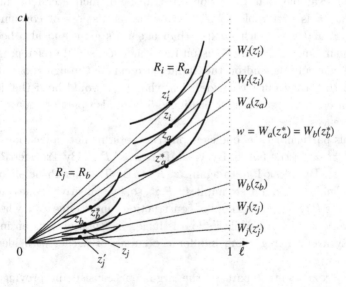

Fig. 6.

Separability, it must necessarily be the case that

$$(z_a^*, z_b^*, z_i, z_j) P_{\{a,b,i,j\}}(z_a, z_b, z_i, z_j).$$

By the above argument producing an infinite inequality aversion among agents with identical preferences (from Transfer Principle and Hansson Independence), one also sees that, by reducing the inequality between agents a and i,

$$(z_a, z_b^*, z_i, z_j') P_{\{a,b,i,j\}}(z_a^*, z_b^*, z_i', z_j')$$

and between agents b and j,

$$(z_a, z_b, z_i, z_j) P_{\{a,b,i,j\}}(z_a, z_b^*, z_i, z_j').$$

As a consequence, by transitivity one has

$$(z_a^*, z_b^*, z_i, z_j) P_{\{a,b,i,j\}}(z_a^*, z_b^*, z_i', z_j'),$$

from which Separability entails that

$$(z_i, z_j) R_{\{i,j\}}(z_i', z_j').$$

We would have obtained the desired strict preference $(z_i, z_j) P_{\{i,j\}}(z_i', z_j')$ by referring, in the previous stages of this argument, to another allocation (z_i'', z_j'') Pareto-dominating z', instead of z' itself. Then, from Separability again, one can finally derive the conclusion that $z \, P \, z'$ in the initial economy.

From this intuitive proof, one sees that it is the combination of Transfer Principle and Hansson Independence which leads to focusing on the worst-off, and that it is the combination of Laisser-Faire and Separability which singles out $W_i(z_i)$ as the proper measure of individual situations.

This theorem does not give a full characterization of social preferences, because it does not say how to compare allocations for which $\min_i W_i(z_i) = \min_i W_i(z_i')$. But for the purpose of evaluating taxes and finding the optimal tax, the description given in the theorem is sufficient to yield precise results, as we will show in the next section. Moreover, the theorem does not say how to define the social ranking within the subset of allocations such that $(0,0) P_i z_i$ for some i, but it says that such allocations are low in the social ranking and again that is sufficient for the purpose of tax applications.

As an additional illustration of this result, let us briefly examine how other kinds of social preferences fare with respect to the axioms. In order to simplify the discussion, we restrict our attention to how social preferences rank allocations z such that $z_i\,R_i(0,0)$ for all i. First, consider social preferences based on $\sum_i W_i(z_i)$ instead of $\min_i W_i(z_i)$:

$$z\,R\,z' \Leftrightarrow \sum_i W_i(z_i) \geq \sum_i W_i(z_i').$$

Such social preferences violate Transfer Principle and Laisser-Faire. Social preferences based on the median $W_i(z_i)$ would, in addition, violate Separability. Now, consider social preferences similar to those retained in Choné and Laroque (2001), and based on leximin$_i$ $C_i(z_i)$,[9] where

$$C_i(z_i) = \max\{c \in \mathbb{R}_+ \mid z_i R_i(0, c)\}.$$

Such social preferences satisfy all our axioms except Laisser-Faire. Consider social preferences based on leximin$_i$ $V_i(z_i)$, where

$$V_i(z_i) = \max\{t \in \mathbb{R} \mid \forall \ell, z_i\,R_i(\ell, t + w_i \ell)\}.$$

These social preferences satisfy all our axioms except Transfer Principle. As a final example, consider utilitarian social preferences based on $\sum_i U_i(z_i)$, where U_i is an exogenously given utility function representing R_i. Such social preferences require more information (the U_i functions) than the social preferences studied in this paper, and therefore do not fit exactly in our framework. One can nonetheless examine whether they satisfy some of our axioms. They fully satisfy Weak Pareto and Separability. They also satisfy Transfer Principle when the utility functions are concave in c (and when two agents with identical preferences also have identical utility functions). They do not satisfy Laisser-Faire, except on the subdomain of utility functions which are quasi-linear in c, and do not satisfy Hansson Independence on any reasonable domain.

4. Tax Redistribution

4.1. Setting

In this section, we examine the issue of devising the redistribution system under incentive-compatibility constraints and with the objective of

---

[9]Leximin is the lexicographic extension of maximin (when the smallest value is equal, one looks at the second smallest value, and so on).

achieving the best possible consequences according to the above social preferences. As is standard in the second-best context, whose formalism dates
back to Mirrlees (1971), we assume that only earned income $y_i = w_i\ell_i$ is
observed, so that redistribution is made via a tax function $\tau(y_i)$. This tax
is a subsidy when $\tau(y_i) < 0$. Individuals are free to choose their labour
time in the budget set modified by the tax schedule. The government is
assumed to know the distribution of types (preferences, earning abilities)
in the population but ignores the characteristics of any particular agent.
Since it is easy to forecast the behaviour of any given type of agent under a
tax schedule, knowing the distribution of types enables the government to
forecast the social consequences of any tax function. It may then evaluate
or choose a tax function in view of the foreseen social consequences.

Under this kind of redistribution, agent i's budget set is defined by (see
Figure 7(a)):

$$B(\tau, w_i) = \{(\ell, c) \in X \mid c \leq w_i\ell - \tau(w_i\ell)\}.$$

Notice that $-\tau(0)$ is the minimum income granted to agents with no earnings. It is convenient to focus on the earnings–consumption space, in which
the budget is defined by (see Figure 7(b)):

$$B(\tau, w_i) = \{(y, c) \in [0, w_i] \times \mathbb{R}_+ \mid c \leq y - \tau(y)\}.$$

We retain the same notation for the two sets since no confusion is possible.
Similarly, in our figures z_i will simultaneously denote the bundle (ℓ_i, c_i) in
one space and the bundle $(y_i, c_i) = (w_i\ell_i, c_i)$ in the other space.

In the earnings–consumption space, one can define individual preferences R_i^* over earnings–consumption bundles, and they are derived from

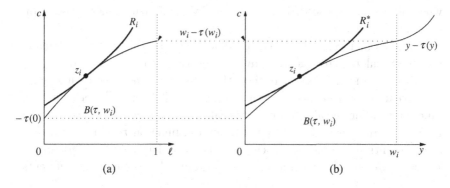

(a)　　　　　　　　　　　(b)

Fig. 7.

ordinary preferences over labour–consumption bundles via

$$(y,c)R_i^*(y',c') \Leftrightarrow \left(\frac{y}{w_i},c\right)R_i\left(\frac{y'}{w_i},c'\right).$$

The fact that all agents are submitted to the same constraint $c \leq y - \tau(y)$ implies that for any pair of agents i,j, when i chooses (y_i,c_i) in $B(\tau,w_i)$ and j chooses (y_j,c_j) in $B(\tau,w_j)$, one must have $(y_i,c_i)R_i^*(y_j,c_j)$ or $y_j > w_i$.

Conversely,[10] any allocation z satisfying

$$\text{for all } i,j, (y_i,c_i)R_i^*(y_j,c_j) \quad \text{or} \quad y_j > w_i \quad \text{(self-selection constraints)}$$

is incentive-compatible and can be obtained by letting every agent i choose her best bundle in a budget set $B(\tau,w_i)$ for some well-chosen tax function τ. This tax function must be such that $y - \tau(y)$ lies nowhere above the envelope curve of the indifference curves of the population in the (y,c)-space, and intersects this envelope curve at all points (y_i,c_i) for $i = 1,\ldots,n$. By monotonicity of individual preferences, we may restrict attention to tax functions τ such that $y - \tau(y)$ is non-decreasing.

An allocation is *feasible* if it satisfies

$$\sum_{i=1}^{n} c_i \leq \sum_{i=1}^{n} y_i.$$

A tax function τ is *feasible* if it satisfies

$$\sum_{i=1}^{n} \tau(w_i \ell_i) \geq 0$$

when all agents choose their labour time by maximizing their satisfaction over their budget set.

Consider an incentive-compatible allocation z. By the assumptions made on individual preferences, the envelope curve of the agents' indifference curves in (y,c)-space, at z, is then the graph of a non-decreasing, non-negative function f defined on an interval $S(z) \subset [0, \max_i w_i]$. Let τ be a tax function yielding the allocation z. It is called *minimal* when $y - \tau(y) = f(y)$ for all $y \in S(z)$, or equivalently when any tax function τ' which yields the same incentive-compatible allocation z is such that $\tau'(y) \geq \tau(y)$ for all $y \in S(z)$. Concretely, when a tax τ is not minimal, one can devise tax cuts

---

[10]See, e.g., Stiglitz (1987, pp. 1002–1004) or Boadway and Keen (2000, pp. 737–738).

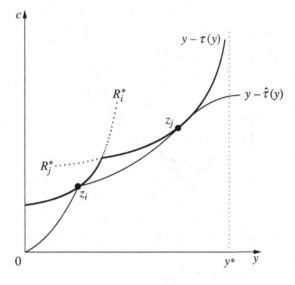

Fig. 8.

which have no consequence on the agents' behaviour and on tax receipts (because no agent has earnings in the range of the tax cuts). Figure 8 illustrates this, with a minimal tax τ and a non-minimal tax $\hat{\tau}$. When $\max_i w_i \notin S(z)$, then there is y^* such that $\lim_{y \to y^*, y < y^*} f(y) = +\infty$ (see Figure 8). In this case, by convention we let any corresponding minimal tax have $\tau(y) = -\infty$ (or equivalently $y - \tau(y) = +\infty$) for all $y \geq y^*$. When $z_i R_i(0,0)$ for all i, then $0 \in S(z)$, so on the interval $[0, \max_i w_i]$ there is only one minimal tax τ corresponding to z.[11]

In the following, we explore the evaluation of taxes for the class of social preferences highlighted in Theorem 1. This means that an incentive-compatible allocation z is socially preferred to another incentive-compatible allocation z' whenever

$$\min_i W_i(z_i) > \min_i W_i(z_i').$$

The way $W_i(z_i)$ is computed in the earnings–consumption space is illustrated in Figure 9.

---

[11]The definition of $\tau(y)$ for $y > \max_i w_i$ does not matter. By convention, for all tax functions considered in this paper, we let $\tau(y) = \tau(\max_i w_i)$ for all $y > \max_i w_i$.

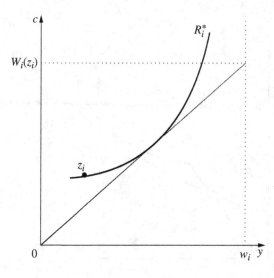

Fig. 9.

4.2. Two agents

As an introductory analysis, consider the case of a two-agent population $\{1, 2\}$. Assume that $w_1 < w_2$. As a consequence, agent 2's budget set always contains agent 1's one. And if agent 1's labour time is positive at the laisser-faire allocation z^*, necessarily $W_1(z_1^*) < W_2(z_2^*)$ since $W_i(z_i^*) \geq w_i$ for $i = 1, 2$, with equality $W_i(z_i^*) = w_i$ when the agent has a positive labour time. (If an agent is so averse to labour that $\ell_i^* = 0$, then $W_i(z_i^*)$ equals the marginal rate of substitution at $(0, 0)$, which is greater than or equal to w_i.)

If the agents have the same preferences $R_1 = R_2$, then the optimal tax is the one which maximizes the satisfaction of agent 1 (since agent 2's budget set contains agent 1's one, in the case of identical preferences one has $W_2(z_2) \geq W_1(z_1)$ in any incentive-compatible allocation). This result extends immediately to a larger population: When all agents have the same preferences, an optimal tax is one which, among the feasible tax functions, maximizes the satisfaction of the agents with the lowest wage rate.

In the general case when the agents may have the same or different preferences (assuming that agent 1 has a positive labour time at the laisser-faire allocation), then either the optimal tax achieves an allocation such that $W_1(z_1) = W_2(z_2)$, or it maximizes the satisfaction of agent 1 over the set of feasible taxes. The argument for this fact is the following. Starting from the laisser-faire z^* where $W_1(z_1^*) < W_2(z_2^*)$, one redistributes from agent 2 to agent 1, and this increases $W_1(z_1)$ and decreases $W_2(z_2)$, following the second-best Pareto frontier. When one reaches the equality $W_1(z_1) = W_2(z_2)$, redistribution has to stop, since, by Pareto-efficiency, there is no other allocation with a greater $\min_i W_i(z_i)$. But an alternative possibility is that the incentive-compatibility constraint $(y_2, c_2)R_2^*(y_1, c_1)$ puts a limit on redistribution, which occurs when the point maximizing agent 1's satisfaction is reached. Then, the inequality $W_1(z_1) < W_2(z_2)$ remains at the optimal tax.

Figure 10 illustrates these two possibilities. In (a), the optimal allocation has $W_1(z_1) = W_2(z_2)$. The fact that it does not maximize the satisfaction of agent 1 is transparent in this example because agent 2's self-selection constraint is not binding — note that the allocation is then first-best efficient. In (b), the optimal allocation maximizes the satisfaction of agent 1 and $W_1(z_1) < W_2(z_2)$.

4.3. *General population*

Let us now turn to the case of a larger population. The computation of the optimal tax is quite complex in general, in particular because the population is heterogeneous in two dimensions, preferences and earning ability.[12] We

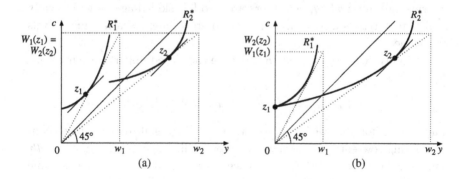

Fig. 10.

---

[12] Actually, since the set of individual preferences is itself infinitely multi-dimensional, this is a problem of screening with, *a priori*, infinitely many dimensions of heterogeneity (but the population is finite in our model). The fact that the complexity of the multidimensional screening problem increases with the number of dimensions is shown in Matthews and Moore (1987).

will, however, be able to derive some conclusions about, first, the part of the tax schedule which should be the focus of the social planner and, second, some features of the optimal tax.

The main difficulty in such an analysis comes from the theoretical possibility of observing ranking reversals, with high-skilled agents earning lower incomes than low-skilled agents. In the standard setting with agents differing only in the skill dimension, this is usually excluded by the Spence–Mirrlees single-crossing assumption. In the current multi-dimensional setting, it would be exceedingly artificial to exclude such reversals, since agents with slightly different wages may obviously have quite different preferences, and it would be questionable to assume that high-skilled agents are always more hardworking than low-skilled agents. Fortunately, it appears that the real difficulty does *not* lie with individual reversals, that is, with the fact that *some* high-skilled agent may earn less than *some* low-skilled agent. For our purposes, we only need to exclude the possibility of observing gaps in the distribution of earnings of low-skilled agents, with such gaps filled only with high-skilled agents. That is, we need to exclude the possibility of having, say, a succession of intervals $[0, y_1], (y_1, y_2), [y_2, w]$, such that agents with wage rate w earn only incomes in the intervals $[0, y_1]$ and $[y_2, w]$, whereas in the earnings interval (y_1, y_2) one only finds agents with skill $w' > w$. Excluding this possibility is quite natural. This can be done by assuming that whenever some high-skilled agents are ready to have earnings in some intermediate interval (y_1, y_2), there are also low-skilled agents with locally similar preferences in the (y, c)-space who are willing to earn similar levels of income.

Formally, let $uc((y_i, c_i), w_i, R_i^*)$ denote the closed upper contour set for R_i^* at (y_i, c_i):

$$uc((y_i, c_i), w_i, R_i^*) = \{(y, c) \in [0, w_i] \times \mathbb{R}_+ \mid (y, c) R_i^* (y_i, c_i)\}.$$

The assumption that we introduce says that a high-skilled agent, when contemplating low earnings, always finds low-skilled agents who have *locally* similar preferences in the (y, c)-space. Let $w_m = \min_i w_i$. We assume throughout this section that $w_m > 0$.

Assumption (Low-Skill Diversity). *For every agent i, and every (y, c) such that $y \leq w_m$, there is an agent j such that $w_j = w_m$ and $uc((y, c), w_j, R_j^*) \subseteq uc((y, c), w_i, R_i^*)$.*

Figure 11 illustrates this configuration. The inclusion of upper contour sets means that whenever agent i chooses (y_i, c_i) in a budget set, there is a

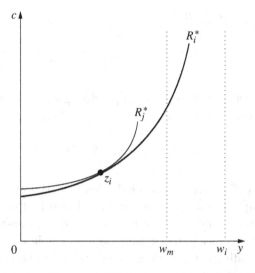

Fig. 11.

low-skilled agent j who is willing to choose the same bundle (y_i, c_i) from the same budget set (for another bundle, it may be another low-skilled agent).

This assumption is of course rather strong for small populations. As explained above, however, what is needed for the results below is only that there be no gap in the distribution of earnings for low-skilled agents. More precisely, the consequence of Low-Skill Diversity that is used below is that for all incentive-compatible and feasible allocations, the envelope curve in (y, c)-space of the indifference curves of low-skilled agents coincides over the interval $[0, w_m]$ of earnings with the envelope curve of the whole population. This weaker assumption is quite natural for large populations, and Low-Skill Diversity is probably the simplest assumption on the primitives of the model which guarantees that it will be satisfied.

The first result in this section has to do with translating the abstract objective of maximizing $\min_i W_i(z_i)$ into a more concrete objective about the part of the agents' budget set which should be maximized.

Theorem 2. *Consider two incentive-compatible allocations z and z' obtainable with two minimal tax functions τ and τ', respectively, such that $\tau(0) < 0$ and $\tau'(0) \leq 0$. If social preferences satisfy Transfer Principle, Laisser-Faire, Weak Pareto, Hansson Independence and Separability, then z is socially preferred to z' whenever the maximal average tax rate over low* *incomes $y \in [0, w_m]$ is smaller in z:*

$$\max_{0 \leq y \leq w_m} \frac{\tau(y)}{y} < \max_{0 \leq y \leq w_m} \frac{\tau'(y)}{y}.$$

The proof of this result (see the Appendix) goes by showing that this inequality on tax rates entails that

$$\min_i W_i(z_i) > \min_i W_i(z_i'),$$

so one may apply Theorem 1 to conclude that z is socially preferred. Note that $\tau(0) < 0$ implies that $z_i P_i(0,0)$ for all i. The priority of the worst-off in social preferences, combined with the assumption of Low-Skill Diversity, is the key factor that leads to focusing on earnings in the range $[0, w_m]$. The measure of individual situations by $W_i(z_i)$, on the other hand, is the key ingredient for taking the average tax rate $\tau(y)/y$ as the relevant token. Indeed, consider on Figure 12 that the graph of $y - \tau(y)$ over the range $[0, w_m]$ coincides (by Low-Skill Diversity and the assumption that the tax function is minimal) with the envelope curve of low-skilled agents' indifference curves. As shown in the figure, the smallest value of $W_i(z_i)$ for the low-skilled agents is then found by looking for the ray that is tangent to

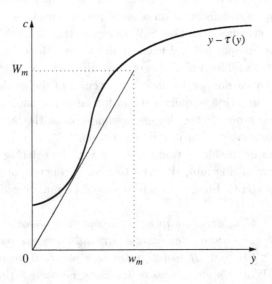

Fig. 12.

this portion of the graph, and therefore equals

$$W_m = w_m \times \min_{0 \leq y \leq w_m} \frac{y - \tau(y)}{y}.$$

It turns out that this is actually the smallest value of $W_i(z_i)$ over the whole population. The conclusion of Theorem 2 immediately follows.

This result has three features which deserve some comments. First, this result does not only provide information about the optimal tax, saying that it must minimize

$$\max_{0 \leq y \leq w_m} \frac{\tau(y)}{y},$$

but also gives a criterion for the assessment of suboptimal taxes. Given the fact that political constraints and disagreements often make the computation of the optimal tax look like an ethereal exercise, it is quite useful to be able to say something about realistic taxes and piecemeal reforms in an imperfect world.

Second, it provides a very simple criterion for the observer who wants to compare taxes. The application of the criterion requires no information about the population characteristics, except the value of w_m, which, in practice, may be thought to coincide with the legal minimum wage.[13] Therefore, there is no need to measure $W_i(z_i)$ for every individual, nor even to estimate the distribution of $W_i(z_i)$ over the population. A simple examination of the tax schedule yields a definite answer.

Third, the content of the criterion itself is quite intuitive. It says that the focus should be on the maximum average tax rate $\tau(y)/y$ over low earnings. Near the optimal tax, low earnings will actually be subsidized, that is, $\tau(y)$ will be negative over this range. Then, the criterion means that the *smallest average rate of subsidy should be as high as possible*, over this range. Interestingly, when w_m tends to zero, the criterion boils down to comparing the value of the minimum income (or demogrant) $-\tau(0)$, and advocates that it should be as high as possible.

It may be useful here to illustrate how the simple comparison criterion provided in the above result can be applied. The next figure presents the 2000 budget set for a lone parent with two children in the U.S.[14]

---

[13]Except, perhaps, when there is more than frictional unemployment. See below.

[14]In this paper, we do not deal with the issue of unequal household sizes. Theorem 2 does however apply to any subpopulation of households of a certain kind. The case of lone parents with children is probably the most relevant if one wants to focus on the subgroup of the population which is the worst-off in all respects.

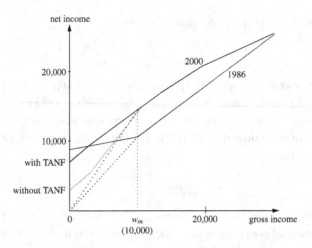

Fig. 13. The U.S. reform.
Source: Brewer (2000), Ellwood (2000).

Net income is computed including income tax, social security contributions, food stamps and Temporary Assistance to Needy Families (TANF), a scheme which replaced the Aid to Families with Dependent Children (AFDC) programme in 1996.[15] Since the TANF is temporary (it has a five-year limit), it is also relevant to look at the budget set after withdrawal of TANF. This is drawn on the figure with a dotted line. An approximate representation of a 1986 (pre-reform) budget is also provided, in order to assess the impact of the reform. The reform has had a positive impact according to the criterion provided in Theorem 2, as shown by the dotted rays from the origins. The conclusion remains even when withdrawal of TANF is considered.

In the following theorem, we provide more information about the optimal tax.

Theorem 3. *Assume that there exists a feasible (not necessarily incentive-compatible) allocation z such that $z_i \, P_i(0,0)$ for all i. If z^* is an optimal (incentive-compatible) allocation for social preferences satisfying Transfer Principle, Laisser-Faire, Weak Pareto, Hansson Independence and*

---

[15]The TANF programme is managed at the State level. Figures corresponding to Florida are retained in Figure 8.

Separability, then it can be obtained with a tax function τ^* which, among all feasible tax functions, maximizes the net income of the hardworking poor, $w_m - \tau(w_m)$, under the constraints that

$$\frac{\tau(y)}{y} \leq \frac{\tau(w_m)}{w_m} \quad \text{for all } y \in (0, w_m],$$

$$\tau(y) \geq \tau(w_m) \quad \text{for all } y,$$

$$\tau(0) \leq 0.$$

The initial assumption made in the theorem simply excludes the case when the zero allocation is efficient and there is therefore no interesting possibility of redistribution. The three constraints listed at the end of the statement mean, respectively, that the average tax rate on low incomes is always lower than at w_m, that the tax (subsidy) is the smallest (largest) at w_m, and that the tax (subsidy) is non-positive (non-negative) at 0.

This result does not say that every optimal tax must satisfy these constraints, but it says, quite relevantly for the social planner, that there is no problem, i.e. no welfare loss, in restricting attention to taxes satisfying those constraints, when looking for the optimal allocation. This result shows how the social preferences defined in this paper lead to focusing on the hardworking poor, who should get, in the optimal allocation, the greatest *absolute amount* of subsidy, among the whole population. However, the taxes computed for those with a lower income than w_m also matter, as those agents must obtain at least as great a *rate of subsidy* as the hardworking poor.

Theorem 3 is illustrated in Figure 14. From the point $(w_m, w_m - \tau(w_m))$ one can construct the hatched area delimited by an upper line of slope 1 and a lower boundary made of the ray to the origin (on the left) and a flat line (on the right). Now, Theorem 3 says that computing the optimal tax may, without welfare loss, be done by maximizing the second coordinate of the point $(w_m, w_m - \tau(w_m))$ under the constraint that the income function $y - \tau(y)$ is located in the corresponding hatched area. It is useless to consider income functions which lie outside this area.

Interestingly, the shape of this area implies that the marginal tax rate over incomes below w_m is, on average, non-positive.

As explained above, when there are agents with almost zero earning ability, our results boil down to a simple maximization of the minimum income. The case of a zero w_m can be related to productive disabilities but also to involuntary unemployment. Since unemployment may be viewed

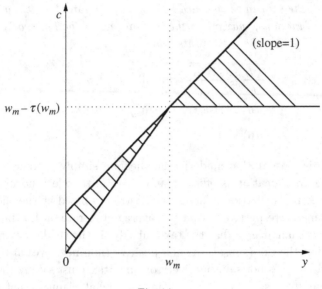

Fig. 14.

as nullifying the agents' earning ability, this result should best be interpreted as suggesting that the focus of redistributive policies should shift
from the hardworking poor to the low-income households when the extent
of unemployment is large, and especially when long-term unemployment is
a significant phenomenon. Then, for instance, the assessment of the welfare
reform in the U.S., as illustrated in Figure 13, would be much less positive since the minimum income has been reduced (and the temporariness
of TANF would appear quite questionable in this context). On the other
hand, physical disabilities and unemployment are more or less observable
characteristics, which may elicit special policies toward those affected by
such conditions, as can be witnessed in many countries.[16] If this is the
case, then the above result should apply to the rest of the population, and
the relevant value of w_m is then likely to be the minimum legal hourly
wage. Nonetheless when unemployment takes the form of constrained part
time jobs (a less easily observable form than ordinary unemployment), this
should also be tackled by considering it as a reduction of the agents' earning
ability.

---

[16]Observation of disabilities and involuntary unemployment is, however, imperfect. For
an analysis of optimal taxation under imperfect tagging, see Salanié (2002).

5. Conclusion

In this paper, we have examined how two fairness principles, a weak version of the Pigou–Dalton transfer principle and a laisser-faire principle for equal-skill economies, single out particular social preferences and a particular measure of individual situations. Such social preferences grant absolute priority to the worst-off, in the maximin fashion. This result[17] might contribute to lending more respectability to the maximin criterion, which is sometimes criticized for its extreme aversion to inequality.[18]

The measure of individual situations obtained here is the tax-free wage rate which would enable an agent to maintain her current satisfaction. This may be viewed as a special money-metric utility representation of individual preferences. The choice of this measure, however, did not rely on introspection or a philosophical examination of human well-being. It derived from the fairness principles (especially the laisser-faire principle), and the analysis did not require any other informational input about individual welfare than ordinal non-comparable preferences. The famous impossibility of social choice (Arrow's theorem) was avoided by weakening Arrow's axiom of Independence of Irrelevant Alternatives in order to take account of the shape of individual indifference curves at the allocations under consideration. It must be stressed that we do not consider W_i as the only reasonable measure of individual situations. In Fleurbaey and Maniquet (2005), alternative social preferences, using different measures, are defended on the basis of other ethical principles. Our purpose is not to defend a single view of social welfare, but to clarify the link between fairness principles and concrete policy evaluations. "It is a legitimate exercise of economic analysis to examine the consequences of various value judgments, whether or not they are shared by the theorist" (Samuelson, 1947, p. 220).

The second part of the paper studied the implications of such social preferences for the evaluation of income tax schedules, under incentive constraints due to the unobservability of skills and the possibility for agents to freely choose their labour time in their budget set. The main result was the discovery of a simple criterion for the comparison of tax schedules, based on the smallest average subsidy (or greatest average tax rate) for low incomes. Another result was that the average marginal tax rate for low

---

[17]Similar derivations of the maximin criterion have also been obtained in different contexts by Fleurbaey (2001) and Maniquet and Sprumont (2004).

[18]It has always been, however, one of the prominent criteria in the literature of optimal taxation. See, e.g., Atkinson (1973, 1995) and, more recently, Choné and Laroque (2001).

incomes should optimally be non-positive, and that the hardworking poor should receive maximal subsidies, under the constraint that lower incomes should not have a lower rate of subsidy than the hardworking poor. This constraint is important. It forbids policies which harshly punish the agents working part time and give exclusive subsidies to full-time jobs. In addition, various forms of unemployment can be taken into account by revising the distribution of earning abilities in the population, leading to a reduction of w_m and therefore to a more generous policy toward low incomes.

There are many directions in which this line of research can be pursued. In particular, the model can be enriched so as to study such issues as savings and the taxation of unearned income, or different consumption goods and the interaction between income taxation and commodity taxation.

Appendix: Proofs

Lemma 1. *If social preferences satisfy Transfer Principle, Weak Pareto and Hansson Independence, then for any pair of allocations z, z' and any pair of agents i, j with identical preferences R_0, such that*

$$z_i' \, P_0 \, z_i \, P_0 \, z_j \, P_0 \, z_j' \, R_0 \, (0,0)$$

and $z_k \, P_k \, z_k'$ for all $k \neq i$, j, one has $z \, P \, z'$.

Proof. Let z, z' satisfy the above conditions. By Hansson Independence, we can arbitrarily modify the preferences R_0 at bundles which are not indifferent to one of the four bundles z_i, z_j', z_j, z_j'. Let f_i, g_i, f_j, g_j be the functions whose graphs are the indifference curves for R_0 at these four bundles, respectively. Let f^* be the function whose graph is the lower boundary of the convex hull of

$$(0, f_i(0)) \cup \{(\ell, c) \mid c \geq g_i(\ell)\},$$

and f_j^* be the function whose graph is the lower boundary of the convex hull of

$$(0, g_j(0)) \cup \{(\ell, c) \mid c \geq f_j(\ell)\}.$$

These functions are convex, and their graphs can be arbitrarily close (w.r.t. the sup norm) to two indifference curves for R_0. We will indeed assume that there is an indifference curve for R_0, between f_i and g_i, arbitrarily close to the graph of f_i^*, and another one, between f_j and g_j, arbitrarily close to f_j^*.

By construction there exists ℓ_1 such that

$$g_i(\ell_1) - f_i^*(\ell_1) < f_j^*(\ell_1) - g_j(\ell_1),$$

and similarly

$$f_i^*(0) - f_i(0) = 0 < f_j(0) - f_j^*(0) = f_j(0) - g_j(0).$$

Therefore, one can find $c_i^1, c_i^2, c_j^1, c_j^2$ such that

$$g_i(\ell_1) - f_i^*(\ell_1) < c_i^1 - c_i^2 = c_j^2 - c_j^1 < f_j^*(\ell_1) - g_j(\ell_1),$$
$$c_i^2 < f_i^*(\ell_1) \le g_i(\ell_1) < c_i^1,$$
$$g_j(\ell_1) < c_j^1 < c_j^2 < f_j^*(\ell_1).$$

and $c_i^3, c_i^4, c_j^3, c_j^4$ such that

$$0 < c_i^3 - c_i^4 = c_j^4 - c_j^3 < f_j(0) - f_j^*(0),$$
$$c_i^4 < f_i(0) = f_i^*(0) < c_i^3,$$
$$f_j^*(0) < c_j^3 < c_j^4 < f_j(0).$$

Define z^1, z^2, z^3, z^4 by

$$z_k \, P_k \, z_k^4 = z_k^3 \, P_k \, z_k^2 = z_k^1 \, P_k \, z_k'$$

for all $k \ne i, j$, and

$$z_k^1 = (\ell_1, c_k^1), \quad z_k^2 = (\ell_1, c_k^2), \quad z_k^3 = (0, c_k^3), \quad z_k^4 = (0, c_k^4)$$

for all $k = i, j$.

By Transfer Principle, one has

$$z^2 \, R \, z^1 \quad \text{and} \quad z^4 \, R \, z^3.$$

By Weak Pareto (and the assumption about indifference curves close to f_i^* and f_j^*),

$$z \, P \, z^4, \quad z^3 \, P \, z^2 \quad \text{and} \quad z^1 \, P \, z'.$$

By transitivity, one concludes that $z \, P \, z'$. $\qquad \square$

Lemma 2.   *If social preferences satisfy Transfer Principle, Laisser-Faire, Weak Pareto, Hansson Independence and Separability, then for any pair of allocations z, z' and any pair of agents i, j, such that*

$$W_i(z_i') > W_i(z_i) > W_j(z_j) > W_j(z_j'),$$

$z_i\, P_i(0,0)$ *and* $z_k = z_k'$ *for all* $k \neq i$, j, *one has* $z\, P\, z'$.

Proof.   Let z and z' be two allocations satisfying the above conditions. Necessarily $W_j(z_j) > 0$, and since $z_i\, P_i(0,0)$ there exists $\hat{z}_i$ such that $W_i(z_i) > W_i(\hat{z}_i) > W_j(z_j)$. Let a and b be two new agents with $w_a = w_b = w = W_i(\hat{z}_i)$, and with preferences $R_a = R_i$ and $R_b = R_j$. Let z^* be a laisser-faire allocation for the two-agent economy $\{a, b\}$, and (z_a, z_b) be another allocation such that

$$W_i(z_i) > W_a(z_a) > w > W_b(z_b) > W_j(z_j)$$

and

$$c_a + c_b < w(\ell_a + \ell_b),$$

which means that (z_a, z_b) is inefficient. Therefore, there exists $(\tilde{z}_a, \tilde{z}_b)$ such that $\tilde{c}_a + \tilde{c}_b \leq w(\tilde{\ell}_a + \tilde{\ell}_b)$ and $\tilde{z}_a\, P_a\, z_a$, $\tilde{z}b\, P_b\, z_b$.

For any population A, let R_A denote the social preferences for the economy with population A. By Laisser-Faire,

$$z^* R_{\{a,b\}} (\tilde{z}_a, \tilde{z}_b)$$

and by Weak Pareto,

$$(\tilde{z}_a, \tilde{z}_b) P_{\{a,b\}} (z_a, z_b)$$

so by transitivity,

$$z^* P_{\{a,b\}} (z_a, z_b).$$

Therefore, by Separability,

$$(z_a^*, z_b^*, z_i, z_j) P_{\{a,b,i,j\}} (z_a, z_b, z_i, z_j).$$

We will now use the fact that

$$z_i'\, P_i\, z_i\, P_i\, z_a\, P_i\, z_a^*$$

and

$$z_b^*\, P_j\, z_b\, P_j\, z_j\, P_j\, z_j'.$$

Let z_i^-, $z_i'^+$ and z_a^- be such that

$$z_i'^+ \, P_i \, z_i' \, P_i \, z_i \, P_i \, z_i^- \, P_i \, z_a \, P_i \, z_a^- \, P_i \, z_a^*,$$

and similarly, let $z_j'^+$, $z_j'^{++}$ and z_b^{*+} be such that

$$z_b^{*+} \, P_j \, z_b^* \, P_j \, z_b \, P_j \, z_j \, P_j \, z_j'^{++} \, P_j \, z_j'^+ \, P_j \, z_j'.$$

Since

$$z_j'^+ \, P_i \, z_i^- \, P_i \, z_a^- \, P_i \, z_a^*$$

and $z_b^{*+} \, P_j \, z_b^*$, $z_j'^{++} \, P_j \, z_j'^+$, one can refer to Lemma 1, and conclude that

$$(z_a^-, z_b^{*+}, z_i^-, z_j'^{++}) P_{\{a,b,i,j\}} (z_a^*, z_b^*, z_i'^+, z_j'^+).$$

Similarly, since

$$z_b^{*+} \, P_j \, z_b \, P_j \, z_j \, P_j \, z_j'^{++}$$

and $z_i \, P_i \, z_i^-$, $z_a \, P_i \, z_a^-$, one obtains

$$(z_a, z_b, z_i, z_j) P_{\{a,b,i,j\}} (z_a^-, z_b^{*+}, z_i^-, z_j'^{++}).$$

By transitivity, one then has

$$(z_a, z_b, z_i, z_j) P_{\{a,b,i,j\}} (z_a^*, z_b^*, z_i'^+, z_j'^+),$$

and therefore

$$(z_a^*, z_b^*, z_i, z_j) P_{\{a,b,i,j\}} (z_a^*, z_b^*, z_i'^+, z_j'^+).$$

Separability then entails that

$$(z_i, z_j) R_{\{i,j\}} (z_i'^+, z_j'^+),$$

and by Weak Pareto one actually gets

$$(z_i, z_j) P_{\{i,j\}} (z_i', z_j').$$

From Separability again, one can finally derive the conclusion that $z \, P \, z'$ in the initial economy. □

Proof of Theorem 1.

(i) Let z and z' be two allocations such that $z_i\, P_i(0,0)$ and $z'_i\, R_i(0,0)$ for all i, and

$$\min_i W_i(z_i) > \min_i W_i(z'_i).$$

Then, by monotonicity of preferences, one can find two allocations x, x' such that for all i, $z_i\, P_i\, x_i\, P_i(0,0)$, $x'_i\, P_i\, z'_i$, and there exists i_0 such that for all $i \neq i_0$

$$W_i(x'_i) > W_i(x_i) > W_{i_0}(x_{i_0}) > W_{i_0}(x'_{i_0}).$$

Let $(x^k)_{1 \le k \le n+1}$ be a sequence of allocations such that for all $i \neq i_0$,

$$x_i^i = \cdots = x_i^1 = x'_i,$$
$$z_i\, P_i\, x_i^{n+1} = \cdots = x_i^{i+1} = x_i,$$

while

$$x_{i_0} = x_{i_0}^{n+1}\, P_{i_0}\, x_{i_0}^{n-1}\, P_{i_0} \cdots P_{i_0} x_{i_0}^{i_0+1} = x_{i_0}^{i_0}\, P_{i_0} \cdots P_{i_0}\, x_{i_0}^1 = x'_{i_0}.$$

One sees that for all $k \neq i_0$, $x_k^{k+1}\, P_k(0,0)$ and

$$W_k(x_k^k) > W_k(x_k^{k+1}) > W_{i_0}(x_{i_0}^{k+1}) > W_{i_0}(x_{i_0}^k),$$

while for all k, and all $i \neq i_0$, k, $x_i^{k+1} = x_i^k$. By Lemma 2, this implies that $x^{k+1}\, P\, x^k$ for all $k \neq i_0$, while $x^{i_0+1} = x^{i_0}$.

By Weak Pareto, $x^1\, P\, z'$, and $z\, P\, x^{n+1}$. By transitivity, $z\, P\, z'$.

(ii) Consider allocations z and z' such that $z_i\, P_i(0,0)$ for all i and $(0,0)\, P_{i_0}\, z'_{i_0}$ for some i_0. By Hansson Independence, social preferences over $\{z, z'\}$ are not altered if the indifference curve for i_0 at $(0,0)$ is assumed to be such that $W_{i_0}(0,0) < \min_i W_i(z_i)$. Let z'' be such that $z''_{i_0} = (0,0)$ and for all $i \neq i_0$, $z''_i\, P_i(0,0)$ and $z''_i\, P_i\, z'$. One has $\min_i W_i(z''_i) \le W_{i_0}(0,0) < \min_i W_i(z_i)$ and by Theorem 1(i), $z\, P\, z''$. By Weak Pareto, $z''\, P\, z'$. Therefore, $z\, P\, z'$.

Proof of Theorem 2. Consider an allocation z such that $z_i\, R_i(0,0)$ for all i, and the (unique) related minimal tax function τ. Since τ is minimal, the income function $y - \tau(y)$ coincides with the envelope curve of the population's indifference curves in (y,c)-space, at z.

We first prove the following fact: Over $[0, w_m]$, the income function $y - \tau(y)$ coincides with the envelope curve of the indifference curves of the agents from the w_m subpopulation. Consider the set delimited by the envelope curve of all agents' indifference curves over this range:

$$([0, w_m] \times \mathbb{R}_+) \cap \left(\bigcup_i uc((w_i\ell_i, c_i), w_i, R_i^*) \right)$$

$$= \bigcup_i (uc((w_i\ell_i, c_i), w_i, R_i^*) \cap ([0, w_m] \times \mathbb{R}_+)).$$

If the stated fact did not hold, then one would find some (y_0, c_0) such that

$$(y_0, c_0) \in \bigcup_i (uc((w_i\ell_i, c_i), w_i, R_i^*) \cap ([0, w_m] \times \mathbb{R}_+)),$$

$$(y_0, c_0) \notin \bigcup_{i : w_i = w_m} (uc((w_i\ell_i, c_i), w_i, R_i^*) \cap ([0, w_m] \times \mathbb{R}_+)).$$

The first statement means that there is some i such that

$$(y_0, c_0) \in uc((w_i\ell_i, c_i), w_i, R_i^*) \cap ([0, w_m] \times \mathbb{R}_+),$$

implying

$$uc((y_0, c_0), w_i, R_i^*) \subseteq uc((w_i\ell_i, c_i), w_i, R_i^*).$$

By the Low-Skill Diversity assumption, there is j with $w_j = w_m$ such that

$$uc((y_0, c_0), w_j, R_j^*) \subseteq uc((y_0, c_0), w_i, R_i^*),$$

and therefore

$$uc((y_0, c_0), w_j, R_j^*) \subseteq uc((w_i\ell_i, c_i), w_i, R_i^*).$$

A consequence of this inclusion is that for any (y, c) such that $(y, c) P_j^*(y_0, c_0)$, one has $(y, c) P_i^*(w_i\ell_i, c_i)$. Since

$$(y_0, c_0) \notin \bigcup_{i : w_i = w_m} (uc((w_i\ell_i, c_i), w_i, R_i^*) \cap ([0, w_m] \times \mathbb{R}_+)),$$

one must have $(w_j\ell_j, c_j) P_j^*(y_0, c_0)$, and therefore $(w_j\ell_j, c_j) P_i^*(w_i\ell_i, c_i)$. Now, this violates the incentive-compatibility condition. We obtain a contradiction, which proves the stated fact.

Let

$$W_m = w_m \min_{0 \le y \le w_m} \frac{y - \tau(y)}{y}.$$

By the above fact,

$$W_m = w_m \min \left\{ \frac{c}{y} \middle| (y, c) \in \bigcup_{i : w_i = w_m} uc((w_i \ell_i, c_i), w_i, R_i^*) \right\},$$

which equivalently reads

$$W_m = w_m \min_{i : w_i = w_m} \min \left\{ \frac{c}{y} \middle| (y, c) \in uc((w_i \ell_i, c_i), w_i, R_i^*) \right\}.$$

Now, one has, by definition:

$$W_i(z_i) = w_i \min \left\{ \frac{c}{y} \middle| (y, c) \in uc((w_i \ell_i, c_i), w_i, R_i^*) \right\}.$$

Therefore, W_m is the minimum value of $W_i(z_i)$ over the w_m subpopulation.

Similarly, for agents with a higher w, the minimum value of $W_i(z_i)$ is greater or equal to

$$W_{(w)} = w \min_{0 \leq y \leq w} \frac{y - \tau(y)}{y}.$$

It may be strictly greater than $W_{(w)}$ because, contrary to the case of $w = w_m$ where the Low-Skill Diversity assumption applied, the envelope curve of indifference curves for agents with wage rate $w > w_m$ may be above the envelope curve of all agents' indifference curves over the range $[0, w]$. Notice that, for any w, either

$$W_{(w)} = w - \tau(w)$$

or

$$W_{(w)} = w \frac{y_0 - \tau(y_0)}{y_0} \quad \text{for } y_0 < w.$$

Since $y - \tau(y)$ is non-decreasing, the first expression is non-decreasing in w, and this is also trivially true for the second expression. As a consequence, $W_{(w)}$ is non-decreasing in w, so that $W_{(w)} \geq W_m$, and *a fortiori* W_m is indeed the minimum value of $W_i(z_i)$ over the whole population.

We want to compare z and z', as given in the statement of the theorem. Let

$$W_m' = w_m \min_{0 \leq y \leq w_m} \frac{y - \tau'(y)}{y}.$$

As $\tau(0) < 0$ and $\tau'(0) \leq 0$, one has $z_i P_i(0, 0)$ and $z_i' R_i(0, 0)$ for all i, so that Theorem 1(i) applies: Allocation z is socially preferred to z' whenever

$W_m > W'_m$. This inequality is equivalent to

$$\min_{0 \le y \le w_m} \frac{y - \tau(y)}{y} > \min_{0 \le y \le w_m} \frac{y - \tau'(y)}{y},$$

or equivalently,

$$\max_{0 \le y \le w_m} \frac{\tau(y)}{y} < \max_{0 \le y \le w_m} \frac{\tau'(y)}{y}.$$

This concludes the proof. □

We need three lemmas for the proof of Theorem 3. These lemmas deal with the possibility of finding incentive-compatible allocations in a neighbourhood of allocations satisfying some properties.

Lemma 3. *Let $f : \mathbb{R}_+ \to \mathbb{R}_+$ be an arbitrary non-decreasing function, and z an incentive-compatible (not necessarily feasible) allocation.*

(i) *Assume that $c_i < f(y_i)$ for all i. Then, for any $\varepsilon > 0$ there exists an incentive-compatible allocation z' such that $(\ell_i, c_i + \varepsilon) P_i z'_i P_i z_i$ and $c'_i \le f(y'_i)$ for all i, and $\sum_i (c'_i - y'_i) \le \sum_i (c_i - y_i) + \varepsilon$.*

(ii) *Assume that $0 < c_i \le f(y_i)$ for all i. Then for any ε such that $0 < \varepsilon < \min_i c_i$ there exists an incentive-compatible allocation z' such that $z_i R'_i z'_i P_i (\ell_i, c_i - \varepsilon)$ and $c'_i \le f(y'_i)$ for all i, and $\sum_i (c'_i - y'_i) < \sum_i (c_i - y_i)$.*

Proof.

(i) Let $z_i^+ = (\ell_i, c_i + \varepsilon/n)$ for all i. Let g be a function whose graph in (y, c)-space coincides with the envelope curve of the agents' indifference curves at z^+. Since $z_i^+ P_i z_i$ for all i and $(y_i, c_i) R_i^*(y_j, c_j)$ for all i, j such that $y_j \le w_i$, implying $(y_i, c_i^+) P_i^*(y_j, c_j)$ for all i, j such that $y_j \le w_i$, one has $c_i < g(y_i)$ for all i. Let $\eta = \min_i(\min\{f(y_i), g(y_i)\} - c_i)_{i=1,\dots,n}$. One has $(y_i, c_i^+) R_i^*(y_j, c_j + \eta)$ for all i, j such that $y_j \le w_i$, and therefore $(\ell_i, c_i + \varepsilon) P_i(y_j/w_i, c_j + \eta)$ for all i, j such that $y_j \le w_i$.

For any i, k in $\{1, \dots, n\}$, let

$$v_i(y_k, c) = \begin{cases} \min\{x \ge 0 \mid (0, x) R_i^*(y_k, c)\} \\ \qquad \text{if } y_k \le w_i \text{ and } (y_k, c) R_i^*(0, 0), \\ -\max\{y \ge 0 \mid (y, 0) R_i^*(y_k, c)\} \\ \qquad \text{if } y_k \le w_i \text{ and } (0, 0) P_i^*(y_k, c), \\ -w_i - y_k/(1 + c) \text{ if } y_k > w_i. \end{cases}$$

For all y_k, this "value function" is continuous and strictly increasing in $c \geq 0$, and it represents i's preferences R_i^* over the subset of (y_k, c) such that $y_k \leq w_i$.

We now focus on allocations $(y_i', c_i')_{i=1,\ldots,n}$ such that for some permutation π on $\{1, \ldots, n\}$ and for some vector $(d_1, \ldots, d_n) \geq 0$, one has $(y_i', c_i') = (y_{\pi(i)}, c_{\pi(i)} + d_{\pi(i)})$ for all i. The initial allocation $(y_i, c_i)_{i=1,\ldots,n}$ is obtained by π being the identity mapping and $(d_1, \ldots, d_n) = 0$. It is "envy-free" in the sense that for all i, k, $v_i(y_i, c_i) \geq v_i(y_k, c_k)$. This is an immediate consequence of the fact that for any i, k, $(y_i, c_i) R_i^*(y_k, c_k)$ if $y_k \leq w_i$, and $v_i(y_i, c_i) \geq -w_i > v_i(y_k, c_k)$ if $y_k > w_i$.

We can then apply the "Perturbation Lemma" in Alkan, Demange and Gale (1991, p. 1029) to conclude that there is another envy-free allocation $(y_i', c_i')_{i=1,\ldots,n}$, for some π and some d such that $0 < d_i < \eta$ for all i.

The allocation z' defined by $z_i' = (y_i'/w_i, c_i')$ for all i satisfies the desired properties. By envy-freeness one has $v_i(y_i', c_i') \geq v_i(y_k', c_k')$ for all i, k, and in particular for k such that $\pi(k) = i$, $v_i(y_i', c_i') \geq v_i(y_i, c_i + d_i) > v_i(y_i, c_i)$. Since $v_i(y_i, c_i) \geq -w_i$ for all i, this implies $v_i(y_i', c_i') > -w_i$ for all i. Therefore, $y_i' \leq w_i$ for all i and $(y_i', c_i') R_i^*(y_k', c_k')$ for all i, k such that $y_k \leq w_i$, which means that z' is incentive-compatible.

By construction, $(y_i', c_i') < (y_{\pi(i)}, c_{\pi(i)} + \eta)$. Since $(\ell_i, c_i + \varepsilon) P_i(y_j/w_i, c_j + \eta)$ for all i, j such that $y_j \leq w_i$, it follows that $(\ell_i, c_i + \varepsilon) P_i z_i'$ for all i. In addition $v_i(y_i', c_i') > v_i(y_i, c_i)$ implies $z_i' P_i z_i$.

Finally,

$$\sum_i (c_i' - y_i') \leq \sum_i (c_i - y_i) + n\eta < \sum_i (c_i - y_i) + \varepsilon.$$

(ii) Let $m = \max_i(c_i - y_i)$. Let $M = \{i \mid c_i - y_i > m - \varepsilon/2\}$. Notice that for all i,

$$\frac{\varepsilon}{2} < \varepsilon < c_i \leq y_i + m.$$

For all $i \in M$, let $\hat{c}_i = y_i + m - \varepsilon/2 > 0$, and let (y_i', c_i') be a best bundle for i in the subset $\{(y_k, \hat{c}_k)_{k \in M}, (y_k, c_k)_{k \notin M}\}$. For $i \notin M$, let $z_i' = z_i$.

The allocation z' is incentive-compatible. Indeed, for every $i \in M$, (y_i', c_i') is her best bundle in $\{(y_k, \hat{c}_k)_{k \in M}, (y_k, c_k)_{k \notin M}\}$ and therefore also in $\{(y_k, c_k')_{k \in M}, (y_k, c_k)_{k \notin M}\} \subseteq \{(y_k, \hat{c}_k)_{k \in M}, (y_k, c_k)_{k \notin M}\}$. And since $\hat{c}_k < c_k$ for $k \in M$, the fact that for any $i \notin M$, (y_i', c_i') is a best bundle in the subset $\{(y_k, c_k)_{k \in M}, (y_k, c_k)_{k \notin M}\}$ entails that it is *a fortiori* a best bundle in $\{(y_k, c'_k)_{k \in M}, (y_k, c_k)_{k \notin M}\} \subseteq \{(y_k, \hat{c}_k)_{k \in M}, (y_k, c_k)_{k \notin M}\}$.

For every $i \in M$, $z_i \, R_i \, z'_i \, P_i(\ell_i, c_i - \varepsilon)$, because $(y'_i, c'_i) R_i^*(y_i, \hat{c}_i)$ and $\hat{c}_i = y_i + m - \varepsilon/2 \geq y_i + (c_i - y_i) - \varepsilon/2 > c_i - \varepsilon$. For every $i \notin M$, $z_i = z'_i \, P_i(\ell_i, c_i - \varepsilon)$.

The fact that $\hat{c}_i \leq c_i$ for all $i = 1, \ldots, n$ implies that $\hat{c}_i \leq f(y_i)$ for all i and thereby guarantees that $c'_i \leq f(y'_i)$ for all i.

Finally,

$$\sum_i (c'_i - y'_i) = \sum_{i \in M} (c'_i - y'_i) + \sum_{i \notin M} (c'_i - y'_i)$$

$$\leq \sum_{i \in M} (m - \varepsilon/2) + \sum_{i \notin M} (c_i - y_i) < \sum_i (c_i - y_i).$$

$\square$

Lemma 4. *Let A be the set of allocations z which are feasible, incentive-compatible, and such that $z_i \, P_i(0,0)$ for all i. Let B be the set of allocations z which are feasible, incentive-compatible, and such that $z_i \, R_i(0,0)$ for all i. Let U_i be a continuous representation of R_i, and let $U(z)$ denote $(U_1(z_1), \ldots, U_n(z_n))$. If A is not empty, then for any $z \in B \backslash A$, there is $z' \in A$ such that $U(z')$ is arbitrarily close to $U(z)$.*

Proof. Let $z \in B \backslash A$ and assume $A \neq \emptyset$.

(1) If $\sum_i (c_i - y_i) < 0$, then by Lemma 3(i), for any $\varepsilon > 0$ there exists an incentive-compatible allocation z' such that $(c_i + \varepsilon, \ell_i) P_i \, z'_i \, P_i \, z_i$ for all i, and $\sum_i (c'_i - y'_i) \leq \sum_i (c_i - y_i) + \varepsilon$. If $\varepsilon < |\sum_i (c_i - y_i)|$, then z' is feasible and belongs to A. Since ε is arbitrarily small, $U(z')$ is arbitrarily close to $U(z)$.

(2) If $\sum_i (c_i - y_i) = 0$:

(2-i) If $\max_i (c_i - y_i) = 0$, then $c_i = y_i$ for all i. Let τ be the minimal tax implementing z (i.e. $y - \tau(y)$ coincides on $[0, \max_i w_i]$ with the envelope curve of the agents' indifference curves in (y, c) space).

(2-i-a) If there exists y_0 such that $\tau(y_0) > 0$, then consider agent i such that $z_i \, I_i(\frac{y_0}{w_i}, y_0 - \tau(y_0))$, and let $z_i^- = (\frac{y_0}{w_i}, y_0 - \tau(y_0))$. One has $c_i^- - y_i^- = -\tau(y_0) < 0$, so that the allocation (z_i^-, z_{-i}) may be dealt with as in case (1) in order to find $z' \in A$ with arbitrarily close utilities.

(2-i-b) If $\tau(y) \leq 0$ for all y, let $J = \{i \mid z_i \, P_i(0,0)\}$ and $K = \{i \mid Z_i \, I_i(0,0)\}$. The set J is non-empty, otherwise A would be empty (because, then, for all $i, (0,0)$ is a best allocation for R_i^* in $\{(y, c) \mid c \leq y\}$). And $c_i > 0$ for all $i \in J$. Define $z_i^- = (0,0)$ for all $i \in K$

and $z_i^- = z_i$ for all $i \in J$. The allocation z^- is feasible (recall that $c_i = y_i$ for all i), incentive-compatible and Pareto-indifferent to z. Let f be a function whose graph, in (y, c)-space, coincides with the envelope curve of the indifference curves at z^- of agents from K. Since for any $i \in K$, $j \in J$, either $(0,0)R_i^*(y_j, c_j)$ or $y_j > w_i$, one has $c_j \leq f(y_j)$ or $y_j > \max_{i \in K} w_i$ for all $j \in J$. By extending $f(.)$ over the interval $(\max_{i \in K} w_i, +\infty)$, one can easily have $c_j \leq f(y_j)$ for all $j \in J$. By Lemma 3(ii), for any η such that $0 < \eta < \min_{j \in J} c_j$ there exists $(z_j')_{j \in J}$ which is incentive-compatible for the subpopulation J and such that $z_j R_j z_j' P_j(\ell_j, c_j - \eta)$ and $c_j' \leq f(y_j')$ for all $j \in J$, and $\sum_{j \in J}(c_j' - y_j') < \sum_{j \in J}(c_j - y_j)$. By taking η sufficiently small one can have $z_j' P_j(0,0)$ for all $j \in J$. Let g be a function whose graph, in (y, c)-space, coincides with the envelope curve of the indifference curves at z' of agents from J. One has $c_i^- = 0 < g(y_i^-) = g(0)$ for all $i \in K$. Let $0 < \varepsilon < \sum_{j \in J}(c_j - y_j) - \sum_{j \in J}(c_j' - y_j')$. By Lemma 3(i), there exists $(z_i')_{i \in K}$ which is incentive-compatible and such that $(c_i^- + \varepsilon, \ell_i^-)P_i z_i' P_i z_i^-$ and $c_i' \leq g(y_i')$ for all $i \in K$, and $\sum_{i \in K}(c_i' - y_i') \leq \sum_{i \in K}(c_i - y_i) + \varepsilon$. The allocation z' is in A and is as desired.

(2-ii) If $\max_i(c_i - y_i) > 0$: Let

$$M = \Big\{ i \in \{1, \ldots, n\} \mid c_i - y_i = \max_j(c_j - y_j) \Big\}.$$

Since $\sum_j(c_j - y_j) \leq 0$, $M \subsetneq \{1, \ldots, n\}$.

(2-ii-a) If there is $i \in M$ such that $(y_i, c_i)I_i^*(y_{j_0}, c_{j_0})$ for some $j_0 \notin M$, then let $(y_i^-, c_i^-) = (y_{j_0}, c_{j_0})$. Let $0 < \varepsilon < c_i - y_i - (c_i^- - y_i^-)$. By Lemma 3(i) there exists an incentive-compatible allocation z' such that $(c_i^- + \varepsilon, \ell_i^-)P_i z_i' P_i z_i^-$ and $(c_j + \varepsilon, \ell_j)P_j z_j' P_j z_j$ for all $j \neq i$, and

$$\sum_i(c_i' - y_i') \leq c_i^- - y_i^- + \sum_{j \neq i}(c_j - y_j) + \varepsilon < \sum_j(c_j - y_j) \leq 0.$$

(2-ii-b) If there is $i \in M$ such that $z_i I_i(0,0)$, then let $z_i^- = (0,0)$. The rest of the argument is as in case a. (2-ii-c) If none of the cases a–b holds, then for all $i \in M$, $z_i P_i(0,0)$ and $(y_i, c_i)P_i^*(y_j, c_j)$ (or $y_j > w_i$) for all $j \notin M$. This case is dealt with similarly as the case i-b, by taxing agents from M at the benefit of the others.   □

Lemma 5. *If there is a feasible allocation z such that $z_i P_i(0,0)$ for all i, then there is a feasible and incentive-compatible allocation z such that $z_i P_i(0,0)$ for all i.*

Proof. Let $z^* = ((0,0), \ldots, (0,0))$. It is feasible and incentive-compatible. Let $f : \mathbb{R}_+ \to \mathbb{R}_+$ be a function whose graph coincides on $[0, \max_i w_i]$ with the envelope curve in (y, c)-space of individual indifference curves at z^*. If $f(y) \geq y$ for all $y \in [0, \max_i w_i]$, then z^* is Pareto-efficient and there is no feasible allocation z such that $z_i \, P_i(0,0)$ for all i. Therefore, $f(y_0) < y_0$ for some $y_0 \leq \max_i w_i$. Let i_0 be an agent such that $(0,0) I_{i_0}^*(y_0, f(y_0))$. The allocation z' such that $(y'_{i_0}, c'_{i_0}) = (y_0, f(y_0))$ and $(y'_j, c'_j) = (0,0)$ for all $j \neq i_0$ is incentive-compatible and such that $\sum_i c'_i < \sum_i y'_i$. By Lemma 3, there exists another feasible and incentive-compatible allocation z such that for all i, $z_i \, P_i \, z'_i$. $\qquad\square$

Proof of Theorem 3. Consider an optimal allocation z^*. Suppose there is i such that $(0,0) P_i z_i^*$. Since by Lemma 5, there is a feasible and incentive-compatible allocation z such that $z_i \, P_i(0,0)$ for all i, then by Theorem 1(ii) $z \, P \, z^*$ and this contradicts the assumption that z^* is optimal. Therefore, one must have $z_i^* R_i(0,0)$ for all i. There is a (unique) minimal tax function τ such that the income function $y - \tau(y)$ coincides with the envelope curve of the population's indifference curves in (y, c)-space, at z^*. In particular, $\tau(0) \leq 0$.

Let the sets A and B be defined as in Lemma 4. We have just proved that $z^* \in B$. We now show that

$$\min_i W_i(z_i^*) = \max_{z \in B} \min_i W_i(z_i).$$

Suppose not. This may be either because $\max_{z \in B} \min_i W_i(z_i)$ does not exist, or because $\min_i W_i(z_i^*) < \max_{z \in B} \min_i W_i(z_i)$. In both cases, there exists $z \in B$ such that $\min_i W_i(z_i^*) < \min_i W_i(z_i)$. By Lemma 4, there exists $z' \in A$ such that $W(z')$ is arbitrarily close to $W(z)$, so $\min_i W_i(z_i^*) < \min_i W_i(z'_i)$. This implies $z' \, P \, z^*$, which contradicts the assumption that z^* is optimal.

The fact that $\min_i W_i(z_i^*) = \max_{z \in B} \min_i W_i(z_i)$ means that z^* is obtained by a tax which, among all feasible taxes such that $\tau(0) \leq 0$ (and $y - \tau(y)$ is non-decreasing), maximizes $\min_i W_i(z_i)$ at the resulting allocation z. It remains to show that there is no restriction in adding the other conditions stated in the theorem, and that under these conditions maximizing $\min_i W_i(z_i)$ is equivalent to maximizing $w_m - \tau(w_m)$.

By the proof of Theorem 2,

$$\min_i W_i(z_i^*) = W_m = w_m \min_{0 \leq y \leq w_m} \frac{y - \tau(y)}{y}.$$

At a laisser-faire allocation z^{LF}, one has $W_i(z_i^{LF}) \geq w_i$ for all i, so

$$\min_i W_i(z_i^{LF}) \geq w_m.$$

A fortiori, at the optimum,

$$W_m = \min_i W_i(z_i^*) \geq w_m.$$

Let a new tax be defined by

$$\tau^*(y) = \max\{\tau(y), w_m - W_m\}.$$

This tax function is feasible, because it cuts all subsidies greater than a constant, $W_m - w_m \geq 0$, so that no agent's tax may decrease (and no subsidy increase), even after she adjusts her choice. Moreover,

$$\min_{0 \leq y \leq w_m} \frac{y - \tau^*(y)}{y} = \min_{0 \leq y \leq w_m} \left\{ \frac{y - \tau(y)}{y}, \frac{y - (w_m - W_m)}{y} \right\}$$

$$= \min \left\{ \min_{0 \leq y \leq w_m} \frac{y - \tau(y)}{y}, \min_{0 \leq y \leq w_m} 1 + \frac{W_m - w_m}{y} \right\}$$

$$= \min \left\{ \frac{W_m}{w_m}, 1 + \frac{W_m - w_m}{w_m} \right\}$$

$$= \frac{W_m}{w_m} = \min_{0 \leq y \leq w_m} \frac{y - \tau(y)}{y}.$$

The tax function τ^* need not be minimal. Let z^{**} be an allocation obtained with τ^*, and chosen so that $z_i^{**} = z_i^*$ for all i such that $\tau(y_i^*) \geq w_m - W_m$. Let τ^{**} be the corresponding minimal tax function. One has $\tau^{**} \leq \tau^*$, and therefore

$$\min_i W_i(z_i^{**}) = w_m \min_{0 \leq y \leq w_m} \frac{y - \tau^{**}(y)}{y} \geq w_m \min_{0 \leq y \leq w_m} \frac{y - \tau^*(y)}{y} = W_m.$$

In addition, since $\tau^* \geq \tau$, necessarily $z_i^* R_i z_i^{**}$ for all i, implying $W_i(z_i^{**}) \leq W_i(z_i^*)$ for all i. Therefore

$$\min_i W_i(z_i^{**}) \leq \min_i W_i(z_i^*) = W_m,$$

and then

$$\min_i W_i(z_i^{**}) = W_m.$$

The allocation z^{**} has been constructed so that for every i, either $z_i^{**} = z_i^*$ and $\tau^*(y_i^{**}) = \tau(y_i^*)$, or $\tau^*(y_i^{**}) > \tau(y_i^*)$. Suppose there is i

such that $\tau^*(y_i^{**}) > \tau(y_i^*)$. Then one has $\sum_i \tau^*(y_i^{**}) > 0$, meaning that $\sum_i c_i^{**} < \sum_i y_i^{**}$. By Lemma 3(i), this inequality contradicts the fact that z^{**} maximizes $\min_i W_i$ over B. Therefore, there is no i such that $\tau^*(y_i^{**}) > \tau(y_i^*)$, and for all i, $z_i^{**} = z_i^*$. This means that τ^* implements z^*.

By construction, for all $y \geq 0$, $\tau^*(y) \geq w_m - W_m$, and as shown above, for all $y \leq w_m$,

$$W_m \leq w_m \frac{y - \tau^*(y)}{y},$$

so

$$w_m - W_m \leq \tau^*(y) \leq y \left(1 - \frac{W_m}{w_m}\right).$$

For $y = w_m$, this entails: $\tau^*(w_m) = w_m - W_m$. Therefore, $\tau^*(y) \geq \tau^*(w_m)$ for all $y \geq 0$.

Moreover, for all $y \in [0, w_m]$,

$$\tau^*(y) \leq y \left(1 - \frac{W_m}{w_m}\right) = y \left(1 - \frac{w_m - \tau^*(w_m)}{w_m}\right) = y \left(\frac{\tau^*(w_m)}{w_m}\right),$$

entailing $\tau(0) \leq 0$ and, for $y \in (0, w_m]$,

$$\frac{\tau^*(y)}{y} \leq \frac{\tau^*(w_m)}{w_m}.$$

Since $W_m = w_m - \tau^*(w_m)$, maximizing W_m is equivalent to maximizing $w_m - \tau^*(w_m)$. $\square$

Acknowledgments

We thank Dilip Abreu, Faruk Gul, Eric Maskin, Pierre Pestieau, John Roemer and H. Peyton Young for very useful discussions, two anonymous referees, Juuso Välimäki, and seminar participants at CORE, U. de Lyon, U. de Montpellier, U. de Pau, Yale U. and the Fourgeaud-Roy seminar (Paris) for their comments, and Giunia Gatta for her help with the presentation of the paper. The paper was written while the second author was a member of the Institute for Advanced Study (Princeton, NJ); the exceptional research atmosphere at the Institute is gratefully acknowledged. This paper presents research results of the Belgian Programme on Interuniversity Poles of Attraction initiated by the Belgian State, Prime Minister's Office, Science Policy Programming.

References

1. A. Alkan, G. Demange and D. Gale. 'Fair allocation of indivisible goods and criteria of justice', *Econometrica* **59** (1991), 1023–1040.
2. M. Armstrong. 'Multiproduct nonlinear pricing', *Econometrica* **64** (1996), 51–75.
3. K. J. Arrow. *Social Choice and Individual Values*, Wiley: New York. 1951.
4. A. B. Atkinson. 'How progressive should income tax be?', in M. Parkin and A. R. Nobay (eds.), *Essays in Modern Economics*, London: Longmans. 1973.
5. A. B. Atkinson. *Public Economics in Action*, Oxford: Clarendon Press. 1995.
6. T. Besley and S. Coate. 'The design of income maintenance programs', *Review of Economic Studies* **62** (1995), 187–221.
7. R. Boadway and M. Keen. 'Redistribution', in A. B. Bourguignon and F. Bourguignon (eds.), *Handbook of Income Distribution*, Vol. 1, Amsterdam: North-Holland. 2000.
8. R. Boadway, M. Marchand, P. Pestieau and M. Racionero. 'Optimal redistribution with heterogeneous preferences for leisure', *Journal of Public Economic Theory* **4**(4) (2002), 475–498.
9. W. Bossert, M. Fleurbaey and D. Van de Gaer. 'Responsibility, talent, and compensation: A second-best analysis', *Review of Economic Design* **4** (1999), 35–55.
10. M. Brewer. 'Comparing in-work benefits and financial work incentives for low-income families in the U.S. and the U.K.', WP #00/16 Institute for Fiscal Studies. 2000.
11. P. Chone and G. Laroque. 'Optimal incentives for labor force participation', *Journal of Public Economics*, forthcoming. 2001.
12. P. Diamond. 'Optimal income taxation: An example with a U-shaped pattern of optimal marginal tax rates', *American Economic Review* **88**(1) (1998), 83–95.
13. R. Dworkin. 'What is equality? Part 2: Equality of resources', *Philosophy and Public Affairs* **10** (1981), 283–345.
14. U. Ebert. 'A reexamination of the optimal nonlinear income tax', *Journal of Public Economics* **49** (1992), 47–73.
15. D. T. Ellwood. 'The impact of the earned income tax credit and social policy reforms on work, marriage, and living arrangements', *National Tax Journal* **53** (2000), 1063–1075.

16. M. Fleurbaey. 'The Pazner-Schmeidler social ordering: A defense', *Review of Economic Design*, forthcoming. 2001.

17. M. Fleurbaey and F. Maniquet. 'Fair allocation with unequal production skills: The no-envy approach to compensation', *Mathematical Social Sciences* **32** (1996a), 71–93.

18. M. Fleurbaey and F. Maniquet. 'Utilitarianism versus fairness in welfare economics', in M. Salles and J. A. Weymark (eds.), *Justice, Political Liberalism and Utilitarianism: Themes from Harsanyi and Rawls*, Cambridge: Cambridge University Press, forthcoming. 1996b.

19. M. Fleurbaey and F. Maniquet. 'Fair allocation with unequal production skills: The solidarity approach to compensation', *Social Choice and Welfare* **16** (1999), 569–583.

20. M. Fleurbaey and F. Maniquet. 'Fair social orderings', *Economic Theory*, forthcoming. 2001.

21. M. Fleurbaey and F. Maniquet. 'Fair orderings with unequal production skills', *Social Choice and Welfare* **24** (2005), 93–127.

22. M. Fleurbaey, K. Suzumura and K. Tadenuma. 'Arrovian aggregation in economic environments: How much should we know about indifference surfaces?', *Journal of Economic Theory*, forthcoming. 2003.

23. M. Fleurbaey and A. Trannoy. 'The impossibility of a paretian egalitarian', *Social Choice and Welfare* **21** (2003), 243–264.

24. B. Hansson. 'The independence condition in the theory of social choice', *Theory and Decision* **4** (1973), 25–49.

25. F. Maniquet and Y. Sprumont. 'Fair production and allocation of an excludable nonrival good', *Econometrica* **72** (2004), 627–640.

26. S. Matthews and J. H. Moore. 'Optimal provision of quality and warranties: An exploration in the theory of multidimensional screening', *Econometrica* **55** (1987), 441–467.

27. J. Mirrlees. 'An exploration in the theory of optimum income taxation', *Review of Economic Studies* **38** (1971), 175–208.

28. J. Mirrlees. 'Notes on welfare economics, information and uncertainty', in M. Balch, D. McFadden and S. Wu (eds.), *Essays in Equilibrium Behavior under Uncertainty*, Amsterdam: North-Holland. 1974, pp. 243–258.

29. E. Pazner. 'Equity, nonfeasible alternatives and social choice: A reconsideration of the concept of social welfare', in J. J. Laffont (ed.), *Aggregation and Revelation of Preferences*, Amsterdam: North-Holland. 1979.

30. J.-C. Rochet and P. Chone. 'Ironing, sweeping and multidimensional screening', *Econometrica* **66** (1998), 783–826.

31. E. Sadka. 'On income distribution incentive effects and optimal income taxation', *Review of Economic Studies* **43** (1976), 261–268.

32. B. Salanie. 'Optimal demogrants with imperfect tagging', *Economics Letters* **75** (2002), 319–324.

33. P. A. Samuelson. *Foundations of Economic Analysis*, Cambridge, MA: Harvard University Press. 1947.

34. J. K. Seade. 'On the shape of optimal tax schedules', *Journal of Public Economics* **7** (1977), 203–236.

35. J. E. Stiglitz. 'Pareto efficient and optimal taxation and the new welfare economics', in A. J. Auerbach and M. Feldstein (eds.), *Handbook of Public Economics*, Vol. 2, Amsterdam: North-Holland. 1987.

36. M. Tuomala. *Optimal Income Tax and Redistribution*, Oxford: Oxford University Press. 1990.

CHAPTER 9

Help the Low Skilled or Let the Hardworking Thrive? A Study of Fairness in Optimal Income Taxation

Marc Fleurbaey and François Maniquet

ABSTRACT. In a model where agents have unequal wages and heterogeneous preferences, we study the optimal redistribution via an income tax, when the social objective is based on a combination of efficiency and fairness principles, and when incentive issues are taken into account. We show how some fairness principles entail specific features for the optimal taxes, such as progressivity or tax exemption for incomes below the minimum wage.

Marc Fleurbaey, CNRS-CERSES, Centre Universitaire des Saints-Pères, 45 rue des Saints-Pères, 75270 Paris cedex 06, France (marc.fleurbaey@univ-paris5.fr). François Maniquet, CORE (Université Catholique de Louvain), 34 Voie du Roman Pays, 1348 Louvain-la-Neuve, Belgium (maniquet@core.ucl.ac.be).

This paper is based on a previous draft entitled "Optimal Income Taxation: An Ordinal Approach." We thank L. Gevers for stimulating conversations, M. Kaneko, L. Kranich, R. Kranton, and M. Morelli, as well as the editor and two anonymous referees for valuable comments on earlier drafts, and participants at seminars in Aix-Marseille III, CORE, U. of Exeter, K.U. Leuven, U. of Montreal, FUNDP Namur, U. of Keio, U. of Tsukuba and Paris, and at various conferences in Cergy, Toulouse, Quimper, Tuscaloosa, Vancouver, and Lille for their comments. Financial support from European TMR Network FMRX-CT96-0055 is gratefully acknowledged. This paper presents research results of the Belgian Program on Interuniversity Poles of Attraction initiated by the Belgian State, Prime Minister's Office, Science Policy Programming.
Received June 19, 2003; Accepted September 5, 2006.

Journal of Public Economic Theory **9**(3): 467–500, 2007.

1. Introduction

Redistribution via an income tax does not only involve considerations of inequality reduction or of efficiency losses but also and, maybe primarily, of fairness. Is it fair to try to reduce income inequalities indiscriminately, when some are due to unequal earning abilities while others are simply due to different consumption-leisure preferences? Is it fair to impose a high marginal tax rate on those who have the lowest wages? In this paper, we analyze these issues by establishing a rigorous connection between axioms of fairness and features of the income tax schedule.

We consider a model in individuals differ in their earning ability as well as their consumption-leisure preferences. We show how to define social preferences that incorporate efficiency concerns and fairness requirements. Two main fairness requirements are referred to here. The first one defends inequality reductions between agents who have identical preferences and differ in their earning ability. The second one is oriented toward the respect of individual consumption-leisure preferences and goes against redistribution between agents with the same earning ability. These two requirements can be related to ethical principles that are well known in the fairness literature, and it has now been well established that there is a tension between them (see, e.g., Fleurbaey, 1995). But this tension offers an interesting ethical choice about which value should have priority over the other: Help the low skilled agents, or let the hardworking reap the benefits of their work? This dilemma has echoes in recent debates about the welfare state. Depending on which value is given the lead, one obtains two different kinds of social objectives, leading potentially to different tax schedules.

In this paper, we study the consequences of such alternative social preferences for tax design. First we briefly summarize the axiomatic analysis of fairness requirements and of the social preferences which can be characterized on their basis (see Fleurbaey and Maniquet, 2005 for the detailed study), and then we focus on the derivation of the optimal tax.

The computation of the optimal tax for a population which is heterogeneous in two dimensions (skill and preferences) is a difficult exercise for which no general solution exists.[1] But we will be able to describe at least what part of the agents' budget set created by the tax schedule should

---

[1] On double heterogeneity, see, for example, Seade (1979), dealing with commodity taxation, or Chone and Laroque (2005). The multidimensional screening problem has received much more attention in nonlinear pricing (see, e.g., Wilson, 1993, Rochet and Chone, 1998).

be the focus of the social planner and to determine some features of the optimal tax. The main result is that the two kinds of social preferences mentioned above converge in order to grant tax exemption to incomes below the minimum wage, that is, a zero marginal tax rate for those incomes (the minimum wage is the income earned by those who work full time at the smallest wage rate, and an agent with any wage rate may earn less than this amount by working part time). But we also show under what circumstances it is legitimate to choose the tax that maximizes the minimum income (the transfer paid to agents who earn nothing), as advocated by promoters of the basic income proposal.

Our result of a zero marginal tax rate for the whole interval of incomes below the minimum wage is unusual in the optimal tax literature. In some cases, we cannot even exclude a negative marginal tax rate in this interval. Some recent papers (Saez, 2002; Choné and Laroque, 2005) have obtained the possibility of zero or negative marginal tax rate by focusing on the case when agents either work full time or do not work at all. Our own result is not due to this assumption, since in our models agents have access to a continuum of labor quantities. Boadway *et al.* (2002) study a framework with double heterogeneity and continuous labor similar to ours and with a utilitarian social welfare function in which heterogeneous individual utility functions are given specific weights. They study a population with only two kinds of individual preferences and two skill levels, yielding four types of agents and three levels of incomes (they assume that "lazy" high skilled are indistinguishable from "crazy" low skilled). They obtain the possibility of a zero tax rate for the lowest income (and also of a negative tax rate for the highest income) only when the social objective gives such a high priority to hardworking agents that redistribution is made, regressively, from low incomes to high incomes. In contrast, our result is that low income earners not only have a zero marginal tax rate but also receive the greatest positive transfer among the whole population. We interpret our result as due to an assumption of a richer distribution of types (in particular, that there are agents with minimal productivity and sufficiently diverse preferences) and above all as due to social objectives that, as explained above, are neutral with respect to individual preferences and do not call for any redistribution among agents with identical productivity. We come back on the comparison between Boadway *et al.*'s (2002) result and ours at the end of Section 4.

As mentioned above, our ethical requirements are inspired by similar requirements studied in the literature on fairness (see Fleurbaey, 1995). But that literature is devoted to determining the first-best allocations (for a recent survey, see Moulin and Thomson, 1997) and ignores distortionary taxation. An important feature of fairness concepts is that they do not involve interpersonal *utility* comparisons but instead rely on comparisons of personal *resources* and how these resources are valued by individual noncomparable ordinal preferences.

On the other hand, the literature on optimal taxation usually relies, after Mirrlees (1971), on an additive social welfare function, which aggregates individual utilities (two recent, and quite synthetic, contributions have been made in Atkinson, 1995 and Diamond, 1998). The choice of individual utility functions is problematic for this approach, so that researchers often focus on results that are robust to the specification of the utility function. This difficulty is particularly acute when agents have heterogeneous preferences, as in Boadway *et al.* (2002) where weights are introduced in the social welfare function and results appear to be sensitive to how agents' different utility functions are weighted. Our approach can be seen as supplementing the theory of optimal taxation by relating particular measures of individual well-being to fairness justifications and by showing that only a subset of the efficient taxation systems is compatible with the resulting social preferences.

As a matter of fact, there already is a small literature on equality of resources applied to optimal taxation. Indeed, our work elaborates on an early attempt made in Bossert, Fleurbaey, and Van de gaer (1999), which deals with linear tax. Related papers are by Roemer *et al.* (2000) and Schokkaert *et al.* (2004), who also focus on linear taxation. But none of these works rely on thoroughly constructed and axiomatically justified social preferences, and in particular, the social objectives used in Roemer *et al.* (2000) and Schokkaert *et al.* (2001) depend on the arbitrary choice of an interpersonally comparable representation of individual well-being, as in the welfarist literature (although they also consider "objective" indices that may not represent the agents' personal preferences, in violation of the Pareto principle).

The paper is organized as follows. In Section 2, we present the model and notations. In Section 3, we introduce fairness principles and the related social preferences. In Section 4, we study the case where agents have either a low or a high skill and either a low or a high willingness to work, which illustrates the logic of the optimal tax in a simple way. In Section 5, we tackle the general case, and we derive the main results of the paper. In Section 6, we give some concluding comments. All the proofs are gathered in the Appendix.

2. The Model

There are two goods: labor and consumption. A *bundle* for agent i is a pair $zi = (\ell_i, c_i)$, where ℓ_i is the labor and c_i is the consumption. The agents' *consumption set* X is defined by the conditions $0 \le \ell_i \le 1$ and $c_i \ge 0$.[2]

The population contains n agents. Agents have two characteristics, their personal preferences over the consumption set and their personal skill, measured by their wage rate. For any agent $i = 1, \ldots, n$, *personal preferences are* denoted by R_i and $z_i R_i z_i'$ (respectively, $z_i P_i z_i'$ and $z_i I_i z_i'$) means that bundle z_i is weakly preferred (respectively, strictly preferred, indifferent) to bundle z_i'. We assume that individual preferences are continuous, convex, and monotonic in the sense that for any $(\ell_i, c_i), (\ell_i', c_i') \in X$,

$$\ell_i \le \ell_i' \quad \text{and} \quad c_i > c_i' \Rightarrow (\ell_i, c_i) P_i (\ell_i', c_i').$$

We will say that preferences R_i exhibit a lower willingness to work than R_i' if they satisfy the following property: for any $(\ell_i, c_i), (\ell_i', c_i') \in X$,

$$\ell_i' > \ell_i \quad \text{and} \quad (\ell_i', c_i') R_i (\ell_i, c_i) \Rightarrow (\ell_i', c_i') P_i (\ell_i, c_i),$$
$$\ell_i' < \ell_i \quad \text{and} \quad (\ell_i', c_i') R_i' (\ell_i, c_i) \Rightarrow (\ell_i', c_i') P_i (\ell_i, c_i).$$

This means that any pair of indifference curves, one for R_i and one for R_i', cross at most once in the (ℓ, c) space, as illustrated in Figure 1, so that facing any kind of budget, agent R_i chooses a lower labor time than R_i'.

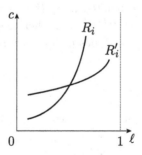

Fig. 1. Indifference curves of different agents cross at most once in the (ℓ, c) space.

---

[2] Our analysis can easily be refined to take account of unequal time available for labor, when agents are constrained by family duties, for instance.

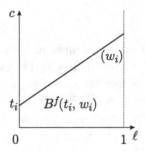

Fig. 2. First-best budgets in the (ℓ, c) space.

For further reference it is useful to define the preferences R^c of agents who are only interested in their consumption (they have the highest willingness to work): For any $(\ell_i, c_i), (\ell_i', c_i') \in X$,

$$(\ell_i', c_i')R^c(\ell_i, c_i) \Leftrightarrow c_i' \geq c_i.$$

Agent i's *skill* or *wage rate* is denoted by w_i and is measured in consumption units, so that w_i is the amount of consumption that agent i can afford when working $\ell_i = 1$ in the absence of tax or transfer. Wage rates are assumed to be fixed, as in a constant returns to scale technology. The maximal and minimal skills in the population are denoted as w_M and w_m, respectively.

An allocation $(z_1, \ldots, z_n) \in X^n$ is feasible if $\sum_{i=1}^{n} c^i \leq \sum_{i=1}^{n} w_i \ell_i$. An agent i is said to be taxed (respectively, subsidized) at an allocation when $c_i < w_i \ell_i$ (respectively, $c_i > w_i \ell_i$).

In the first-best context, redistribution can be made via lump-sum transfers. Such transfers will be denoted as t_i (for agent i). This means that agent i's first-best budget set $B^f(t_i, w_i)$ is then (see Figure 2 — on figures we adopt the convention that slopes of lines are indicated in parentheses below the lines):

$$B^f(t_i, w_i) = \{(\ell, c) \in X | c \leq t_i + w_i \ell\}.$$

The budget constraint for the redistribution agency is then simply

$$\sum_{i=1}^{n} t_i \leq 0.$$

In the second-best context, we assume that only earned income $y_i = w_i \ell_i$ is observed, so that redistribution is made via a tax function $\tau(y)$. The tax

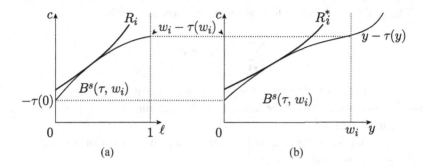

Fig. 3. Second-best budgets (a) in the (ℓ, c) space and (b) in the (y, c) space.

may turn into a subsidy when $\tau(y) < 0$. Under this kind of redistribution, agent i's budget is defined by (see Figure 3a)

$$B^s(\tau, w_i) = \{\ell, c) \in X | c \le w_i \ell - \tau(w_i \ell)\}.$$

It is convenient to focus on the earnings-consumption space, in which the budget is defined by (see Figure 3b; we retain the same notation as no confusion is possible)

$$B^s(\tau, w_i) = \{(y, c) \in [0, w_i] \times \mathbb{R}_+ | c \le y - \tau(y)\},$$

and individual preferences R_i^* over income-consumption bundles can be defined, when $w_i > 0$, by[3]

$$(y, c) R_i^*(y', c') \Leftrightarrow \left(\frac{y}{w_i}, c\right) R_i \left(\frac{y'}{w_i}, c'\right). \tag{1}$$

The incentive compatibility constraint can then be formulated by the condition that for all agents i and j,

$$(y_i, c_i) R_i^*(y_j, c_j) \quad \text{or} \quad y_j > w_i.$$

The second part of the condition follows from our assumption that labor time is bounded above. We will illustrate its role in Section 4.

---

[3]When $w_i = 0$, then R_i^* is defined over $\{0\} \times \mathbb{R}_+$, and $(0, c) R_i^*(0, c')$ if and only if $c \ge c'$.

The budget constraint for the redistribution agency is

$$\sum_{i=1}^{n} \tau(w_i \ell_i) \geq 0.$$

We will say that a tax function τ is *feasible* if it satisfies the above constraint when all agents choose their labor time by maximizing their satisfaction over their budget set.

We restrict our attention to functions τ, which are continuous and such that $y - \tau(y)$ is nondecreasing.

3. Social Preferences

Help the low skilled or let the hardworking thrive? This alternative refers to two ethical principles, which we now proceed to formalize in the current model.

The reduction of inequalities due to unequal earning abilities should not be simply formulated in terms of disposable income, since efficiency alone would normally require a high-skilled agent to work more than a low skilled agent, and in terms of equity, working more may justify consuming more. Things are even more complex when preferences differ, too. But consider two agents with identical preferences and unequal skills. Then a reasonable objective is to avoid that they end up with bundles they both consider to be of unequal values, according to their identical preferences. In other words, the objective would be that they end up with bundles they deem equally valuable, that is, on the same indifference curve. Formulating such an objective in terms of a property that social preferences should satisfy, we require that reducing the indifference curve gap between two agents with identical preferences be a social improvement.

Help Low Skilled: *It is a social improvement to change an allocation by modifying the bundles of two agents i and j who have identical preferences R, from z_i, z_j to z_i', z_j', so that*

$$z_i P z_i' P z_j' P z_j.$$

The second ethical idea on which we focus here is that differences in preferences, in contrast to skills, may justify inequalities. In symmetry to the above principle, this is best applied to a pair of agents with identical skills, so as to avoid any issue of redistribution for unequal skills. If two agents have the same skill level, and the same budget, but one chooses to work hard while the other works less, this ethical view says that there is nothing objectionable about the resulting inequality. There are famous defenses of this kind of principle (e.g., Dworkin, 1981; Rawls, 1982), and they rely on the ideal of neutrality as regards individual preferences and choices.

This idea suggests that ideally redistribution should be made independently of preferences. That is, agents' preferences should never, by themselves, be a reason for redistributing resources. In a first-best context, it is actually possible to achieve this state of affairs by giving any agent i a lump-sum transfer t_i that does not depend on her preferences and letting her choose in the budget set $B^f(t_i, w_i)$. As a consequence, in the context of comparing allocations, it is interesting to focus on allocations that are obtainable via lump-sum transfers. Such allocations are those where every agent chooses her best bundle in a budget set of the $B^f(t_i, w_i)$ kind. The idea that redistribution should not depend on preferences clearly pushes in this case in the direction of reducing the inequality of budgets, and therefore the inequality in lump-sum transfers, for agents with equal skill. This is what the following condition states formally.[4]

Let Hardworking Thrive: *It is a social improvement to change an allocation obtainable via lump-sum transfers by modifying the lump-sum transfers of two agents i and j who have the same skill, from t_i, t_j to t'_i, t'_j, so that*

$$t_i > t'_i > t'_j > t_j.$$

Help Low Skilled and Let Hardworking Thrive can be directly related to the principles of "compensation" and "natural reward" coined in Fleurbaey (1995), where they are shown to conflict with each other. The two requirements formulated here are also mutually incompatible, as can be shown with a simple example. The Help Low Skilled principle focuses on indifference curves, whereas the Let Hardworking Thrive principle focuses on budgets. An agent with a low indifference curve compared to another may have a high budget with respect to a third one, and this may entail contradictory injunctions, as illustrated in Figure 4, where the Help Low Skilled principle says that agents 1 and 2 should be helped at the expense of agents 3 and 4, whereas the Let Hardworking Thrive principle advocates the contrary.

---

[4]An interesting consequence of giving agents with equal skill the same budget is that they will not envy each other: $z_i R_i z_j$ for all i, j in a subpopulation with equal skill. This "no-envy among equally skilled" was the condition retained to express this ethical principle in Fleurbaey and Maniquet (1996) in a study of first-best allocation rules.

Marc Fleurbaey and François Maniquet

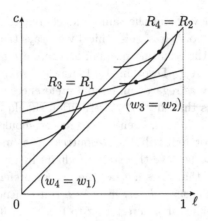

Fig. 4. Social preferences cannot simultaneously satisfy Help The Low Skilled and Let Hardworking Thrive.

This conflict between principles implies that the social decision maker has to choose which of the two principles must have priority. Is it necessary to emphasize that this ethical dilemma is at the core of current debates about the welfare state? And it seems to go across the political spectrum, since one can read in the U.S. Democratic Party platform: "We must bring all Americans who are willing to work hard into the circle of prosperity." In the platform of the U.K. Labour Party, one finds, "Our values: (...) reward for hard work."[5]

What we want to do here is to analyze the consequences of such ethical choices. Depending on which principle is preferred, a different kind of social preferences is obtained. Two kinds of social preferences are prominent in this context, as can be seen from the axiomatic analysis presented in Fleurbaey and Maniquet (2005). We here proceed directly with the presentation of these two kinds of social preferences.

We first have to define the notion of implicit budget associated with an agent's indifference curve and a wage rate w, which is the budget with a line of slope w that is tangent to the agent's indifference curve. Figure 5 illustrates this notion in the (ℓ, c) space (Figure 5a) and in the (y, c) space (Figure 5b).

The implicit budget of agent i at bundle z is formally defined as the set

$$\mathbb{B}(z, w, R_i) = B^f(t, w),$$

[5]See http://www.democrats.org/issues/platform/platform.html#progress and http://www.labour.org.uk/.

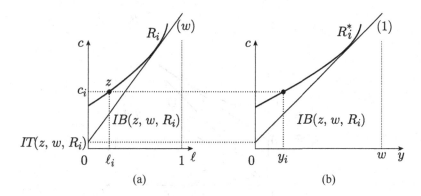

Fig. 5.   Implicit budgets (a) in the (ℓ, c) space and (b) in the (y, c) space.

where t is computed as the minimal transfer such that there is $x \in B^f(t, w), xR_iz$. Such a t will be called as the implicit transfer of agent i at bundle z, and denoted as $IT(z, w, R_i)$. This expression, viewed as a function of z, corresponds to a particular money-metric utility function. This measure of individual well-being does not require any information about individuals' subjective utility, and depends only on ordinal noncomparable preferences about consumption and labor.

The first social preferences focus on the implicit transfers with respect to a reference skill $\tilde{w}$. They are dubbed "egalitarian-equivalent" by reference to their similarity with Pazner and Schmeidler's concept (1978).

Definition 1.   (Egalitarian-equivalent social preferences EE). *Apply the maximin criterion to the vector*

$$(IT(z_1, \tilde{w}, R_1), \ldots, IT(z_n, \tilde{w}, R_n)),$$

for some chosen $\tilde{w}$.

EE preferences give priority to the agents with the lowest $IT(z_i, \tilde{w}, R_i)$. As can be checked easily, EE preferences satisfy the Help Low Skilled principle and satisfy the Let Hardworking Thrive principle only for the special case of two agents having their identical skill precisely equal to $\tilde{w}$.

EE preferences are actually not uncommon in the optimal tax literature, and, for instance, Atkinson (1995) or Chone and Laroque (2005) study EE preferences with $\tilde{w} = 0$ (in this case, $IT(z_i, 0, R_i)$ is equal to the consumption level where agent i's indifference curve crosses the axis). Usually the representation of individual well-being by $IT(z_i, 0, R_i)$ is presented as a more or less natural choice of utility function. In particular, when individual

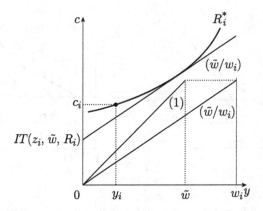

Fig. 6.   The construction of egalitarian-equivalent social preferences in the (y, c) space.

preferences are representable by a quasilinear utility function $c_i - v(\ell_i)$, such that $v(0) = 0$, one indeed has

$$c_i - v(\ell_i) = I\!T((\ell_i, c_i), 0, R_i).$$

What our approach provides is a rationale for the choice of $I\!T(z_i, \tilde{w}, R_i)$ as a measure of individual situations and an interpretation in terms of resources rather than subjective utility.

Since $I\!T(z_i, \tilde{w}, R_i)$ is a particular representation of i's preferences, EE preferences satisfy the weak Pareto principle (an allocation where all agents are better off is socially strictly better).[6] In the second-best context, one finds $I\!T(z_i, \tilde{w}, R_i)$ on the (y, c) space by taking the line of slope $\tilde{w}/w_i$, which is tangent to agent i's indifference curve. The graphical construction is shown in Figure 6.

In the first-best context, the socially preferred allocation for EE preferences displays full equality of the $I\!T(z_i, \tilde{w}, R_i)$, and is described in Figure 7. It has all agents indifferent between their bundle and their best bundle in an equal budget with slope $\tilde{w}$. The bundles of resources that agents actually consume need not be on the boundary of this equal budget, as an agent's skill may differ from $\tilde{w}$.

EE preferences rely on the $\tilde{w}$ parameter. The consequences of the choice of this parameter are illustrated in Figure 8, where agent 1 has preferences that exhibit a lower willingness to work than agent 2. With a low

---

[6]Fleurbaey and Maniquet (2005) actually characterize the leximin version of *EE*, that is, the lexicographic extension of the maximin (see, e.g. Sen 1986). The social preferences then satisfy the Strong Pareto principle.

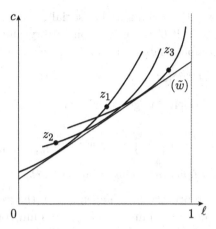

Fig. 7. A first-best socially optimal allocation for egalitarian-equivalent social preferences.

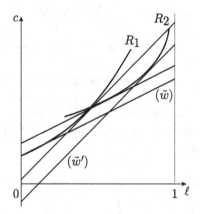

Fig. 8. Two different reference parameter for egalitarian-equivalent social preferences.

$\tilde{w}$, EE preferences are relatively favorable to agent 1, because this agent is then considered to be the worse off, as measured by the implicit transfer $I\!T(z_i, \tilde{w}, R_i)$, and is therefore given priority by the maximin criterion. And symmetrically, a higher $\tilde{w}' > \tilde{w}$ entails that agent 2 is considered worse off in terms of $I\!T(z_i, \tilde{w}, R_i)$, and therefore relatively favored. In summary, EE preferences are neutral about preferences for agents with $w_i = \tilde{w}$, are biased toward the "hardworking" for agents with $w_i < \tilde{w}$, and conversely for $w_i > \tilde{w}$.

For the definition of the second kind of social preferences, we introduce the following convention. If U is a continuous utility function defined over X and $B \subset X$ is a compact subset of bundles (such as a budget set), then

$$U^{\max}(B) = \max\{U(z)|z \in B\}.$$

Definition 2.   (Equivalent-budget social preferences EB). *Apply the maximin criterion to the vector*

$$(\tilde{U}^{\max}(\mathit{I\!B}(z_1, w_1, R_1)), \ldots, \tilde{U}^{\max}(\mathit{I\!B}(z_n, w_n, R_n))),$$

where $\tilde{U}$ is any utility function representing some chosen preferences $\tilde{R}$.

EB preferences give priority to the agents with the worst $\mathit{I\!B}(z_i, w_i, R_i)$ according to $\tilde{R}$. The notion of implicit budget was illustrated on Figure 5.

EB preferences satisfy the Let Hardworking Thrive principle, but satisfy the Help Low Skilled principle only for the special case of two agents having their identical preferences equal to $\tilde{R}$.

Notice that the expression $\tilde{U}^{\max}(\mathit{I\!B}(z_i, w_i, R_i))$ is increasing with i's satisfaction. Therefore EB preferences satisfy the Pareto principle, and this guarantees that fairness requirements will never be allowed to entail inefficiency in the chosen allocations.

In the second-best context, one finds ($\mathit{I\!B}(z_i, w_i, R_i)$ in the (y, c) space by looking for the line of slope 1, which is tangent to agent i's indifference curve. In order to evaluate this implicit budget with $\tilde{R}$, one has to rescale $\tilde{R}$ to agent i's consumption set in this space, as explained in Equation (1) and shown in Figure 9.

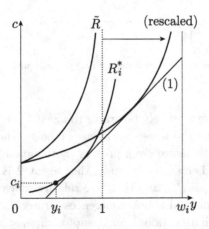

Fig. 9.   The construction of equivalent-budget social preferences in the (y, c) space.

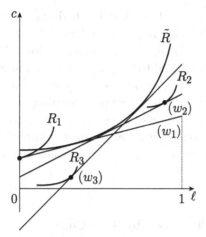

Fig. 10. A first-best socially optimal allocation for equivalent-budget social preferences.

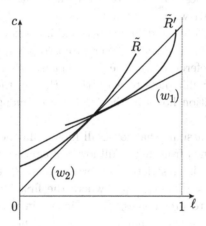

Fig. 11. Two different reference preferences for equivalent-budget social preferences.

In the first-best context, EB preferences lead to a fully egalitarian situation, in the sense that all the agents' implicit budgets are deemed equivalent by preferences $\tilde{R}$ as shown in Figure 10.

EB preferences rely on the $\tilde{R}$ preferences as a crucial parameter. The choice of this parameter has nothing to do with favoring agents who have such preferences, but only with guaranteeing that the Help Low Skilled principle will be fully satisfied for them. Practically, the choice of $\tilde{R}$ influences the degree of redistribution. Examine Figure 11, where agent 1 has a smaller skill $w_1 < w_2$, and two implicit budgets are represented (we do not represent preferences of agents 1 and 2 as they would not influence the degree of redistribution). Preferences $\tilde{R}$ exhibit a lower willingness to work than $\tilde{R}'$. Choosing $\tilde{R}$ will lead to little redistribution in favor of agent 1, as agent 2's implicit budget is considered the worse of the two. In contrast, choosing $\tilde{R}'$ will entail a high degree of redistribution in favor of agent 1, because implicit budgets are now assessed by comparing consumption levels associated with larger labor time, so that the implicit budget of the low wage rate agent (agent 1) is deemed worse than that of the high-skilled agent.

4. Optimal Tax: The Two-by-Two Case

In the previous section, we have described social preferences and their consequences in the first-best context. We now turn our attention to the second-best context, and start with a preliminary analysis of the case where skills can be either low or high and preferences exhibit either a low or a high willingness to work. More precisely, there are two possible skills, $w_1 < w_2$, and two possible preferences (in the (ℓ, c) space), R_1 and R_2 such that R_1 exhibits a lower willingness to work than R_2 (i.e. the Mirrlees-Spence single crossing condition holds in the (ℓ, c) space among agents with the same skill).

Furthermore, we assume that low-skill high willingness to work agents cannot be distinguished from high-skill low willingness to work ones. That is, let $R_i^*|_A$ denote the restriction of preferences R_i^* to a subset A of bundles. Then, $R_{12}^* = R_{21}^*|_{[0,w_1] \times \mathbb{R}_+}$, where the first index refers to skill and the second one to preferences. To fix ideas (in particular for graphical illustrations), we assume that there is one agent of each type in the population.

Let us begin by illustrating the influence of our assumption that labor time is bounded above on the incentive constraints. Figure 12 depicts two incentive compatible and (second-best) efficient allocations where it is not true that $z_{12}R_{12}^*z_{21}$, but $y_{21} > w_1$. In part (a) of the picture, $z_{21}I_{21}^*z_{12}$ whereas in part (b) $z_{21}P_{21}^*z_{12}$ (by incentive compatibility, we cannot have $z_{12}P_{21}^*z_{21}$). Let us observe that both parts are consistent with our assumption that $R_{12}^* = R_{21}^*|_{[0,w_1] \times \mathbb{R}_+}$. In this case, the constraint $\ell_{12} \leq 1$ prevents the planner from proposing bundle (y_{21}, c_{21}) to agents 12 and benefiting from the fact that $\tau(y_{21}) > \tau(y_{12})$.

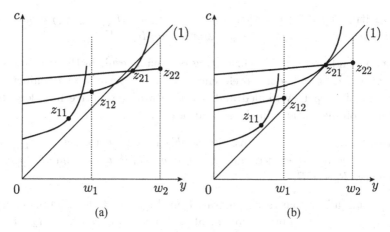

Fig. 12. Incentive compatible and (second-best) efficient allocations (a) where $z_{21} I_{21}^* z_{12}$ and (b) where $z_{21} P_{21}^* z_{12}$.

To simplify the exposition and to be able to compare our results with the literature, we now add the assumption that $z_{12}^* = z_{21}^*$.[7] Consequently, we can do as if there were three groups of agents. A group of agents with low skill and low willingness to work, a group with high skill and high willingness to work, and a mixed group gathering the other agents (let us note that the single crossing condition then also holds in the (y, c) space). An allocation $(y_{ij}, c_{ij})_{i,j \in \{1,2\}}$ is incentive compatible if $(y_{12}, c_{12}) = (y_{21}, c_{21})$ and

$$(y_{11}, c_{11}) R_{11}^* (y_{21}, c_{21}), (y_{12}, c_{12}) R_{12}^* (y_{22}, c_{22}),$$
$$(y_{22}, c_{22}) R_{22}^* (y_{12}, c_{12}), (y_{21}, c_{21}) R_{21}^* (y_{11}, c_{11}).$$

The first two conditions are upward conditions (no agent should be willing to mimic an agent with the same willingness to work but a higher skill), and the last two are downward conditions (no agent should be willing to mimic an agent with the same willingness to work but a lower skill).

Four social preferences are of particular interest in this model, the *EE* preferences with either w_1 or w_2 as reference skill, and the *EB* preferences with either R_1 or R_2 as reference preferences. We can derive the following preliminary results. The first result states that redistribution between high willingness to work agents must go from high-skilled to low skilled agents, with three out of our four social preferences.

---

[7]This could follow, for instance, from the assumption that agents 12 never choose $\ell_{12} = 1$ when their marginal after-tax income is lower or equal to w_1.

Proposition 1.   *The incentive constraint $(y_{22}, c_{22}) R_{22}^*(y_{12}, c_{12})$ is binding in all cases but when the social preferences are $R_1 - EB$.*

The second proposition, illustrating our main result in the two-by-two case, proves that the social preferences derived from our two conflicting principles of Help Low Skilled and Let Hardworking Thrive may lead to similar recommendations in the second best.[8]

Proposition 2.   *An incentive compatible allocation $(y_{ij}, c_{ij})_{i,j \in \{1,2\}}$ is optimal for social preferences $w_1 - EE$ if and only if it is optimal for social preferences $R_2 - EB$.*

Optimal allocations are illustrated in Figure 13. In Figure 13(a), $(z_{11}, z_{12} = z_{21}, z_{22})$ is optimal for social preferences $w_1 - EE$ and $R_2 - EB$. The argument can be developed geometrically. First, the indifference curves of both types of low-skilled agents are tangent to the same budget of slope 1. This implies that $I\!B((\ell_{11}, c_{11}), w_1, R_1) = I\!B((l_{12}, c_{12}), w_1, R_2)$, so that the $w_1 - EE$ and $R_2 - EB$ well-being indices are equalized among low-skilled agents. Moreover, the budget of slope $\frac{w_1}{w_2}$ represents the same implicit budget rescaled so as to fit the consumption set of high-skilled agents. Given that indifference curves of agents 22 can be obtained by a corresponding rescaling of those of agents 12, the incentive compatibility constraint $z_{22} R_{22}^* z_{12}$ guarantees that $I\!\Gamma((\ell_{22}, c_{22}), w_1, R_2) \geq I\!\Gamma((\ell_{12}, c_{12}), w_1, R_2)$, so that the indifference curve of agents 22 must be above the line of slope $\frac{w_1}{w_2}$ (illustrating Proposition 1, as equalizing the well-being measures is impossible among high willingness to work agents). Consequently, low-skilled agents have the lowest $w_1 - EE$ well-being indices. Also, the dashed indifference curve is a rescaling of the appropriate indifference curve of the reference agent (an agent with preferences R_2) and, as explained above, this curve lies below the indifference curve of agents 22 through z_{22}, so that, again, low-skilled agents have the lowest $R_2 - EB$ well-being indices. Now, the incentive compatibility constraints are binding in such a way that it is no longer possible to increase the welfare of any of the low-skilled agents, proving that the allocation is $w_1 - EE$ and $R_2 - EB$ optimal.

In Figure 13(b), $(z_{11}, z_{12} = z_{21}, z_{22})$ is optimal for social preferences $w_2 - EE$. Again, the indices are equalized among low-skilled agents, which is illustrated by the fact that both indifference curves are tangent to the same line of slope $\frac{w_2}{w_1}$, and the welfare of no low-skilled agent can be increased

---

[8]In the case of only two agents, optimal allocations for $w_2 - EB$ and $R_1 - EB$ also coincide.

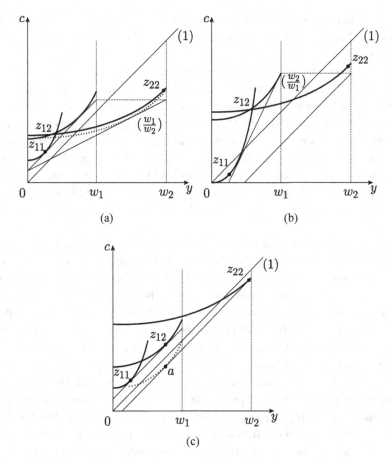

Fig. 13. Optimal second-best allocations (a) for social preferences $w_1 - EE$ and $R_2 - EB$, (b) for social preferences $w_2 - EE$, and (c) for social preferences $R_1 - EB$.

without violating an incentive compatibility constraint. Let us observe that, as suggested by the figure, it could be the case that $(0, 0)\ P_{11}^* z_{11}$, that is, agents 11 would be forced to work.

In Figure 13(c), $(z_{11}, z_{12} = z_{21}, z_{22})$ is optimal for social preferences $R_1 - EB$. First, the reference agent (an agent with preferences R_1) is indifferent between the implicit budgets of all low-skilled agents (as they all have their indifference curves tangent to the same 45° line). Secondly, the rescaled indifference curve matching preferences R_{21}^* is tangent (at point a) to agents' 22 implicit budget, which means that the relevant index has been equalized among agents of all three relevant groups (agents 21 have a higher index level but this cannot be avoided as they cannot be distinguished from agents 12). Let us observe that, in this example, the allocation is also first-best efficient.

Those figures illustrate the effect of the choice of w_i or R_i on the resulting optimal allocation. It confirms what we said about first-best optimal allocations. When social preferences are of the EE type, a larger reference skill benefits the low-skilled hardworking agents (agents 12). When social preferences are of the EB type, a lower willingness to work of the reference preference benefits the high-skilled hardworking agents (and hurts all the other agents). We see that EE preferences lead to more redistribution than EB preferences, but the difference is not as large as could be expected given that, as proven by Proposition 2, the sets of optimal allocations intersect.

The taxation is never progressive among low-skilled agents. Indeed, the amount transferred to low-skilled hardworking agents is always at least as large as the amount transferred to low-skill low willingness to work agents (those transfers are measured by the vertical distance between the bundles agents are assigned and the no tax 45° line). Moreover, in two cases, with $w_1 - EE$ and $R_2 - EB$ social preferences (see Figure 13a), it is strictly larger. We need to qualify this result, however. With $w_1 - EE$ preferences, the difference in the amount received by agents 12 and 11 depends on the shape of the indifference curve of agents 11, given that the incentive compatibility constraint $z_{11} R_{11}^* z_{21}$ is binding. Had they been linear with a slope equal to 1, both groups would have received the same transfer (bundle z_{12} would have been on the frontier of the same implicit budget set as z_{11}). As we will see in the next section, when the number of agents is large, preferences are sufficiently diverse, and the reference skill is the lowest skill in the population, low-skilled agents indeed receive the same transfer. With another reference skill, in our case with w_2, the transfer paid to agents 12 is strictly larger than the one paid to agents 11 independently of the shape of the preferences. The resulting tax system is therefore regressive for low incomes (the marginal rate of tax is, on average, negative). This result will still hold with a large number of agents.

All the tax systems we justify with EE or EB social preferences are progressive if we regard larger incomes: The tax paid by agents 22 is always larger than the one paid by any other agent. This result, however, does not extend to a larger population.

Finally, let us observe that, even if our social preferences are of the maximin type, they may lead to a very limited redistribution, as exemplified by the $R_1 - EB$ preferences. The intuition for this result is the following one. The well-being index associated with EB preferences is equalized among agents when an agent with reference preferences is indifferent between the implicit budgets of all agents, and, in particular, is indifferent between having a low or a high skill. But the transfer that is necessary for an agent with a low willingness to work to be indifferent between budgets corresponding to a low and a high skill is lower than the transfer necessary for an agent with a high willingness to work. At the limit, an agent with so low a willingness to work that she always chooses not to work (she has indifference curves with slope greater than w_M) does not need any transfer to be indifferent between having a low or a high skill. Consequently, if these preferences are the reference ones, then the laissez-faire is optimal.

Boadway *et al.* (2002) study the same two-by-two model under the assumption that preferences are quasilinear in leisure and there is no upper bound on the labor time. They show that when social preferences are utilitarian, the optimal allocations can be associated with a list of binding incentive compatibility constraints very different from what we obtain here. In particular, it may be the case that redistribution benefits the 22 agents. This cannot occur here as those agents always have larger index of well-being and we apply the maximin criterion. This proves that allocations maximizing one of the social preferences discussed in this paper form a strict subset of the second-best efficient allocations.

Closer to what we develop here, they study the consequences of a family of utilitarian social preferences which give absolute priority to low-skilled agents in the sense that the weight assigned to the others' utility is zero, whereas the weights given to the utilities of low and high willingness to work agents, among the low-skilled, may vary. Let us call those functions utility maximin functions. Boadway *et al.* (2002) also reach the conclusion that redistribution may be regressive among low-skilled agents. Actually, the set of allocations which are optimal for one of their utility maximin functions coincide with the set of optimal allocations we would obtain with $\tilde{w} - EE$ social preferences by letting $\tilde{w}$ vary over $\mathbb{R}_+$. Indeed, by a slight generalization of our study of $w_1 - EE$ and $w_2 - EE$ above, we can show that if an allocation is incentive compatible, the low-skilled agents are always those having the lowest well-being index, so that maximizing one of those social preferences boils down to maximizing a utilitarian social welfare function where the weights assigned to high-skilled agents are zero. Moreover, if we take $\tilde{w} = 0$, the $\tilde{w} - EE$ force us to maximize the welfare of agents 11, and, as $\tilde{w}$ increases, the $\tilde{w} - EE$ objective becomes that of maximizing a utilitarian social welfare function where the weight of 11 agents decrease and that of 12 agents increase (and the other weights remain zero). This equivalence between our $\tilde{w} - EE$ preferences and the Boadway *et al.* maximin only holds, however, when there are two kinds of individual preferences in the population. As shown in the next section, in the general case, $\tilde{w} - EE$ preferences will still lead to allocations having the property that the indifference curves of all low-skilled agents are tangent to the same line of slope $\frac{\tilde{w}}{w_m}$, whereas utility maximin social preferences may select other allocations.

Let us complete this section by mentioning a last feature of the optimal allocations identified here. Recall that agents 12 and 21 are indistinguishable in the (y, c) space. Consequently, as soon as an allocation $(z_{11}, z_{12} = z_{21}, z_{22})$ is second-best efficient, it remains so independently of how the total measure of agents 12 and 21 is distributed among the two types. Moreover, given that our objectives are egalitarian, and our indices of well-being are indeed equalized among agents 11 and 12, optimality of the selected allocations is preserved after a resizing of subgroups 12 and 21 that does not affect their total size (with an obvious discontinuity when the proportion of agents 12 reaches 0). This contrasts with the outcome of a utilitarian objective where an increase in the relative size of a group of agents always benefits these agents.

5.   Optimal Tax: The General Case

We now consider the case of a general population. What we do in this section is an analysis of how the search for the optimal tax function can be translated into simple objectives about the shape of the function of disposable income, and we derive some conclusions about the shape of the optimal tax function.

5.1.   *The case $w_m = 0$*

Let us focus, first, on the case when $w_m = 0$, and let us assume moreover that there are agents with a zero skill, for every type of preferences R in the population.[9] For any tax function, the budget set of such agents in the (ℓ, c) space is the flat line with intercept $-\tau(0)$. In every preference class, these agents have the lowest budget, hence the lowest indifference curve, and therefore the lowest $\mathit{\Pi}(z_i, \tilde{w}, R_i)$.

---

[9] For instance, the distributions of w and R are independent, and the minimum value for w is zero.

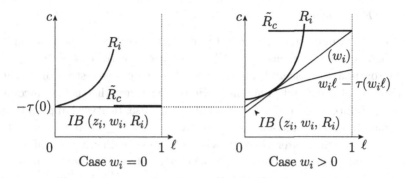

Fig. 14. The equivalent-budget social preferences with reference preferences $\tilde{R} = R^c$.

Therefore the optimal tax for EE preferences must maximize the welfare of agents with zero skill. Such agents have heterogeneous preferences, which may a priori render this maximization ambiguous, but fortunately here, maximizing their welfare is, for all kinds of individual preferences R, tantamount to maximizing $-\tau(0)$.

A similar reasoning can be made for *EB* preferences based on the highest willingness to work preferences $\tilde{R} = R^c$. For any tax function, the agents with zero skill necessarily have the following implicit budget:

$$\{(\ell, c) \mid 0 < c < -\tau(0)\}$$

And this is always the worst implicit budget for preferences R^c, because all other agents are at least as well off as at the bundle $(0, -\tau(0))$, and therefore their implicit budget must have a maximal consumption that is greater than or equal to $-\tau(0)$, as shown in Figure 14.[10]

We have therefore proved the following result.

Theorem 1. *If every preference class contains agents with zero skill, then the optimal tax for all EE preferences, and for EB preferences with $\tilde{R} = R^c$, maximizes the minimum income $-\tau(0)$.*

When the reference preferences are different from R^c, then *EB* preferences lead to tax systems which are similar to those obtained when $w_m > 0$. We come back to those cases in Section 5.3.

---

[10]Notice that here we only need the assumption that there is at least one agent in the population with a zero wage.

5.2.   *EE tax when* $w_m > 0$

Let us now examine the case when the minimum skill in the population is positive, and start by focusing on EE preferences, for the case $\tilde{w} \geq w_m$.

The optimal tax is complex to analyze when there is no restriction on the distribution of skills and preferences. Here, we assume that pretax income is not too informative a signal in the following sense: It never happens that over some interval of income $[y, y']$ with $0 < y < y' \leq w$, one finds only agents with wage greater than w, whereas agents with wage equal to w can be found earning incomes either below y or above y'. We then impose the assumption that over any interval of income $[0, w]$, it is impossible, by only looking at preferences restricted to that interval of income, to identify agents with greater productivity than w and distinguish them, on the basis of their preferences, from agents with productivity w. Let W denotes the set of wage rates in the current profile:

$$W = \{w \in \mathbb{R}_+ \mid \exists i, w_i = w\}.$$

Assumption (No Identification): *For every agent* i, *and every* $w \in W$ *such that* $w < w_i$, *there is another agent* j *such that* $w_j = w$ *and* $R_j^* = R_i^* \mid_{[0,w] \times \mathbb{R}_+}$.

This assumption is a generalization of the assumption made in the previous section, where agents 12 and 21 could not be distinguished. Let us insist that even if No Identification is a strong assumption it is only imposed to exclude the implausible case where fiscal authorities design the tax for some interval $[y, y']$ (and, in particular, apply very high tax rates over that interval) only because they know that nobody among agents having an ability to earn income in the interval $[0, y'']$ for some $y'' > y'$ would ever end up with an income in $[y, y']$.

We obtain the following description of the optimal tax, when it exists. Let $a^+ = \max\{a, 0\}$.

Theorem 2.   *Under the No Identification assumption, a tax function maximizing*

$$\min_i \mathit{\Pi}(z_i, \tilde{w}, R_i),$$

for $\tilde{w} \geq w_m$, *can be computed by minimizing* $\tau(w_m)$ *under the constraint: for all* $y \geq 0$,

$$\tau(w_m) \leq \tau(y) \leq \tau(w_m) + y - w_m + (w_m - y)^+ \left(\frac{\tilde{w}}{w_m}\right).$$

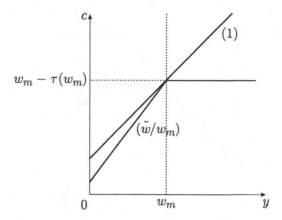

Fig. 15.   Lower and upper bounds on the optimal tax scheme for egalitarian-equivalent social preferences.

Theorem 2 is illustrated in Figure 15: In the income-consumption space, computing the optimal tax amounts to maximizing the height of the point $(w_m, w_m - \tau(w_m))$ under the constraint that the income function $y - \tau(y)$ must be located in the area delineated by the thick lines.

An income function in this area has the following features. First, the agents who earn w_m receive the greatest subsidy, in absolute amount. Secondly, the average marginal tax rate over incomes belonging to the interval $[0, w_m]$ is nonpositive. And in the particular case when $\tilde{w} = w_m$, which is, as explained above, the most generous to low incomes, the lower bound coincides with the upper bound for this interval, so that the marginal tax rate is exactly zero over $[0, w_m]$.

The intuitive argument for this zero marginal tax result goes as follows. Consider any incentive compatible allocation $z = (z_1, \ldots, z_n)$, and let the corresponding tax function τ be defined such that $y - \tau(y)$ is the envelope curve of the agents' indifference curves (in (y, c) space) at z. Consider the family of functions f_α defined by $f_\alpha(y) = \alpha + \min\{y, w_m\}$. There is a maximal α such that for all y, $y - \tau(y) \geq f_\alpha(y)$. Since $y - \tau(y)$ is nondecreasing, necessarily there is $y \in [0, w_m]$ such that $y - \tau(y) = f_\alpha(y)$.

In words, the graph of f_α touches the envelope curve of the agents' indifference curves on $[0, w_m]$, as illustrated in Figure 16. But, by the No Identification assumption, this part of the envelope curve is also the envelope curve of the subpopulation of agents with productivity w_m. Therefore, at z, there is an agent i, with productivity w_m, such that (remember, indeed,

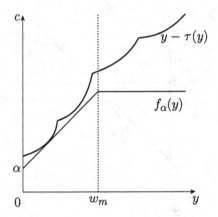

Fig. 16. The graph of fα, touches the envelope curve of the agents' indifference curves on $[0, w_m]$.

how the implicit budget is computed in (y, c) space)

$$I\!\Gamma(z_i, \tilde{w}, R_i) = \alpha.$$

It is easy to check, by the same token, that for all other agents j of the whole population,

$$I\!\Gamma(z_j, \tilde{w}, R_j) \geq \alpha.$$

This is the first part of the argument, allowing us to identify the bundle of the worst-off agent in the economy. The second part is that if one truncates the tax function τ and replaces it with $\tau_0(y) = \max\{\tau(y), -\alpha\}$, one obtains a new allocation that is still feasible. Indeed, τ_0 is obtained from τ by cutting all subsidies greater than α.[11] The change does not affect agents who received less under z (or were taxed), because it cuts apart of their budget which they did not choose anyway, and for all affected agents, the subsidy they receive afterward is smaller. It is then an immediate accounting result that the new tax function is feasible. But it still satisfies $y - \tau_0(y) \geq f_\alpha(y)$ for all y, and therefore, for all i in N, one still has

$$I\!\Gamma(z_i, \tilde{w}, R_i) \geq \alpha.$$

The important point is that, for all $y \leq w_m, y - \tau(y) \geq f_\alpha(y)$ means that $\tau(y) \leq -\alpha$, so that $\tau_0(y) = -\alpha$, implying that τ_0 has a zero marginal tax

---

[11]We can restrict our attention to allocations such that the maximal α is nonnegative, since the laissez-faire allocation yields $\alpha \geq 0$. Therefore, the allocation that maximizes $\min_i I\!\Gamma(z_i, \tilde{w}, R_i)$ has $\alpha \geq 0$.

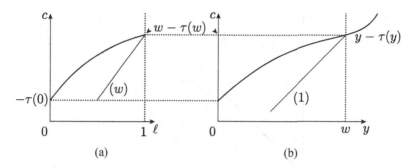

Fig. 17. Identifying the smallest implicit budget (a) in the (l, c) space and (b) in the (y, c) space.

rate over $[0, w_m]$. And this is why the optimal tax may be sought among the subfamily of tax functions displaying this property (see the formal proof of the theorem, for more details). This result does not prove that all taxes maximizing $\min_i \Pi(z_i, \tilde{w}, R_i)$ have this shape. But the theorem proves that there is no loss of social welfare if one restricts his attention to those taxes.

5.3. *EB tax when* $w_m \geq 0$

Let us now turn to EB preferences, for the general case $w_m \geq 0$. It is not obvious to find the minimal $U^{\max}(B(z_i, w_i, R_i))$ over the whole population, because a higher skill does not necessarily mean a larger implicit budget $B(z_i, w_i, R_i)$, since budget frontiers may intersect. In a given subpopulation with skill w, however, a part of the reasoning leading to Theorem 2 still applies, that is, the smallest implicit budget is obtained by the line of appropriate slope that is tangent (from below) to the envelope curve of those agents' indifference curves. In the (ℓ, c) space (Figure 17a), this is the line of slope w. In the (y, c) space (Figure 17b), the slope is 1, and the budget is constrained by $y \leq w$.

It is worthwhile noting here that if a tax function τ is nondecreasing (a case that will be shown to be relevant below), then $y - \tau(y)$ has a slope less than or equal to 1, so that the smallest implicit budget among the subpopulation with skill w is obtained by agents who work full time (as shown in Figure 17b), if there are such agents.

Define the expenditure function $\tilde{E}(w, u)$, relative to reference preferences $\tilde{R}$, as the solution to the equation

$$\tilde{U}^{\max}(B^f(\tilde{E}(w, u), w)) = u.$$

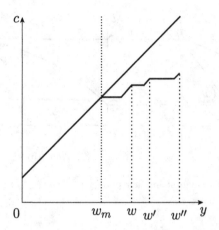

Fig. 18. Lower and upper bounds on the optimal tax scheme for equivalent-budget social preferences.

Theorem 3.   *Under the No Identification assumption, a tax function maximizing*

$$\min_i \tilde{U}^{\max}(I\!B(z_i, w_i, R_i))$$

can be computed by minimizing $\tau(w_m)$ under the constraint: for all $y \geq 0$,

$$\tau(w_m) \leq \tau(y) \leq \min_{w \in W}[(y - w)^+ - \tilde{E}(w, \tilde{U}_0)],$$

where $\tilde{U}_0 = \tilde{U}^{\max}(B^s(-\tau(w_m), w_m))$.

The inequalities obtained in the theorem yield upper and lower bounds for the income function $y - \tau(y)$, which are represented by the thick lines on Figure 18. Again, one observes that the agents who earn $y = w_m$ receive the greatest subsidy over the whole population. And they share this privilege with all agents with a lower income, since the marginal tax rate over the interval $[0, w_m]$ is exactly zero.

On the figure, w_m, w, w', and w'' are consecutive members of W. The intuition for the construction of the upper bound on the tax goes as follows. Within each group of agents having the same wage rate, if the tax is nondecreasing, those working full time have the lowest well-being index (see Figure 17). Given that the social preferences are of the maximin type, we can restrict our attention to those agents. The upper bound is indeed designed in such a way that the well-being index is equalized among agents working full time.

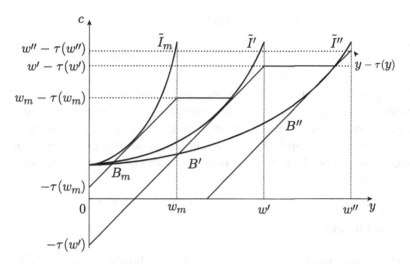

Fig. 19. Identifying the upper bound on the tax scheme for equivalent-budget social preferences.

This is illustrated in Figure 19: For any $w \in W$, the implicit budget of an agent choosing a maximal labor time is equal to $B^f(-\tau(w), w)$, which are referred to B_m, B', and B'' in the figure, for wages w_m, w', and w'', respectively. Equality of $\tilde{U}^{\max}(B^f(-\tau(w), w))$ is achieved among w's when the rescaled indifference curves $\tilde{I}_m, \tilde{I}'$, and $\tilde{I}''$ associated with the same welfare level (they intersect the vertical axis at the same coordinate) are tangent to B_m, B', and B'', respectively.

If we fix $\tilde{U}_0 = \tilde{U}^{\max}(B^f(-\tau(w_m), w_m))$, we need to have $-\tau(w) = \tilde{E}(w, \tilde{U}_0)$. Then, for any y between, say, w' and w'', the tax $\tau(y)$ must satisfy $y - \tau(y) \geq w' - \tau(w')$ and $\tau(y) \leq \tau(w'')$, and the definition of the upper bound follows.

Moreover, for $y \in [0, w_m]$, the only relevant wage is w_m and the restriction on the tax is $\tau(y) \leq \tau(w_m)$. Combined with the lower bound $\tau(y) \geq \tau(w_m)$, we obtain $\tau(y) = \tau(w_m)$ which means that the marginal income tax rate, again, needs to be zero on low incomes.

To study the shape of the function

$$\min_{w \in W} [(y - w)^+ - \tilde{E}(w, \tilde{U}_0)],$$

we can focus, for the sake of simplicity, on the case when W is the interval $[w_m, +\infty[$. For a given y, the expression $(y - w)^+ - \tilde{E}(w, \tilde{U}_o)$ is nondecreasing in w, so that the minimum is attained for $w = y$ if $y \in W$, and for

$w = w_m > y$ otherwise. Then one can write

$$\min_{w \in W} [(y - w)^+ - \tilde{E}(w, \tilde{U}_0)] = -\tilde{E}(\max\{y, w_m\}, \tilde{U}_0).$$

This expression is constant for $y \leq w_m$, and is convex because $\tilde{E}(w, \tilde{U}_0)$ is concave in w. In other words, this function provides an upper bound for the tax function, which has nondecreasing marginal tax rates, a clear case of progressive tax. The optimal tax itself need not be progressive, but it has a progressive upper bound and it coincides with the upper bound as soon as the latter is efficient.[12]

6.   Conclusion

Should we help the low skilled or reward the hardworking? Our analysis is meant to shed light on the implications of this ethical dilemma.

First, recall that the approach adopted in this paper defines social preferences that refer only to individual noncomparable preferences and yet satisfy the Pareto principle and fairness requirements. Such social preferences can be applied in second-best contexts. Consequently, applications need not depend on delicate choices of individual utility functions, and the only data required are the joint distribution of wages and preferences in the population.

Our main result is that, in spite of a definite antagonism between these two goals, as illustrated in the incompatibility between the corresponding requirements in our model, there are interesting convergences between egalitarian-equivalent preferences (which focus on the low skilled) and equivalent-budget preferences (which focus on the hardworking), as far as the optimal tax is concerned. It is as if the second-best context reduced the intensity of this value conflict, as compared to the first-best context.

The tax schemes that turn out to be justified by our analysis have one of the following features: they maximize the basic income, they exhibit a zero marginal tax rate on incomes below the minimum wage (the minimum wage being defined as the earnings of agents working full time at the smallest wage rate) or they are below an upper bound exhibiting increasing marginal tax rates.

---

[12]When, as in our finite model, W is not an interval, it still contains points of this convex function (for all values $w \in W$), so that this general shape is still relevant.

In the above theoretical analysis as well as in potential applications, the determination of the smallest wage rate plays an important role. The minimum legal wage seems a natural candidate (assuming law is respected), but one may also suggest that agents who are constrained in their labor time by an insufficient labor demand, such as the unemployed, may be treated as if their wage rate was zero above their current labor time. Unemployed agents are then equivalent to agents with a zero wage. As a consequence of our analysis, one might suggest that in times of high unemployment, it is reasonable to maximize the minimum income, whereas when unemployment is low it is advisable to seek low marginal rates of taxation for low incomes. A combination of unemployment allowances and tax exemption for low incomes could approximately achieve this goal without requiring any institutional adjustment during the business cycle.[13]

Appendix: Proofs

Proof of Proposition 1: Assume that the constraint (y_{22}, c_{22}) $R_{22}^*(y_{12}, c_{12})$ is not binding, so that $(y_{22}, c_{22})P_{22}^*(y_{12}, c_{12})$. The social preferences under consideration are of the maximin type. Therefore, either equality among the relevant indices is achieved, or an incentive compatibility constraint is binding. Let U_2 be a utility function representing R_2. As the above incentive constraint is not binding, one must have either

$$I\!\!\Gamma\left(\left(\frac{y_{12}}{w_1}, c_{12}\right), w_1, R_2\right) = I\!\!\Gamma\left(\left(\frac{y_{22}}{w_2}, c_{22}\right), w_1, R_2\right),$$

or

$$I\!\!\Gamma\left(\left(\frac{y_{12}}{w_1}, c_{12}\right), w_2, R_2\right) = I\!\!\Gamma\left(\left(\frac{y_{22}}{w_2}, c_{22}\right), w_2, R_2\right),$$

or

$$U_2^{\max}\left(I\!\!B\left(\left(\frac{y_{12}}{w_1}, c_{12}\right), w_1, R_2\right)\right) = U_2^{\max}\left(I\!\!B\left(\left(\frac{y_{22}}{w_2}, c_{22}\right), w_2, R_2\right)\right),$$

implying $(\frac{y_{12}}{w_1}, c_{12})$ $I_2(\frac{y_{22}}{w_2}, c_{22})$. As $w_1 < w_2$, this implies (y_{12}, c_{12}) R_{22}^* (y_{22}, c_{22}), in contradiction with the above assumption. $\qquad\square$

---

[13]Special observable characteristics of unemployed or handicapped agents may justify that they be given a special treatment, with a greater income support, even when these characteristics are not perfectly observed. See Salanié (2002).

Proof of Proposition 2: By Proposition 1, $(y_{22}, c_{22}) I_{22}^*(y_{12}, e_{12})$ in both cases. By assumption, $(y_{12}, c_{12}) = (y_{21}, c_{21})$. That is, $w_1 - EE$ and $R_2 - EB$ can only differ with respect to the relative treatment of agents 11 and 12. But

$$I\!\Gamma\left(\left(\frac{y_{11}}{w_1}, c_{11}\right), w_1, R_1\right) \geq I\!\Gamma\left(\left(\frac{y_{12}}{w_1}, c_{12}\right), w_1, R_2\right) \Leftrightarrow$$

$$I\!B\left(\left(\frac{y_{11}}{w_1}, c_{11}\right), w_1, R_1\right) \geqq I\!B\left(\left(\frac{y_{12}}{w_1}, c_{12}\right), w_1, R_2\right) \Leftrightarrow$$

$$U_2^{\max}\left(I\!B\left(\left(\frac{y_{11}}{w_1}, c_{11}\right), w_1, R_1\right)\right) \geq U_2^{\max}\left(I\!B\left(\left(\frac{y_{12}}{w_1}, c_{12}\right), w_1, R_2\right)\right)$$

for any utility function U_2 representing R_2. Therefore, either equality of the indices is achieved in both cases, or the incentive constraint is binding in both cases.   □

Proof of Theorem 2: Consider a tax function τ^* defined by the fact that the income function $y - \tau^*(y)$ is continuous, nondecreasing, and the part of it lying in the positive orthant is the envelope curve of the population's indifference curves in (y, c) space, at an allocation z^* maximizing $\min_i I\!\Gamma(z_i, \tilde{w}, R_i)$. Let $y^* \geq 0$ be the smallest level of earnings such that $y - \tau^*(y) \geq 0$. By the No Identification assumption, over $[y^*, w_m]$ it is the envelope curve of agents from the w_m subpopulation. Let

$$I\!\Gamma_m = \min\left\{t \in \mathbb{R} \mid \exists \ell \in \left[\frac{y^*}{w_m}, 1\right], t + \tilde{w}\ell = w_m\ell - \tau^*(w_m\ell)\right\}$$

$$= \min\left\{y - \tau^*(y) - \frac{\tilde{w}}{w_m}y \mid y \in [y^*, w_m]\right\}.$$

$I\!\Gamma_m$ is the minimum value of $I\!\Gamma(z_i, \tilde{w}, R_i)$ over the w_m subpopulation. Without loss of generality, we can assume that over $[0, y^*)$ the slope of $y - \tau^*(y) < 0$ is smaller than $\tilde{w}/w_m$, so that one simply has

$$I\!\Gamma_m = \min\left\{y - \tau^*(y) - \frac{\tilde{w}}{w_m}y \mid y \in [0, w_m]\right\}.$$

Similarly, for agents with a higher w, the minimum value of $I\!\Gamma(z_i^*, \tilde{w}, R_i)$ is at least as great as

$$\min\left\{y - \tau^*(y) - \frac{\tilde{w}}{w}y \mid y \in [0, w]\right\}.$$

Since $y - \tau^*(y)$ is nondecreasing, the above expression is nondecreasing in w, so that $I\!\!\Gamma_m$ is indeed the minimum value of $I\!\!\Gamma(z_i^*, \tilde{w}, R_i)$ over the whole population.

Notice that, at a laissez-faire allocation,

$$\min\left\{y - \frac{\tilde{w}}{w_m}y \mid y \in [0, w_m]\right\} = w_m - \tilde{w},$$

so that since z^* maximizes $\min_i I\!\!\Gamma(z_i, \tilde{w}, R_i)$, one has $I\!\!\Gamma_m \geq w_m - \tilde{w}$.

Let a new tax be defined by $\tau^{**}(y) = \max\{\tau^*(y), -I\!\!\Gamma_m - (\tilde{w} - w_m)\}$. This tax function is feasible, because it cuts all subsidies greater than a constant, $I\!\!\Gamma_m + (\tilde{w} - w_m)$, so that no agent's tax may decrease (and no subsidy increase), even after they adjust their choice. Moreover,

$$\min\left\{y - \tau^{**}(y) - \frac{\tilde{w}}{w_m}y \mid y \in [0, w_m]\right\}$$

$$= \min\left\{ \begin{array}{c} \min\left\{y - \tau^*(y) - \frac{\tilde{w}}{w_m}y \mid y \in [0, w_m]\right\}, \\ \min\left\{y + I\!\!\Gamma_m + (\tilde{w} - w_m) - \frac{\tilde{w}}{w_m}y \mid y \in [0, w_m]\right\} \end{array} \right\}$$

$$= \min\left\{ \begin{array}{c} \min\left\{y - \tau^*(y) - \frac{\tilde{w}}{w_m}y \mid y \in [0, w_m]\right\}, \\ I\!\!\Gamma_m. \end{array} \right\}$$

$$= I\!\!\Gamma_m.$$

Since the minimum value of $I\!\!\Gamma(z_i, \tilde{w}, R_i)$ over the w_m subpopulation, under application of τ^{**}, is at least as great as this expression, one obtains that τ^{**} maximizes $\min_i I\!\!\Gamma(z_i, \tilde{w}, R_i)$ as well.

By construction, for all $y \geq 0, \tau^{**}(y) \geq -I\!\!\Gamma_m - (\tilde{w} - w_m)$, and as shown above, for all $y \leq w_m, y - \tau^{**}(y) - \frac{\tilde{w}}{w_m}y \geq I\!\!\Gamma_m$, so that for all $y \leq w_m$,

$$-I\!\!\Gamma_m - (\tilde{w} - w_m) \leq \tau^{**}(y) \leq -I\!\!\Gamma_m + y - \frac{\tilde{w}}{w_m}y.$$

For $y = w_m$, one obtains $\tau^{**}(w_m) = -I\!\!\Gamma_m - (\tilde{w} - w_m)$, implying that for all $y \geq 0, \tau^{**}(y) \geq \tau^{**}(w_m)$. And for all $y \in [0, w_m]$,

$$\tau^{**}(y) \leq y - \frac{\tilde{w}}{w_m}y - I\!\!\Gamma_m = y - \frac{\tilde{w}}{w_m}y + \tau^{**}(w_m) + \tilde{w} - w_m$$

$$\leq \tau^{**}(w_m) + (w_m - y)\left(\frac{\tilde{w}}{w_m} - 1\right).$$

Finally, since $y - \tau^{**}(y)$ is nondecreasing, for all $y > w_m$ one has $\tau^{**}(y) \leq \tau^{**}(w_m) - w_m + y$.

It remains to note that since $I\!\Gamma_m = w_m - \tilde{w} - \tau^{**}(w_m)$, maximizing $I\!\Gamma_m$ is equivalent to minimizing $\tau^{**}(w_m)$. $\qquad\square$

Proof of Theorem 3: Consider a tax function τ^* such that the income function $y - \tau^*(y)$ is continuous, nondecreasing, and the part of it lying in the positive orthant coincides with the envelope curve of the agents' indifference curves at z^*. By the No Identification assumption, the part of this envelope curve over some interval $[0, w]$, for $w \in W$, is also the envelope curve of the indifference curves of the subpopulation with a wage rate no greater than w.

Let

$$\tilde{U}_0 = \min_i \tilde{U}^{\max}(I\!B(z_i^*, w_i, R_i)).$$

Necessarily, $\tilde{U}_0 \geq \tilde{U}^{\max}(B^f(0, w_m))$, since a laissez-faire allocation z^{LF} is such that $\tilde{U}^{\max}(I\!B(z_i^{\mathrm{LF}}, w_i, R_i)) = \tilde{U}^{\max}(B^f(0, w_m)) \geq \tilde{U}(0,0)$ for all i. An allocation at which $\min_i \tilde{U}^{\max}(I\!B(z_i, w_i, R_i))$ is maximized cannot do worse. Notice that

$$\tilde{U}_0 = \tilde{U}^{\max}(B^f(\tilde{E}(w_m, \tilde{U}_0), w_m)) \geq \tilde{U}^{\max}(B^f(0, w_m))$$

implies $\tilde{E}(w_m, \tilde{U}_0) \geq 0$.

Take any $w \in W$, and any $y \leq w$. By the above observation about the envelope curve, there is an agent i such that $w_i \leq w$, and such that $z_i^* I_i(\frac{y}{w_i}, y - \tau^*(y))$, which entails

$$I\!B(z_i^*, w_i, R_i) \subseteq B^f(-\tau^*(y), w_m).$$

Since $\tilde{U}^{\max}(I\!B(z_i^*, w_i, R_i)) \geq \tilde{U}_0$,

$$B^f(-\tau^*(y), w_i) \supseteq B^f(\tilde{E}(w_i, \tilde{U}_0), w_i),$$

or equivalently, $-\tau^*(y) \geq \tilde{E}(w_i, \tilde{U}_0)$. As $\tilde{E}(w_i, \tilde{U}_0)$ is nonincreasing in w_i, and $w \geq w_i$, one obtains $-\tau^*(y) \geq \tilde{E}(w, \tilde{U}_0)$. Take any $y > w$. Since

$y - \tau^*(y)$ is nondecreasing, one has

$$y - \tau^*(y) \geq w - \tau^*(w) \geq w + \tilde{E}(w, \tilde{U}_0),$$

and therefore $\tau^*(y) \leq y - w - \tilde{E}(w, \tilde{U}_0)$. This achieves the proof that for all $y \geq 0$, all $w \in W$,

$$\tau^*(y) \leq (y - w)^+ - \tilde{E}(w, \tilde{U}_0).$$

Define a new tax function τ^{**} by $\tau^{**}(y) = \max\{\tau^*(y), -\tilde{E}(w_m, \tilde{U}_0)\}$. Since it cuts all subsidies greater than $\tilde{E}(w_m, \tilde{U}_0)$, this new tax function is feasible. In addition, it also satisfies the property that for all $y \geq 0$, all $w \in W$,

$$\tau^{**}(y) \leq (y - w)^+ - \tilde{E}(w, \tilde{U}_0).$$

This is due to the fact that if $\tau^{**}(y) = \tau^*(y)$, this immediately follows from the same property of τ^*; and if $\tau^{**}(y) = -\tilde{E}(w_m, \tilde{U}_0)$, then the conclusion is obtained by observing that

$$\tilde{E}(w, \tilde{U}_0) - \tilde{E}(w_m, \tilde{U}_0) \leq 0 \leq (y - w)^+.$$

We now show that at any (incentive-compatible) allocation z^{**} generated by τ^{**}, one has

$$\min_i \tilde{U}^{\max}(I\!B(z_i^{**}w_i, R_i)) = \tilde{U}_0.$$

First, we note that for all $y \leq w_m$, $\tau^{**}(y) = \tau^{**}(w_m) = -\tilde{E}(w_m, \tilde{U}_0)$, since $\tau^*(y) \leq -\tilde{E}(w_m, \tilde{U}_0)$. This entails that all agents from the w_m subpopulation have the implicit budget $B^f(\tilde{E}(w_m, \tilde{U}_0), w_m)$. For all those agents,

$$\tilde{U}^{\max}(I\!B(z_i^{**}, w_i, R_i)) = \tilde{U}^{\max}(B^f(\tilde{E}(w_m, \tilde{U}_0), w_m)) = \tilde{U}_0.$$

More generally, since $(\tau^{**})'(y) = 0$ over $[0, w_m]$ and individual preferences are convex, one can see that for all agents i with $y_i^{**} \leq w_m$, z_i^{**} is the best for R_i over $B^f(\tilde{E}(w_m, \tilde{U}_0), w_i)$, so that

$$I\!B(z_i^{**}, w_i.R_i) = B^f(\tilde{E}(w_m, \tilde{U}_0), w_i),$$

and as $w_m \leq w_i$, $\tilde{E}(w_m, \tilde{U}_0) \geq \tilde{E}(w_i, \tilde{U}_0)$, implying

$$\mathbb{B}(z_i^{**}, w_i, R_i) \supseteq B^f(\tilde{E}(w_i, \tilde{U}_0), w_i),$$

and then

$$\tilde{U}^{\max}(\mathbb{B}(z_i^{**}, w_i, R_i)) \geq \tilde{U}^{\max}(B^f(\tilde{E}(w_i, \tilde{U}_0), w_i)) = \tilde{U}_0.$$

Now consider an agent i with $y_i^{**} > w_m$. Then $w_i > w_m$. One has, for all $y \leq w_i$,

$$z_i^{**} R_i \left(\frac{y}{w_i}, y - \tau^{**}(y) \right).$$

If for all $y \leq w_i, \tau^*(y) \leq -\tilde{E}(w_m, \tilde{U}_0)$, then for all $y \leq w_i$, $\tau^{**}(y) = -\tilde{E}(w_m, \tilde{U}_0)$ and

$$z_i^{**} R_i \left(\frac{y}{w_i}, y + \tilde{E}(w_m, \tilde{U}_0) \right),$$

so that

$$\mathbb{B}(z_i^{**}, w_i, R_i) \supseteq B^f(\tilde{E}(w_m, \tilde{U}_0), w_m),$$

and, since

$$B^f(\tilde{E}(w_m, \tilde{U}_0), w_i) \supseteq B^f(\tilde{E}(w_m, \tilde{U}_0), w_m),$$

one obtains $\tilde{U}^{\max}(\mathbb{B}(z_i^{**}, w_i, R_i)) \geq \tilde{U}_0$.

If there exists $y \leq w_i$ such that $\tau^*(y) > -\tilde{E}(w_m, \tilde{U}_0)$ then, for any such $y, \tau^{**}(y) = \tau^*(y)$. Let

$$y_0 = \arg \max_{0 \leq y \leq w_i} \tau^*(y).$$

Necessarily, $I\!T(z_i^{**}, w_i, R_i) \geq -\tau^*(y_0)$, because

$$I\!T(z_i^{**}, w_i, R_i) \geq - \max_{0 \leq y \leq w_i} \tau^{**}(y) = -\tau^*(y_0).$$

Recollect that $y - \tau^*(y)$ is the envelope curve of the agents' indifference curves at z, and that, by the No Identification assumption, over the interval $[0, w_i]$, it is the envelope curve for the subpopulation with wage no greater than w_i. Then there exists an agent j with wage $w_j \in [y_0, w_i]$, such that

$$\mathit{\Pi}(z_j, w_j, R_j) \leq -\tau^*(y_0) \leq \mathit{\Pi}(z_i^{**}, w_i, R_i),$$

implying

$$\mathit{B}(z_i^{**}, w_i, R_i) \supseteq \mathit{B}(z_j, w_j, R_j).$$

Since one has $\tilde{U}^{\max}(\mathit{B}(z_j, w_j, R_j)) \geq \tilde{U}_0$, this implies $\tilde{U}^{\max}$ $(\mathit{B}(z_i^{**}, w_i, R_i)) \geq \tilde{U}_0$.

The tax function τ^{**} satisfies the constraint enunciated in the theorem. It remains to show that one must seek to minimize $\tau^{**}(w_m)$. This is an immediate consequence of the fact that

$$\min_i \tilde{U}^{\max}(\mathit{B}(z_i^*, w_i, R_i)) = \tilde{U}_0 = \tilde{U}^{\max}(B^f(-\tau^{**}(w_m), w_m)). \qquad \square$$

References

1. A. B. Atkinson. *Public Economics in Action*. Oxford: Clarendon Press. 1995.
2. R. Boadway, M. Marchand, P. Pestieau and M. Racionero. 'Optimal redistribution with heterogeneous preferences for leisure', *Journal of Public Economic Theory* **4** (2002), 475–498.
3. W. Bossert, M. Fleurbaey and D. van de Gaer. 'Responsibility, talent, and compensation: A second-best analysis', *Review of Economic Design* **4** (1999), 35–55.
4. P. Chone and G. Laroque. 'Optimal incentives for labor force participation', *Journal of Public Economics* **89** (2005), 395–425.
5. P. Diamond. 'Optimal income taxation: An example with a U-shaped pattern of optimal marginal tax rates', *American Economic Review* **88** (1998), 83–95.
6. R. Dworkin. 'What is equality? Part 2: Equality of resources', *Philosophy and Public Affairs* **10** (1981), 283–345.
7. M. Fleurbaey. 'Equality and responsibility', *European Economic Review* **39** (1995), 683–689.
8. M. Fleurbaey and F. Maniquet. 'Fair allocation with unequal production skills: The no-envy approach to compensation', *Mathematical Social Sciences* **32** (1996), 71–93.

9. M. Fleurbaey and F. Maniquet. 'Fair orderings with unequal production skills', *Social Choice and Welfare* **24** (2005), 1–35.

10. M. Kaneko and K. Nakamura. 'The Nash social welfare function', *Econometrica* **47** (1979), 423–435.

11. J. Mirrlees. 'An exploration in the theory of optimum income taxation', *Review of Economic Studies* **38** (1971), 175–208.

12. H. Moulin and W. Thomson. 'Axiomatic analysis of resource allocation problems', in K. J. Arrow, A. K. Sen and K. Suzumura (eds.), *Social Choice Re-examined*, Macmillan: London and St Martin's Press: New York. 1997.

13. E. Pazner and D. Schmeidler. 'Egalitarian-equivalent allocations: A new concept of economic equity', *Quarterly Journal of Economics* **92** (1978), 671–687.

14. J. Rawls. 'Social unity and primary goods', in A. Sen and B. Williams (eds.), *Utilitarianism and Beyond*, Cambridge: Cambridge University Press. 1982.

15. J. C. Rochet and P. Chone. 'Ironing, sweeping, and multi-dimensional screening', *Econometrica* **66** (1998), 783–826.

16. J. E. Roemer, R. Aaberge, U. Colombino, J. Fritzell, S. P. Jenkins, A. Lefranc, I. Marx, M. Page, E. Pommer, J. Ruiz-Castillo, M. J. San Segundo, T. Tranaes, A. Trannoy, G. G. Wagner and I. Zubiri. 'To what extent do fiscal regimes equalize opportunities for income acquisition among citizens?' *Journal of Public Economics* **87** (2003), 539–565.

17. E. Saez. 'Optimal income transfer programs: Intensive versus extensive labor supply responses', *Quarterly Journal of Economics* **117** (2002), 1039–1073.

18. B. Salanié. 'Optimal demogrants with imperfect tagging', *Economics Letters* **75** (2002), 319–324.

19. E. Schokkaert, D. van de Gaer, F. Vandenbroucke and R. Luttens. 'Responsibility-sensitive egalitarianism and optimal linear income taxation', *Mathematical Social Sciences* **48** (2004), 151–182.

20. J. K. Seade. 'Non linear prices with multidimensional consumers', Bellcore, Livinston N. J., Mimeo. (1979).

21. A. K. Sen. 'Social choice theory', in K. J. Arrow and M. D. Intriligator (eds.), *Handbook of Mathematical Economics*, Amsterdam: North-Holland. 1986.

22. R. B. Wilson. *Nonlinear Pricing*. Oxford: Oxford University Press. 1993.

CHAPTER 10

Kolm's Tax, Tax Credit, and the Flat Tax

Marc Fleurbaey and François Maniquet

1. Introduction

In several of his recent contributions, most notably Kolm (2004), Serge-Christophe Kolm has developed a solution to the macro-justice problem which he calls Equal Labor Income Equalization (ELIE). It consists in a particular labor income taxation scheme that he advocates as the ideal compromise between freedom and equality requirements.

The ELIE proposal is, in essence, a first-best taxation scheme involving a parameter, k, which can be thought of as being the share of every individual's labor time which is equally shared within society. At an ELIE allocation, earning ability is taxed in such a way that the net income an individual would get should he choose to work precisely k is equalized among individuals. If an individual's earning ability is s, he pays the tax ks and receives a universal grant g. Therefore, if he works exactly k at the wage rate s, his net income is g, independently of s. Individuals choosing to work more than k are paid marginally at their wage rate; that is, the marginal tax on earnings is zero. Individuals choosing to work less than k have to "buy" their leisure, and have to do so at its marginal value as well.

Implementing the ELIE scheme requires the earning ability of each individual to be observable. If the earning ability is not observable, then Kolm's

M. Fleurbaey *et al.* (eds.), *Social Ethics and Normative Economics,*
Studies in Choice and Welfare, DOI 10.1007/978-3-642-17807-8_9.
© Springer-Verlag Berlin Heidelberg 2011

proposal needs to be adapted into a second-best version. This is what we study in this article.

In order to refine the ELIE scheme for the second-best context, we will begin by defining a social ordering function compatible with ELIE. A social ordering function defines a complete ranking of the set of allocations for each profile of the population characteristics. The social ordering function, which we define below and which we axiomatize, rationalizes ELIE in the sense that the ELIE allocations maximize the social ordering function in the special case in which the information is complete. Moreover, we believe it incorporates the basic fairness principles underlying ELIE and thereby extends the thrust of the ELIE idea to the comparison of arbitrary allocations.

Then, we use this social ordering function to derive taxation schemes under different information settings. First, we look at the case in which the earning ability cannot be observed but incomes and labor times are observable. Consequently, the wage rate can be deduced from the observables, but individuals may still decide to take jobs at wage rates lower than their actual earning ability. This is the same informational framework as in Dasgupta and Hammond (1980). We prove that under certain conditions, the resulting taxation scheme is similar to Kolm's proposal regarding incomes earned by individuals working more than k, but differs substantially for the other individuals.

Second, we look at the case in which only income, but not labor time nor the wage rate, is observable. This is the typical case considered in the optimal income taxation literature, following Mirrlees (1971). We derive some insights about the optimal income tax scheme, in particular that taxation of incomes at a constant marginal tax rate equal to k appears as an important benchmark. We therefore establish a surprising connection between ELIE and the flat tax.

This connection is loose, however, for low incomes. Indeed, we also show that in both of the informational contexts studied here, one feature of the first-best version of ELIE is preserved at the optimal second-best tax: low incomes up to the lowest earning ability should have a marginal tax of zero. This is a notable result in the light of recent reforms of the welfare state in which efforts have been made to reduce the marginal tax on low incomes.[1]

---

[1]This practical evolution has already found echoes in economic theory. See, e.g., Choné and Laroque (2005), Boadway, Marchand, Pestieau, and del Mar Racionero (2002), and Fleurbaey and Maniquet (2006, 2007).

A related analysis is made by Simula and Trannoy (2011), who observe that if all individuals work more than k at the ELIE first-best allocation, then ELIE is incentive-compatible when labor time is observable. For the case in which only income is observable, they suggest seeking an incentive-compatible allocation that is as close as possible to ELIE. There are three main differences with our approach. First, we study economies with heterogeneity in skills and preferences, whereas Simula and Trannoy examine economies with heterogeneity in skills only. Second, we use a different social welfare function (more specifically a different social ordering function), to which we give axiomatic foundations. Third, we do not restrict attention to situations in which all individuals work more than k. When some individuals work less than k, the first-best ELIE allocation is not always incentive-compatible even when labor time is observable, as we will show below.

In Section 2, we present the model and define our social ordering function. In Section 3, we provide an axiomatic justification for it. In Section 4, we study the optimal tax scheme when both labor times and incomes are observable. In Section 5, we examine the optimal tax scheme when only incomes are observable. Section 6 offers concluding comments.

2. The Model

Our model is identical to the one Kolm used to develop his ELIE proposal. This model was introduced in the axiomatic literature on fairness by Pazner and Schmeidler (1974). It generalizes the model of Mirrlees (1971) by allowing individuals to have different preferences, not only different earning abilities. There are two goods, labor time (l) and consumption (c). The population of an economy is finite. If the set of individuals in an economy is N, each individual $i \in N$ has a *production skill* $s_i \geq 0$, which enables him to produce the quantity $s_i l_i$ of the consumption good with labor time l_i. This individual can also choose to work at a lower productivity (wage rate) $w_i \leq s_i$, in which case his earnings are equal to $w_i l_i$. Individual i also has *preferences* represented by an ordering R_i over bundles $z_i = (l_i, c_i)$, where $0 \leq l_i \leq 1$ and $c_i \geq 0$. Let $X = [0, 1] \times \mathbb{R}_+$ denote an individual's labor-consumption set. We assume that the wage rate w_i does not directly affect an individual's satisfaction.

We study the domain $\mathscr{E}$ of economies defined as follows. Let $\mathscr{N}$ denote the set of non-empty finite subsets of the set of positive integers $\mathbb{N}_+$ and $\mathscr{R}$ denote the set of continuous, convex, and strictly monotonic (negatively in labor, positively in consumption) orderings over X. An *economy* $e = (s_N, R_N)$ belongs to the domain $\mathscr{E}$ if $N \in \mathscr{N}, s_N \in \mathbb{R}_+^N$, and $R_N \in \mathscr{R}^N$ that is,

$$\mathscr{E} = \bigcup_{N \in \mathscr{N}} (\mathbb{R}_+^N \times \mathscr{R}^N).$$

Let $e = (s_N, R_N) \in \mathscr{E}$. An *allocation* is a vector $x_N = (w_i, z_i)_{i \in N} \in \mathbb{R}_+^N \times X^N$. It is *feasible* for e if $w_i \le s_i$ for all $i \in N$ and

$$\sum_{i \in N} c_i \le \sum_{i \in N} w_i l_i.$$

Because w_i does not affect i's satisfaction, we will generally restrict attention to bundle allocations $z_N = (z_i)_{i \in N} \in X^N$ in the context of social evaluation.[2] Bundle allocations will also be called allocations for short when there is no risk of confusion. Let $Z(e)$ be the subset of X^N for which $l_i = 0$ for all $i \in N$ such that $s_i = 0$. We will restrict attention to this subset, as it does not make sense in any first-best or second-best context to make an individual work when his productivity is nill. This restriction is useful because it simplifies the presentation of our social ordering.

A *social ordering* for an economy $e = (s_N, R_N) \in \mathscr{E}$ is a complete ordering over the set $Z(e)$ of (bundle) allocations. A *social ordering function* (SOF) $\mathbf{R}$ associates a social ordering $\mathbf{R}(e)$ to each economy $e \in \mathscr{E}$. We write $z_N \mathbf{R}(e) z_N'$ to denote that allocation z_N is at least as good as z_N' in e. The corresponding strict social preference and social indifference relations are denoted $\mathbf{P}(e)$ and $\mathbf{I}(e)$, respectively. Following the social choice tradition initiated by Arrow (1951), we require a social ordering to rank all allocations in $Z(e)$, not just the feasible allocations.[3] We depart, however, from Arrow's legacy by letting the social ordering depend on s_N, not just on R_N. We do this because fairness principles may recommend treating individuals differently depending on their earning ability. As it turns out, this happens with ELIE.

Our next objective in this section is to define the social ordering function that we consider to be associated with Kolm's ELIE proposal. To do so requires introducing some terminology. Let $e = (s_N, R_N) \in \mathscr{E}$ and let $i \in N$.

---

[2]At the cost of heavier notation, we could always deal with allocations x_N and deduce from the Pareto principle the fact that only z_N really matters.

[3]Although we think that it is less justified, we could have restricted the definition of a social ordering function to feasible allocations and still derive the same results.

For $A \subseteq X$, let $m(R_i, A) \subseteq A$ denote the set of bundles (if any) that are the best in A for the preferences R_i; that is,

$$m(R_i, A) = \{z_i \in A | \forall z_i' \in A, \ z_i R_i z_i'\}.$$

For $z_i = (l_i, c_i) \in X$ and $s_i \in \mathbb{R}_+$, let $B(z_i, s_i) \subseteq X$ denote the *budget set* obtained with s_i for which z_i is on the budget frontier:

$$B(z_i, s_i) = \{(l_i', c_i') \in X | c_i' - s_i l_i' \leq c_i - s_i l_i\}.$$

In the special case in which $s_i = 0$ and $c_i = 0$, we adopt the convention that

$$B(z_i, s_i) = \{(l_i', c_i') \in X | c_i' = 0, l_i' \leq l_i\}.$$

Let ∂B denote the upper frontier of the set B. Also, let $IB(z_i, s_i, R_i) \subseteq X$ denote the *implicit budget* at z_i, which is defined to be the budget set with slope s_i having the property that i is indifferent between z_i and his preferred bundle in that budget set:

$IB(z_i, s_i, R_i)$

$$= B(z_i', s_i) \text{ for any } z_i' \text{ such that } z_i' I_i z_i \quad \text{and} \quad z_i' \in m(R_i, B(z_t', s_t)).$$

By the strict monotonicity of preferences, this definition is unambiguous. See Figure 1 for an illustration of this construction. Notice that the bundle z_i need not belong to the implicit budget. Also note that implicit budgets

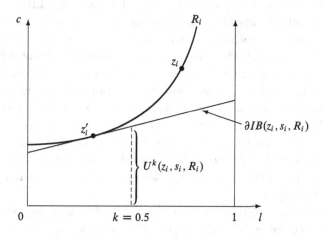

Fig. 1. Implicit budget and utility function.

provide a set representation of the preferences of individual i in e in the sense that

$$z_i R_i z_i' \Leftrightarrow IB(z_i, s_i, R_i) \supseteq IB(z_i', s_i R_i).$$

We are now equipped to define the SOFs that will be used in the subsequent discussion. We consider a family of SOFs, parameterized by a coefficient $k \in [0, 1]$. For each $k \in [0, 1]$, the corresponding SOF will be denoted $\mathbf{R}^k$. Each SOF in the family is based on a specific utility representation of the preferences, and it compares allocations by applying the leximin aggregation rule to the utility vectors derived from these numerical representations.

Assuming that a parameter $k \in [0, 1]$ has been chosen, let us begin by defining the utility functions. Let $e = (s_N, R_n) \in \mathscr{E}$ and let $i \in N$. The utility function $U^k(\cdot, s_i, R_i)$ is constructed as follows: $U^k(z_i, s_i, R_i)$ is the vertical coordinate of the bundle with abscissa k on the frontier of the implicit budget of individual i at z_i. Formally,

$$U^k(z_i, s_i, R_i) = u \Leftrightarrow (k, u) \in \partial IB(z_i, s_i, R_i).$$

This construction is illustrated in Figure 1 for the case $k = 0.5$. Observe that this construction works only for bundles such that $(k, 0) \in IB(z_i, s_i, R_i)$ when $s_i > 0$. Let $Y^k(e)$ denote the subset of $Z(e)$ for which this condition is satisfied for all $i \in N$.

Such utility indexes depend on k and also on s_i, not just on R_i. This dependence is justified by the fact that the philosophy of ELIE is not welfarist. These utility indexes in fact measure how well-off an individual is in terms of budget opportunities, not in terms of subjective satisfaction or happiness. Even though these indexes are ordinally consistent with each individual's preferences, the interpersonal comparisons they generate are basically resourcist, not welfarist. Moreover, the principles underlying ELIE stipulate that individuals are partly (depending on k) entitled to enjoy the benefits of their own productivity, so it is normal for the corresponding indexes to be sensitive to k and to individual skills. It must be emphasized that the axiomatic justification that is offered in the next section provides a joint derivation of the social aggregation rule and of these utility indexes from basic principles.

The social ordering $\mathbf{R}^k(e)$ on $Y^k(e)$ is obtained by applying the leximin criterion to vectors of U^k utility levels. The definition of the leximin criterion is the following. For two vectors of real numbers u_N, u_N', one says that u_N is weakly better than u'_N for the leximin criterion, which will be denoted here by

$$u_N \geq_{lex} u'_N,$$

when the smallest component of u_N is not lower than the smallest component of u'_N, and if they are equal, the second smallest component is not lower, and so forth.

k-**Leximin** ($\mathbf{R}^k$). For all $e = (s_N, R_N) \in \mathscr{E}$ and all $z_N, z'_N \in Y^k(e)$,

$$z_N \mathbf{R}^k(e) z'_N \Leftrightarrow u_N \geq_{lex} u'_N,$$

where, for all $i \in N$, $u_i = U^k(z_i, s_i, R_i)$ and $u'_i = U^k(z'_i, s_i, R_i)$.

This SOF is illustrated in Figure 2 for a two-individual economy $e = ((s_1, s_2), (R_1, R_2)) \in \mathscr{E}$. We see in the figure that $s_1 < s_2$ and that the preferences R_1 are less leisure oriented preferences than R_2. The allocations $z_N = (z_1, z_2)$ and $z'_N = (z'_1, z'_2)$ have to be compared. First, the implicit budgets associated with the four bundles are identified. Then, on the frontier of each budget, the bundle with abscissa k is identified. The vertical coordinates of these bundles are denoted by $u_1, u_2, u'_1,$ and u'_2 in the figure (corresponding respectively to $U^{0.5}(z_1, s_1, R_1)$, $U^{0.5}(z_2, s_2, R_2)$,

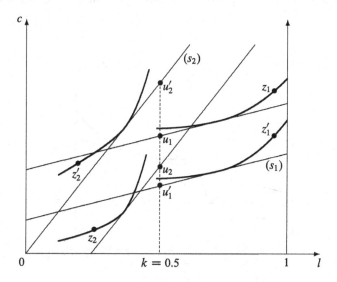

Fig. 2.   Illustration of the k-Leximin social ordering function (SOF).

$U^{0.5}(z_1', s_1, R_1)$, and $U^{0.5}(z_2', s_2, R_2)$). We observe that $u_1' < u_2 < u_1 < u_2'$. These inequalities imply that $z_N \ \mathbf{P}^{0.5}(e) z_N'$.

We do not study the extension of $\mathbf{R}^k(e)$ to $Z(e) \backslash Y^k(e)$, as this is of little consequence for the study of taxation. It is easy to find reasonable extensions. For instance, when $(k, 0) \notin IB(z_i, s_i, R_i)$ and $s_i > 0$, one can define

$$U^k(z_i, s_i, R_i) = u \Leftrightarrow (k - u, 0) \in \partial IB(z_i, s_i, R_i),$$

which yields $u < 0$. With this extended definition of U^k, $\mathbf{R}^k$ satisfies the axioms introduced in the next section over $Z(e)$.

The aim of a SOF is to give precise policy recommendations as a function of the informational conditions describing the set of tools available to the policy maker. If the informational conditions are those of a first-best world, then maximizing the social ordering $\mathbf{R}^k(e)$ on the set of feasible allocations leads to the ELIE allocations corresponding to parameter k. Indeed, at a (first-best) Pareto-efficient allocation, one has $w_i = s_i$ and $B(z_i, s_i) = IB(z_i, s_i, R_i)$ for all $i \in N$. A best allocation for $\mathbf{R}^k(e)$ is such that, in addition, the U^k utility levels are equalized, which implies that all budget set frontiers cross at a bundle with abscissa k. An example is given in Figure 3, for the same economy as above.

In the next section, we provide axiomatic foundations for this family of SOFs.

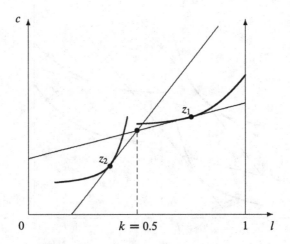

Fig. 3.   First-best allocation for k-Leximin.

3. Axiomatic Foundations

The family of SOFs inspired by Kolm's ELIE proposal, which we call the k-Leximin SOFs, satisfy a set of axioms that we define in this section. We also show that every SOF satisfying this set of axioms must satisfy a maximin property, which makes the SOF close to a k-Leximin SOF. The material in this section draws on previous work in which we have provided a similar axiomatic characterization of a family of SOFs containing the $\mathbf{R}^k$.[4] We present a variant of that characterization here in order to highlight the relationship between the k-Leximin SOF on the one hand and Kolm's fairness principles and his justification of ELIE on the other.

We begin with the key axiom establishing this relationship. This axiom is consistent with Kolm's idea that incomes should be equal among individuals working k. Let $e = (s_N, R_N) \in \mathscr{E}$ and $z_N, z'_N \in Z(e)$. Assume that z_N and z'_N differ only in the bundles of two individuals, say $p, q \in N$, and that in both allocations, p and q each freely choose to work k in a budget set determined by a lump-sum transfer and his own skill level. Using the notation of the preceding section, it follows that for $j = p, q$, one has $l_j = l'_j = k, Z_j \in m(R_j, B(z_j, s_j))$, and $z'_j \in m(R_j, B(z'_j, s_j))$. Assume, moreover, that p and q do not have the same consumption level in z_N, for instance, $c_p > c_q$. We then regard individual p as relatively richer than individual q. The social situation is not worsened, the axiom says, if $c_p > c'_p > c'_q > c_q$, so that the inequality in consumption between p and q is reduced in z'_N.[5]

k-Equal Labor Consumption Equalization. For all $e = (s_N, R_N) \in \mathscr{E}$, all $p, q \in N$, and all $z_N, z'_N \in Z(e)$ for which $z_i = z'_i$ for all $i \neq p, q$, if

(i) $l_p = l'_p = l_q = l'_q = k$;
(ii) $c_p > c'_p > c'_q > c_q$;
(iii) for all $j \in \{p, q\}, z_j \in m(R_j, B(z_j, s_j))$ and $z'_j \in m(R_j, B(z'_j, s_j))$, then $z'_N \mathbf{R}(e) z_N$.

Our next axiom captures the idea that individuals should be held responsible for their preferences and that society should not treat them

---

[4]See Fleurbaey and Maniquet (2005). For first-best allocation rules, see also Fleurbaey and Maniquet (1996) and Maniquet (1998).

[5]This kind of inequality reduction principle can be traced back to Hammond (1976, 1979). What is specific here is that it is applied to consumption rather than welfare, and for special amounts of labor.

differently — which, in this context, means that it should not tax them differently — on the sole basis that they have different preferences. This idea is also an important tenet of Kolm's conception of fairness. Consequently, if two individuals have the same skill but possibly different preferences, then they should be given the same treatment, which we interpret as requiring the social evaluation to focus on the opportunities available to them rather than their particular choice of consumption and labor.

Consider two individuals p and q endowed with the same skill s and facing different budget sets $B(z_p, s)$ and $B(z_q, s)$. One set contains the other, so the corresponding individual can be regarded as being relatively richer than the other. Assume, now, that we permute their budget sets. By doing so, we may have increased or decreased the observed inequality in consumption or in labor time, depending on these individuals' preferences. Nevertheless, the axiom states that the resulting allocation is equally fair (or equally unfair) as the initial one, because the distribution of budget sets is unchanged.[6] Formally,

Budget Anonymity. For all $e = (s_N, R_N) \in \mathscr{E}$, all $p, q \in N$ for which $s_p = s_q$, and all $z_N, z'_N \in Z(e)$ for which $z_i = z'_i$ for all $i \neq p, q$, if

(i) $B(z'_p, s_p) = B(z_q, s_q)$ and $B(z'_q, s_q) = B(z_p, s_p)$;
(ii) for all $j \in \{p, q\}$, $z_j \in m(R_j, B(z_j, s_j))$ and $z'_j \in m(R_j, B(z'_j, s_j))$, then $z'_N \mathbf{I}(e) z_N$.

The third axiom is the classical Strong Pareto axiom.

Strong Pareto. For all $e = (s_N, R_N) \in \mathscr{E}$ and all $z_N, z'_N \in Z(e)$, (i) if $z_i R_i z'_i$ for all $i \in N$, then $z_N \mathbf{R}(e) z'_N$ and (ii) if, in addition, $z_j P_j z'_j$ for some $j \in N$, then $z_N \mathbf{P}(e) z'_N$.

The last axiom is a separability condition. It states that when an individual has the same bundle in two allocations, the ranking of these two allocations should remain the same if this individual were simply absent from the economy. Let $|N|$ denote the cardinality of N.

Separation. For all $e = (s_N, R_N) \in \mathscr{E}$ with $|N| \geq 2$ and all $z_N, z'_N \in Z(e)$, if there exists a $j \in N$ such that $z_j = z'_j$, then

$$z_N \mathbf{R}(e) z'_N \Rightarrow z_{N \setminus \{j\}} \mathbf{R}(e') z'_{N \setminus \{j\}},$$

where $e' = (s_{N \setminus \{j\}}, R_{N \setminus \{j\}}) \in \mathscr{E}$.

---

[6]We could as well formulate an axiom that requires inequality reduction in budget sets for agents with the same skill. The rest of the analysis would follow with little modification.

As can be easily checked, the k-Leximin SOFs presented in the previous section satisfy our four axioms. Moreover, any SOF satisfying these axioms must rank allocations exactly like a k-Leximin SOF whenever the lowest levels of utility U^k differ in the allocations being compared.

Proposition 1. *For all $k \in [0, 1]$:*

(i) *On $Z(e)$, the k-Leximin SOF satisfies k-Equal Labor Consumption Equalization, Budget Anonymity, Strong Pareto, and Separation.*

(ii) *If a SOF satisfies k-Equal Labor Consumption Equalization, Budget Anonymity, Strong Pareto, and Separation, then it satisfies the following property: for all $e = (s_N, R_N) \in \mathcal{E}$ and all $z_N, z'_N \in Y^k(e)$, if*

$$\min_{i \in N} U^k(z_i, s_i, R_i) > \min_{i \in N} U^k(z^i, s_i, R_i),$$

then $z_N \boldsymbol{P}(e) z'_N$.

The proof of (ii) is provided in the Appendix.

4. Second Best: Observable Labor Time

We now turn to second-best situations. In this section, we assume that the planner only observes earnings $w_i l_i$ and labor time l_i, so that she can deduce wage rates w_i, but she does not observe the individuals' earning abilities s_i. Any individual can choose to work at a lower wage rate than his maximum possible, $w_i < s_i$, if this is in his interest.[7] Observe that, in Figure 4 (a variant of Figure 3 with two more individuals), individual 2 would prefer to have individual 3's bundle rather than his own. It would be advantageous for him to work at the same wage rate as individual 3 because this would give him access to individual 3's bundle. Therefore, the ELIE first-best allocation is not, in general, incentive-compatible in this context.[8]

---

[7]Observe that the first-best ELIE allocation can be implemented when s_i is observable, even if individual preferences are private information.

[8]In anticipation of concepts to be introduced in this section, we may note that the allocation depicted in Figure 3 is incentive-compatible because neither individual would want to mimic the other. But this allocation cannot be implemented by the menu of budget sets shown in Figure 3 because individual 2 would like to be able to choose from individual 1's budget set and can work at $w_2 = s_1$ (in contrast, individual 1 is unable to work at $w_1 = s_2$). Another menu must be offered in order to implement the allocation (e.g., offer a menu such that for the two skill levels of these individuals, the post-tax budget set is the same and coincides with the intersection of the budget sets in the figure).

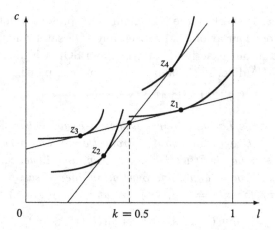

Fig. 4. An Equal labor income equalization (ELIE) allocation that is not incentive compatible.

Because the wage rates w_i are (indirectly) observed, the planner can offer a tax function on earnings, $\tau_w : [0, w] \to \mathbb{R}$, that is specific to each value of w. Individual i will then choose w_i and (l_i, c_i) to maximize his satisfaction subject to the constraints that $w_i \leq s_i$ and $c_i \leq w_i l_i - \tau_{w_i}(w_i l_i)$. One can have $\tau_{w_i}(w_i l_i) < 0$, in which case the tax turns into a subsidy. When $c_i = w_i l_i - \tau_{w_i}(w_i l_i)$ for all $i \in N$, the allocation is feasible if and only if $\sum_{i \in N} \tau_{w_i}(w_i l_i) \geq 0$.

In this context, an *incentive-compatible* allocation $x_N = (w_N, z_N)$ is obtained when no individual envies the bundle of any other individual working at a wage rate he could earn: for all $i, j \in N$, if $s_i \geq w_j$, then $(l_i, c_i) R_i (l_j, c_j)$. This definition does not refer to tax menus, but there is a classical connection between incentive-compatibility and taxes which takes the following form in the current context. First, every allocation obtained by offering a menu $\{\tau_w\}$ and letting the individuals choose their wage rate and bundle subject to the skill constraint $w_i \leq s_i$ and the budget constraint $c_i \leq w_i l_i - \tau_{w_i}(w_i l_i)$ is incentive-compatible.

Conversely, every incentive-compatible allocation can be obtained by offering a menu of tax functions $\{\tau_w\}$ and letting the individuals choose their wage rate and bundle subject to the skill constraint $w_i \leq s_i$ and the budget constraint $c_i \leq w_i l_i - \tau_{w_i}(w_i l_i)$. For instance, the tax function τ_w can be defined so that the graph of $f_w(l) = wl - \tau_w(wl)$ in the (l, c)-space is the lower envelope of the indifference curves of all individuals i such that $w_i \geq w$. For future reference, let this menu of taxes be called the "envelope menu". Note the following fact: when $w > w'$, the set of individuals i for whom $w_i \geq w'$ contains the set of individuals for whom $w_i \geq w$, so that the lower envelope of the indifference curves of the former set is nowhere above the lower envelope for the latter set. In other words, the envelope menu $\{\tau_w\}$ satisfies the following "nesting property": for all $w > w'$ and all $l \in [0,1], wl - \tau_w(wl) \geq w'l - \tau_{w'}(w'l)$. In conclusion, every incentive-compatible allocation can be implemented by a tax menu $\{\tau_w\}$ satisfying the nesting property.

Because w_i does not affect i's satisfaction directly, it is inefficient to let him work at a wage $w_i < s_i$. Fortunately, it is always possible to replace an incentive-compatible allocation $x_N = (w_N, z_N)$ by another allocation $x'_N = (s_N, z_N)$ in which every individual works at his potential and obtains the same bundle as in x_N. This is possible because for all $i, j \in N, s_i \geq s_j$ implies $s_i \geq w_j$, so that if for all $i, j \in N, (l_i, c_i)R_i(l_j, c_j)$ whenever $s_i \geq w_j$, then one also has $(l_i, c_i)R_i(l_j, c_j)$ whenever $s_i \geq s_j$, which is equivalent to saying that x'_N is incentive-compatible. Therefore, from now on we will focus on bundle-allocations z_N and simply assume that $w_i = s_i$ for all $i \in N$.

Let us now fix $e = (s_N, R_N) \in \mathscr{E}$. Let $\underline{s}$ denote the lowest component in s_N. Our first result is that an optimal allocation for $\mathbf{R}^k(e)$ can be obtained by a menu $\{\tau_w\}$ such that the individuals with the lowest skill face a zero marginal tax. This result is obtained with the following assumption.

Restriction 1. For all $i \in N$, there exists a $j \in N$ such that $s_j = \underline{s}$ and $R_j = R_i$.

This restriction is quite natural for large populations. It is satisfied when preferences and skills are independently distributed, but it is much weaker than that.

Proposition 2. *Assume that earnings and labor times (but not skills) are observable. Let $e = (s_N, R_N) \in \mathscr{E}$ satisfy Restriction 1. Then, every second-best optimal allocation for $\mathbf{R}^k(e)$ can be obtained by a menu $\{\tau_w\}$ for which $\tau_{\underline{s}}$ is a non-positive constant-valued function.*

Proof. At a laissez-faire allocation, $z_N^L, U^k(z_i^L, s_i, R_i) = ks_i$ for all $i \in N$. Therefore, at this allocation, $\min_{i \in N} U^k(z_i^L, s_i, R_i) = k\underline{s}$.

Let z_N^* be an optimal allocation for $\mathbf{R}^k(e)$. The structure of the argument is the following. If z_N^* cannot be obtained by a menu $\{\tau_w\}$ for which $\tau_{\underline{s}}$ is a non-positive constant-valued function, then it is possible to define a new menu $\{\hat{\tau}_w\}$ for which $\hat{\tau}_{\underline{s}}$ is a non-positive constant-valued function, with a corresponding allocation $\hat{z}_N$ such that $\min_{i \in N} U^k(\hat{z}_i, s_i, R_i) \geq \min_{i \in N} U^k(z_i^*, s_i, R_i)$ and such that there is a budget surplus, which proves that z_N^* is not optimal (because the budget surplus can be redistributed so as to increase the welfare of all agents).

Because $z_N^* \mathbf{R}^k(e) z_N^L$, necessarily $\min_{i \in N} U^k(z_i^*, S_i, R_i) \geq k\underline{s}$. Let $\{\tau_w\}$ be the envelope menu implementing z_N^*. By construction, the graph of $f_{\underline{s}}(l) = \underline{s}l - \tau_{\underline{s}}(\underline{s}l)$ is the lower envelope of the indifference curves of all $i \in N$ at z_N^*. Consider now the lower envelope of the indifference curves of individuals $i \in N$ for which $s_i = \underline{s}$ and suppose that it lies above $f_{\underline{s}}(l)$ for some $l \in [0,1]$. By Restriction 1, this implies that there are i, j such that $R_i = R_j$, $s_i = \underline{s}$, $s_j > \underline{s}$, and the indifference curve of i at z_i^* is above that of j at z_j^*, which contradicts incentive-compatibility. Therefore, the graph of $f_{\underline{s}}(l)$ is also the lower envelope of the indifference curves of the individuals $i \in N$ for which $s_i = \underline{s}$.

Let $a = \max \tau_{\underline{s}}$. One must have $a \leq 0$ for the following reason. For any individual $i \in N$,

$$U^k(z^*, s_i, R_i) = \min\{c - s_i l | (l, c) R_i z_i^*\} + k s_i.$$

Because the graph of $f_{\underline{s}}$ is the envelope curve of the indifference curves of the individuals i for which $s_i = \underline{s}$, necessarily there is one such i for whom

$$\min\{c - s_i l | (l, c) R_i z_i^*\} = -\max \tau_{\underline{s}}.$$

For this individual, then, $U^k(z_i^*, s_i, R_i) = -a + k\underline{s}$. Recall that $U^k(z_i^*, s_i, R_i) \geq k\underline{s}$. Therefore, $a \leq 0$.

Let $\hat{\tau}_{\underline{s}}(\underline{s}l) = a$ for all $l \in [0,1]$. The menu $\{\tau_w | w > \underline{s}\} \bigcup \{\hat{\tau}_{\underline{s}}\}$ (i.e., $\hat{\tau}_{\underline{s}}$ replaces $\tau_{\underline{s}}$) still satisfies the nesting property. In every allocation $\hat{z}_N$ obtained with this new menu, all $i \in N$ for which $s_i = \underline{s}$ receive the subsidy $-a$ and have $U^k(\hat{z}_i, s_i, R_i) = -a + k\underline{s}$. For $i \in N$ for which $s_i > \underline{s}$, $U^k(\hat{z}_i, s_i, R_i) = U^k(z^*, s_i, R_i)$. Therefore, $\min_{i \in N} U^k(\hat{z}_i, s_i, R_i) \geq \min_{i \in N} U^k(z_i^*, s_i, R_i)$. Suppose that for some $i \in N$ for which $s_i = \underline{s}, z_i^*$ is no longer in the budget set. This implies that $\tau_s(s_i l_i^*) < a$ and that when choosing from the new menu, i gets a lower subsidy (namely, $-a$). If there is such an individual, then the new menu generates a budget surplus. This budget surplus can be redistributed so as to increase $\min_{i \in N} U^k(z_i^*, s_i, R_i)$, in contradiction to the assumption that z_N^* was optimal for $\mathbf{R}^k(e)$.[9] In conclusion, z_N^* must still be implementable with the new menu. $\quad\square$

---

[9]For the proof that a budget surplus always makes it possible to obtain another incentive-compatible allocation in which every individual is strictly better-off, see Fleurbaey and Maniquet (2006, Lemma 3).

By a similar argument, one can show that every optimal allocation can be obtained by a tax menu for which the graph of $f_w(l) = wl - \tau_w(wl)$ lies in the dashed area depicted in Figure 5.

Our next result focuses on the case in which the lower bound of such areas is binding. Such a situation makes the configuration of budget lines the closest possible, given the incentive-compatibility constraints, to the first-best ELIE configuration that was shown in Figures 3 and 5. This case is illustrated in Figure 6.

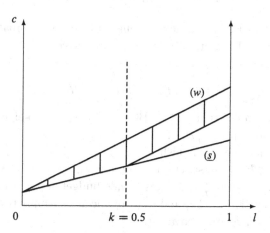

Fig. 5.   The dashed area contains optimal budget curves for w.

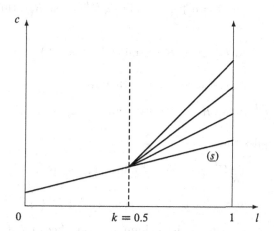

Fig. 6.   Illustration of Proposition 3.

Proposition 3. *Assume that earnings and labor times (but not skills) are observable. Let $e = (s_N, R_N) \in \mathscr{E}$ satisfy Restriction 1 and let $b \geq 0$. For each w, let τ_w be defined by: $\tau_w(wl) = (w - \underline{s})l - b$ for $l \leq k$ and $\tau_w(wl) = (w - \underline{s})k - b$ for $l \geq k$. If an allocation obtained with the menu $\{\tau_w\}$ is second-best Pareto-efficient, then it is second-best optimal for $\mathbf{R}^k(e)$.*

Proof. Let z_N^* be an allocation obtained with $\{\tau_w\}$. By construction, one has

$$\min_{i \in N} U^k(z_i^*, s_i, R_i) = b + k\underline{s}.$$

Assume that z_N^* is Pareto-efficient among all incentive-compatible feasible allocations. Let z_N be another feasible and incentive-compatible allocation for which for some $i \in N$,

$$U^k(z_i, s_i, R_i) > U^k(z_i^*, s_i, R_i).$$

This inequality implies that $z_i P_i z_i^*$. Because z_N^* is Pareto-efficient, there is another $j \in N$ for whom $z_j^* P_j z_j$.

Two cases must be distinguished.

Case 1: $l_j^* < k$. By Restriction 1, there is an $i_0 \in N$ for which $s_{i_0} = \underline{s}$ and $R_{i_0} = R_j$. Because $l_j^* < k, z_j^*$ is in i_0's budget set (see Figure 6) and $z_{i_0}^* I_{i_0} z_j^*$. The fact that $z_j^* P_j z_j$ and that, by incentive-compatibility, $z_j R_j z_{i_0}$ implies that $z_{i_0}^* P_{i_0} z_{i_0}$ or, equivalently,

$$U^k(z_{i_0}, s_{i_0}, R_{i_0}) < U^k(z_{i_0}^*, s_{i_0}, R_{i_0}).$$

Because $U^k(z_{i_0}^*, s_{i_0}, R_{i_0}) = b + k\underline{s} = \min_{i \in N} U^k(z_i^*, s_i, R_i)$, this inequality implies that

$$\min_{i \in N} U^k(z_i, s_i, R_i) < \min_{i \in N} U^k(z_i^*, s_i, R_i).$$

Case 2: $l_j^* \geq k$. By construction, one then has

$$U^k(z_j^*, s_j, R_j) = b + k\underline{s} = \min_{i \in N} U^k(z_i^*, s_i, R_i),$$

which again implies that

$$\min_{i \in N} U^k(z_i, s_i, R_i) < \min_{i \in N} U^k(z_i^*, s_i, R_i).$$

In conclusion, z_N cannot be better than z_N^* for $\mathbf{R}^k(e)$. $\qquad \square$

This result may seem to have limited scope because it is generally unlikely that the menu $\{\tau_w\}$ as defined in the proposition generates a second-best efficient allocation. But one can safely conjecture that if the allocation obtained with this menu is not too inefficient, then the optimal tax menu is close to $\{\tau_w\}$. Note that for $k = 0$, this menu corresponds to the laissez-faire policy (one must then have $b = 0$), which yields an efficient allocation and is indeed optimal for $\mathbf{R}^0(e)$. The likelihood that the optimal menu is close to $\{\tau_w\}$ therefore increases as k gets smaller.

In practice, a menu like $\{\tau_w\}$ is easy to enforce (assuming that labor time or wage rates are observable), and one can then proceed to check if it generates large inefficiencies.

5. Second Best: Unobservable Labor Time

We now turn to a different second-best context in which we assume that the planner only observes earned incomes $yi = w_i l_i$ and is unable to identify the individuals' wage rates, as in the classical literature following Mirrlees (1971). Therefore, redistribution is now made via a single tax function τ. Observe that, in this context, it is always best for every individual $i \in N$ to earn any given gross income by working at his maximal wage rate $w_i = s_i$ because with the tax only depending on yi and not on w_i or l_i, doing so minimizes l_i for a fixed level of consumption. We can therefore focus on bundle-allocations z_N and simply assume that $w_i = s_i$ for all $i \in N$.

With this kind of redistribution, individual i's budget set is defined by (see the left-hand panel in Figure 7):

$$B^\tau(s_i) = \{(l, c) \in X | c \le s_i l - \tau(s_i l)\}.$$

It is convenient to focus on the earnings-consumption space in which the budget set is defined by (see the right-hand panel of Figure 7; we retain the

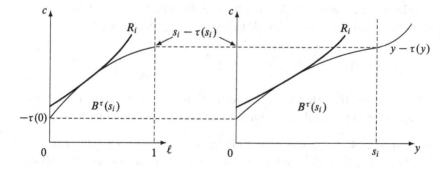

Fig. 7. Preferences over consumption-leisure and over consumption-earnings.

same notation B^τ as no confusion is possible):

$$B^\tau(s_i) = \{(y,c) \in [0,s_i] \times \mathbb{R}_+ | c \leq y - \tau(y)\}.$$

In the right-hand panel of Figure 7, the indifference curve has been rescaled so that the choice of labor time in $[0,1]$ is equivalent to a choice of earnings in $[0,s_i]$.

An incentive-compatible allocation z_N, in this context, is obtained when no individual envies the *earnings*-consumption bundle of any other individual earning a level of gross income that he could earn: for all $i,j \in N$, if $s_i \geq y_j$, then $(l_i,c_i)R_i(y_j/s_i,c_j)$.

Every allocation obtained by offering budget sets defined by a tax function τ is incentive-compatible. Conversely, every incentive-compatible allocation can be obtained by offering a tax function τ and letting every individual $i \in N$ choose his bundle in the budget set $B^\tau(s_i)$. For instance, the tax function τ can be defined so that the graph of $f(y) = y - \tau(y)$ in the (y,c)-space is the lower envelope of the indifference curves of all individuals in this space at the allocation under consideration.

For any $e = (s_N,R_N) \in \mathscr{E}$, let $S = \{s_i | i \in N\}$, $\underline{s} = \min S$, and $\bar{s} = \max S$. As in the previous section, our reasoning below does not require a specific number of individuals, but it is clear that we think of economies with a finite but large number of individuals. In particular, we will impose a restriction on the population of individuals so that the pre-tax income cannot be too informative a signal. According to this restriction, over any interval of earnings $[0,s]$, it is impossible by only looking at preferences over *earnings* and consumption restricted to that interval of earnings to identify individuals with greater productivity than s and to distinguish them, on the basis of their preferences, from individuals with productivity s.

Restriction 2. For all $i \in N$ and all $s \in S$ for which $s < s_i$, there exists a $j \in N$ such that $s_j = s$ and for all $(y,c),(y',c') \in [0,s] \times \mathbb{R}_+$:

$$\left(\frac{y}{s_j},c\right) R_j \left(\frac{y'}{s_j},c'\right) \Leftrightarrow \left(\frac{y}{s_i},c\right) R_i \left(\frac{y'}{s_i},c'\right).$$

Our next result is that with this restriction, the zero marginal tax result still holds for low-skilled individuals when labor time is unobservable.

Proposition 4. *Assume that only earnings are observable. Let $e = (s_N,R_N) \in \mathscr{E}$ satisfy Restriction 2. Then, every second-best optimal allocation for $\mathbf{R}^k(e)$ can be obtained by a tax function τ that is constant over $[0,\underline{s}]$.*

Proof. This proposition is a corollary of Theorem 3 in Fleurbaey and Maniquet (2007) because the preferences $\mathbf{R}^k(e)$ coincide with "Equivalent-Budget" social preferences (defined in that article) for reference preferences $\tilde{R}$ with indifference curves having cusps when $\ell = k$ and a marginal rate of substitution at any point $(l, c) \neq (k, c)$ that is lower than $\underline{s}$ if $l < k$ and greater than $\bar{s}$ if $l > k$. □

We now focus on a particular kind of tax function which satisfies this property, what will be called a *k-type tax*. It is defined as follows:

(i) for all $y \in [0, \underline{s}], \tau(y) = \tau(0) \leq 0$;
(ii) for all $s, s' \in S$ for which $s < s'$ and $s < s_i < s'$ for no $i \in N$ and for all $y \in [s, s']$,

$$\tau(y) = \min\{\tau(0) + k(s - \underline{s}) + (y - s), \tau(0) + k(s' - \underline{s})\}.$$

This formula calls for some explanation. This tax function is piece-wise linear. For low incomes in the segment $[0, \underline{s}]$, the tax function is constant with a fixed subsidy of $-\tau(0)$. Then comes a segment $[\underline{s}, y^1]$ for some y^1 between $\underline{s}$ and the next element s^1 of S on which the rate of taxation is one hundred percent. Of course, no individual is expected to earn an income in this interval. The next segment is the interval $[y^1, s^1]$ on which there is a zero marginal tax rate. Then, the function continues with successive pairs of intervals, one with a one hundred percent marginal tax and the other with a zero marginal tax. The key feature of this tax function is that the points $(s, \tau(s))$, for $s \in S$, are colinear and the slope of this line is precisely k; that is, for all $s, s' \in S$,

$$\frac{\tau(s) - \tau(s')}{s - s'} = k.$$

When S is a large set with elements spread over the interval $[\underline{s}, \bar{s}]$, the tax function is therefore approximately a flat tax (constant marginal tax rate) except for the $[0, \underline{s}]$ interval on which it is constant.

The corresponding budget set, whose upper boundary is given by $y - \tau(y)$, is illustrated in Figure 8, where the indifference curves of five individuals (rescaled so as to fit into (y, c)-space) are also depicted.

An interesting property of a *k*-type tax function τ is that for all $i \in N$, if i chooses a bundle that is on the segment with slope 1 (zero marginal tax) just below s_i, then

$$U^k(z_i, s_i, R_i) = -\tau(0) + k\underline{s}.$$

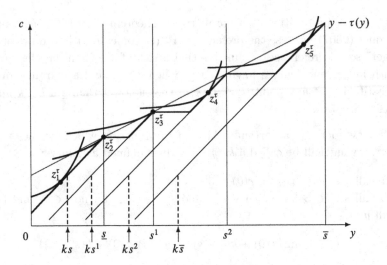

Fig. 8.　Illustration of a k-type tax.

Let us prove this fact (called *Property P* for future reference) by focusing, for clarity but without loss of generality, on individual 4 in Figure 8, assuming that $s_4 = s^2$. From the second term in the definition of τ, one has

$$\tau(y_4) = \tau(0) + k(s^2 - \underline{s}).$$

Bundle z_4 is optimal for R_4 in the budget set for which this level of tax is lump-sum. Therefore, one simply has

$$U^k(z_4, s_4, R_4) = -\tau(y_4) + ks^2$$
$$= -\tau(0) + k\underline{s},$$

which shows that Property P holds. Note that the quantity $-\tau(0) + k\underline{s}$ is independent of s_i. This tax function therefore equalizes U^k across individuals who work full time or just below full time. This equality can be seen in Figure 8 by observing that the vertical lengths at $k\underline{s}, ks^1, ks^2$, and $k\bar{s}$ between the horizontal axis and the lines of slope 1 corresponding to each of these values of s are all the same.

From Figure 8, it is also clear that an individual who chooses a bundle on a lower segment of the budget set must have a greater implicit budget and, hence, that $-\tau(0) + k\underline{s}$ is a lower bound for $U^k(z_i, s_i, R_i)$ for all $i \in N$. Note that this lower bound is attained at least by all $i \in N$ for which

$s_i = \underline{s}$. Therefore, every allocation z_N obtained with a k-type tax is such that $\min_{i \in N} U^k(z_i, s_i, R_i) = -\tau(0) + k\underline{s}$.

This observation is important in order to obtain the next result.

Proposition 5. *Assume that only earnings are observable. Let $e = (s_N, R_N) \in \mathscr{E}$ satisfy Restriction 2. If an allocation obtained with a k-type tax is second-best Pareto-efficient, then it is second-best optimal for $\mathbf{R}^k(e)$.*

Proof. Let z_N be an allocation obtained by a k-type tax function τ. The value of $\min_{i \in N} U^k(z_i, s_i, R_i)$ is $-\tau(0) + k\underline{s}$, as explained in the paragraph preceding the proposition. Assume that z_N is Pareto-efficient in the set of incentive-compatible feasible allocations.

Let z'_N be another feasible and incentive-compatible allocation (not necessarily obtained by a k-type tax function) for which not all individuals are indifferent between z_i and z'_i. By the Pareto-efficiency of z_N, there must be some $i \in N$ for which $z_i P_i z'_i$ or, equivalently, $U^k(z_i, s_i, R_i) > U^k(z'_i, s_i, R_i)$.

Two cases must be distinguished.

Case 1. The earnings y_i are on the last segment of i's budget set (i.e., the segment with slope 1 just below s_i). In this case, by Property P, one has

$$U^k(z_i, s_i, R_i) = -\tau(0) + k\underline{s} = \min_{i \in N} U^k(z_i, s_i, R_i),$$

so that $U^k(z_i, s_i, R_i) > U^k(z'_i, s_i, R_i)$ implies

$$\min_{i \in N} U^k(z_i, s_i, R_i) > \min_{i \in N} U^k(z'_i, s_i, R_i)$$

and, therefore, $z_N \mathbf{P}^k(e) z'_N$.

Case 2. The earnings y_i are on the last segment of the budget set for some $s < s_i$. By Restriction 2, there exists a j for which $s_j = s$ and j has the same preferences as i over bundles (y, c) with $y \in [0, s]$. The fact that $z_i P_i z'_i$ then implies that $z_j P_j z'_j$ because if j could obtain a bundle (y', c') that is at least as good as (y_j, c_j), then i could also have it. As a consequence,

$$U^k(z_j, s_j, R_j) = -\tau(0) + k\underline{s} > U^k(z'_j, s_j, R_j),$$

implying that

$$\min_{i \in N} U^k(z_i, s_i, R_i) > \min_{i \in N} U^k(z'_i, s_i, R_i)$$

and, therefore, $z_N \mathbf{P}^k(e) z'_N$.

In conclusion, z_N is optimal for $\mathbf{R}^k(e)$. $\qquad\square$

Determining the conditions under which a k-type tax is actually second-best Pareto-efficient is beyond the scope of this article. It is clear that this is more likely to be the case for low values of k. Let us, nevertheless, mention the example provided in Fleurbaey and Maniquet (1998) of a Pareto-efficient flat tax of 50% in a model of double heterogeneity with quasi-linear preferences and a uniform distribution of tastes.

Even if no allocation obtained with a k-type tax function is efficient, the k-type tax functions are nonetheless interesting benchmarks because of the property that individuals working full time have the minimum value of $U^k(z_i, s_i, R_i)$, whatever their skill. Because two different k-type tax functions (for the same k) define nested budget sets (one function always dominates the other), it is a valuable exercise to seek the lowest feasible k-type tax function, and we conjecture that the optimal tax function is often close to it for low values of k. (For $k = 0$, the lowest feasible k-type tax function is the laissez-faire policy $\tau = 0$, which is optimal for $\mathbf{R}^0(e)$.)

6. Concluding Comments

Kolm's ELIE proposal strikes the imagination because it yields a simple configuration of budget sets. Such a configuration, however, is not compatible with incentives in general when individuals' potential earnings are not observable (even when, as Kolm assumes, labor time is observable). Our purpose in this article has been to extend the ELIE concept into a full social ordering that can serve to rank all allocations, and to examine the optimal tax that one derives from this ordering in the two prominent second-best contexts studied in the optimal taxation literature.

We have seen that one feature of the ELIE first-best configuration is preserved in the two second-best contexts studied here: the low-skilled individuals should face a zero marginal tax rate. This is a rather striking feature of a tax rule. It contrasts markedly with classical results obtained with standard social welfare functions in the optimal taxation literature when individuals are assumed to have the same preferences over labor and consumption and to differ only in their skills.[10] But it is consonant with recent reforms of income tax and income support institutions in countries like the United States and the United Kingdom.

---

[10]See, e.g., Diamond (1998).

Another, perhaps more surprising, result is the connection between ELIE and the flat tax proposal. For tax functions that depend only on total earnings (and do not depend on labor time or the wage rate), ELIE can be roughly summarized as "a zero marginal tax up to the lowest wage and a constant marginal tax rate k beyond that". When the lowest wage rate is zero (for instance, because of unemployment), this description boils down to a flat tax at rate k.

A full description of the optimal tax has not been provided in this article because it is extremely difficult to provide a precise description of the set of feasible taxes in a model with multi-dimensional heterogeneity of individuals. This leaves opportunities for future research. But it may be worth stressing that the social ordering function proposed in this article can easily be used to evaluate any feasible allocation when the distribution of the population characteristics is known, and in previous works we have shown how to make evaluations directly from the budget set generated by the tax function.[11] This evaluation can be done as well with $\mathbf{R}^k$. For instance, in the framework of the previous section, one can evaluate an arbitrary tax function by seeking the lowest k-type tax function that lies nowhere below it. When political constraints make the optimal tax out of reach, this kind of criterion can serve to evaluate piecemeal reforms of suboptimal tax functions.

It is also possible to evaluate taxes in the case in which different industries or types of jobs display different informational constraints, so that for some individuals s_i is observable, for others only y_i and w_i (or l_i) are observable, and for the rest only y_i is observable. The evaluation then consists in computing the minimum of $U^k(z_i, s_i, R_i)$ for each category of individuals, using the results of this article, and then maximizing the smallest of these three values.

Acknowledgments

We would like to thank participants in the conference organised in Caen in honor of Serge-Christophe Kolm and Serge Kolm himself for numerous stimulating discussions. This article has also benefited from comments by Maurice Salles, John Weymark, and a referee.

---

[11] See Fleurbaey (2006) and Fleurbaey and Maniquet (2006).

Appendix

In this Appendix, we prove Proposition 1.(ii) That is, we show that if a SOF satisfies k-Equal Labor Consumption Equalization, Budget Anonymity, Strong Pareto, and Separation, then it satisfies the following property: for all $e = (s_N, R_N) \in \mathcal{E}$ and all $z_N, z'_N \in Y^k(e)$, if

$$\min_{i \in N} U^k(z_i, s_i, R_i) > \min_{i \in N} U^k(z'_i, s_i, R_i),$$

then $z_N \mathbf{P}(e) z'_N$.

Step 1. We first prove that for all $e = (s_N, R_N) \in \mathcal{E}, p, q \in N$, and $z_N, z'_N \in Y^k(e)$ for which $z_i = z'_i$ for all $i \neq p, q$, if

$$U^k(z_p, s_p, R_p) < U^k(z'_p, s_p, R_p) < U^k(z'_q, s_q, R_q) < U^k(z_q, s_q, R_q),$$

then $z'_N \mathbf{R}(e) z_N$. Let $z_N^1, z_N^2 \in Y^k(e)$ be defined as follows. For all $j \in \{p, q\}: z'_j I_j z_j, z_j^2 I_j z'_j, z_j^1 \in IB(z'_j, s_j, R_j);$ and $z_j^2 \in IB(z'_j, s_j, R_j);$ whereas for all $j \notin \{p, q\}: z_j^1 = z_j$ and $z_j^2 = z'_j$. By Strong Pareto,

$$z_N \mathbf{I}(e) z_N^1 \quad \text{and} \quad z'_N \mathbf{I}(e) z_N^2.$$

We now define $M = \{a, b\} \in \mathcal{N}$ with $a, b \notin N, s_a = s_p, s_b = s_q$, and $R_a = R_b \in \mathcal{R}$ such that when facing budget sets with slope s_p and s_q, respectively, the two individuals in M choose a labor time equal to k. Let $z_a^1, z_b^1, z_a^2, z_b^2 \in X$ be defined by

$$z_a^1 \in m(R_a, B(z_p^1, s_a)),$$
$$z_b^1 \in m(R_b, B(z_q^1, s_b)),$$
$$z_a^2 \in m(R_a, B(z_p^2, s_a)),$$
$$z_b^2 \in m(R_b, B(z_q^2, s_b)).$$

We must prove that $z'_N \mathbf{R}(e) z_N$. On the contrary, assume that $z_N \mathbf{P}(e) z'_N$. Then, by Strong Pareto,

$$(z_{N \setminus \{p,q\}}, z_p^1, z_q^1) \mathbf{P}(e) (z'_{N \setminus \{p,q\}}, z_p^2, z_q^2).$$

By Separation,

$$(z_{N \setminus \{p,q\}}, z_p^1, z_q^1, z_a^2, z_b^2) \mathbf{P}(e') (z'_{N \setminus \{p,q\}}, z_p^2, z_q^2, , z_a^2, z_b^2),$$

where $e' = ((s_N, s_a, s_b), (R_N, R_a, R_b))$.[12] By Budget Anonymity, swapping the budgets of individuals p and a, as well as those of q and b, one gets

$$(z_{N\backslash\{p,q\}}, z_p^2, z_q^2, z_a^1, z_b^1)\mathbf{I}(e')\,(z_{N\backslash\{p,q\}}, z_p^1, z_q^1, z_a^2, z_b^2).$$

Observe that $c_a^1 < c_a^2 < c_b^2 < c_b^1$ and $\ell_a^1 = \ell_a^2 = \ell_b^1 = \ell_b^2 = k$. By k-Equal Labor Consumption Equalization,

$$(z_{N\backslash\{p,q\}}, z_p^2, z_q^2, z_a^2, z_b^2)\mathbf{R}(e')(z_{N\backslash\{p,q\}}, z_p^2, z_q^2, z_a^l z_b^l).$$

By transitivity, if we gather the above relations, we get

$$(z_{N\backslash\{p,q\}} z_p^2, z_q^2, z_a^2, z_b^2)\mathbf{P}(e')\,(z'_{N\backslash\{p,q\}} z_p^2, z_q^2, z_a^2, z_b^2),$$

an obvious contradiction.[13]

Step 2. Let $e = (s_N, R_N) \in \mathscr{E}$ and $z_N, z'_N \in Y^k(e)$. Assume that

$$\min_{i\in N} U^k(z_i, s_i, R_i) > \min_{i\in N} U^k(z'_i, s_i, R_i)$$

and $z'_N\mathbf{R}(e)z_N$. Choose $p \in N$ so that $U^k(z'_p, s_p, R_p) = \min_{i\in N} U^k(z'_i, s_i, R_i)$. Let $z_N^1 \in Y^k(e)$ be such that $U^k(z_p^1, s_p, R_p) = U^k(z'_p, s_p, R_p)$ and for all $j \in N\backslash\{p\}$,

$$U^k(z_j^1, s_j, R_j) > \max\{U^k(z_j, s_j, R_j), U^k(z'_j, s_j, R_j)\}.$$

By Strong Pareto, $z_N^1\mathbf{P}(e)z'_N$. Choose $z_N^2 \in Y^k(e)$ so that for all $j \in N\backslash\{p\}$,

$$\min_{i\in N} U^k(z_i, s_i, R_i) > U^k(z_j^2, s_j, R_j) > U^k(z_p^2, s_p, R_p) > U^k(z_p^1, s_p, R_p).$$

By an iterative application of Step 1, we can prove that $z_N^2\mathbf{R}(e)z_N^1$. That is, for each $j \in N\backslash\{p\}$, we apply the argument in Step 1 to individuals j and p, decreasing the index of j to $U^k(z_i^2, s_i, R_i)$ while at the same time slightly increasing that of individual p, calibrating such increases so that p's

---

[12]If z_N and z'_N are feasible, then so are z_N^1 and z_N^2, but $(z_{N\backslash\{p,q\}}, z_p^1, z_q^1, z_a^2, z_b^2$ and $(z'_{N\backslash\{p,q\}}, z_p^2, z_q^2, z_a^2, z_b^2)$ need not be. This is, therefore, where the proof needs to be changed if we want to restrict the definition of SOF to feasible allocations. But the required change is minor: an agent c should be added who has a sufficiently large skill, a sufficiently large labor time, and a sufficiently low consumption that the resulting allocation is feasible.

[13]Recall that $z_{N\backslash\{p,q\}} = z'_{N\backslash\{p,q\}}$.

index reaches $U^k(z_p^2, s_p, R_p)$ when p is paired with the last individual from $N\backslash\{p\}$. By transitivity, we get $z_N^2 \mathbf{P}(e) z_N$, contradicting Strong Pareto.

References

1. K. J. Arrow. *Social Choice and Individual Values*. New York: Wiley. 1951.
2. R. Boadway, M. Marchand, P. Pestieau and M. del Mar Racionero. 'Optimal redistribution with heterogeneous preferences for leisure', *Journal of Public Economic Theory* **4** (2002), 475–498.
3. P. Choné and G. Laroque. 'Optimal incentives for labor force participation', *Journal of Public Economics* **89** (2005), 395–425.
4. P. Dasgupta and P. J. Hammond. 'Fully progressive taxation', *Journal of Public Economics* **13** (1980), 141–154.
5. P. A. Diamond. 'Optimal income taxation: An example with a U-shaped pattern of optimal marginal tax rates', *American Economic Review* **88** (1998) 83–95.
6. M. Fleurbaey. 'Social welfare, priority to the worst-off and the dimensions of individual well-being', in F. Farina and E. Savaglio (eds.), *Inequality and Economic Integration*. London: Routledge. 2006, pp. 225–268.
7. M. Fleurbaey and F. Maniquet. 'Fair allocation with unequal production skills: The no-envy approach to compensation'. *Mathematical Social Sciences* **32** (1996), 71–93.
8. M. Fleurbaey and F. Maniquet. 'Optimal income taxation: An ordinal approach'. Discussion Paper No. 9865, CORE, Université Catholique de Louvain. 1998.
9. M. Fleurbaey and F. Maniquet. 'Fair orderings with unequal production skills', *Social Choice and Welfare* **24** (2005), 93–128.
10. M. Fleurbaey and F. Maniquet. 'Fair income tax', *Review of Economic Studies* **73** (2006), 55–83.
11. M. Fleurbaey and F. Maniquet. 'Help the low-skilled or let the hard-working thrive? A study of fairness in optimal income taxation'. *Journal of Public Economic Theory* **9** (2007), 467–500.
12. P. J. Hammond. 'Equity, Arrow's conditions, and Rawls' difference principle', *Econometrica* **44** (1976), 793–804.
13. P. J. Hammond. 'Equity in two-person situations', *Econometrica* **47** (1979), 1127–1136.

14. S.-C. Kolm. *Macrojustice: The Political Economy of Fairness.* Cambridge: Cambridge University Press. 2004.
15. F. Maniquet. 'An equal-right solution to the compensation-responsibility dilemma', *Mathematical Social Sciences* **35** (1998), 185–202.
16. J. A. Mirrlees. 'An exploration in the theory of optimum income taxation', *Review of Economic Studies* **38** (1971), 175–208.
17. E. Pazner and D. Schmeidler. 'A difficulty in the concept of fairness', *Review of Economic Studies* **41** (1974), 441–443.
18. L. Simula and A. Trannoy. 'When Kolm meets Mirrlees: ELIE', in M. Fleurbaey, M. Salles and J. A. Weymark (eds.), *Social Ethics and Normative Economics: Essays in Honour of Serge-Christophe Kolm.* Berlin: Springer. 2011, pp. 193–216.

Author Index

Abreu, 233
Aczél, 48
Alkan, 6
Alkan, Demange, 228
Armstrong, 193
Arneson, v, xiv, 5, 82
Arnsperger, 28, 84
Arrow, xviii, 149, 150, 153, 154, 168,
    171, 219, 278
Athanasiou, vi
Atkinson, 193, 219, 240
Aumann, 33

Becker, 84
Bergson-Samuelson, xviii
Besley, 194
Blackorby, 62, 65, 66
Boadway, 193, 194, 208, 239, 240,
    257, 258, 276
Bossert, v, xvii, 28, 53, 54, 57, 58, 82,
    127, 128, 153, 194, 240

Campbell, 153
Capéau, 147
Cappelen, xvii
Casal, vi
Champsaur, 13, 83
Chaudhuri, 170
Choné, 193, 194, 202, 206, 219, 238,
    239, 276
Christiano, vi
Chun, 33
Clayton, vi
Coate, 194

Cohen, v, xiv, 5, 82
Consistency, 119

d'Aspremont, vi, 55, 63, 65, 157
Daniel, 4, 18, 19, 170
Dasgupta, 85, 276
Diamantaras, 19, 170
Diamond, 193, 240, 296
Dworkin, v, xiv, 4, 13, 14, 21, 68, 82,
    84, 94, 132, 154, 198, 245

Ebert, 193

Feldman, 17, 170
Fleming, 55, 65, 157
Fleurbaey, xv, xvii, xviii, 35, 38, 48,
    53, 56–58, 64, 82, 83, 87, 89, 96, 99,
    100, 110, 112, 115, 117, 118, 123,
    127–129, 132, 136, 141–143, 147,
    150, 153, 154, 162–165, 170, 171,
    194, 196, 202, 219, 238–240, 245,
    246, 276, 283, 288, 296, 297
Fleurbaey-Bossert, 61
Foley, 83

Gale, 228
Gaspart, 134, 147
Gatta, 233
Gevers, v, 53, 55, 63, 65, 83, 89, 100,
    118, 144, 147, 157, 237
Gibbard-Satterthwaite, xviii
Gini, 65
Gotoh, vi
Gul, 233

Hammond, vi, 85, 100, 158, 159, 276, 283
Hansson, xviii, 153, 169
Hausman, vi

Iturbe-Ormaetxe, v, xvii, 4, 20, 28, 48, 128

Jackson, xviii

Kaneko, 237
Keen, 208
Kelly, 153
Kirman, 17, 170
Kolm, v, xvii, 28, 115, 129, 275, 277, 278, 283, 284, 296, 297
Kranich, 54, 59, 61, 64, 237
Kranton, 237

Laroque, 13, 83, 100, 193, 194, 202, 206, 219, 238, 239, 276
Le Breton, 153, 169

Maniquet, xv, 33, 57, 89, 99, 100, 110, 112, 115, 117, 118, 123, 128, 129, 132, 136, 141–143, 150, 153, 154, 162–165, 170, 171, 194, 202, 219, 238, 245, 246, 276, 283, 288, 296, 297
Marchand, 193, 276
Mas-Colell, 118
Maschler, 33
Maskin, v, xviii, 6, 53, 89, 137, 233
Michel, 100
Mirrlees, xvii, 85, 125, 153, 193, 202, 240, 276, 277, 291
Mongin, v, xviii, 28, 33
Morelli, 237
Moreno-Ternero, vi
Moulin, v, 28, 33, 88, 93–95, 100, 111, 113, 118–121, 128, 143, 154, 240

Nash, 65
Nieto, xvii, 4, 20, 28, 48, 128
Nozick, 109–111, 122
Nussbaum, v

O'Neill, 33
Ok, 54, 64

Pareto, xiii, xviii
Pazner, xvii, xviii, 4, 16, 18, 35, 42, 84, 85, 87, 92, 94, 98, 123, 129, 138, 153, 167, 169, 170, 277
Pestieau, 193, 233, 276

Racionero, 193, 276
Rawls, xiv, 54, 68, 82, 109, 110, 154, 245
Rochet, 193, 238
Roemer, v, xiv, 4, 7, 16, 21, 28, 35, 37, 41, 54, 57, 58, 61, 64, 82, 110, 111, 113, 114, 119–121, 128, 153, 171, 233, 240

Sadka, 193
Saez, 239
Salles, 297
Samuelson, 219
Schmeidler, xvii, 4, 16, 35, 42, 84, 85, 87, 92, 94, 98, 123, 129, 138, 153, 167, 170, 277
Schokkaert, 153, 240
Seade, 193, 238
Sen, xiv, 15, 42, 59, 82, 150, 159
Shenker, 119, 143
Silvestre, 114
Simula, 277
Sjöström, xviii
Sprumont, vi, xvii, 53, 57, 128, 219
Stiglitz, 208
Suppes, 59, 159
Suzumura, vi, 170
Svensson, 6

Tadenuma, vi, 170
Thomson, v, xviii, 19, 28, 33, 37, 55, 64, 84, 87, 88, 92, 93, 100, 110, 113, 118, 119, 143, 144, 154, 158, 170, 240
Tinbergen, 83
Trannoy, 196, 277
Tungodden, vi, xvii

Tuomala, 193

Vallentyne, v
Valletta, vi
Van de Gaer, vi, 128, 194, 240
Van Parijs, v, 13, 14, 20, 28, 48, 82
Varian, 83, 84, 87, 92, 94, 129, 132, 170
Vohra, 87, 116
Voorhoeve, vi

Waldron, 110
Walras, 14
Weymark, vi, 297
Williams, v
Wilson, 238

Yoshihara, vi
Young, 39, 40, 233

Zeckhauser, 21

Subject Index

adaptive preferences, 15
allocation rule, xvii
anonymity, 36, 63
average compensation, 45

'balanced' solution, 18
bankruptcy, 33
basic income, xxi, 239, 266
Blackorby, 55
budget anonymity, 284

capabilities, 7, 42, 150
compensation, 4, 8, 9, 21, 55, 58–61
compensation for acknowledged
    handicap, 9
compensation principle, xx
compensation problem, 7
concrete fair division problems, 5
conditional equality, 41
CONRAD, 7
consistency, 35, 37, 39, 55, 64, 65,
    143, 158
continuity, 36, 158
contraction independence, 93
cost sharing, 34

earned income tax credit, xx
efficiency, xiii, xv, xix
efficiency–equity trade-off, 192
egalitarian, xiii, xix
egalitarian-equivalent, 42
ELIE, 275
ELIE allocations, 282
equal access, 172
equal opportunities, 5, 35
equal profit Walrasian rule, 99
equal resource for equal handicap, 9,
    37

equal right, 128, 131
equal welfare for $\tilde{R}$-reference
    preferences, 88
equal welfare for equal preference, 8,
    38, 87, 136
equal welfare for uniform preferences,
    96, 136
equal welfare in equal-preference
    economies, 160
equality of opportunity, xiv, 53, 54,
    58, 61
equality of resources, xiv, 4, 35
equality of utilities, xiv
equality of welfare, 5, 35
expansion invariance, 37
expensive tastes, 8, 21
extended auction, 14
extended preferences, 6

fair division, 3
fairness, xv, xvii, xxi
flat tax, 276, 293, 297
full-income-fair, 92
'full incomes', 84
fundamental preference, 16

general incompatibility, 12
generalized utilitarian, 166

Hammond compensation, 159
Hammond equal access, 161
Hammond equal treatment of Equals,
    168
Hansson independence, 200
happiness, xiv
hardworking, 238
hardworking poor, 193, 217
help low skilled, 244

implementation, xviii, xix
implicit budget, 156, 246, 279
impossibility result, 10
incentive-compatibility constraints,
 206
incentive-compatible, 286, 292
income taxation, xvii, xx, 57
independence conditions, xviii, xx
independence of irrelevant
 alternatives, 150, 167
independence of irrelevant
 alternatives for allocation rules, 171
independence of non-indifferent
 alternatives, 169
independence of unfeasible bundles,
 169
individual preferences, xv
indivisibles, 6
inequality measurement, xix
informational basis, 67
intensity of envy, 19
internal resources, xiv, 4
interpersonal comparisons, xiv, 150

k-equal labor consumption
 equalization, 283
k-leximin, 281
k-type tax, 293

laisser-faire, 192, 198
laisser-faire in equal skill economies,
 161
let hardworking thrive, 245
leximin, 42, 163, 206, 280

maximin, xix, 42
minimal compensation, 60
minimal Hammond compensation,
 160
minimal Hammond equal access, 161
minimal responsibility, 61
minimal Suppes compensation, 160
minimal Suppes equal access, 161
minimax envy, 19

money-metric utility, 219
monotonicity, 89
'μ-balanced' solution, 18

no envy, 4, 13, 15, 17, 35, 83, 84, 170
no envy among equally skilled, 87, 136
no envy among uniformly skilled, 96,
 136
non-discrimination, 92, 144
non-existence of efficient envy-free
 allocations, 16

opportunities, 284
opportunity set, 128, 160
optimal income tax, 191
optimal tax, 258
optimal taxation, xix
ordinal non-comparability, 67, 68
ordinal non-comparable preferences,
 6, 56, 192, 219
ordinalism, 154

Pareto optimality, 86
partial compensation, 12, 34
participation, 94, 132
Pigou–Dalton principle, 192
Pigou–Dalton transfer principle, xix,
 196
population monotonicity, 37
preferences, xvi, 7, 34
preferences monotonicity, 137
principle of compensation, xv, xxi
principle of natural (or liberal)
 reward, xv
principle of responsibility, xxi
principle of responsibility or
 neutrality, xv
principles of compensation, xix
priority to the worst-off, 202
progressive tax, 266
pure compensation model, xvi

$\tilde{R}$-conditional equality, 41
reference parameters, 173

reference welfare equivalent budget, 83, 90
reforms, 297
replication invariance, 144
resource equality, 12
resource monotonicity, 37
respecting individual preferences, 198
responsibility, xix, 55, 60, 61
responsibility principle, xx
rights arbitration model, 9
rights arbitration problem, 3
role of economists, xiii

schooling, 57
second-best context, 266, 276
sensitiveness, 46
separability, 65, 200
separation, 284
$\tilde{s}$-implicit-budget generalized utilitarian, 166, 167
$\tilde{s}$-implicit-budget leximin, 163, 165
skill solidarity, 137
social choice, 150, 278
social choice in economic environments, 167
social choice theory, xviii
social indifference, 62
social ordering function, xvii, 157
solidarity, 37
Strong Pareto, 157, 284
Suppes compensation, 159
Suppes equal access, 161
Suppes equal treatment of equals, 168

tax reforms, xix
theory of fair allocation, xviii
transfer principle, 196

undominated diversity, 20
unemployment, 217
unequal production skills, 81, 149
unequal skills, 191
"utilitarian" reward principle, xv
utilitarianism, 54
utility, 66, 68, 82, 152, 171, 202, 240, 280
utility functions, 6

wage-equivalent leximin function, 164
Weak Pareto, 157
wealth-fair, 84, 92
welfare, xiv, 7
welfare economics, xiii, 150
welfare equality, 12
welfare lower bound, 96, 128
welfarism, 53, 62, 63
welfarist, 15, 193, 280
welfarist criterion, 10
well-being index, xx
work-alone lower bound, 95

x^*-equal right, 134

$\tilde{y}$-egalitarian-equivalent, 42

zero marginal tax rate, 239, 266, 292, 296